"There is no sport that reflects the place w[...]
quite like soccer. Athlete-activist Gabriel [...]
to a place where other sports writers fear t[...]
tell you how soccer explains the world while offering means to improve it."
—Dave Zirin, author of *Bad Sports*

"In an era when football appears captured by the forces of money and
power, straitjacketed by the needs of corporations and international
bureaucracies, Gabriel Kuhn's *Soccer vs. the State* is a wondrous
reminder of all the times and ways and places where football has slipped
its chains and offers what it always promised: new solidarities and
identities a site of resistance, a celebration of spontaneity and play."
—David Goldblatt, author of *The Ball Is Round: A Global History of Soccer*

"The personal commitment and experiences that Kuhn brings to the
text, combined with his accessible prose, make this book appealing
to a large and diverse audience of sports academics from multiple
disciplines and to a general public of radical fans and non-fans alike."
—Melissa M. Forbis in *Journal of Sport History*

"Kuhn is impressive in his global and historical scope, and in
acknowledging gender and sexuality questions as well as those of class
and race, as he looks at issues ranging from the exploitation of African
players to the way the World Cup has been abused politically."
—Tom Davies in *When Saturday Comes*

"In 1971, my sister Meredith and I successfully disrupted the Australia
vs. South Africa rugby encounter at the Sydney Cricket Ground as anti-
apartheid activists. This demonstrated not only the intrinsic relationship
between sport and politics but also the significance of sport as a vehicle
for political protest. *Soccer vs. the State* shows how activists and players
alike have made use of this in football, the world's most popular
and most beautiful game—an encouraging and inspiring read!"
—Verity Burgmann, professor of political science, Melbourne University

"Gabriel Kuhn has written the program notes for the most important
match of all, The People's Game vs. Modern Football."
—Mark Perryman, cofounder of Philosophy Football

"If you are a soccer fan, this book is a must,
especially if your politics lean left."
—Ron Jacobs in *Counterpunch*

Soccer vs. the State
Tackling Football and Radical Politics
Gabriel Kuhn

BTL

Soccer vs. the State: Tackling Football and Radical Politics
Gabriel Kuhn

© PM Press 2019

Published by:
PM Press
PO Box 23912
Oakland, CA 94623
www.pmpress.org

Cover by John Yates/Stealworks
Interior design by briandesign

ISBN: 978-1-62963-572-9
Library of Congress Control Number: 2018931524
10 9 8 7 6 5 4 3 2 1

This edition first published in Canada in 2018 by Between the Lines
401 Richmond Street West, Studio 281, Toronto, Ontario, M5V 3A8, Canada
1-800-718-7201
www.btlbooks.com

Canadian cataloguing information is available from Library and Archives Canada.

ISBN 978-1-77113-380-7 Soccer vs. the State paperback
ISBN 978-1-77113-381-4 Soccer vs. the State epub
ISBN 978-1-77113-382-1 Soccer vs. the State pdf

Printed in the USA by the Employee Owners of Thomson-Shore in Dexter, Michigan.
www.thomsonshore.com

Contents

Preface to the Second Edition

The first edition of this book came out eight years ago. In broad strokes, the world of soccer still looks the same: there is an increasingly commercialized game of professionals at the top, managed by corrupt administrators and greedy corporations, and a grassroots game at the bottom that provides millions of people with joy, confidence, and a sense of community. This book looks at the contradictions within the world of soccer and the efforts to bring out the best in it. Football occupies the minds and hearts of millions of people, and even for those who don't share this passion, the sport is too big and influential to be ignored. Football is a beautiful game, but the dreadful economic, social, and political realities we live under cast dark shadows over it. Football cannot change the world, but it can be part of the process.

Except for the correction of a few factual errors and misspellings, no changes have been made to the original text. The notes have been updated. A 67-page appendix covers important developments since 2011. Further bits of information are woven into the outline of the chapters below.

I owe great thanks to everyone who contributed texts, photos, and artwork to this book. All interviews and reprints are listed under "Inserts"; all photographers and artists, as well as relevant information about their contributions and their work, can be found under "Images." "Resources" includes information about books, magazines, films, music, and online resources of relevance for the political soccer fan. The section has been updated for this edition.

Soccer vs. the State starts with a chapter on political soccer history, "Truths and Myths about Football as a Working-Class Sport." In the last few years, researchers have unearthed formerly neglected material, most notably on the role that the club Académica de Coimbra played in the struggle against the Portuguese military dictatorship and colonial empire in the 1960s and early 1970s, and on the organized soccer leagues of South African freedom fighters incarcerated on Robben Island.

Chapter 2, "Radical Debates on Football," discusses relevant questions for the politically inclined football fan: Is soccer an opiate for the masses? How does it relate to nationalism? Is fan violence a problem? How far has

commercialization come? How widespread is bigotry? How does soccer relate to realpolitik?

Concerning the latter, the recent past has provided some telling examples. In Turkey, president Recep Tayyip Erdoğan has been trying to influence the football league to gain political advantage for many years. In Liberia, former world-class striker George Weah's second bid for presidency was successful when he won the 2017 presidential elections.

Numerous examples have proven how big a factor nationalism still is in soccer. In Kurdistan, Amed SK, playing in the third Turkish league, has become a symbol for the resistance movement. Dalkurd FF, a football club founded by Kurds in Sweden in 2004 has become an ambassador for the Kurdish people far beyond Sweden's borders; as of 2018, the club is playing in the country's top division. Kurdistan also participates in tournaments arranged by the Confederation of Independent Football Associations (ConIFA), alongside other self-identified nations not recognized by FIFA, such as Catalonia. There are notable Catalan football personalities who support the independence movement, including Barcelona defender and Spanish international Gerard Piqué as well as star manager Pep Guardiola, currently coaching Manchester City.

Among certain FIFA members, tensions remain high. Competitive matches between Armenia and Azerbaijan, or between Gibraltar and Spain, are prevented by particular drawing procedures. Serbia and Albania, however, met in the qualifying rounds for the 2016 Men's European Championship. The game in Belgrade had to be abandoned after forty-two minutes, when a drone carrying the flag of Great Albania descended on the field, causing a melee among players, coaching staff, and spectators. The division of Syria is reflected by two different teams claiming to represent the country. While the official squad, loyal to Assad, made an unexpected run to the play-offs for a spot in the 2018 Men's World Cup (losing to Australia), exiled players founded the Free Syrian National Team. The question of national identity has become increasingly ambiguous in a globalized world. If the 2022 Men's World Cup will indeed be held in Qatar, it has to be expected that very few of the players representing the host nation will have been born or raised in the country—the majority will be players nationalized for the occasion.

The commercialization of football is about to spiral out of control. Here are only a few of the many staggering figures: in 2017, Brazilian star player Neymar was traded for USD 250 million from Barcelona to Paris St. Germain. That same year, Cristiano Ronaldo earned USD 90 million from his Real Madrid salary and endorsements. The English Premier League makes at least USD 3 billion each year from television rights.

As the 2018 Deloitte Football Money League Report shows, the gap between the rich and the poor is widening. Leading European clubs such as Chelsea, Manchester City, and Paris St. Germain have become commercial showpieces of foreign multibillionaires. One third of the tickets for European Men's Champions League finals is reserved for sponsors. With all the money in circulation, it is of little surprise that match fixing has emerged as a serious problem in the last decade, affecting games even in the most prestigious leagues. Trials for tax evasion and fraud have become a regular feature in the life of top officials and players, including icons such as Neymar, Cristiano Ronaldo, and Lionel Messi. Bayern Munich president Uli Hoeneß was sentenced to three and a half years in prison in 2014.

Cinderella stories such as 5000:1 outsider Leicester City winning the Premier League in 2016, or the team from Eibar, a Basque town of 27,000 people, establishing itself in the Spanish La Liga, are but the exceptions that confirm the rule. Professional soccer has become an orchestrated spectacle for the masses controlled by big money. The writing on the wall has been there for a long time. Already in 1995, former professional Garry Nelson wrote in his splendid book *Left Foot Forward*: "Every time a dad in Devon buys a United shirt for his kid, it's bad news for Plymouth, Torquay and Exeter." If any doubt remained, the disgraceful FIFA scandal of 2015 has proven how rotten the system is. Resistance is increasing, however, involving unexpected agents. In July 2018, Fiat workers in Italy went on strike after a 105-million-euro trade of Cristiano Ronaldo to Juventus Turin was announced. As Fiat and Juventus are controlled by the same holding company, the workers felt the money should have been spent on improving their wages and working conditions instead.

Bigotry still haunts football culture. Despite many campaigns against racism, black players are still targets of taunts and insults. Only drastic reactions create headlines, for example when Kevin-Prince Boateng, at the time

playing for AC Milan, walked off the field during a 2013 preseason game in Busto Arsizio, or when Emmanuel Frimpong, representing the Russian side FC Ufa, was red-carded in 2015 after giving monkey-chanting fans the finger.

Headlines were also created by German midfielder Thomas Hitzlsperger in 2014, when, after he had ended his career, he became the first prominent footballer since Justin Fashanu to come out as gay. In 2011, Anton Hysén, a lower-league player in Sweden and the son of Liverpool legend Glenn Hysén, had a much-noticed coming-out

in the Swedish football magazine *Offside*. That same year, Jaiyah Saelua became the first transgender player to compete in a men's FIFA competition, representing American Samoa.

Stories about the abuse of young athletes by coaching and medical staff have shaken the sports world in the past ten years, with some horrific cases coming to light. This did not pass by soccer either. The revelations made in 2016 by Andy Woodward, a former English professional and victim of sexual abuse, were groundbreaking and caused investigations that led to the arrest and imprisonment of several perpetrators.

Chapter 3, "Radical Interventions in the Professional Game," is dedicated to different forms of political activism in football.

Social justice campaigns receive increasing support. Current examples include Common Goal, with professional players pledging to donate 1 percent of their income to football charities, and Soccer Without Borders, which invests in youth soccer projects in low-income communities. Many football-based initiatives were founded in Europe in 2015 in connection with many refugees arriving from the Middle East, Asia, and Africa. While few of these initiatives have a radical political profile, many of them prove football's ability to build community, making an important difference for people starting new lives in Europe.

Soccer events are regularly used by political activists as a stage to protest and raise concerns. When the men's U20 of China was supposed to play the 2017–2018 season in Germany's Regionalliga Südwest (fourth tier) as an out-of-competition team, the unconventional experiment came to an abrupt halt after just one match, when pro-Tibet activists unrolled Tibetan flags on the stands; fearing similar incidents in subsequent games, Chinese leaders ordered the team to return home. Greenpeace activists have repeatedly disrupted European Champions League games to protest against the natural gas giant Gazprom, one of the tournament's main sponsors. Members of the Russian activist group Pussy Riot invaded the pitch during the final of the 2018 Men's World Cup, denouncing political repression under the Putin regime. In Iran, the ban of women spectators from soccer matches remains a highly charged political issue.

And in Brazil, mass protests erupted during the 2013 Confederations Cup, targeting the government's priorities, as it was investing more money in the upcoming 2014 Men's World Cup than in the country's social services and educational institutions.

Soccer is not only used as a platform by political activists, however. Even if it is a minority, there are supporters, players, and sometimes even managers and officials, who try to change the game from within. One of the most prominent such figures, former Brazilian star player Sócrates, passed away in December 2011. Emerged as a new hero among leftist supporters has Kurdish-German striker Deniz Naki. After playing for Germany's U21 national team and a three-year stint with St. Pauli, Naki continued his career in Turkey, where he came under increasing pressure for his open support of the Kurdish liberation movement. In 2015, he signed with Amed SK, a Kurdish club playing in Turkey's third league. In January 2018, Naki barely escaped an assassination attempt during a visit to Germany. Meanwhile, he was banned from playing soccer in Turkey by the Turkish Football Association. At the time of writing, he resides at an unknown location.

Other players have spoken out politically with less drastic consequences. In 2017, Megan Rapinhoe joined the anthem protests of kneeling NFL players, while Michael Bradley, captain of the U.S. men's team, commented on President Trump's immigration policies thus: "When Trump was elected, I only hoped that the President Trump would be different than the campaigner Trump. That the xenophobic, misogynistic and narcissistic rhetoric would be replaced with a more humble and measured approach to leading our country. I was wrong. And the Muslim ban is just the latest example of someone who couldn't be more out of touch with our country and the right way to move forward."

Serbian defender Neven Subotić has castigated global injustice and the effects of capitalism not just in football but in society at large. He also heads a foundation that provides clean drinking water and sanitation facilities in Ethiopia. In 2011, Sporting Gijón defender Javi Poves raised eyebrows when he retired from the game stating: "What I've seen from within makes it clear: professional football is only money and corruption. It's capitalism, and capitalism is death. I don't want to be part of a system based on people earning money at the expense of the deaths of others in South America, Africa and Asia. To put it simply, my conscience will not let me continue with this."

A player who received much political attention was the Palestinian Mahmoud Sarsak, who, in 2012, went on a three-month hunger strike to protest his imprisonment by Israeli authorities. The political convictions of Sarsak, an alleged Islamic Jihad member, remain unclear, however. The same is true for Syrian goalkeeper Abdul Baset al-Sarout, who became a rebel commander in the fight against the Assad regime. In Bahrain, sev-

eral football players were arrested in connection with anti-government protests in 2011; the national team players Mohamed Hubail and Ali Said were sentenced to prison terms.

To look for pronounced leftist values among soccer players remains a daunting task. In a 2018 interview, a leftist soccer icon of the 1970s, the Italian Paolo Sollier, was asked how difficult he thought it was to be a left-wing football player today. His response is telling: "I don't know. I have never met one."

The FC St. Pauli remains a professional club of a special kind. It is sometimes overly romanticized—even St. Pauli has to obey football's governing bodies, field a competitive team, and make money—but the club's management has repeatedly proven its sympathies for the left-wing fan base. In 2017, for example, it allowed activists who had descended on Hamburg to protest the G20 summit to stay on the grounds of the Millerntor Stadium.

Other soccer clubs that have made political statements in recent years include the Greek teams of AEL Larissa and Acharnaikos, whose players staged a sit-in protest before a game in 2016 to protest the treatment of refugees in the country. In October 2017, Hertha BSC Berlin players took a knee before a Bundesliga match to express solidarity with the NFL anthem protests.

The management of SV Babelsberg 03, playing at the fourth level of German football, is also in tune with the club's left-wing fan base. In the spring of 2018, the club risked forced relegation when it refused to pay a fine of 7,000 euros to the Northeastern German Football Association after some of its supporters had confronted neo-Nazi fans of Energie Cottbus. The matter was finally resolved, when the FA promised to invest the fine paid by Babelsberg into an antiracism campaign. In England, Forest Green Rovers FC (also a fourth-tier team) prides itself on being "the greenest football club in the world" and "the first and only vegan football club."

The politics of football supporters remain as diverse as they have always been. Some are antifascists, others right-wingers, and all of them might be against "modern football." This makes clear-cut distinctions sometimes difficult. Recently, for example, Millwall supporters, long accused of racism and belligerence, have become anti-gentrification poster children, as they fiercely oppose commercial development projects around their homeground, the infamous Den. In Germany, Ultras of all colors have campaigned against Monday evening games and the emergence of the RB Leipzig, sponsored by Red Bull, as a new Bundesliga powerhouse. Ultras have fought for democratization in the Middle East and for ethnic cleansing in Ukraine. In Germany, an odd formation called Hooligans against Salafists has stirred up anti-Muslim sentiments.

In some cases, of course, the political persuasion of football supporters is very clear. Showan Shattak, a cofounder of the Swedish branch of Football Fans against Homophobia, became a symbol for antifascist supporters when he was almost killed by neo-Nazis in his hometown of Malmö, returning home from a rally on International Women's Day 2014. In Greece, Ultra groups have been strongly involved in migrant justice campaigns. In Spain, the Bukanero supporters of Rayo Vallecano have been active in the Movimiento 15-M. In North America, left-wing support is growing, exemplified by groups such as Gorilla FC in Seattle, the Timbers Army in Portland, and Front Commun in Montreal. And in places far off the radar of Western sports media, most notably in Indonesia, political radicals fill the ranks of highly committed Ultra groups.

An increasing number of left-leaning supporters fed up with the hyper-commercialization of the professional game are turning to lower leagues to live out their passion. In France, third-tier Red Star FC has emerged as an antifa favorite, and in England, left-wing support has grown strong around the amateur sides of Lewes FC, Clapton FC, and Dulwich Hamlet. In 2010, Non-League Day was introduced by English fans, a celebration of amateur soccer that has expanded to many countries around the world.

An important day for many football supporters, no matter their politics, was September 12, 2012, when the Independent Hillsborough Panel declared that Liverpool fans were not to blame for the 1989 tragedy at the Hillsborough football stadium in Sheffield. On April 15 that year, a human crush during an FA semifinal game between Liverpool FC and Nottingham Forest caused the deaths of nearly a hundred supporters and injuries and trauma among hundreds more. According to the Independent Hillsborough Panel's report, the human crush had been caused by insufficient safety precautions, irresponsible police actions, and the delayed response by emergency services.

The Hillsborough Justice Campaign is still active and has been driven by football supporters—from Liverpool and beyond—for almost three decades.

Another expression of the often-admirable dedication of football supporters is the increasing number of fan-owned clubs. Much has happened in recent years for the pioneering projects featured in the original edition of this book: AFC Wimbledon have advanced to League One (third tier in English football), where they meet the Milton Keynes Dons, the official successor to Wimbledon FC that the AFC Wimbledon founders refused to support. The FC United of Manchester has opened its own stadium, Broadhurst Park, in 2015. And Austria Salzburg advanced all the way to Austria's second league before bankruptcy forced the club back into the amateur leagues. This might be seen as proof that there is no place for fan-owned clubs in professional football, but whether that's a bad thing is another question. In any case, neither the Salzburg experience nor the early failure of *deinfussballclub.de* at SC Fortuna Köln has stopped new fan-owned clubs from emerging, such as AKS Zły in Warsaw, or HFC Falke in Hamburg, founded by disgruntled Hamburger SV fans. In Portsmouth, a fan cooperative saved the club from bankruptcy in 2013, with the fans deciding four years later to sell the club again to an investor, hoping that this would help it return to the Premier League. Time will tell how wise the decision was. The bankruptcy of 1860 Munich in the summer of 2017 caused unusual reactions among the club's fans: they celebrated the forced relegation to the amateur leagues, since it meant an end to sharing the highly unpopular Allianz Arena with city rival Bayern Munich, and a return to the beloved and picturesque Stadium at the Gründwalder Straße.

The final chapter, "Alternative Football Culture," focuses on people playing and enjoying football apart from the professional game. Three-sided football now has its own World Cup; the first was held in Silkeborg, Denmark, at the Museum Jorn, dedicated to the artist Asger Jorn, credited with conceiving the game. There is an ever-increasing number of alternative clubs, tournaments, and leagues, focusing on joy and community rather than on performance and competition. Several examples are presented in the appendix.

Football is intrinsically political. Under the right circumstances, it can contribute to radical change. To illustrate the former and to strengthen the latter is the purpose of this book.

Foreword

My first football match, an FA Cup replay between my hometown Burnley FC and visitors Chelsea, took place in 1970. Despite growing up playing football, talking about football and wanting to be a footballer, the rush and push of that game, as a nine-year-old, shocked me—on the pitch and on the terraces, so potent, exciting and colourful! So much life and noise squashed into such a small place.

By the time of my first music concert, by a local punk band in a town centre youth club seven years later, I'd been told I wasn't going to make it as a footballer and had taken instead to playing music, talking about music and wanting to be a musician. Still, that first concert was, like my first football match, potent, exciting and colourful; a place of life and noise.

These two events, as if in a secret pact, joined together and combined to energise, delight and frustrate me from that day to this. As with music, having football in my life wasn't a choice. Once bitten, the bug wouldn't leave. I did realise, though, that I had the power to interpret and organise this obsession; I could choose how to dress up my infatuation with this simple game. In short, I could complicate it. Learn its weaknesses and strengths, put it in context, criticise and praise, adorn and strip away. None of this prodding diminished my love for the game; if anything, my passion for the underdog—politically, socially, culturally—has given meaning to an increasingly distant top-layer of football. (In pubs and on terraces around the world I've gladly supported any number of teams in the hope of them beating Man Utd/Real Madrid/Bayern Munich).

Football is a complicated game. This book—veering between love affair and put-down, between pro- and anti-, between football's potential and football's ignorance—sets out to prod and poke its fingers into that big, messy personal passion we have for the game. It's a remarkable collection. It displays both football's traditional masculinity, conservatism, racism, homophobia and nationalism alongside the game's saviours, the activists and autonomous organisations who are gradually changing the way football is played, watched and regulated.

It also contrasts the revolting corporate colossus of the most 'successful' clubs with the honest, inspiring and groundbreaking work done by grassroots alliances and fan clubs. What the book reminds us of is that despite the damage done to the game by the billionaire owners and TV franchises, the heart of football is still defiantly where it was at the game's inception: twenty-two players kicking a ball around a field and an audience of several thousand mainly working class supporters celebrating their communal solidarity. The book's conclusion is worth the price of admission (through the turnstiles, of course) alone.

The first time I heard our song 'Tubthumping' being played at Turf Moor (home of Burnley FC) I was in the toilets behind the main stand having a piss. And believe it or not, the synthesis of a lifelong love of the culture and context of both music and football came together right there in that smelly urinal. It didn't matter then that I didn't think it was particularly representative of the band, or that people had little idea of the song's meaning—all that mattered was that we'd somehow (briefly) become part of the fabric of a working class popular culture, football culture. Never mind the years of writing slyly anarchist rallying-calls: that's my team, running out onto the pitch to my song while I'm down here zipping up my flies! I've never finished a piss so fast in my life.

I love football. I hate football too, sometimes—but never for long enough to dent that complicated passion. If you're like me, this book will prod and poke at you, instruct you, and remind you of your initial introduction to football's excitement and potency. How could anyone read Zapatista Subcomandante Marcos' mischievous letter to the president of Inter Milan without laughing along? Or fail to agree with the 1917 Argentinean anarchist journal *La Protesta*'s denunciation of the "pernicious idiotization caused by the constant running after a round object"? So much life and noise . . . squashed into such a small book.

Boff Whalley, Chumbawamba
November 2010

Introduction

A few months ago I was tabling at a media fair in Germany. Early in the second day, the flow of visitors was rather slow and I started chatting with an Argentinean friend who had a stall nearby. In a swift thirty minutes, we covered a number of issues: anarchism vs. communism, the German autonomous movement, the overall crisis of the left, the future of radical publishing, etc. Then we started talking football—three hours later, we were still at the same topic. We had discussed the 2010 Men's World Cup in South Africa, corrupt football associations, fan cultures in South America and Europe, the origins of our favorite clubs, and many pressing issues like the biggest upsets, the most beautiful goals, and the worst referee's calls in the history of the game. Eventually, we had to relieve the folks who had attended to our stalls although we were long from finished.

This book is for two kinds of people: those who have similar discussions all the time; and those who have always wondered how politically inclined folks can enjoy them. The intention is to provide an overview of the connections between football and radical politics—politics that pursue fundamental social change in order to create egalitarian communities comprised of free individuals. The focus will be on three main aspects: 1) manifestations of radical politics in the professional game; 2) radical soccer fan culture; 3) the radical soccer underground that has spread across the world.

On a personal level, the motivation was simple. For a long time, I have been trying to reconcile a deeply rooted passion for soccer with my political convictions.

In 1987, at the age of fifteen, I was on the roster of FC Kufstein, a semi-professional second-league team in Austria. That very season, the club celebrated its biggest success in history. I was a substitute when a 2-1 win over FC Salzburg secured a birth in the play-off tournament for promotion to the country's top division. After losses against the later Champions League contenders Sturm Graz and Austria Salzburg we failed, but those were exciting weeks.

Although I enjoyed the status I gained as a semi-professional soccer player among my peers, the travels around the country, the Italian training camps, and the days off school, I decided to quit soccer only two years later, after graduating high school. At that point, radical politics had become my new number-one passion and many of my beliefs clashed with the world of soccer as I knew it: the competitiveness, the sexism, racism, and homophobia, the close contact with authoritarian managers, greedy sponsors, corrupt presidents, and despicable politicians. I returned to soccer only half a year later, when I realized that it was still more fun to earn money as a student playing football than waiting tables.

I started regularly for the FC Kufstein as an eighteen-year-old, hoping that I would attract the attention of a first division club—after all, the childhood dream of becoming a professional player had not evaporated just because I was now fascinated by armed guerrilla struggle, squatting, and anarchist theory. The next season, we had a new manager, and things changed, as they often do in these cases. I returned late from my summer vacation, was benched for "lacking the right attitude," resented the new coaching staff, and instead of fighting for my spot on the team I showed up for practice just to collect the paycheck. In the summer of 1992, after much ado about contracts, transfer fees, and club ownership rights, I quit semi-professional soccer for good. I played two more years in minor leagues to have fun and get some exercise, and in 1994 I moved to the U.S. and mainly played basketball.

In the decade that followed, I did a lot of traveling and joined pick-up games from Vanuatu to South Africa. I watched football in corrugated-iron shacks in Burkina Faso, in uninspiring motels in China, and in activists' homes in New Zealand. I hardly ever talked about my years as an aspiring football professional. It seemed like this period of my life was long gone, something I needed to justify rather than to be proud of, and of no relevance whatsoever for my existence as a mature grown-up.

The truth, though, is that my footballing years have had a profound impact on my personality, my relationships with others, and my view of the world. The famous remark by Albert Camus, "what I know most surely about morality and the duty of man I owe to [football],"[1] deeply resonates with me. Outside of personal matters—family, friends, love—the strongest emotions of my life are tied to the game: pleasure and joy as well as disappointment, embarrassment, and feelings of deceit and betrayal. Football unraveled many myths, as I played with and against Austrian national team players, revered heroes of mine. Football taught me how to work with people to achieve a mutual goal even if you have little in common. Football demonstrated how folks turn into liars and cheaters when blinded by money and fame. Football sharpened my class politics, as I came from an artists' home while my teammates were predominantly working-class. Football taught me about labor relations, as I left my dirty gear at every practice for underpaid staff to clean. Football shaped my sense of home as I played for the youth teams of the province I grew up in, the Tyrol. And

then, of course, there is the infamous irrationality: the passion that you develop as a child and never lose, no matter how pathetic it appears and how often it leads to actions that seem unthinkable under other circumstances—like embracing drunken British backpackers and football-crazy Thais on Bangkok's Khao San Road at five in the morning after Manchester United's last-minute turnaround against the despised Bayern Munich in the 1999 European Champions League Final. There are more staggering reports from others. Toni Negri stated in a recent interview that when Italy won the 1982 Men's World Cup, "it was the only day in which we embraced with the guards."[2] Argentinean political prisoners have told similar stories in connection with Argentina's 1978 Men's World Cup victory.[3] However, as Claudio Tamburrini, an Argentinean philosopher, writer, and ex-goalkeeper, who was imprisoned at the time, says: "Sport is a powerful political weapon. We should never surrender it into enemy hands."[4] If this book can make a small contribution to this task, I would be thrilled.

The main text of the book is based on an "Anarchist Football (Soccer) Manual" that I wrote and published with Alpine Anarchist Productions in 2005. The text has been updated and significantly altered, but the handbook character remains: at its core, it provides concise information about the many aspects of the world of football that are of interest to the radical fan. Some of these are dealt with in more depth in the many articles, essays, and interviews included here. These are partly reprints of texts that are difficult to access or forgotten, partly first-time English translations of foreign-language pieces, and partly original contributions to this book. All interviews were conducted by me unless noted otherwise. The terms *soccer* and *football* are used synonymously throughout.

The illustrations have been collected from a variety of sources. I am greatly indebted to all the people who have provided material, lending crucial support to this project!

History: Truths and Myths about Football as a Working-Class Sport

Radical football fans like to portray the game as a traditional working-class sport. This is true in certain ways, and false in others.

Soccer historians have cited evidence of football-like games in many cultures. Apparently, such games have been played among Romans, Egyptians, Assyrians, Persians, and Vikings as well as in ancient Chinese and Japanese societies.[5] This book's focus, however, is the modern-day game of association football, as it was established in England in the 1860s.

Football games in England date back at least 800 years. They have been described as "slightly structured battles between the youth of neighbouring villages and towns," with an unlimited number of players, no set time, and no referees. The games were played "for settling old scores, land disputes, and engaging in 'manly,' tribal aggression."[6] Apparently, some of them could go on for days. Even though the ball is generally referred to as "a leather-bound inflated pig's bladder"[7] some historians suggest that enemies' skulls were used as well.[8]

Traditional English football games were people's events, attracting large and excited crowds, which, in their "unruliness," offended Puritan principles, worried political authorities, and upset merchants who lost profit. "As early as the 14th century there were calls for controls on the game. These stemmed not so much from moral disquiet about the violent consequences of football but from the fact that, by driving ordinary citizens away from the market towns on match days, it was bad for business."[9]

The royals had other concerns. Supposedly, King Edward III of England banned the game in 1349 because it kept his bowmen from

practicing their archery skills. Numerous legal attempts were made at suppressing the game over the centuries—all to no avail.

In the 19th century, a much more effective way of "taming the game" was found: football was incorporated into the public school system. This was a reflection of industrialization and urbanization, which had eradicated many areas where the traditional games had been played, and of new mechanisms of social control.

Once the game had entered public schools, it was increasingly regulated. But football remained a fairly violent sport for some time. According to one report, "the enemy tripped, shinned, charged with the shoulder, got you down and sat upon you . . . in fact might do anything short of murder to get the ball from you."[10] "Weak" boys suffered bullying from their stronger peers, and scores were settled between "rough" working-class and "soft" middle-class kids, whose parents began to worry about their safety.

In 1828, Dr. Thomas Arnold, headmaster at the School of Rugby (yes, that's where the name derives from) cast a first set of rules to "pacify" football. In the words of a group of football historians, "the real violence on the football field was ritualized by regulation."[11] Football became a sport to keep working-class youth out of trouble and to instill gentleman-like qualities in the players. Even the churches started to embrace the game, hoping that it would keep youths from drinking and idling.

The Rugby regulations found wide acceptance, yet interpretations varied from school to school for some decades. With the desire for increased inter-school contests came finally the wish for a commonly accepted book of rules. In 1863, representatives of ten schools and one football club met at the Freemason's Tavern in London to discuss the most disputed aspects of the game: shin-kicking, tripping, and carrying the ball. After weeks of discussion, traditionalists split from reformists. The former eventually founded the Rugby Football Union in 1871. The latter founded the first Football Association (FA) on October 26, 1863. This marks the beginning of the modern-day game of football—or "soccer," a variation of "association"—although it would take another six years to create the distinct position of the goalkeeper, to ban any handling of the ball for outfield players, and to reduce the number of players to eleven. By 1871, the game had pretty much taken on the form that characterizes it to this day.

The same year, the FA's club membership reached fifty and the first FA Cup, the world's oldest football competition, was played, the Wanderers FC beating the Royal Engineers AFC 1-0 in the final. 1872 saw the first international encounter between England and Scotland, a 0-0 draw. Scotland was represented by its oldest club, Queen's Park. The Scottish FA was founded in 1873, that of Wales in 1875, and that of Ireland in 1880.

Scholars have argued that the 19th-century regulation of the game reflected the emergence of bourgeois-capitalist society: prescribing the number of players and the size of the field has been linked to the standard-ization of measuring size and weight for economic interests; the league's tables have been compared to the demands of bookkeeping; stipulating the time of play has been tied to the rigorous supervision of working hours.[12] There probably lies some truth in these claims, yet they hardly discredit the game as a mere capitalist invention. Commonly accepted rules are pre-requisites for games to spread globally, which creates enormous potential for international community building. Besides, soccer might be framed by a number of regulations, yet they are simple and few and leave plenty of space for creative innovation—one of the game's most beautiful aspects.

The class character of football changed in the late 19th century. When the game was being tamed, football was predominantly played by the middle and upper classes; as one Marxist paper puts it, "by young men whose future careers were as bankers, captains of industry or administrators of empire."[13] Through the introduction of professional teams in the 1880s, however, football became increasingly attractive for workers. Middle-class and upper-class folks played football for recreation, but their professional ambitions lay elsewhere. For working-class folks, however, playing football professionally became a tempting alternative to toiling in a factory. While the middle and upper classes arrogantly snubbed the professionalization of the game, the working classes embraced it as an early form of social ascent.

The prominence of working-class players in the professional game also had an effect on the spectators, who wanted to see their mates play. Football became the favorite pastime of the work-ing classes, while rugby was the preferred football game among the middle and upper classes, still embracing ideals of "noble amateurism."

Blackburn Olympic counts as the first working-class team to win the FA Cup in 1883, a time that saw some of England's biggest clubs emerge with working-class rosters: the Arsenal team was formed by workers from the Royal Arsenal in Woolwich, West Ham United by work-ers from Thames Ironworks, Manchester United by Lancashire and Yorkshire Railway workers, and Southampton FC by workers from the Woolston shipyard.

However, although the players in these clubs were workers who attracted a largely working-class audience, the teams were founded, financed, and administered by capitalist industry. This means that from its beginnings as a professional enterprise, football was economically and politically depen-dent on and controlled by the middle and upper classes.

It was not only factory workers who founded clubs, but also churches. Even if their interest was less economic, the intention was to oversee the workers' leisure activities. Many of England's most prominent clubs were founded on this basis: Aston Villa emerged from a Birmingham bible class, Birmingham City from the Holy Trinity Church, Everton from Liverpool's St. Domingo's Congregational Church Sunday School, and the Bolton Wanderers from the Christ Church in the city's Egerton neighborhood.

The first soccer league was formed in England in 1888 by William McGregor, a Scottish shopkeeper and the chairman of Aston Villa. The development that football took was not to the liking of the defenders of Victorian conservatism. The festival character of working-class soccer matches seemed to recall the atmosphere at traditional inter-village football games. The upper classes saw soccer as an excuse for "rowdy" folks to gather and hence as a threat to the public order. These fears reinforced the image of soccer as a working-class sport.

The early game's class character was the same almost everywhere it spread. In the context of the British Empire, it is interesting to note that wherever the British ruled—South Asia, South Africa, Australia/New Zealand—rugby and cricket were groomed as dominant sports; wherever British workers ventured—first and foremost Continental Europe and South America—it was soccer that had a much bigger impact.

On the European continent, soccer arrived early. The Netherlands and Denmark founded national football associations as early as 1889, with Switzerland, Belgium, and Italy following shortly after. In 1900, football made its first appearance at the Olympics as a demonstration sport; it was included as an official event by 1908.

The *Fédération Internationale de Football Association* (FIFA), today arguably one of the most powerful organizations in the world, was founded in Paris in 1904 by seven members: France, Belgium, Denmark, the Netherlands, Spain, Sweden, and Switzerland. Germany cabled its intention to join the same day.

Political controversies were a big factor in FIFA from its inception. In 1908, Austria successfully objected to the membership of Bohemia and Hungary on the grounds that these were Austrian territories. Why Scotland, Wales, and Northern Ireland were still allowed as independent FIFA members was never explained to any satisfaction.

The British associations had joined FIFA a year after its foundation but were not very active in the organization. The motive was thinly veiled snobbery: British football officials saw their teams above all other football-playing nations.

From 1919 to 1946, the British associations basically boycotted FIFA, officially to avoid organizing with World War I enemies. In light of this, it becomes understandable why the 0-1 loss to the United States at England's first-ever World Cup appearance in 1950 marks one of the very special moments in football history.

In its beginnings, football was predominantly a men's sport, but not exclusively so. Women had participated in British village football games, but were excluded from the sport when it became restricted to boys' schools in the 1800s. When club football became popular in the late 19th century, however, women soon formed their own teams.

The first organized matches took place in the 1890s, and women's football became highly popular. During World War I, with the majority of male players at the front, women's games were scheduled regularly, often advertised as charities to raise money for the war. The popularity continued after the war's end.

The most popular of the women's teams were the Dick, Kerr's Ladies, founded in 1917 by W.B. Dick and John Kerr, Scottish factory owners in Preston, England. In 1920, on Boxing Day, the Dick, Kerr's Ladies beat their closest rival, St. Helen's Ladies, 4-0 at Goodison Park in Liverpool in front of 53,000 people, still a record for women's games in England. Regular attendance at men's games was much lower at the time.

The game set off alarm bells at the headquarters of the English FA, which began to perceive women's football as a serious threat to the men's game. In a scandalous move, the English FA banned women's football from all FA grounds in 1921, which effectively meant an end to organized women's football. The explanation given was that "football is quite unsuitable for females and ought not to be encouraged."[14]

The Dick, Kerr's Ladies made headlines one more time when they toured the United States in 1922. They played some of the country's best men's sides and won three out of seven games.

THE FAMOUS DICK KERR INTERNATIONAL LADIES' A.F.C., WORLD'S CHAMPIONS, 1917-25.
RAISED OVER £70.000 FOR EX-SERVICE MEN, HOSPITALS AND POOR CHILDREN.
WINNERS OF 7 SILVER CUPS AND 3 SETS OF GOLD MEDALS.

The English FA's ban of women's football, replicated by some other national football associations, also hindered its international expansion. There exist hardly any records of organized women's football between 1920 and 1970. This allowed football to develop its staunchly male character, also on the terraces. While women reportedly attended football games at the beginning of the 20th century in fair numbers, there were hardly any female spectators left by the 1930s and the few women who defied their de facto exclusion were considered to "invade male territory."

The English FA ban on women's soccer was eventually lifted in 1971. The only notable football nation that kept a longer ban was Paraguay, where women were prohibited from organized football until 1979.

Soccer had reached South America almost as early as Continental Europe. Argentina had its own Football Association by 1893, Chile two years later, and Uruguay by 1900. The *Confederación Sudamericana de Fútbol* (CONMEBOL) was founded in 1916. By 1920, *fútbol rioplatense*, the soccer played in Uruguay and Argentina, had become a worldwide sensation. Uruguay dominated the Olympic football tournaments of 1924 and 1928, and the *fútbol rioplatense* was regarded the best in the world—at least by everyone but the English who remained convinced of their own game's superiority.

The sociocultural development of football in South America was similar to the one in Europe. The first clubs were mostly founded by expatriates, but the sport was fast embraced by the working classes. In the early 20th century, there were probably more clubs founded by workers themselves than in Europe. However, as Maurice Biriotti del Burgo explains, those in power soon tried to take control:

> In the early years of the century, many old-style establishments—not only football clubs but also factory management boards and the like— representatives of Latin America's elite, made attempts to form relationships with working-class teams. At times this took the form of patronage, with an established club funding an affiliated local team. At other times, it took on other dimensions—managers encouraging the creation of football sides among the workers to engender company loyalty and, perhaps more importantly, to divert employees' attentions away from the more damaging spectre of industrial unrest. In these early relationships formed between the elite and the masses in football, can be seen the origins of one of the most compelling arguments in the analysis of football in Latin America: that football serves as an opiate of the masses, an instrument of mass control, a social adhesive binding the most volatile and precarious of ethnic and political mixes.[15]

The "opiate of the masses" argument was widespread among early-20th-century socialists both in Europe and in South America. Football was seen as a distraction from the political struggle, as a means by the powerful to keep the workers complacent, as a potential tool for nationalism, as a formula to pit workers against workers in competition, and as a way to create stars, thereby undermining workers' solidarity.

▌Football!

Leaflet published by the anarcho-syndicalist Freie Arbeiter-Union Deutschlands [Free Workers' Union Germany] in 1921.

May God punish England! Not for nationalistic reasons, but because the English people invented football!

Football is a counterrevolutionary phenomenon. Proletarians between the age of eighteen and twenty-five, i.e., exactly those who have the strength to break their chains, have no time for the revolution because they play soccer!

No matter how much effort you put into advertising political meetings, no one attends. Meanwhile, thousands, even tens of thousands, of proletarians gather around big city football fields every Sunday. We can find the worker with his wife and kids, holding his breath while following a soulless ball's every move. As if the answer to the social question, as if life and happiness depended on whether it flies to the left or to the right.

It is like a disease, like a fever. Whether the state is about to crumble, whether the troops of the Entente prepare for war, whether political gangs threaten each other with weapons, whether the blood of the workers is spilled by green, blue, white, and yellow police units, is all irrelevant; the only thing that matters is whether "Unity Athletics" or "Muscular Wasting FC" will be victorious in next weekend's encounter.

The situation is bizarre. Almost all of these young men who break each other's shinbones are proletarians—as if their muscles were not abused enough during the weekly drudgery! Would it not be a natural and pleasant change if Sunday were used for training their neglected brain muscles? But no—they want to do anything but think!

The one who laughs behind the scenes is the capitalist. He knows that he will only be in danger once the workers start to ponder. This is why he keeps them from pondering by all means possible. Sponsoring sports, which will destroy all of the workers' intellectual capabilities, is one of the most effective. The bourgeois press, usually eager to save space, fills page after page with football news. On these pages, the poor proletarian boys—who are only an undefined "mass" during the week, mere "numbers"—find their names printed. There they can read that Fritze Müller made a wonderful cross, and that Karl Meier defended the goal magnificently. In the illustrated supplement, the whole team can even find their picture!

Translated by Gabriel Kuhn.

However, many socialists soon realized that football was becoming an integral part of working-class culture and they reacted. In the 1920s, a number of socialist football clubs were founded. The idea was to place the game in a sound ideological environment, but also to use it to strengthen socialist and collective values. These developments were particularly strong in Argentina.

■ Agnostics and Believers, Workers and Bosses

Osvaldo Bayer

In the first two decades of the century—in the course of not even a generation—football, like the children of European immigrants, became part of daily life in Argentina. In each neighborhood, one or two clubs were founded. They were called *Club Social y Deportivo*, "Social and Sports Clubs." In the language of Buenos Aires that meant "Milonga and Football."

The anarchists and socialists were alarmed. Instead of attending political meetings and gatherings, the workers went to dance tango on Saturday and to watch football on Sunday. In 1917, the anarchist journal *La Protesta* denounced the "pernicious idiotization caused by the constant running after a round object." They compared the effects of football with those of religion, summarizing their critique in the slogan, "The Mass and the Ball: The Worst Drugs for the People."

Eventually, however, the anarchists and social-  ists also had to adapt, and it did not take long before they were involved in founding their own clubs in workers' neighborhoods. There were, for example, the Mártires de Chicago in La Paternal, named in honor of the workers killed in the United States while fighting for the eight-hour work day; later, the name was changed to Argentinos Juniors, a designation somewhat less compromising. There was also El Porvenir, indicating the utopian vision of its founders. And there was Chacarita Juniors, founded in a libertarian library on May 1, the workers' day. Given the enthusiasm of the people, the old ideologues had to revise their perspective: they now welcomed football as a communitarian game that helped unite people—but they were still opposed to football as a spectacle that mesmerized the masses.

Football kept on growing. Stands were erected around the fields to provide more space for spectators. The organization of the game became increasingly complicated. Political and economic interests played a big part, the competition increased, referees were suspected of accepting bribes—football was no longer a mere game, it had become a business.

Players who had always been amateurs were suddenly lured to clubs for money, the best of them ending up at the clubs that were financially strongest. In the early 1920s, there was a clear division between "big" and "small" teams.

These were not the only borders created by football—there were more. First, within Argentina, the people of Rosario wanted their city to be the country's football capital, challenging the clubs of Buenos Aires. Secondly, with respect to Uruguay, football further fueled the long-standing rivalry across the Río de la Plata. The term *fútbol rioplatense* emerged, uniting the antagonists at least rhetorically. *Fútbol rioplatense*: a magic term indicating a special style of football, soon to be famous around the world.

In 1919, the great era of Boca Juniors began. The club won its first title and had fans that constituted a twelfth player. A reality and a myth were born, having their origin on a bench on the Plaza Solís in the predominantly Genovese neighborhood of Boca. Boca Juniors was formed in 1905, four years after Atlético River Plate. Its humble founders crossed many barren fields until they made their home behind a coal bunker on the island of Demarchi. When they were kicked out, they found a temporary refuge in the Wilde neighborhood. Eventually, they moved back to Boca, and in 1923 they ended up at Brandsen y Del Crucero, where *La Bombonera*, their stadium, was built and where they remain to this day. The names of some of the players in the blue-and-golden shirts have become legendary: Tesorieri, Calomino, Canaveri, and Garassino, who played all eleven positions.

In 1920, Boca and River, the clubs that would become the biggest rivals, still shared championships: one won the "Association" title, the other the "Amateur" league.

Spectators no longer came to just watch their teams—they came to watch their idols. One of them was Pedro Calomino, cheered on by the Boca fans in Genovese Spanish: *"idáguele Calumín, dáguele!"*—"Do it, Calumín, do it!"

Calomino was always oblivious to the stands. He stood on the field, waited for the ball, and then made defenders dizzy with his incredible dribbles. He was the inventor of the *bicicleta*, the "step over." Another Boca idol was Américo Tesorieri, called "Mérico" by the fans. They loved to see him jump, and Mérico did them the favor: slim, delicate, and flexible, he moved like a cat, or like a ballet dancer, complementing the curves of the ball with elegant motions. He was a goalkeeper who reminded you of Mozart's music.

The River fans had their own goalkeeping ace: Carlos Isola, dubbed the "Rubber Man." He had an incredible eye for the ball—he did not catch it, he seduced it! He was a circus artist, an aerial acrobat, a juggler.

In 1921, the big question was which goalkeeper would represent Argentina at the South American Championship, held in Buenos Aires. The choice was Tesorieri, and he justified his selection in an impressive manner: he did not concede a single goal! The final was the one that had to be expected: Argentina vs. Uruguay. The goal securing the 1-0 victory for Argentina was scored by Julio Libonatti from Rosario's Newell's Old Boys. The crowd of 25,000 was ecstatic; they had come to celebrate football as the festival of the people. There were no fences and it was easy to invade the pitch after the final whistle. The spectators carried the hero from Rosario on their shoulders, shouting, "To the Teatro Colón, to the Teatro Colón!" They marched to the city centre, still carrying Libonatti, until some decided that the Teatro Colón was not good enough—it had to be the Casa Rosada on the Plaza de Mayo! So there they went with the triumphant gladiator they were ready to baptize Cesar. But Julio Libonatti never acted as a tenor in the Teatro Colón and never entered the Casa Rosada either. Instead, he moved to Italy, bought by Torino, launching the exodus of Argentina's best players—a colonial drain that hurts Argentinean football to this day.

Huracán is a club that comes from a proletarian neighborhood, Nueva Pompeya. Their logo is a little globe—it is the globe of Jorge Newbery, the famous pilot, who never came back from his last journey. The club was founded on a sidewalk meeting, and "Huracán" was spelt without an H. Maybe the founders lacked knowledge in spelling, but not in football. In 1921 and in 1922, they were champions of the Association League. Their indisputable hero was Guillermo Stábile, called "The Infiltrator," because he joined the attack from behind, always knowing when the ball would arrive in the penalty area. Later, Stabile would be one of the first to practice what had become a new profession: that of the football manager.

Huracán had another glorious striker: Cesáreo Onzari, who is responsible for the name *gol olímpico*, which indicates a goal scored directly from a corner kick. This was in 1924. The Uruguayans had proven the *fútbol rioplatense* to be the best in the world by winning the Olympic football tournament in Paris. When they returned to America, the Argentineans challenged them and beat them 2-1 with Onzari scoring directly from a corner kick. Only a few months earlier, the International Football Association Board had decided at a meeting in England that direct goals from corner kicks would count. The *gol olímpico* is one of the most beautiful goals there is; in fact, it should count double, just for the beauty of the ball's curve.

In 1922, another club rose to fame. It came from Avellaneda and was called Independiente. The libertarian name implied rebellion. It was chosen by Argentinean employees of a big British company who were not allowed to join the official company's team. Their name and the red color of their shirts made them dangerous in the eyes of the authorities. The club was founded at a coffee table in the city center but soon moved to an affordable location in Avellaneda, very close to Racing Club. This is when the rivalry with Racing and the identification with the proletarian neighborhood began.

In 1926, Independiente realized the dream of all football players and supporters: they became unbeaten champions. Not a single game was lost, and the memory of the first official game they played in 1907, a 1-22 defeat against Atlanta, was finally erased. There were players on the team who went straight to heaven in the eyes of the fans, like the five musketeers who formed the attack: Canaveri, Lalín, Ravaschino, Seoane, and Orsi. It was the birth of the *Diablos Rojos*, the "Red Devils," whose artistry in the penalty area hypnotized the audience, not least because the players were from their own neighborhood. The "negro" Seaona made his opponents look like fire hydrants, while "Mumo" Orsi destroyed the defense. Gaucho singers even composed a song for the champions:

> *Ha de gritar el que pueda*
> *siguiendo nuestra corriente*
> *hurras al Independiente*
> *del pueblo de Avellaneda.*

But the *Diablos Rojos* did not forget Boca. In 1925, Boca Juniors were crowned *Campeón de Honor* by the Argentinean Football Association after a remarkable tour of Europe. The Europeans wanted to see more of the *fútbol rioplatense*, which the Uruguayans had displayed so compellingly, and Boca did not disappoint. They played nineteen games, won fifteen, and lost only three.

Even though the best of Argentinean football was traveling to Europe, the local fans had no reason to complain—especially not those of Racing, nicknamed *La Academia*, which had a pair of strikers delighting the crowds with both finesse and efficiency: Natalio Perinetti and Pedro Ochoa. Ochoa had a great admirer in Carlos Gardel, who even dedicated a tango to him: *Ochoíta, el crack de la afición*.

1927 saw Argentina's footballers unite for a sweeping triumph at the South American Championship in Lima: seven goals against Bolivia, five against Peru, and no less than three against Uruguay. The doors stood wide open for the Olympics in Amsterdam in 1928. The Argentineans felt strong and had lost their inferiority complexes towards the Uruguayans. When the team returned from Lima by train, the masses gathered at the station in the Retiro district of the capital. The joy knew no limits and President Alvear forgot his aristocratic manners, embracing Bidoglio, Recanatini, Carricaberry, and Zumelzú, the main men behind the triumph.

Soon, new saints came marching in. Their colors were red and blue and their name was San Lorenzo de Almagro. They were the national champions of 1927, the first year that all of Argentina's teams were united in one league. The club had been founded as Forzosos de Almagro on the grounds of a church, before the name was changed to San Lorenzo, honoring the church's priest Lorenzo Massa, a tireless supporter. It should be added, though, that some less pious fans insist to this day that the name is a reference to the Battle of San Lorenzo, an important event in the Argentine War of Independence. Regardless, the believers and the agnostics always forget their quarrels when *Los Azulgranas*, the "Men in Red-and-Blue," score, and they are all happy to call them *Los Santos*, the "Saints"—except for their opponents, who prefer *Los Cruevos*, the "Crows." Other nicknames are *Los Gauchos de Boedo*, after the district they hail from, and *El Ciclón*, a reference to the line of strikers who secured the 1927 title: Carricaberry, Acosta, Maglio, Sarrasqueta, and Foresto.

Their eternal rival, Huracán, took the championship in 1928, and the following year the winner came from La Plata: it was the Club de Gimnasia y Esgrima, also known as *El Expreso*. It had been founded by aristocrats, fine gentlemen who wanted to practice manly sports. Among them were names like Olazábal, Perdriel, Alconada, Huergo, Uzal, Uriburu, and one that should not be forgotten: Ramón L. Falcón, the Chief of Police who was responsible for the massacre of the workers at the Plaza Lorea in Buenos Aires on May 1, 1909.

The gentlemen began to play football with the English sailors in the nearby port. But as the years went by, the high society players were replaced by workers, and the students in the stands mixed with migrants from the surrounding countryside. The champion team included two players who were off to a magnificent career: the defender Evaristo Delovo and the striker Francisco Varallo.

Football and cinema became the preferred forms of entertainment in Buenos Aires. Cinemas opened in every neighborhood, while the football clubs were looking for better grounds. The rich clubs grew increasingly unhappy with wooden stands and wanted to build with solid cement. In 1928, Independiente inaugurated the first proper stadium in the country; it could hold up to 100,000 people.

But Argentineans did not only go to the cinema and to the stadium in the 1920s. In 1927, like all over the world, thousands gathered on the streets to protest the assassination of the workers Sacco and Vanzetti, condemned to the electric chair by the North American justice system.

Osvaldo Bayer is an Argentinean historian, writer, and activist. This is a chapter from the book *Fútbol Argentino* (Buenos Aires: Editorial Sudamericana, 1990). Translated by Elnura y Hefe.

The German-speaking world saw an interesting development in football in the 1920s and early 1930s, when workers-only clubs were founded. From 1920 to 1933, Germany brandished its own workers' league. It was organized by the socialist *Arbeiter-Turn- und Sportbund* [Workers' Gymnastics and Sports Association] (ATSB), alongside the official league of the German FA. This was a unique endeavor in football history. The ATSB was dissolved by the Nazis in 1933.

The Nazis also eradicated the strong Jewish influence on European soccer. Walther Bensemann was not only involved in the foundation of Eintracht Frankfurt and Karlsruher SC but also founded *Kicker*, the most popular German soccer journal to date. Notable clubs with strong Jewish roots are Racing Club de Paris, Bayern Munich, Ajax Amsterdam, Austria Vienna, and MTK Budapest.

In Austria and Hungary, the Jewish influence on soccer was particularly strong. While Hungary's national team often fielded a majority of Jewish players, an all-Jewish club, Hakoah Vienna, won the Austrian Championship in 1925. Hakoah was also the first team to beat an English side in England when they routed West Ham United 5-1 in 1923. Noteworthy anecdotes from the team's history include the 1925 Vienna Championship Final, in which goalkeeper Alexander Fabian broke his arm and—substitutions not being allowed at the time—swapped position with a forward only to secure Hakoah's win by scoring the decisive goal.

In 1926, Hakoah embarked on a very successful tour of the United States, playing in front of record-breaking crowds. A May 1, 1926, game at the polo grounds in New York City attracted a crowd of 46,000—a U.S. record for soccer games until 1977, when the Pelé-led New York Cosmos attracted crowds of over 70,000.

A few Hakoah players stayed in the United States, partly due to the relative lack of anti-Semitism, partly due to financial lure: Hakoah's most prominent player, the Hungarian Béla Guttmann, was contracted by the New York Giants.

Against common perception, soccer was a fairly well-established sport in the United States at the time. Prominent schools like Harvard and Princeton had started to organize intramural football competitions in the 1820s. The Oneida club, formed in Boston in 1862, became the first soccer club outside of England. In 1866, Beadle & Company of New York City published a set of rules for both Association Football and the "Handling Game" (Rugby). An important event for the history of North American sports was Harvard's 1874 decision to follow rugby rather than soccer rules. Yale and Princeton followed suit, and in 1876, Harvard, Princeton, and Columbia formed the Intercollegiate Football Association, from which American football gradually emerged as a distinct game.

Soccer was still widely played, however, especially by the working classes, while the middle and upper classes followed the Ivy League schools' embrace of rugby. The fact that the U.S. working classes at the time consisted largely of impoverished European immigrants marked soccer as a "foreign" sport—a reputation still upheld by some U.S. conservatives.

New Jersey, Pennsylvania, New York, the New England states, and the Canadian province of Ontario were the first heartlands of North American soccer. The game reached the Midwest in the 1880s and the West Coast by the end of the century. In 1884, immigrants from Britain formed the American Football Association, the United States and Canada played their first international in 1885 (1-0 Canada), and in 1904, a demonstration soccer tournament was played at the Olympics in St. Louis. The Challenge Cup, today known as the U.S. Open Cup, a soccer tournament open to all teams willing to enter, was introduced in 1914 and remains one of the continent's oldest team sport competitions. The significance of the United States for the development of soccer is not least confirmed by U.S. missionaries founding the first Brazilian soccer club for nationals—not just expats—at São Paulo's Mackenzie College in 1898.

By the 1920s, several leagues had been formed across the continent. Of particular interest from a left-wing perspective was the involvement of Nicolaas Steelink in the California Soccer League. Steelink, a Dutch immigrant and successful youth player in the Netherlands, became an IWW activist in the United States and was imprisoned for two years in the early 1920s. After his release, he was an influential figure in U.S. soccer for fifty years and was included in the U.S. Soccer Hall of Fame.

■ Soccer Lover, Labor Organizer Steelink Dies

Tucson Citizen, April 26, 1989
Karen Enquist

Nicolaas Steelink, ardent soccer player and labor union organizer, died Friday at age 98.

Mr. Steelink was born Oct. 5, 1890, in Amsterdam, the Netherlands. He came to the United States from his native Holland in 1912 and settled in Seattle. In 1914, he moved to Los Angeles and, concerned about the poor working conditions that prevailed at the time, joined the Industrial Workers of the World.

Because of his political views and intense involvement in the IWW, he was arrested for syndicalism—an effort to put trade unions in control of production and distribution at manufacturing plants. At age 30, he was sentenced to two years in San Quentin Prison in California.

As he became older, Mr. Steelink became less active politically and more active physically in his first love, soccer, according to Leslie Forster, a chemistry professor at the University of Arizona and a friend of Mr. Steelink.

When he was young, Mr. Steelink played soccer on one of Europe's foremost youth soccer teams, Holland Steamship. After moving to California he organized the California Soccer League in 1958, an organization composed of hundreds of teams and thousands of members today.

Mr. Steelink was inducted into the U.S. Soccer Hall of Fame in 1971 and is also in the California Soccer League Hall of Fame.

Mr. Steelink retired from his profession of accounting in 1965 and moved to Tucson in 1973. He was a referee for the Pima County Junior Soccer League until he was almost 90.

Mr. Steelink also liked to exercise his mind. He spent some of his spare time translating literary works from his native Dutch to English. He was the only person to do a complete translation of the published works of Dutch philosopher Eduard Douwes Dekker, which he donated to the University of Arizona Library in 1977.

He is survived by his son, Cornelius, a chemistry professor at UA, four grandchildren, and three great-grandchildren.

The 1920s are considered the Golden Era of North American soccer. The American Soccer League, founded in 1921, was financially strong and attracted a number of European players. In 1930, the U.S. team traveled as a favorite to the first Men's World Cup in Uruguay and took third place behind the hosts and Argentina. However, the tournament marked the end of U.S. soccer's heyday. Hit hard by the depression of the 1930s, the game was soon surpassed in popularity by both baseball and American football. Fierce battles between competing soccer associations and failed attempts at various professional leagues contributed to further demise. The stunning 1-0 victory over England at the 1950 World Cup in Brazil was an exceptional event during a decades-long drought. Luckily, soccer was recognized as a National Collegiate Athletic Association (NCAA) sport in 1950. This at least kept it alive on the college level.

In Europe, major changes occurred with the rise of fascism in the 1930s and with World War II. Mussolini used the 1934 Men's World Cup in Italy as a fascist showcase. Hitler outlawed all socialist and Jewish clubs. When the Nazis saw their darling team Schalke 04 lose the 1941 German Championship to Rapid Vienna, they blamed the "Jewization" of Austrian football for the loss. Vienna had introduced Continental Europe's first professional football league in 1924.

World War II caused the Men's World Cups of 1942 and 1946 to be cancelled. However, football soon recovered and regained popularity around the world.

The *Union of European Football Associations* (UEFA) was founded in Basel, Switzerland, in 1954. It has always been the most influential association within FIFA and has turned into a powerful organization in its own right. In 1955, UEFA organized the first European club competition, and in 1960 the first Men's European Championship.

The *Asian Football Confederation* (AFC) was founded in Manila in 1954. Football had reached most Asian countries through European colonizers and traders. In many parts of the continent, the game developed into the most popular team sport, although in certain regions there has been stiff competition by cricket (South Asia) and baseball (East Asia). Today, several professional leagues have been established, most notably in Japan and in China. Overall, however, the European leagues, in particular the English Premier League remain far more popular. The Thai edition of Manchester United's club magazine has sold up to 100,000 copies per issue.

The Japanese J. League was originally modeled after professional sports leagues in the United States and controlled by big business, although some structural changes have been made in recent years. Nonetheless, it still attracts many European and Latin American star players beyond their peak who end their careers there with generous salaries. The Chinese Super League, founded in 2004, has been marred by scandals, financial difficulties, and allegations of match-fixing, but is still expanding.

Notable is the relative strength of women's football in Asia. The first Women's World Cup was hosted in China in 1991, and the Chinese team came in second at the 1999 World Cup after losing the final to the United States in a legendary penalty shoot-out. North Korea also has a strong women's side.

In men's football, South Korea, semifinalist at the 2002 Men's World Cup, has been Asia's powerhouse for a couple of decades.

The earliest teams in the Middle East were founded by European expatriates, but clubs were soon organized by nationals. Today, football is very popular in the Arab nations of the Middle East and of North Africa. The Gulf States spend a lot of money on their national sides and Saudi Arabia emerged as a strong international contender in the 1990s.

Football is also highly popular in Israel, where the identity of soccer clubs—like most social bodies—is deeply entrenched in the country's political history. Hapoel teams have traditional connections to the trade union movement and the Labor Party—the most prominent today is Hapoel Tel Aviv. Maccabi teams used to represent the mainstream Zionist movement—Maccabi Haifa is one of the best-known. Beitar teams have traditional ties to the "Zionist revisionism" of Zeev Jabotinsky and are the most right-wing—the most notorious Beitar club is Beitar Jerusalem, whose supporters reject Arab players on the team and openly display anti-Arab sentiments.

The *Confédération Africaine de Football* (CAF) was founded in Addis Abeba, Ethiopia, in 1957. It has sometimes been hailed as the first pan-African organization, although such claims seem disputable: there were only four founding members (Ethiopia, the Sudan, Egypt, and South Africa), the Pan-African Congress by W.E.B. Du Bois was already organized in 1900, and Marcus Garvey founded several organizations with a pan-African outlook. However, football played an important role in Africa's decolonization process. Some of the earliest clubs founded on the continent by Africans, like the Egyptian side Al-Ahly in 1907, played an important role for African pride and self-esteem. For some of Africa's most important politicians of the postcolonial period, like Ghana's Kwame Nkrumah and Guinea's Ahmed Sékou Touré, soccer was an important part in the African nation-building process.

A particular situation emerged in South Africa, where soccer became the most popular sport for the Black community, while Whites preferred cricket and rugby. This marked yet another chapter in the history of soccer as a "low-class" and "underdog" sport. Most of the leading teams in South Africa today, like the Orlando Pirates or the Kaizer Chiefs, have their roots in the townships of a segregated country.

Given the lack of money and infrastructure for local leagues, African soccer has become closely tied to the European game. Football fans follow the European leagues more than the local ones, and every player's ambition is to eventually play there. Ever since regulations on foreign players on European club teams were abandoned in the mid-1990s, there has been an exodus of African football talent to Europe. Thousands of Africans earn their money in leagues all over the continent, and, with the exception of South Africa, it is hard to find players on an African Men's World Cup squad who play club football on the continent: at the 2010 Men's World Cup, Algeria and Ghana had three out of twenty-three, Cameroon one, and Nigeria zero. (Mind you, this economic inequity is not only apparent in the case of African teams. They are also reflected in the squads of relatively poor European countries: at the 2010 Men's World Cup, both the Slovakian and Slovenian sides had only two players from their national leagues, respectively.)

The transfer of African players to Europe has become a lucrative business, haunted by exploitation and fraud. "Football Academies" have mushroomed all over Africa—many with honest intentions, but some using people's desperation and their dreams to take the little they have. The many football agents are divided into sincere folks and crooks. Thousands of African football hopefuls are left penniless in Africa or stranded in Europe every year.

■ Ivorian Teens' Football Dreams Shattered

In March 2007, the Mali authorities alerted IOM [International Organization for Migration] of the presence of a large group of 34 young boys in a villa in Sikasso. The boys turned out to be members of an amateur football club from Abidjan in Ivory Coast. They had been promised contracts with European football clubs and had therefore agreed to travel with the club president and a manager to Europe via Mali. The parents of the boys had each paid about 450 euro to the player agent for the journey. Once in Sikasso, they joined a smaller group of boys already held in the villa. 11 of them escaped and alerted the Malian authorities, which arrested the manager and the president, and requested IOM's assistance for the voluntary return and reintegration of the boys home. The press briefing of IOM concerning this story further revealed that the boys were smuggled into Mali in late December and experienced rough living conditions. They were all aged between 16 and 18 years and coming from Yopougon, a municipality in the outskirts of Abidjan.

Excerpt from *The Muscle Drain of African Football Players to Europe: Trade or Trafficking?* by Jonas Scherrens, European Master in Human Rights and Democratisation, 2006–2007

Organizations have sprung up to try to counteract the exploitation of African players by agents and clubs. *Foot Solidaire*, founded by the ex-Cameroon professional Jean-Claude Mbvoumin, is one example.

Given the global economic imbalance, the desire of Africans to play in Europe is more than understandable. At the same time, it contributes to the structural problems that many African football nations have to struggle with, namely a lack of resources and of local infrastructure. This is undoubtedly one reason why—despite Africa being hailed as a future soccer giant since the 1990s and despite significant international success on the youth level (Ghana and Nigeria dominated the U17 Men's World Cups in the 1990s)—an African team, male or female, has yet to reach a World Cup semifinal. With players dispersed far and wide, with poor local facilities, and with frequent changes of managing staff, it is hard to plan far ahead.

■ Football in Africa

Interview with Daniel Künzler

You are a sociologist and you have spent a lot of time in Africa. What motivated you to write a book about Africa and football?
I've been interested in football since my childhood. I mainly knew about African football through African players in my favorite club, FC Zürich, for example Ike Shorunmu and Shabani Nonda, and from watching African national teams play in the World Cup. Thirteen years ago I traveled to Africa for the first time. Since then, I have visited over twenty African countries. During my travels, I encountered football in all sorts of contexts. Football is a subject that allows you to connect with Africans very quickly, especially men, but also women. Despite the different experiences and possibilities, especially financially, we can discuss football as equals. It is also a subject that touches on many issues that take the conversation way beyond football itself.

When I moved to West Africa in 2003 to work there for two years, I began collecting information on African football more systematically. It became increasingly clear to me that football was a very useful vehicle to study and to present African societies. I first turned the material I gathered into a course at the University of Zurich. I thought it was a good introduction to Africa for students who did not know much about the continent. Later, I decided to write a book.

What are your first associations when it comes to "football and politics" in Africa?
In general, the political aspects of football in Africa are much more obvious than, say, in Switzerland. To begin with, this is certainly connected to the personal character of political power in vast parts of Africa, meaning that power is tied to particular individuals rather than to particular posts or functions. In this context, the powerful use different strategies to secure their followers' loyalty. Instrumentalizing football and football players belongs to these strategies. Important games are attended by huge delegations of politicians, trophies are presented by state presidents, and successful national teams are brought home by charter planes, are personally received by the president, and generously rewarded with gifts. National holidays are declared to guarantee the population's support. All these are examples for symbolic politics in which ritual is more important than content.

Politicians also tend to disregard divisions of powers. They put pressure on national football associations and national team managers. Whether FIFA likes it or not: the national football associations in Africa are hardly independent from the state. Political power struggles are also the cause for the frequent changes of national team managers. New managers are often hired shortly before big tournaments with the demand to deliver good results—not in the future, but right now! Under such circumstances, long-term development becomes very difficult.

In authoritarian states, the political influence is particularly pro-nounced: the authoritarian governments attempt to steer the activities of civil society by controlling the media, trade unions, and other organizations. The lack of political pluralism has a paradoxical consequence: relatively "non-political" events like football matches become overly politicized. Authoritarian rulers often attempt to control and to instrumentalize football, for example by presenting the success of a team as their personal success. Many people are quite aware of this.

However, football stadiums can also be sites for expressing dissatisfaction with authoritarian regimes. A defeat in football can also become a defeat for an authoritarian ruler. The football stadiums of Africa—like those of other continents—are locations of power as much as locations of opposition or counterpower. Football is a medium to execute power *and* to resist power.

Here is a recent example of how rulers can exploit football for their interests: The Men's Africa Cup of Nations 2010 in Angola was used by the rebel group *Frente para a Libertação do Enclave de Cabinda* [Front for the Liberation of the Enclave of Cabinda] (FLEC) to draw attention to their cause with an attack on the bus carrying the team of Togo, which left three people dead. The incident allowed the Angolan President José Eduardo dos Santos to crack down on dissidents. Furthermore, while the population was distracted by the football tournament, the Angolan parliament abolished popular vote for the presidency, effectively paving the way for Santos to remain in power until 2022—by then, he will have ruled Angola for forty-three years.

Is there anything like a left-wing football history or culture in Africa?
I would say that hardly any individuals or parties in sub-Saharan Africa could even be placed on the political left-right continuum. Is there even a noteworthy organized left in Africa? Parties represent regions or individuals rather than clear political programs. The same goes for football clubs: they represent a certain area, a certain neighborhood (for example, "autoch-thonous" or "migrant" people), or a certain social group (for example, the educated), whereby the backgrounds of the players often matter little. Sometimes, clubs might be defined in socioeconomic terms: "the club of

the rich" or "the club of the poor." Notable examples include the rivalries between Jeunesse Sportive de Kabylie ("rich Kabyles") and Union Sportive de la Médina d'Alger ("working-class Kabyles") in Algeria, and between ASEC Mimosas ("rich merchants") and Stella Club d'Adjamé ("the poor") in the Ivory Coast. Sometimes, ethnic and regional identities play into this as well, for example in Tanzania, where Samba is regarded as the club for the "educated Africans and Arabs," while Yanga (Young Africans FC) goes as the club for the "poor coastal people." But to speak of a "left wing football culture" would go too far. This is also true for clubs that derived from workplace teams, from railway workers, from civil servants, from customs officers, or from security forces like the army or the police.

There were socialist African states in which football played an important role. Ahmed Sékou Touré, the former Guinean President, was passionate about football and under his reign some clubs from Guinea were very strong, especially in the 1970s. At the time, important football games were prioritized over all else, players were appointed to specific teams, and contacts abroad were prohibited. Schools and factories were closed to enable people to go support certain teams. Touré's favorite club, Hafia Conakry, dominated the national league and won the African Cup of Champions three times. Horoya de Conakry won the African Cup Winners' Cup once. Touré enjoyed presenting the trophies and regularly received players. However, when Hafia Conakry lost in the final of the 1976 African Cup of Champions to MC Algers—at the time even an ideological ally—the players were publicly accused of "betraying the revolution," "dishonoring ideological education," and "causing national mourning."

The national team encounters between the "revolutionary socialist" Guinea and the "reactionary capitalist" Ivory Coast or between Guinea and the France-loyal Senegal were at times representative duels between two different political systems. Similar ideological contests happened between the Ivory Coast and Ghana and between Congo-Brazzaville and Zaïre, today's Democratic Republic of Congo. Mobutu, Zaïre's President, was everything but a socialist, but there were similarities in how football was used by the governments of Zaïre and Guinea. In both countries, people still recall the football successes of the 1970s. Right-wing and left-wing dictatorships instrumentalized football in similar ways.

Male African players have long attracted international attention—what is the situation of women's football on the continent?
There is a fairly long history of organized women's football in South Africa; it goes back to the 1960s—to a time when women's football was still officially prohibited in Germany. In other African countries, like the predominantly Muslim Senegal and Nigeria, women's clubs were formed

in the 1970s. They were sponsored by football-passionate men, successful women entrepreneurs, and the wives of known politicians. In the beginning, the national football associations did not show much assistance. Today, however, there are leagues for women's teams in several African countries. Some female African players also migrated, for example to the USA or Northern Europe. Unsurprisingly, though, much less money is involved in these transfers than in those of male players.

The powerhouse of women's football in Africa is Nigeria, which has won all African Championships but one. On a global scale, Nigeria reached the quarterfinals of the World Cup in 1999 and of the Olympic Games in 2004. They rose to the top much faster than the men's team. International competitions are also increasingly shown on TV, which means that the women's game becomes more popular, also in other countries.

Among FIFA referees, there are a disproportionately high number of African women, especially compared to the strongest nations in women's football. At the same time there are—just like in Europe—few female managers. National women's teams are almost exclusively coached by men. The South African manager Fran Hilton-Smith is a great exception. Women in football are confronted with many stereotypes. They always have to work twice as hard as the men, and their achievements are often belittled.

In the administrative bodies, women are highly underrepresented too. Burundi's football association is headed by a woman, Lydia Nsekera. Liberia even makes a bigger exception: for some time, the most important posts in football were held by women when Jamesetta Howard was the Minister of Sports and Izetta Wesley the President of the Football Association. The President of the State, Ellen Johnson-Sirleaf, also actively supports women's football. In other African countries, we find few women in leading positions. FIFA also sets a negative example: no women hold important positions there either. At the same time, FIFA provides more financial support for women's football in Africa than most of the national football associations.

There are definitely fewer material resources for the women's game than for the men's. Critics often point out that African states almost exclusively sponsor men in sports generally. In various countries of Eastern and Southern Africa, netball is a very popular sport among women, but receives little official support. It is seen as a "women's sport," a label that illustrates the cultural construction of barriers to perpetuate social privilege. Of course this is a phenomenon not exclusive to Africa.

A topic that, in recent years, has been raised repeatedly in connection with football in Africa are the bad conditions under which many African footballers play in Europe, and the sometimes deceitful methods with

which they are recruited. In some cases, people even speak of a new "slave trade." What is your view of the problem?

I find the comparison to the slave trade rather problematic. There are no Africans leading groups of young footballers at gunpoint to ports where representatives of Manchester United and Chelsea haggle over the best deals. I also don't think that African footballers see themselves as slaves. However, this is not to say that there aren't problems with regard to the migration of African footballers.

The migration itself can take on different forms. Some players come to Europe on their own, sometimes illegally, using money that their family raised for them to make the journey. These players use regular migration routes. Others are brought to Europe—and, increasingly, to Asia—by both European and African agents for test matches, sometimes under false promises. Quite often a lot of money is involved. Some agents are former players, some are managers, and some are mere businessmen. Only very few of those who play in test matches end up with contracts. Players who do not succeed are often abandoned by their agents and left to fend for themselves. Many of them do not dare to return home as losers, and stay illegally. There are probably several thousand failed football migrants in Europe. Those who do find clubs often become dependent on them and accept very poor salaries in lower leagues. There are reports from many European countries that indicate that African players are underpaid. Many of these players are very young—and the average age continues to drop. Overall, there is an increasing number of African players on European teams, especially in France, Belgium, Portugal, and Germany. They play both in professional and amateur leagues.

In particular, those who play for little pay in amateur leagues are dependent on their clubs. They have hardly any social security. At the same time, their salary is usually still above what they could earn in their home countries. There are few alternatives for them in Africa. Even university diplomas don't guarantee employment. Common forms of social mobility, defined by education and integration in the economic system, have long stopped working in Africa due to economic and political crises. Formal education is by no means a guarantee for social success—yet it has become mandatory to even have a chance. Young Africans can't be blamed if they quit school and—sometimes against the explicit wish of their parents, sometimes encouraged by them—try to find their luck in one of the many African football academies. These differ largely: some are very serious and have had great success; some are treacherous and only pull money out of the pockets of desperate people.

Since the end of the 1980s, football academies in Africa have literally exploded. They are usually founded by current or former African players, by European or African clubs, or by European or African businessmen. For

European clubs, they allow a cheaper and more goal-oriented education of promising African talents. The children who are recruited become younger and younger. In most African countries, there is no organized youth football for players of different age and skill groups. Most football associations focus almost exclusively on the national team and leave the development of young players to private initiatives and businesses like the academies. The poor infrastructure and the insufficient organization of African football are further factors that push players abroad. The political and economic difficulties add to this. Migration is therefore something that many African players aspire to, even when they are fully aware of the implied difficulties.

How do you think that the situation can be improved?
I think that curbing football migration is neither realistic nor desirable for the players. It is also problematic to impose restrictions on agents because they usually find ways to bypass them and African agents would suffer first. What seems crucial is to take the wider picture into account: the exploitation and the dependency of African players often relates to immigration laws, especially when residency permits are tied to work contracts. This is where things have to change. There is a fair amount of awareness as far as the conditions for African players in the higher leagues of professional football are concerned, but here "discrimination" is a bigger problem than "exploitation." I believe that more attention has to be paid to the conditions under which Africans play in the lower leagues. It would also be an important move to establish football academies that provide decent general education as well. But even that would remain on the level of fighting symptoms. Any long-term solution can only come from improving the living conditions in Africa and from making African leagues more attractive to local players.

Do you think that football can have a positive influence on the social development of African countries?
I am very skeptical when it comes to presenting football *per se* as some kind of a social savior. Football can unite and it can divide; it can create and it can destroy. Its role depends on the interests and values of those who use it. There are certainly encouraging examples in many countries where people tie football to positive social policies and where the game is part of a "grassroots" effort to achieve certain development goals—we can name projects like the Mathare Youth Sports Association and the Baba Dogo Sports Association in Nairobi, Kenya, as well as the Bosco United Sports Association in Liberia. At the same time, I'm rather skeptical when people involved in development cooperation praise football as a means to teach disadvantaged adolescents that social interaction needs rules; too often this reminds of colonial attempts to use football as a means to instill

European formality, discipline, and punctuality among Africans. Of course it is also true that changes on a micro-level often clash with structural problems like weak institutions, corruption, and nepotism.

Football will continue to arouse passions in Africa, among players and spectators alike. It allows for moments of "normality" in lives characterized by many difficulties and instabilities. Football can empower and help overcome challenges, but it can also be a means of escape that leaves social problems unaddressed. Again, football can be a means of domination and a means of resistance. The only thing that's certain is that African football will remain the topic of many exciting discussions!

Daniel Künzler teaches sociology, social policy, and social work at the University of Fribourg and is the author of *Fußball in Afrika: Mehr als Elefanten, Leoparden und Löwen* [Football in Africa: More Than Elephants, Leopards, and Lions] (Frankfurt am Main: Brandes und Apsel, 2010).

The *Confederation of North, Central American, and Caribbean Association Football* (CONCACAF) was founded in Mexico City in 1961.

Given the small size of most Caribbean island nations, the international success of their football teams is limited. Cuba sent a team to the Men's World Cup in 1938, Haiti represented the region at the Men's World Cup in 1974, Jamaica made a much publicized appearance at the Men's World Cup in 1998, and Trinidad and Tobago qualified for the 2006 Men's World Cup in Germany. No women's team has yet had an impact on the international level.

The main power in Central American football is Mexico, a country with a long and rich football history and one of the few to host the Men's World Cup twice, in 1970 and in 1986. Honduras, El Salvador, and Costa Rica have all had appearances at the Men's World Cup. Mexico has also fielded a side at the Women's World Cup in 1999.

The *Oceania Football Confederation* (OFC) was founded in 1966. Both Australia and New Zealand have had national football associations since the late 19th century. However, as in the United States, other sports came to define national identity, in this case rugby and cricket. As an Australian journalist notes, "soccer flounders wherever it fails to take hold in a nation's working class."[16]

Rugby has also been the dominant sport in Pacific Island nations and territories, with the exception of French Polynesia and New Caledonia, the latter even sporting a member of France's winning squad at the 1998 Men's Soccer World Cup with Christian Karembeu.

Australia is the region's most successful soccer nation, although New Zealand teams have been both at Men's and at Women's World Cups, with a convincing performance by the men's side in South Africa in 2010.

Australian club football has been dominated by teams representing the country's diverse ethnic communities, mainly Croats, Italians, Greeks, and Turks. At times, this has led to hostile confrontations between supporters. In 2005, the A-League was introduced, which since 2007 also includes a New Zealand team, the Wellington Phoenix. On January 1, 2006, Australia left the Oceania Football Confederation to join the Asian Football Confederation, hoping for more regular high-level competition.

▊ Soccer Down Under

Interview with Nick A.

For most, soccer is not the first ball game that comes to mind when thinking of Australia. Cricket and rugby seem to occupy the hearts and minds. Can you tell us a little about the status of soccer down under?
First, there is much conjecture in Australia about what to name the sport: football or soccer. Football, or footy, is appropriated by Rugby League, Union and Australian Rules football, thus confusing the issue. However, I will refer to the round-ball game as football. After all, it is the sport in which you use your foot the most, no?

Certainly in Australia, football does not share the status of sports such as cricket, Rugby League and Australian Rules Football. While at a grassroots level the number of participating registered players exceeds all of these sports, racist attitudes towards the sport and a complicit capitalist media have consistently relegated the importance of football within the cultural psyche of the island-continent's population. However, with a new professional league run by one of Australia's wealthiest men (the Men's league began in 2005, the Womyn's in 2009), huge increases in corporate funding and overt attempts to de-ethnicize the game by denying its history, it seems the game's status is moving towards a "palatable" societal acceptance exemplified through greater media exposure. Now that the ethnic non-Anglo "baggage" has been sidelined, capitalist vultures are swooping. I see this as a very troubling trend.

Yet, the story and traditional status of football as a minnow in Australia is intricately entwined with ethnic diversity and the consequences of migration. This history is important to explore in order to more fully understand the sport's current status. Football's greatest triumphs and most forgettable disgraces in one form or another revolve around the multicultural history of the sport. The heavy involvement of ethnic communities (Turkish, Greek, Italian, Portuguese, Serbian, Bosnian, Croatian, Macedonian, Hungarian, etc.) formidably influenced the development of the sport within Australia. Consequently, football was seen as the sport of the non-Anglo migrant class and duly disrespected, mocked and vilified by the wider Anglo-community and racist capitalist media. Football's traditional and contemporary subservience to the more Anglo-dominated Rugby League, Rugby Union and Australian Rules Football, arguably stemmed from these historical circumstances.

It is the case, however, that football's early years had an Anglo-history in Australia; the first leagues between 1850 and 1920 were dominated by Scottish, Irish, and English migrants. While remnants of this still continue, after WWII football witnessed an explosion of non-Anglo players, clubs and supporters as the Australian State gradually began to relax its White Australia Immigration Policy allowing Southern and Eastern Europeans to migrate from their war-ravaged homelands. They brought their beloved sport with them, building clubs and community centres around football and their shared cultural backgrounds. More recent migration from Southeast Asia and the Middle East continued this trend.

Often oppressed by a discriminatory society that demanded English-speaking workers and as such paid pittance to those that had not yet learnt the dominant tongue, these alienated working-class migrants sought relief from a racist capitalist society through football. In addition, these new communities became acutely aware of racist attitudes towards the Indigenous population. Charlie Perkins, former Secretary of the Department of Aboriginal Affairs and the second Indigenous Australian to graduate from University, insisted that the Greek and Croatian soccer clubs in Adelaide were the first Australians to recognise him as a person to be treated equally. In this climate teams like South Melbourne Hellas, Sydney Olympic, Sydney Croatia, Preston Macedonia, Marconi Fairfield, Adelaide Juventus, Bonnyrigg White Eagles, Sydney Hakoah, St George Budapest, Footscray Jugoslav United, and Associazione Poli-sportiva Italo Australiana formed the backbone of the new wave of football.

In accordance with this new wave, football was long abused and critiqued as the sport of "wogs"; a crude and vulgar term employed to denigrate Southern and Eastern European migrants. "Wogball" was their sport—a term that even entered the lexicon of the Macquarie Colloquial Australian Dictionary.

In fairness, diasporic nationalism and its ugly manifestation of ethnic rivalry played into the hands of the Anglo-dominated media. Crowd violence between Greek and Macedonian teams and Serbian and Croatian, to name but a few, stoked the fire of intolerance towards these new migrants. "How dare they bring their violence here" sniped the media. Whilst these events could be counted on two hands, mainstream capitalist media ate it all up. With little to no television coverage of matches, the only highlights we saw were those of tensions between crowds.

With this background, I suggest that the current commercialisation of the game and the attempts to de-ethnicize the game are a blessing and a curse. With the advent of a new highly professional league replacing the old national league, for both men and womyn, nationalist-driven crowd violence has ceased and this can only be a great thing. Crowd numbers have risen on the whole and media exposure is increasing which encourages more individuals to take up the sport (or sport in general), thus contributing to the physical and mental health of society. Moreover, with the advent of a womyn's league, gender imbalances that have stained the sport are ever so slowly eroding. As with everywhere though, there is a stark gendered distinction between salaries for professionals. Notwithstanding, at least there is a senior league to which womyn can aspire to play in, as well as some media coverage. It should be noted however that Pay TV (FoxSports) owns the rights to the male league and the Government broadcaster (the ABC) provides only limited coverage for the womyn's league.

Yet concurrently, corporate interests have bleached the game of its ethnic history, instead regionally delineating between teams. While any reduction in racially motivated violence is to be applauded, at the same time the migrant history—their struggles in the face of abject racism spurned by a complicit state—are forgotten. In a way this reverse multiculturalism is a troubling trend. It seems a history of racism is whitewashed.

For migrants, children of migrants and grandchildren of migrants, ethnicity is not so easily dismissed. When the Italian national team is victorious internationally for example, the Italian diasporas hit the streets of Sydney, Melbourne, or Adelaide celebrating the successes. The same can be said of the Greek, Croatian, and Serbian diasporas to name but a few. Perhaps controversially, I would suggest this is what makes the sport attractive to some activists. Sure, such support is still a form of nationalism/patriotism, but in a way it is subconsciously acknowledging the fragility of these concepts. Without wishing to generalise too much, based on my own observations I see the same supporters equally as excited when Australia are successful. This may seem to be imbued with notions of national pride and identity, but at the same time, it is a wavering and transient national pride shared between locations, suggesting an erosion of sharp nationalist distinctions.

Another attraction for some activists to football in Australia is that unlike the more aggressive and physically violent sports of rugby and Australian Rules Football, football tends to be less about brute physical force, instead encouraging a more enjoyable and less violent experience. This tends to allow for more mixed-gendered games—at least in the random pick-up park setting. Moreover, one can quite easily join a pick-up game at a local park where games occur regularly. These games are often, though certainly not always, organised by a group of migrants such as Japanese and Koreans in the inner city of Sydney, Irish, Scottish, and English in the Eastern Suburbs of Sydney or Afghani and Iranians in the Western Suburbs of Sydney (to name but a few). These occur throughout Australia.

In this sense a case could certainly be made that some forms of football are political and not purely recreational. As I outlined, football for early Australian non-Anglo migrants was emancipatory. It allowed some escape from the oppression of a racist society. It allowed them an escape from the capitalist forces that drove wage-slavery. I don't wish to overstate this element of the sport. However, as new migrants arrive in Australia, suffering similar oppression and racism, we can again see football providing a space for resistance to the system. Moreover with less of the violent brutish elements of the other dominant sports in Australia (except for cricket), there are more avenues for mixed-gendered games.

Can you tell us something about the situation in New Zealand as well?
Rugby Union is unequivocally the dominant sport in New Zealand. Nonetheless football, or soccer as it is mainly referred to in New Zealand, has of late enjoyed a rise in popularity and play. This is in part due to the "All Whites" qualification for the 2010 Men's FIFA World Cup, only the second time in the nation's history. (The New Zealand team is nicknamed All Whites because of their shirt color and in contrast to the Rugby team's nickname, All Blacks. It is not an issue of skin color.) World Cup qualification has been made somewhat easier for New Zealand now that Australia has left the Oceania Confederation to join Asia. Australia traditionally—while not always—were victors in the cross-Tasman matches. Oceania is the only confederation without a guaranteed World Cup spot. It currently shares a half spot with the Asian Confederation. Personally, I was stoked when New Zealand qualified. Always nice to see a minnow rise!

Another account for the rise of New Zealand football may lie at the domestic level, with the relative recent successes of the Wellington Phoenix club in the A-league. The A-league with corporate support is significantly more publicized than the New Zealand domestic league. Wellington is the only New Zealand club playing in the Australian-based league and recently made the play-offs for the first time, in 2010. This caused crowd numbers to swell. By playing in the A-league, Wellington is the only club playing in an Asian Football Confederation (AFC)-sanctioned league that is not from a state within the confederation. The AFC has threatened Wellington with expulsion from the A-league in 2011 if they do not move to Australia. Yet FIFA seems to be suggesting otherwise. Time will tell how this battle between corrupt elites unfolds.

What does "activist"/"radical" soccer in Australia look like? Do you get together for pick-up games? Are there teams? Tournaments? Leagues?
To the best of my knowledge, radical football in Australia in the sense that your question is asking is almost non-existent. The activist community are yet to regularly organise around radical football ideas.

However, some of the collective members involved with the Anarchist Infoshop Jura Books organised a "People's World Cup" staged on the opening day of the South African 2010 Men's World Cup. Held in Sydney, the football match borrowed and adapted anarcho-football rules and style of play. In particular, 11 vs. 11 with any player able to substitute back for either team without formal restrictions on substitutions. Naturally, it was not gender restrictive, encouraging all to play. Moreover, the general theme of the event loosely aimed to subvert the primacy of nationalism and patriotism during the Men's World Cup period. Jura also organised a People's Kitchen on the day, a Food Not Bombs style of setup.

Australia aims to host the Men's Soccer World Cup, one of the world's most esteemed events, in 2022: will you line up as volunteers, or will you be out on the streets protesting?
The question as to whether anarchists in Sydney will protest the Men's World Cup if Australia wins the bid is very interesting. I can't speak for everyone so this is strictly my opinion.

I am reasonably certain that to some extent I will protest; whether it is against the gender discrimination of the event, FIFA's corruption and corporate pollution of the sport, or the overt nationalism. For sure. However, as I outlined in the history of the sport in this country, to some extent I would be cautious of a broadside attack if it played into the hands of a racist media thirsting for more opportunities to critique football-loving migrants. That will be a tough decision. Some interesting collective discussions await!

Nick A. is an Anarcho-footballer, teacher, and collective member of the Anarchist Infoshop Jura Books in Sydney. His dream is to one day score with his talentless left foot.

In the United States, the National American Soccer League (NASL) revived the professional game in the 1970s. At its peak, the New York Cosmos, signing players like Pelé and Franz Beckenbauer, drew crowds of 70,000. However, poor financial management caused the league to fold in 1984. The current Major League Soccer (MLS) was founded in 1993.

The failure of soccer to establish itself as a dominant professional sport in North America has led to a class identity that differs from other continents. While migrant working-class communities, mainly from Latin America, make up a sizable portion of the game's supporters, soccer has in

many ways become the favorite middle-class sport in the U.S. Amateurism is one aspect of this. Compared to the highly commercialized baseball, American football, basketball, and hockey leagues, with their outrageous salaries and controversial stars, soccer has gained the reputation of a "clean," "family-oriented" sport, conveyed in media imagery of healthy soccer kids and the by now infamous soccer moms. As a sport, soccer ties very much into Puritan notions of U.S. liberalism. In an interview with *The Global Game*, Simon Kuper said:

> I think soccer in America is sort of this Ben and Jerry's-style, upper-middle-class American culture which reacts against a lot of the things in mainstream American culture. It's not the only thing soccer is in America. It is so widely played and it's also an immigrant game, but I think that's part of the culture that it has there. And it's seen as a kids' game, as a girls' game, so it's a liberal game.[17]

From a progressive perspective, the prominent role of women in U.S. soccer is undeniably a positive development. The United States was a central factor in the resurgence of the women's game in the last twenty years. FIFA organized the first Women's World Cup in 1991, women's football was included in the Olympic schedule in 1996, and several professional leagues have sprung up since, in countries like the United States, Germany, and Sweden. In 1999, the U.S. women's team won the World Cup in a dramatic penalty shoot-out against China in front of a crowd of 90,185 in Pasadena, California, at the best-attended women's sports event in history.

Women are also increasingly entering the game in other positions, as club officials, players' agents, and referees. Notable examples include Delia Smith, the famous vegetarian chef and author of *Bean Book*, who is a majority shareholder of Norwich, and Rosolla Sensi, who has been presiding over AS Roma since 2008, inheriting her father's position.

However, there remain huge gender discrepancies. The overall allocation of funds for the women's game is still only a fraction of the money moved in men's soccer; the income gaps between professional male and female players are enormous; and even in Sweden, arguably one of the countries most actively supporting women's soccer, training fields for women's sides remain covered in snow long after the men's fields have been cleared for spring practice.

Indicative of the gender stereotypes still alive in football were the reactions to Swedish author and journalist Åsa Linderborg's recent suggestion to appoint Pia Sundhage, the current manager of the U.S. women's side, as the head coach of Sweden's men's team. Apart from some outright misogynous comments, no one took the idea seriously, even if it was appreciated as a neat political gesture.

Because soccer is seen as a liberal sport, it is susceptible to conservative critique in the United States. Soccerphobia has taken on absurd dimensions among the country's political right. In 1986, Jack Kemp, a former quarterback for the Buffalo Bills, argued in Congress against a U.S. bid for hosting the 1994 Men's World Cup, proclaiming that "a distinction should be made that football is democratic, capitalism, whereas soccer is a European socialist [sport]."[18]

To this day, there are websites portraying soccer as a "communist" and "gay" sport. Famously, right-wing radio and television host Glenn Beck ranted during the 2010 Men's World Cup in South Africa: "We don't want the World Cup. We don't like the World Cup. We don't like soccer. We want nothing to do with it!"[19]

What is interesting is that soccer's identity as a "liberal sport," a "college sport," and an "immigrant's sport" has long made it one of the most popular sports in the United States. It is shortsighted to assess the popularity of a sport simply by the amounts of money moved in professional leagues. Exactly because soccer retains some of its "non-professional" identity, it is hugely popular on an amateur and grassroots level. In a 2008 article in the *Guardian*, Steven Wells wrote:

> America's soccerphobes no longer speak for America. They are a frightened, ignorant, embattled, and increasingly bitter minority—an ugly coalition of young fogies, laddish homophobes, snarling misogynists,

neo-con nogoodniks and gobbledygook-spewing, tin-foil-hat-wearing, knuckle-gnawing nutjobs. And let's not forget the ever-present and always unfunny comedy-of-conformity-spewing sports hacks.[20]

Among working-class-oriented historians of soccer there have been claims that the game itself expresses working-class values, like camaraderie, commitment, and sacrifice. The Italian socialist Gianni Brera interpreted the Italian *catenaccio*, a tactical approach made famous by manager Nereo Rocco in the 1960s and focusing on physical and defensive play, as an expression of working-class ethics. Brera saw *catenaccio* related to the poor's tough life and struggle.

In South America, the aesthetics of the game were considered a more important aspect. South Americans have taken a lot of pride in playing styles they see as distinct from the physicality of the European game, be it the Italian *catenaccio*, the British *kick and run*, or the German *Kampfgeist* [fighting spirit]. In the public eye, Europeans went out onto the pitch to "work," while South Americans went out to "play." As one writer put it: "In the popular imagination, the Latin American football variant is synonymous with emotion, ecstasy, fantasy, spontaneity, instinct, rhythm, and unpredictability."[21] This was famously summarized in the Brazilian notion of *futebol arte*. Leftists, too, based their understanding of football on such distinctions. The famous Argentinean manager César Luis Menotti distinguished between "right-wing football" and "left-wing football." The former meant football in which "only the result counts and in which the players are degraded to mercenaries, paid to secure victory at all costs"; the latter meant football that "celebrated intelligence and creativity" and that "wanted the game to be a festival."[22]

The aesthetic dimensions of the game have been so central to South American identity that huge public debates erupted when in the 1980s and 1990s managers like the Argentinean Carlos Bilardo or the Brazilian Carlos Alberto Parreira changed their national sides' tactics to what they considered a more effective, "European" way of playing.

If we look at the role of the working classes in football today, one aspect remains firmly in place: the vast majority of professional footballers have working-class backgrounds. In *Soccernomics*, Simon Kuper and Stefan Szymanski dismiss the argument that it is the lack of economic opportunities that drives working-class kids to try harder in soccer than their middle-class and upper-class peers. They argue that if the argument were true, working-class kids would also "do better in school and in jobs outside soccer."[23] For Kuper and Szymanski, the only reason why working-class kids excel in soccer is the fact that they play long hours when they are young. While this is certainly a factor, it seems problematic to ignore the economic and social injustice of class societies. Many fields other than sports and entertainment remain closed to ambitious working-class folks, no matter how hard they try. Working-class kids lack access to reputable schools, are neglected by teachers, and find themselves outside of the social networks that bring job opportunities. They do not have the options of studying abroad, of traveling around the world, or of "gaining life experience" as bohemians financed by their parents. They are also more ready to accept the authoritarian structures of club football. While middle-class and upper-class folks are prone to giving up potential soccer careers for "higher" values, working-class folks have little choice.

The connections between football and working-class culture have always been ambivalent. As one article put it, "though soccer may have been played by workers, it was always as a professional game controlled and directed by the upper classes."[24] This, of course, does not render football's working-class dimensions irrelevant. No aspect of working-class culture has developed independently from capitalism, and football's working-class ties remain meaningful for socialist politics. However, it is problematic to claim that the rapid commercialization of the game during the last decades has "stolen" the game from the workers—the game was never fully theirs. More accurately, the recent development of football has often reduced the role of working-class people to those of willful players ("entertainers") and television-bound supporters ("consumers"). Resistance against these developments is a central theme of this book.

■ Football and Working-Class Life

Interview with Alf Algemo

When you first heard about the topic for this interview, you said that ideally I would talk to someone one hundred years old, not seventy-five like you—apparently, significant changes occurred from one generation to the next. Can you summarize those?
Football was always strongly rooted in the Swedish working class, but its significance changed in the 1950s due to the economic boom and a dramatic change in people's living conditions. Until the 1940s, most working-class families in Stockholm lived in a very cramped environment. It was natural to seek activity outside of it. Sports clubs—their football sections being by far the most accessible and popular—provided an essential meeting point for many workers and their children: a place to escape the limited space at home and to meet fellow workers outside of the workplace. Sports clubs were central to working-class culture. Not only did they strengthen the sense of community but they also fulfilled an important social role in very concrete ways. For example, the club I have been involved with for about sixty years, Kungsholms Sportklubb, regularly organized fundraising events to buy clothes and shoes for children of the

poorest families. There was even a group within the club, the "Twelve KSK Brothers," which was set up to administer social services. Club members also helped each other out in various ways, which sometimes had ironic consequences: I remember one of our best players leaving for a club that had many builders because he needed to renovate his house.

Middle-class and upper-class folks also played football, but the game was less tied into their everyday lives—it was more of a leisure activity. When Swedish society became increasingly affluent in the 1950s and when the social democratic government introduced policies against extreme class divides, the social significance of football for working-class communities diminished. However, the consequences of what I experienced as a youth are long-lasting. I still meet regularly with a group of folks who I had played football with when we were kids. The bond that was created at the time and a very basic sense of solidarity are still there. Of course, we all went our different ways in life and some had more luck than others, but when we meet it still feels the same way it did on the football field where we were all equals.

Was playing football a big part of your childhood?
You bet! We played for hours in what we called "rabbit cages": gravel pits surrounded by a wire fence. There wasn't much else to do, and it was hard to pass them on your way home without joining a game—our parents weren't always happy about that, especially not when we were in our Sunday clothes ...

You also told me that you played football at 7 a.m. before going to work?
Yes, that was a common thing in Stockholm. There were even organized leagues. I started to join those games when I was fifteen. If you were there early enough, you always had a chance to play if one of the adults didn't show up.

7 a.m. is very early to play football …
Maybe. But one has to remember that my mother took a tram at 2.20 a.m. every morning to get to her cleaning job. That puts things in perspective …

Was your father a footballer as well?
Not really. He grew up in a farming community in Småland and came to Stockholm in 1908 to look for a job. He ended up working at a brickyard and for the roads office and wasn't all that connected to the city's football culture—but in the wider family, there were some who were active in Kungsholms Sportklubb early on.

How long did you play for the club?
Oh, for a very long time. Simultaneously, I played for several Sunday League clubs. That wasn't really allowed, but I didn't care. Playing in a lot of games was more fun than practicing. I played Sunday League football until I was over fifty …

Until now, you've mentioned the social aspects of football and the joy of playing it. Anything else that was particularly important for you personally?
Football gave me a lot of self-esteem. For working-class kids who didn't necessarily have many prospects in life, football was a way to develop special skills, to gain recognition, and to compete with people from all classes. It allowed you to feel pride and it gave you a sense of achievement.

    It was also a great way to relax and to divert your thoughts from everyday problems—while playing, I was so focused that I forgot everything else.

    Finally, there is the health aspect. I believe that playing football for hours every day as a kid gave me physical strength that I still benefit from. A few years ago, I fell seriously ill but I recovered. I think that football had a lot to do with that.

How have you experienced football as a spectator? Obviously, the professional game has gone through many changes since your youth …
Yes, there is no denying that. It has become a big spectacle and the money involved is just ridiculous. There were no professional players in Sweden when I was young and many of the players who met Brazil in the

1958 Men's World Cup Final had regular day jobs. I remember when, one day, one of my sisters, who seemed gifted in wooing athletes, brought home Knut Nordahl, one of the football gold medalists for Sweden at the 1948 Olympics. It seems unlikely to meet football celebrities that way today.

Do you still go to the stadium a lot?
Not really. Partly I've become too lazy, and partly I no longer enjoy the atmosphere. The emergence of the hooligan problem some decades ago made a big change for me. There was nothing like that in the 1950s when I started to go to the stadium. Sure, there were rivalries between support-ers' groups, but there was no violence. That really turned me off.

Today, the violence has subsided, it seems, but the entire scene is still far removed from what I was used to—even if the game itself has devel-oped in many positive ways. I'm amazed at both the technical and the tactical level of contemporary football.

You support Djurgården—I thought Hammarby was Stockholm's working-class team?
Hammarby has that reputation, yes, but you must remember that they didn't play at the highest level when I got into football. At that time, there were only Djurgården and AIK. AIK definitely had the reputation of being the club for the "finer folks," although they had working-class supporters too, particularly in the environs of their stadium.

Today, there exists a big rivalry between AIK and Hammarby; the former being the rich club from Stockholm's north, the latter the poor club from the south. Djurgården ends up somewhere in the middle and doesn't have a clear political profile. This is exemplified by both Lars Ohly, chairman of Sweden's Left Party, and Fredrik Reinfeldt, the liberal prime minister, supporting the club—Reinfeldt's support is an embarrassment for Djurgården fans like myself, but these contradictions are a part of football too . . .

How do you explain the game's popularity?
That's a good question, actually. Sometimes, when you go from an ice hockey rink to a football pitch, you really wonder: football seems so terribly slow in comparison and nothing happens. Then again, this might be a part of its attraction: you can watch a game and discuss it at the same time; in hockey, things happen so fast that it's often hard to make sense of them.

Most importantly, though, football is easy to emulate. After watching a game, you can pick up a ball, go to the nearest patch of grass, and replay everything you just saw, pretending to be one of the great stars. With hockey, for example, that is near impossible.

In any case, the fascination with football doesn't stop with age. Just the other day, I went down to the sports club with one of my grandchildren and we took turns in shooting free kicks—whenever I managed to put the ball in the upper corner I was as happy as I used to be sixty-five years ago.

Alf Algemo has been living in Stockholm his entire life, working for the roads office as a youth and for forty years in a photocopy and print shop. He has been frequenting the city's football sites from neighborhood playgrounds to the National Stadium.

Radical Debates on Football

Football and Politics

Football is undisputedly the world's most popular game. Three billion people have watched at least some of the live TV coverage of the last Men's World Cup—almost half of the world's population. In 2010, FIFA has more members than the United Nations (208 vs. 192).

The reasons for football's worldwide popularity are various. It is an easy game to play, the rules are simple and straightforward, and all you need is some kind of a ball, a somewhat flat surface, and something that can be used to indicate two goals. Football allows the experience of archetypical warfare in a pacified environment (a common Austrian term for football supporters is *Schlachtenbummler*: a person who travels from battle to battle). Football appeals to deeply rooted notions of collectivity and solidarity ("eleven friends," etc). Football has a long tradition and, in most parts of the world, is an important part of social life ("Let's watch a game!"). Football provides pop cultural icons, special moments, and big tournaments as common social reference points. Football allows for magic experiences and incredible personal stories, such as when no-name goalkeeper Jimmy Glass saved Carlisle United from relegation to amateur football in 1999 with a last-minute goal, only to disappear into anonymity again shortly after.

Finally, due to the relatively low scoring and the many factors that influence a match's outcome, football is prone to sensational victories by outsiders and underdogs—while one exceptional play and a bit of luck can never win you a volleyball or a tennis game, it can secure victory in soccer. Football skeptics have long criticized this aspect of the sport, yet it is undeniably a part of its magic.

The significance of football for many people's lives was maybe most succinctly summed up by Stanley Rous, the former English FA secretary and FIFA president, in 1952: "If this can be termed the century of the common man, then soccer, of all sports, is surely his game.... In a world haunted by the hydrogen and napalm bomb, the football field is a place where sanity and hope are still left unmolested."[25]

Taking such a prominent position in the social world gives football power. The game ignites the masses, creates folk heroes, divides, and unites people. When John Williams, the head of Leicester University's Centre for the Sociology of Sports, notes, "to say 'keep politics out of sport' is like trying to take rain out of the British climate,"[26] or when Chris Bambery from Britain's Socialist Workers Party claims that "sport . . . is totally integrated into a framework of inter-state rivalry, capitalist production and class relations,"[27] then this plays out in football on many levels.

Unfortunately, the most obvious is football's political exploitation by those in power: politicians try to gain public support by identifying with the "people's game"; football victories are turned into political ones; and football tournaments are used to bolster authoritarian regimes. The 1934 Men's World Cup in Italy was a prime example of this. Games were played in the Stadium of the Fascist Party (*Stadio Nazionale PNF*) in Rome and in the Benito Mussolini Stadium (*Stadio Benito Mussolini*) in Turin. The Italian team was celebrated with fascist chants, and fascist symbols were ubiquitous on the terraces. Even a number of foreign delegations paid respect to Mussolini with the fascist salute: Argentineans, Austrians, Brazilians, Spaniards, French, Dutch, and Swiss. Arguably, the Italian victory strengthened the regime and the tournament contributed to its acceptance abroad. Given the fascists' ultra-nationalism, it is somewhat ironic that the victorious Italian side profited from nationalizing three Argentineans shortly before the tournament.

In connection with the event, Mussolini is also credited with inventing the "balcony scene," where political leaders invite successful soccer teams to join them on the balcony of an official building, speaking and waving to the enthused masses below; despite its obvious fascist overtones, the scene has become a must in practically all sports celebrations.

John F. Hobsbawm has argued that football evokes chauvinistic tendencies more so than any other social phenomenon.[28] Simon Kuper has observed that "it is a rare dictator who ignores soccer."[29] National holidays have been declared after soccer victories in Costa Rica, Nigeria, Jamaica, Cameroon, Turkey, and elsewhere. The famous Polish journalist Ryszard Kapuscinski once quoted an exiled Brazilian colleague who claimed after Brazil's World Cup victory in 1970 that "the military right wing can be assured of at least five more years of peaceful rule;"[30] Junta leader Emílio Médici organized a pompous reception for the team in Brasilia.

A special chapter in football's history also belongs to the 1978 Men's World Cup in Argentina. The military had taken control of the country two years earlier and General Jorge Rafael Videla and his cohorts ruled with an iron fist. Thousands of socialists were imprisoned or had "disappeared." Across the world, activists campaigned against the event, calling for a boycott, but hardly anyone complied. The famous Dutch player Johan Cruyff

initially explained his refusal to play at the tournament politically, but later revoked this explanation.

In Argentina, the dissidents were divided over
how to respond to the event. The *Madres de Plaza
de Mayo* staged protests. The armed resistance
groups declared a ceasefire. Meanwhile, the left-
wing Argentinean manager, César Luis Menotti,
claimed that the team was not playing for the dictatorship but for the people. After the victory in the
final, he refused to shake Videla's hand.

To this day, people are undecided about
whether the Argentinean victory helped the military or not. On the one
hand, the regime was able to claim the victory and to unite all Argentineans
under a supposedly common banner; on the other hand, the mass celebrations reminded many Argentineans of powers that were stronger than anything the generals could control.

On a heartening note, the Nazis never managed to use international
football to their advantage. After two losses at home to Switzerland and
Sweden in 1942, the Nazis stopped playing international matches. After
losing to Sweden in Berlin, the Foreign Affairs Secretary Martin Luther
observed that "because victory in this football match is closer to the people's hearts than the capture of some city in the East, such an event must be
prohibited for the sake of the domestic mood."[31]

The Nazis' football legacy is mainly one of oppression. In 1933, they
closed not only the Jewish clubs and those organized in the abovementioned *Arbeiter-Turn- und Sportbund*, but also several others, including
Bavaria's SpVgg Unterhaching, a Bundesliga side in the late 1990s, for
"political unreliability." During their occupation of Kiev, they killed some
of the most prominent Dynamo players in 1942. Although an alleged "death
match" was never played, several of the Dynamo Kiev players were arrested
by the Germans and three of them were ultimately shot.[32]

Footballers also suffered under the Soviet regime. Nikolai Starostin,
who, after the end of his playing career,
founded Spartak Moscow in 1934 as a people's rival to Dynamo (secret police) and
CSKA (army), was imprisoned and exiled
to Siberia from 1942 to 1953.

Also intriguing is the case of Soviet star
striker Eduard Streltsov, who was sent to
prison for five years in 1958, following an
alleged rape. Many insist to this day that
Soviet authorities fabricated the charges
because Streltsov had become a possible

defector. Streltsov successfully returned to football in 1965 and even made the national team again.

In Spain, General Franco appeared able to exploit football for his interests. Fernando María Castiella, longtime Minister of Foreign Affairs under Franco, called Real Madrid "the best embassy we have ever had."[33]

In many countries, clubs were controlled by authoritarian political powers and used for propaganda purposes. Examples reach from Haifa Conakry in Ahmed Sékou Touré's Guinea to Dynamo Berlin in the German Democratic Republic and Al-Rasheed in Saddam Hussein's Iraq. Simon Kuper and Stefan Szymanski have used the term "totalitarian soccer" to describe the phenomenon.[34]

"Totalitarian soccer" can also take on other forms. National teams have been punished by their governments for bad performances. After their poor showing at the 2000 Africa Cup of Nations, the entire Ivory Coast squad was held in a work camp for three days. They were only released when FIFA threatened sanctions. Players of the unsuccessful Zaïre side at the 1974 Men's World Cup in Germany were abandoned by the government, many of them spending the rest of their lives in poverty. The stories about the torture of Iraqi soccer plays at the hands of Saddam Hussein's son Uday, a high sports official, are so outrageous that they seemed unbelievable if it were not for the many eye-witness accounts.

These days, the Prime Minister of Italy and media mogul Silvio Berlusconi also serves as the president of AC Milan, while the multimillionaire Mauricio Macri, former president of Boca Juniors, pursues a political career in Argentina. In Austria, the late right-wing politician Jörg Haider presided over the FC Kärnten, a club representing his home province.

Football tournaments have allegedly also influenced election results, perhaps most notably when the British Prime Minister Harold Wilson partly blamed his surprising defeat in the 1970 general election on England's exit from the Men's World Cup a few days earlier.

Football has also served as a tool in international relations. When Brazil played a friendly in war-torn Haiti in 2004, politicians hardly denied that the game was staged to boost Brazil's chances for a permanent seat in the United Nations Security Council. In other contexts, football reflects geopolitics, for example when Israeli teams play in European competitions rather than in Asian ones, or when military conflicts bar national teams from their home grounds; the Georgian team, for example, was forced to begin its World Cup qualifying campaign in 2008 in Mainz, Germany, because of the country's military confrontation with Russia. Worldwide social and economic injustice is reflected in football when teams from the global South are denied visas for attending tournaments in the global North, a common phenomenon.

Administrative soccer decisions can have huge political implications. Recent examples include FIFA's plans of banning international matches

above an altitude of 3,000 meters, which would deny capital cities like La Paz or Bogotá the right to host international matches. Especially in Bolivia, the plans have been interpreted as an imperialist attack on the country's sovereignty. Similarly, FIFA's ban of the Iranian women's team's jerseys, which include a hijab, has caused accusations of Islamophobia. It is indeed hard not to accuse FIFA of Eurocentrism in the handling of such matters. While hijabs are banned and Hapoel Tel Aviv striker Itay Shechter got booked for celebrating a goal with a kippa and a short prayer in a 2010 UEFA Champions League qualifier against Austria Salzburg, players on European or American sides cross themselves endlessly and even join for collective prayer on the pitch.

FIFA's apparent prioritization of European and American interests also caused huge outrage when the 2006 Men's World Cup was handed to Germany instead of South Africa. FIFA's decision seemed so shady and biased that African nations threatened a boycott. This was avoided when it became clear that South Africa would host the 2010 tournament.

In this context, it should be remembered that no African team was invited to a World Cup tournament until 1970. When, in 1966, one spot was offered to Africa, Asia, and Oceania combined, the African teams withdrew in protest. Even today, European interests remain central. Not only do Men's World Cup kick-off hours follow the best European television times—which forced players to endure soaring midday heat at the 1986 Men's World Cup in Mexico—but the continuing success of European sides at World Cup tournaments is also a self-fulfilling prophecy: out of the thirty-two nations playing at the 2010 Men's World Cup in South Africa, thirteen were European. If Africa were allowed to enter teams in similar numbers, for example, a semifinal berth would be much less of a challenge. Furthermore, the rules of the game are made to this day by the International Football Association Board (IFAB), which, apart from four FIFA representatives, consists of one representative each of the national football associations of England, Scotland, Wales, and Northern Ireland.

FIFA is an extremely powerful and rich organization, rife with corruption and oligarchic structures and tied into many political and economic interests. In its history, it has made a number of scandalous decisions. One of these was the acceptance of a Nazi German team to the 1938 Men's World Cup, although Austria had just been annexed and its best players integrated into the German side—excluding Jews.

The continental and national football associations rarely fare much better. In almost all cases, they are run by people from the political and economic elite. Sometimes, this becomes particularly obvious: longtime German FA president Gerhard Mayer-Vorfelder, for example, was a leading figure in Germany's *Christlich Demokratische Union* (CDU), and the Kuwaiti Sheik Fahad Al Ahmed, who stormed onto the field at the 1982 Men's World Cup after a controversial goal, was a high-ranking government and military official.

The lack of actual knowledge of the game among football officials is notorious. The autobiography of former professional player Len Shackleton contained a section called "What the average director knows about football." It was a blank page.

In the seminal *The Ball Is Round: A Global History of Football*, David Goldblatt speaks of official soccer culture as colonized by the politics of "appeasement"—in his assessment, this explains incidents like the Nazi salutes of English players before an international match against Germany in May 1938.[35]

Finally, here are some further examples of football being caught in the crossfire of political conflict in various ways:

Several football stadiums have been used as detention centers for political opponents. In the 1970s, this was the case in Chile and Argentina. In El Salvador, the national stadium has even been used to carry out televised executions of dissidents. More recently, "illegal" Albanian immigrants have been herded and detained at the football stadium in Bari, Italy.

In 1980, Colombia's *Movimiento 19 de Abril* (M-19) took several diplomats hostage at the Embassy of the Dominican Republic in Bogotá. They had gained entry to the premises by asking to retrieve a soccer ball they had kicked over the fence.

In June 1994, members of the loyalist Ulster Volunteer Force (UVF) entered a bar in the small Catholic village of Loughinisland during an Ireland vs. Italy Men's World Cup game, killing six people and wounding several more.

In 1997, the 126-day hostage drama at the Japanese embassy ended with the Tupac Amaru rebels gathering to play football in the foyer, when a special police unit detonated a bomb, killing most of them instantly.

During the 2010 Africa Cup of Nations in Angola, the bus of the Togolese team was attacked by the *Frente para a Libertação do Enclave de Cabinda* [Front for the Liberation of the Enclave of Cabinda] (FLEC), leaving three people dead.

Football's Role as an "Opiate of the Masses"

Albert Camus, Toni Negri, and Claudio Tamburrini are far from the only intellectuals who have embraced the game of soccer. There are also Vladimir Nabokov, Evelyn Waugh, Pier Paolo Pasolini, and the Latin American writers Eduardo Galeano, Mario Benedetti, and Mario Vargas Llosa, as well as the Peruvian director Francisco Lombardi, president of Sporting Cristal in the 1990s. Nonetheless, in intellectual circles football has often been described as nothing but a circus in which "twenty-two adults run after one ball." Especially among Marxists, the "opiate of the masses" argument has had a very secure place for a long time. The gist of the argument is simple: you give the masses something to be passionate about, and it keeps them from being passionate about political change.

Arguably, the history of soccer confirms this. Fearing the unruliness of the game, the upper classes realized that it could work to their own advantage as a controlled working-class distraction, as a time to forget the hardships of work, and as something to look forward to while toiling away in the factories.

Perhaps even more troubling is the false sense of unity that soccer victories produce. Graciela Daleo remembers celebrating with "the guy who had tortured you with electric drills" after Argentina's Men's World Cup victory in 1978. She says:

> The football thing becomes the dominating thing even in the concentration camp. The torturer who had tortured you when you were kidnapped, if he supported the same club as you did, this terribly mad ghostly bond would be established. Whenever I hear that song by [Joan Manuel] Serrat, "Fiesta," where he sings "the villain and the rich man shake hands, the differences don't matter". . . . I don't know. I've got an anger that has less to do with a sociological analysis and is more a gut reaction: I hate World Cups because they dissolve the class struggle. In a way, during the World Cup it seems we are all the same. We are not all the same.[36]

Andrew Feinstein wrote of similar dynamics in connection with the latest Men's World Cup in South Africa: "The World Cup will create a feel-good factor in South Africa, but when it's all over, the same urgent problems will remain in the world's most unequal country."[37] Dale T. McKinley added to this analysis: "In the case of the 'greatest show on earth,' leaving aside the very real beauty and enjoyment of the game of soccer, the myth-making has created a situation akin to inhaling tik—a short-lived high/euphoria that obscures all reality, followed by a rapid, depressing 'come down' back to that reality."[38]

These sentiments are confirmed by the Ivory Coast player Kolo Touré, when he talks about the effects of soccer victories for the troubled country: "Our job is to try to make people happy and to help them forget everything else. At the same time, we know that we players can't solve all of the country's problems. They wouldn't even disappear if we won the World Cup. People would be happy for two, three weeks—then everything would be again like it was before."[39]

To this day, such observations lead some Marxist theorists to a stern rejection of football. After the South Africa World Cup, Terry Eagleton published an article in the *Guardian* entitled "Football: A Dear Friend to Capitalism." He wrote:

> The World Cup is another setback to any radical change. [. . .] If every rightwing thinktank came up with a scheme to distract the populace from political injustice and compensate them for lives of hard labor, the solution in each case would be the same: football. No finer way of resolving the problems of capitalism has been dreamed up, bar socialism. And in the tussle between them, football is several light years ahead.[40]

Certain historical events confirm Eagleton's concerns. It does indeed seem worrying that thousands of Bangladeshis got so upset about Diego Maradona's exclusion from the 1994 World Cup after a failed drug test that they staged a huge demonstration in Dacca; arguably, there were many more urgent issues to address. There is also truth in the German comedian Klaus Hansen's observation that "football is like democracy: twenty-two people play and millions are watching."

However, while many aspects of football politics give reason to the "opiate of the masses" argument, football is too complex a phenomenon for such a reduction. The game retains many rebellious aspects as well as genuine elements of working-class culture. In a 1998 article, Austrian Marxist Eric Wegner states that

> it has become necessary to partially partake in different forms of capitalist mass culture in order not to become completely isolated and to avoid psychological breakdown. Football has historically not only served the distraction from political and social problems, but also the creation of collective pride and class consciousness [. . .] with a more than average progressive potential.[41]

In July 2010, the Portsmouth Socialist Party branch posted a text expressing similar sentiments, entitled "Workers of the World United: Football and Socialism." Among other things, the authors claimed:

> While it would be correct to say that some in the capitalist class still see football as serving this role [opiate of the masses], it would be patronising in the extreme, to the millions of working class people who watch and play the game, to declare that they've simply been conned or duped, that their love of the sport as entertainment is simply a form of crowd control "brainwashing." Football is a unique cultural phenomenon. No other sport or leisure activity has developed and spread globally like it [. . .] Outside of the trade union movement there are very few areas of modern society where thousands of working class people can gather under a common banner, in support [of] a common cause. While some may cast this aside as mere tribalism, there exist clear feelings of inter-fan solidarity, which if promoted can have a positive great impact on promoting working class consciousness.[42]

Over the last twenty years, the embrace of postmodern diversity and "irrationalism" has given many intellectual closet football fans enough self-confidence to openly voice their passion for the game. It has also become popular to theorize soccer in intellectual forums, and playing the game suddenly gained an air of coolness, as if you dared enter forbidden terrain. In Germany, both the pop culture magazine *Spex* and the radical journal *Die Beute* ran regular football articles in the 1990s. The famed psychoanalyst Klaus Theweleit (*Male Fantasies*) began to publish and lecture about football, and today, before every big tournament, intellectuals profess their love for the game—even if they know nothing about it.

The instrumentalization of football has little to do with the game itself. The powerful instrumentalize everything, including sports, arts, and consumer culture. An "opiate of the masses" is not dependent on football; if football disappears, another opiate will be found. In other words, the solution is not to fight football but to fight a power structure that relies on mass control and distraction.

Nationalism and Sectarianism

A common criticism of football is that it ignites, concentrates, and amplifies nationalistic and sectarian feelings. Looking at the track record of football-related violence this seems hard to deny. To provide just a few examples: in 1930, Argentineans attacked the Uruguayan Consulate in Buenos Aires after their team's loss in the Men's World Cup final; in 1950, the Uruguay players were attacked after beating host Brazil for another Men's World Cup victory; in 1970, the so-called "Football War" between Honduras and El Salvador, following two World Cup qualifying matches, left 6,000 people dead, 12,000 wounded, and 50,000 homeless; in 1990, a Dinamo Zagreb vs. Red Star Belgrade encounter led to widespread rioting between Serbs and Croats, including an on-field brawl in which Ex-Yugoslav and Croatian international Zvonimir Boban famously kicked a police officer; in 2003, a Senegal vs. Gambia game rekindled tensions between the neighboring countries and led to a temporary closure of the border; in 2009, the Egypt vs. Algeria Men's World Cup qualifiers were marred by widespread hostilities.

Northern Ireland has been plagued by a long history of politically motivated football violence. The most notorious event was the Protestant crowd attack on Belfast Celtic players after a game against Linfield in 1948. Belfast Celtic disbanded one year later. The tensions around Derry City games were only resolved when, in 1985, the club left the Northern Irish league to compete in the republic's League of Ireland. In 2002, Neil Lennon, a Catholic playing for Celtic Glasgow, abandoned his international career after death threats in the name of the Loyalist Volunteer Force (LVF) were made before a friendly against Cyprus.

Apart from violent clashes and threats, questions of nation-state identity have impacted football in many ways. In the 1950s, for example, both Turkey and Indonesia refused to play Israel in qualifying matches for the Men's World Cup. There is also a particular rhetoric surrounding certain national encounters, such as those between England and Germany. Before the teams met at the 1990 Men's World Cup, the *Sun* headlined: "We Beat Them In 45 . . . Now The Battle of 90!" Captions before their 1996 European Championship encounter included the *Daily Mirror's* "Achtung Surrender" and the *Sun's* "Let's Blitz Fritz." After the 5-1 thrashing of the German side in Munich in 2001, T-shirts such as *Munich 1-5: Two World Wars and One World Cup* were sold around England. England vs. Argentina games have long been played as ersatz battles for the Falkland Wars, and Dutch player Willem von Hanegem saw games against Germany in the 1970s as a possibility to avenge the death of his father, sister, and two brothers under German occupation during World War II. Football results have also had highly symbolic value in strained nation-state relationships, as when East Germany beat West Germany at the 1974 Men's World Cup, or when Iran beat the United States at the Men's World Cup in 2002.

Clashes between the supporters of rival clubs have led to tragic outcomes, perhaps most famously when thirty-nine people died before the

1985 Men's European Cup final after Liverpool fans charged the supporters of opponent Juventus Turin. Football clubs can indeed become "only a slightly downplayed version of the nation."[43] In 1937, the Italian press reported Bologna's victory over Chelsea as "a brilliant victory for fascist Italy."[44] Particularly well-documented are the conflicts between Celtic Glasgow and Glasgow Rangers supporters, with the former representing the Irish/Catholic community and the latter the British/Protestant.[45]

In all these cases, however, football hardly appears to be the culprit. The "Football War" between Honduras and El Salvador might have been triggered by the countries meeting in a decisive World Cup qualifier, but it was not about football—it concerned land rights and poverty. Likewise, Celtic and Rangers are not responsible for sectarian strife in Ireland and Scotland. It is true that the antagonism played out on the football field and on the stadium terraces might prolong the tensions. However, football also has an enormous power to bring people together. In a non-nationalist and a non-sectarian world, it could not serve nationalistic or sectarian feelings.

In a left-wing context, the discussion of nationalism needs further attention. This is not the forum to decide whether the "nation" is a reactionary concept in itself or whether, especially in an anti-colonial context, it can have liberatory dimensions. However, since the latter has been assumed by many activists and revolutionaries, it has impacted soccer in many ways.

One of the most prominent examples is that of the pre-independence Algerian national team: in 1958, some of the best-known Algerian players left the French league over night, gathered in Tunisia, and formed an "Algerian national team" under the auspices of the *Front de Libération Nationale* (FLN). The team played almost one hundred matches in North Africa, the Middle East, Eastern Europe, and East Asia during a twenty-month period, representing the ambitions of the Algerian people for self-rule.

Today, the Palestinian national team, resurrected in the late 1990s, plays a similar role. Met with many obstacles by the Israeli occupation, reaching from the denial of travel permits to casualties resulting from Israeli military strikes, the team is seen as an important symbol in the Palestinians' quest for independence.

Telling, too, is the response of Roger Milla, Cameroon's 1990 World Cup star, to a question of the French football magazine *France Football* about the win against Argentina and the reactions of President Paul Biya: "An African head of state who leaves as the victor, and who greets with a smile the defeated heads of state! . . . It's thanks to football that a small country could become great."[46] The Senegalese probably thought similarly when their team beat the former colonial power France at the 2002 Men's World Cup, and the same can be said for the Irish after their 1-0 victory over England at the 1988 Men's European Championship. In Africa in the 1950s, Kwame Nkrumah ostentatiously tied football to the history of anti-colonial, pan-African struggle when naming Ghana's football team the Black Stars, a direct reference to Marcus Garvey's Black Star Line.

On a club level, the significance of the Catalan FC Barcelona and the Basque Athletic Bilbao as symbols of anti-Franco resistance is well documented. In the Soviet Union, the sensational 1969 Cup victory of FC Karapty Liv remains celebrated as a manifestation of Ukrainian sovereignty. During the Third Reich, Vienna football terraces often demonstrated Austrian resistance to German annexation through a particularly hostile reception of German teams, and Austria's 3-2 victory over Germany at the 1978 Men's World Cup arguably marked a huge step in the country's emancipation as an independent nation.

In general, though, football's "nation-building" role is a tricky subject. At times, football truly seems to help nationally defined communities overcome internal strife and find collective identity. Recent examples include the triumph of a post-apartheid South African side at the 1996 Africa Cup of Nations; the success of a politically fragmented Ivory Coast at the same tournament in 2006; and Iraq's victory at the 2007 Asia Cup. If nothing else, the Iraqi success "reminded a civilization what 'normal' feels like."[47] However, such moments only bring temporary relief. Just as football cannot be held responsible for causing political conflict, it cannot solve it. The victory of an integrated French side at the 1998 Men's World Cup provides a case in point. Arguably, it helped ease community tensions at the time and diminished the success of the right-wing *Front national* in upcoming elections. However, angry French-Algerians invaded the pitch at the historical first encounter between France and Algeria in 2001, *Front national* leader Jean-Marie Le Pen was a final round candidate in the presidential elections of 2002, and riots rocked predominantly non-white suburbs in France in 2005.

At worst, football's nation-building powers serve reactionary politics. A prime example is the role that football successes played in newly independent Croatia under the authoritarian regime of Franjo Tudjman in the 1990s. In 1954, few were thrilled when Germans celebrated their team's unexpected win at the 1954 Men's World Cup with phrases like *Wir sind wieder wer*: "we are to be reckoned with again."[48]

The crossroads of football and national identity also allow one to examine the formation of the latter in a post-colonial world. In Germany, for instance, many migrants of Turkish and Middle Eastern background very actively support the German national team. To analyze this as a mere gesture of demonstrating one's willingness to "fit in" is too simple—many of the sentiments expressed and the migrants' identification with their new home country are genuine. In fact, the phenomenon expands even beyond Germany's borders. A Latin American friend was appalled when the sizeable Middle Eastern community in Sweden overwhelmingly supported

Germany in their 2010 Men's World Cup quarterfinal against Argentina. Yet, in this duel, it was much easier for members of the community to identify with the German side—they have friends and relatives in Germany, know more about the country, etc.

Interestingly enough, this has created problems for some on the German left. During the tournament in South Africa, a group of autonomist activists removed a huge German flag, worth several hundred euros, from a building in Berlin-Neukölln. "Collecting" German flags during big soccer tournaments has become a favorite pastime for many German anti-nationalists—some bars offer free drinks if you hand in a certain amount. In this case, however, the owner of the flag was a Lebanese shopkeeper who had been living in Germany for twenty years. A long, heated debate ensued over leftist activists "hurting a migrant."

A positive development is to see non-white players representing European countries other than the colonial powers of England, France, and the Netherlands. There are non-white players on all Scandinavian and German-speaking sides, for example. Unfortunately, these changes still meet resistance. In Italy, banners reading "There Is No Black Italian" were hoisted in stadiums when it was suggested that Mario Balotelli, a blessed soccer player of Ghanaian ancestry brought up in Italy, was to be called up for the national team.

In the context of fluctuating citizenship, an increasing number of players are forced to make choices with respect to their footballing allegiance. This can have peculiar consequences. At the 2010 Men's World Cup encounter between Ghana and Germany, Kevin-Prince Boateng represented the former, and his brother Jérôme the latter—the Boatengs have a Ghanaian father but grew up in Germany. Turkey regularly fields players who were born and raised outside of the country. However, cosmopolitan elements are nothing new in football. When the U.S. team sensationally beat England at the 1950 Men's World Cup, the goalscorer, Joe Gaetjens, hailed from Haiti—a U.S. territory at the time.

The integrative potential of football has already been mentioned. At times, it becomes particularly tangible. In Fiji, the town of Ba sees little of the fighting between ethnic Fijians and Fiji-Indians that regularly haunts the islands. The reason given by all of the country's communities is that, for decades, Ba has had a successful integrated soccer club. In Brazil, it has long been argued that issues of racism would be more pronounced if it were not for the national football team uniting players from all backgrounds. In Europe, many clubs founded by migrant communities played an important role for integration. A well-known example is the FBK Balkan, founded in Malmö, Sweden, in 1962. Zlatan Ibrahimović played for the club in his youth. Similar Swedish teams have even advanced to the country's highest league, such as Assyriska and Syrianska FC, both founded in 1974 in Södertälje, home to the world's biggest Assyrian/Syriac community. In Germany, Türkiyemspor Berlin, founded in 1978 in Berlin-Kreuzberg, has received a lot of media attention and was an important factor for the growing recognition of the Turkish community in the country. Several Türkiyemspor clubs have since emerged, not only in Germany but also in a number of other countries, including Australia and the United States.

The integrative potential of football was perhaps most famously exemplified by the game played between British and German soldiers on Christmas Eve 1914 after a spontaneous truce was declared at the Flanders front. Football has served as the basis for many community-building projects since. To name but a few examples: the Football for All campaign aims to undermine sectarian tensions and discrimination in the UK; in Georgia, Atlanta, the Soccer in the Streets project and the Fugees team try to provide poor and migrant children with a sense of belonging and achievement; and in Berlin-Kreuzberg, the women's club BSV Al-Dersimspor became well known for organizing games against Iran's Women's national team, both in Berlin and in Tehran. Recently, the *Institut de Relations Internationales et Strategiques* (IRIS), has been calling for a 2018 Men's World Cup in Israel and Palestine:

> The common organization of the 2018 World Cup in two countries whose inhabitants have been at war for a long time would be a symbol of sport's contribution to peace. Seeing the World Cup take place in the region could serve as an additional motivation for Israelis and Palestinians to sign a peace treaty so long overdue. Let us imagine these two peoples working hand in hand to co-organize the biggest event on the planet [48]

Among tournaments that have been established in an integrative spirit are the International Gay and Lesbian Football Association (IGLFA) World Championship, the Homeless World Cup, the Amputee Football World Cup, and the Come Together Cups in various German cities. Reconciling football games have also been organized on special occasions, for example when several human rights groups, including the *Madres de Plaza de Mayo*, arranged *La otra*

final [The Other Final] in Buenos Aires in 2008 to commonly address the pain related to the 1978 Men's World Cup in Argentina taking place under a military dictatorship. There is even a TV program called *The Team*, which builds on football's unifying powers. The Search for Common Ground project, which produces the program, states:

> In its multi-nation, episodic drama *The Team*, Search for Common Ground has merged the global appeal of soccer/football with soap opera to help transform social attitudes and diminish violent behavior in countries grappling with deeply rooted conflict. The television series addresses the very real divisive issues facing societies in a dozen African, Asian and Middle Eastern countries, using sport as a unifier to surmount barriers. Each production of *The Team* follows the characters on a football team who must overcome their differences—be they cultural, ethnic, religious, tribal, racial or socio-economic—in order to work together to win the game.[49]

With shows in Kenya, Morocco, and the Ivory Coast up and running, additional shows are produced for the Democratic Republic of Congo, Liberia, Nepal, Palestine, and Sierra Leone.

Football-based social projects include *Moving the Goalposts* in Kilifi, Kenya, *L'Athlétique d'Haiti* in Port-au-Prince, and *Gol de Placa* in Rio de Janeiro—many more examples are united in the *streetfootballworld* network.[50] Teams such as the Chosen Few Lesbian Soccer Club of Johannesburg, South Africa, and the Flying Bats Women's Football Club of Sydney, Australia, support lesbians' rights in a heteronormative world. The Pachakuti club in Bolivia, founded by the ex-guerrillero and trade union leader Felipe Quispe Huanca, seeks to unite indigenous people in both an athletic and a political environment. The integrative potential of soccer teams is in many ways encouraging and empowering, and we can rest assured that we will witness many more exciting projects.

Fan Violence

In the 1980s, the image of a drunk, violent, working-class brute in football club colors became synonymous with the image of the football fan in general. Hooliganism received enormous attention in the tabloids, provoked extensive academic work, was the subject of many governmental reports, and caused many new legal measures, including football supporters' data bases, travel bans, and new surveillance technology in the stadiums.

Violence in connection with football matches was not a new phenomenon. In 1909, a riot following a Rangers and Celtic derby involved 6,000 spectators, injured fifty-four policemen, and caused serious damage to the grounds as well as "the destruction of virtually every street-lamp around Hampden."[51] Pitch invasions were a common sight on British grounds for a long time. In general, though, this was nothing that the authorities or the media paid specific attention to.

This changed in the 1960s. Some have blamed television for allowing sensationalized terrace scuffles, thereby helping to create a violence-prone supporters' subculture. As a report noted: "The mass media in general and the national press in particular can take major credit for the public's view of the soccer hooligan as a cross between the Neanderthal Man and Conan the Barbarian."[52]

In reference to a much -publicized riot during a 1961 Sunderland vs. Tottenham game, the *Guardian* wrote that the images "provided ... encouragement to others."[53] Soon, the term "hooligan"—used in Britain for a "street ruffian" since the 1890s—came to signify the "wild" football fan of the 1960s, causing a Victorian moral panic vocalized by the Conservative Party and major newspaper outlets. Yellow press headlines read "Smash These Thugs!" and "Murder on a Soccer Train!" (*Sun*), "Mindless Morons" and "Cage the Animals" (*Daily Mirror*), as well as "Thump and Be Thumped" (*Daily Express*). The hooligan as an uncontrollable maverick fit in neatly with the era's bourgeois fear over rising juvenile crime and delinquency, gangs, and youth violence in general, fueled by the emergence of subcultures such as the Teddy Boys and events like the Notting Hill riots of 1958.

Police statistics show that incidences of violence on match days in English towns never increased by more than a negligible 1 percent—neither in the 1960s nor thereafter. Nonetheless, the hooligan phenomenon induced widespread panic and scholars finally had a football topic worth studying.

The trend continued in the 1970s and '80s. Leeds United was banned for a couple of years from European competition after supporters rioted following the 1975 European Cup Final against Bayern Munich in Paris. Hooligan incidents were increasingly reported from countries other than England as well, most notably from Holland, Germany, and Italy. The notoriety of hooliganism culminated in the events at Brussel's Heysel Stadium in 1985, when thirty-nine people died after clashes preceding the European Cup Final between Liverpool and Juventus. The tragedy seemed to confirm all the horror stories fed to the public. English teams were banned from European competition for five years, and the government plotted drastic measures on the island itself, including an ID card scheme for football fans that even Lord Justice Taylor described as "using a sledgehammer to crack a nut."[54] Even though this particular motion never passed, many others did. Among them were the Public Disorder Act of 1986 that allowed courts to ban fans from football grounds; the Football Spectators Act of 1989 that authorized courts to impose restriction orders on fans, preventing them from attending matches abroad; the Football Offences Act of 1991 that defined new offences of disorderly behavior (namely throwing missiles), taking part in indecent chanting, and entering the pitch without author-ity; the Football (Disorder) Act of 1999 that required courts to issue sta-dium bans on the base of certain convictions and ordering banned fans to hand over their passports; and, finally, the Football Disorder Act of 2000 that abolished the distinction between domestic and international banning orders, effectively preventing all police-registered hooligans from travel-ing abroad.

Both football supporters and left-leaning activists launched widespread protest campaigns against these measures as they threatened the civil liber-ties of thousands of people and were, in modified forms, extended to com-munities way beyond football supporters, for example ravers, travelers, and political protesters. Arguably, the 1994 Criminal Justice Act was built on the legal framework provided by anti-hooligan laws. In the last few decades, travel bans based on anti-hooligan legislation have regularly been used to prevent activists from attending political gatherings.

Football grounds have become increasingly fortified, equipped with special security forces, surveillance cameras, and all-around fences. Arguments about increased stadium safety lack empirical basis. Very often it is the high-security surroundings that provoke supporters and aggravate tensions within the grounds. Some of the grassroots fan initiatives pre-sented later in this book have done decidedly more for stadium security than all law-and-order regulations and riot police units combined. This is particularly true for clubs that engage supporters and take an active part in community life.

The fact that football hooliganism exists cannot be denied and its some-times tragic consequences must not be belittled. It is also true that football-related violence puts a strain on the public that angers many—in Sweden, for example, millions of taxpayers' *kronors* go into policing the matches between Stockholm, Gothenburg, and Malmö teams every year. In other countries, especially in Greece and Italy, hooligan groups have risen to powerful factions within clubs, cooperating with corrupt club officials. In Argentina, the so-called *barra bravas* have even been used as fear-inducing gangs in electoral campaigns. In 2002, the violence got so out of hand that all professional matches were suspended. Hooligan groups—or "firms," as they are often called—have also been regularly infiltrated by the far right.

Still, the "football hooligan problem" has been grossly exaggerated over the last thirty years, especially since it has little to do with football as such. It is well known that hooligans look for an outlet for physical confron-tation and have little interest in the game itself. If they are banned from football grounds, they will not become less violent—they just take their vio-lence somewhere else. Violent confrontations between people, in football stadiums or elsewhere, are a social problem and have to be solved accord-ingly. Football, in fact, can in many ways help keep youth from engaging in violent behavior, as it allows them to express their anger, frustration, and need for attention in socially acceptable ways and provides meaning in what may feel like empty lives.

Unfortunately, sensationalist reporting on hooliganism continues, not least in liberal forums. The widespread attention paid to Željko Ražnatović, a.k.a. Arkan, a former Red Star Belgrade supporter who ended up leading Serbian militias in the war against Croatia, is characteristic. Using Arkan's case to portray all of Red Star Belgrade's supporters as agents of ethnic cleansing is like citing Timothy McVeigh's Oklahoma City bombing as proof that all U.S. soldiers are mass murderers. Such reporting contributes to the ongoing use of football hooliganism as an excuse for increased state control, a pressing issue in the post-9/11 world.

◼ Courts, Police, and Armies in Full Effect

Viktor Györffy

During the 2008 Men's European Championships, there will be "Fan Zones" and "Public Viewing Areas" all over the country. Public streets and squares will be—at least partly—privatized. Municipalities are not only responsible for showing games on huge outdoor screens, but also for enforcing the rights of the championships' exclusive sponsors: only their advertisements may be  seen and only their drinks may be served. Bar and restaurant owners who refuse to comply will see iron fences go up around their properties. Fans who arrive in a T-shirt of the wrong beer company risk being thrown out of the zone, and private security firms will ensure that all these policies are implemented.

With the Euro 08 approaching, the Swiss *Staatsschutzgesetz BWIS*—commonly known as the "Hooligan Law"—has been tightened and a hooligan database has been established. The criteria for inclusion are dubious. A suspicious club official or a criminal complaint filed by the police is enough—a court sentence not necessary. The possible consequences are up to twenty-four hours of police detention, twelve months of location bans, and longtime obligations to register with the police. As media reports have recently revealed, the police also intend to preventively check on fans at home and at work, although no legal precautions have been made for such measures.

Summary procedures are to speed up the judicial process. In Zurich, there are plans for a special "arrest alley" at the *Kasernenareal*, a square in the inner city. State prosecutors, judges, and police are supposed to work in construction trailers. The arrested will be presented in handcuffs before leaving with or without punishment. It is planned to "handle" up to five hundred people a day that way.

During the last few months, several police operations against political protesters seemed to serve as test runs for police activity during the championships: in Lucerne on December 1, in Bern on January 19, and in Basel on January 26. The police arrested people preventively en masse, including accredited journalists. Those arrested were detained for hours. The fact that an arrest needs legal justification—for example, reasonable suspicion of the intent to commit a crime—apparently mattered little. After each operation, the authorities admitted mistakes, but these concerned technicalities, not the operations themselves. Switzerland's intelligence agencies were heavily involved, providing as well as gathering data.

In preparation for the championships, Swiss police went for training abroad, especially to Germany where their colleagues shared experience from the 2006 World Cup. Foreign security personnel will also be present in Switzerland during the tournament. The Swiss forces will be joined by units from Germany and France. We are talking about six hundred policemen. "Experts" and intelligence agents from other countries will be present as well. The Swiss intelligence services will install an international information exchange operating around the clock.

The Swiss Army will probably see its biggest deployment since World War II. What exactly the soldiers are expected to do remains unclear. The ideas range from increased border patrols to logistical aid to security services—and of course, the prevention of possible terrorist attacks. So far, the army has hardly been met with enthusiasm by the Swiss cantons. There is only one thing that the civilian authorities welcome with open arms: the use of unmanned aerial vehicles equipped with cameras. Video surveillance in the stadiums and in public areas will rise to unprecedented heights.

During the championships, basic civil rights, personal freedom, and privacy will come under serious threat. It must be assumed that some of the measures will remain in place long after the tournament. There are already discussions about turning the temporary "Hooligan Law" into something more permanent. Furthermore, it is very common to extend repressive measures designed for a particular group of people to others. Banning people from certain locations is a good example of this. In Switzerland, such a measure was originally introduced in the city of Bern, later incorporated into Swiss immigration law, and now inscribed not only into the "Hooligan Law" but also into the legal codes of several cantons. Likewise, the abovementioned police operations of recent months—justified by the apparent hooligan threat—help prepare for future political protests.

Many of the security measures implemented in light of the European championships reflect the general trend toward ever increasing surveillance and repression. The constantly growing number of surveillance cameras is maybe the most tangible expression of this. Fitting are also new amendments to the National Security Act: the Federal Council tries to exploit the Championships for breaking Swiss taboos like the confidentiality of mail, telephone, and computer communication.

Human rights organizations, fan groups, and lawyers have started to organize with the championships approaching. There will be information events, direct actions, and legal aid, provided by groups like *Demokratische Juristinnen und Juristen Schweiz, grundrechte.ch, augenauf, Rechtsauskunft Anwaltskollektiv*, and *Pikett Strafverteidigung*.

Viktor Györffy works as a lawyer in Zurich and is the president of the civil rights organization grundrechte.ch. This article was first published as "Justiz, Polizei und Armee im Grosseinsatz" in a reader for the event series Fancity 2008 in Zurich's Rote Fabrik (March–July 2008). Translated by Gabriel Kuhn.

The Commercialization of the Game and the "New Football Economy"

Commercial interests have a long history in football. Two players of Darwen, a small Lancashire club that played the Old Etonians in the 1879 English FA Cup quarterfinals, were reportedly the first players ever to receive pay. Seven years later, football professionalism was legalized in Britain. The Baines Cards, the first ever series of collectable sports cards, introduced in 1887, have been called "the first brilliant commercial project to spring from popular sports with mass appeal."[55] In 1888, Small Heath, today Birmingham City, was the first football club to become a limited company. At the time, no FAs had yet been founded outside of Britain.

In Continental Europe, professional football emerged in the 1920s. Vienna introduced the first professional league in 1924. In North America, some clubs paid enough to entice European players to cross the Atlantic. In 1925, Alex McNab, a Scottish star player, got signed for twenty-five dollars a week by Boston's Wonder Works factory team.

However, the commercial beginnings of football were modest, and football players were neither multimillionaires nor celebrities. Most professionals could not rely on football alone. Club owners got some profit out of running their teams, but mainly maintained them to appease their workers, to secure their loyalty, and to boost their prestige:

Most of the early football directors ran football clubs less for direct profit than for the desire to contribute locally to an important community activity, to improve their local status and, yes, to avail themselves of modest business opportunities around the staging of club matches. Directors in the building trade could expect to win the business to build club stands, for example; those in hosiery provided the playing kit; director/bakers sold the club pies for home games. In essence, the club was placed in the trust of local businessmen who benefited in small but significant ways from their work for the club.[56]

In the 1930s, well-known players, the first "football celebrities," began advertising products away from the pitch. Pioneers like Dixie Dean and Stanley Matthews hawked everything from cigarettes to men's clothing.

The commercialization of football grew steadily after World War II, especially once the post-war economic boom hit Europe. Stanley Matthews set a mark again when, in 1951, he was the first player to be paid £20 a week for wearing a particular brand of football boots.

The basis for the "New Football Economy" was laid in the 1960s, a decade that saw the lifting of salary caps as well as the rise of TV culture. Unprecedented amounts of money were poured into football as an industry. It did not take long for these developments to be criticized. *Le Miroir du Football*, a French soccer magazine published from 1960 to 1979 and affiliated to the Communist Party, denounced the commercial interests threatening the "people's character" of the game.

▋ Footballers–Be Aware of Your Power!

Editorial in *Le Miroir du Football*, no. 1, January 1960
François Thébaud

Footballers, my brothers, do you suffer from an inferiority complex?

You are many: five hundred thousand in France, at least twenty million in the world, maybe one hundred million if you count the spectators. But when those in power speak of the "mass sports" of the golden age, they do not think of you.

You are poor. Yet the state refuses to subsidize your sport like it does others.

You are earnest. Yet people bet on your performances, a practice that is degrading your sport, and hand you crumbs of a feast you have not been invited to.

Your game expresses the natural joy of pacifist competition, of the change of fate, of unpredictability. Yet, officially, you are treated like one of the ascetic, "boring" sports.

Your sport causes enthusiasm because in its highest form it becomes art. Yet, whenever we claim as much, it is called an act of "literary hysteria."

Your sport demands intelligence: ever-changing situations require individual initiative as well as collective creativity. Yet the commentators insist on stressing the game's physical aspects.

Your sport demands all athletic qualities: speed, flexibility, technical skill, stamina, and strength; it forms an attractive, natural synthesis of the most diverse physical disciplines; it completes the human being. Yet it is accused of belonging to a selected few.

You, professional footballers, practice a dangerous trade. It is never clear whether you earn enough, and, in any case, it will be little. Yet the system of transfers reduces you to goods, you are denied to partake in the organization of your sport, and you are exposed to sarcastic remarks of people who ignore the technical difficulties of the game and the hardships of your profession.

France has the third best team in the world and some of the best players on the planet. Yet the biggest of your stadiums make your friends from small nations like Uruguay, Switzerland, Belgium, Hungary, and Romania laugh with pity.

Dear footballers, my brothers, you need to grasp your power! It is a power that has allowed FIFA to unite ninety-five nations under its umbrella, without discrimination against race, religious beliefs, and political convictions—this is a number superior to that of the United Nations. It is a power that has allowed countries as opposed as the Soviet Union and Spain to meet in the European Championships.

It is the goal of *Miroir du football* to help you, anonymous and celebrated footballers, managers, spectators of small and big matches, and owners of obscure clubs, to better understand this power, to foster it, to develop it, and to discover its foundations. We are committed to a fight against the chauvinism that rests on the ignorance of the game, against the mercantile exploitation of your passions. In short, we intend to contribute to the greatness of football!

If you search in our pages for material to satisfy nationalist pride, the spirit of the church tower, or the commercial cult of the star player, then put the paper away!

But if you love football for what it is, if you are looking to expand your knowledge about all of the aspects of the game that has conquered the world . . . well, then *Miroir du football* is already your journal!

Translated by Gabriel Kuhn.

The 1966 Men's World Cup in England was an event of particular significance. It introduced many commercial gimmicks that define football culture to this day: an official World Cup song was recorded; a mascot, World Cup Willy, was designed and sold in all shapes and forms; businesses used the event for various PR campaigns—gas stations, for example, offered special "World Cup Medals"; and the interests of media, especially television, determined the kick-off hours. In the midst of all this, the completely unsuspected success by the North Korean team provides us with one of football's most intriguing stories.

■ Red Rice in Middlesbrough: The Axis of Evil as a Four-Man Defense Line

Gerd Dembowski

North Korea, 1966. "The party has decided that you have to win at least one game. Now go and do as you are told!"

This—or something like this—was the order of the "Great Leader" Kim Il Sung as he said goodbye to his envoys after they won the final qualifying game over Australia in Cambodia. And since, as everyone knows, the party is always right, the "red ants"—that's what they were called—were firmly convinced of their communist mission. After all, they had spent two years in a military camp, completely isolated from the world. None of them was married. Their 9-1-1 system, i.e., nine at the front or, alternatively, eleven at the back, demanded unprecedented endurance. It was not by coincidence that the German term *Pferdelunge* [horse lung] was first used by a football reporter during one of their games. No player could be defined as a back or as a forward—the North Korean team of 1966 was a solid, constantly moving collective.

At first, the English did not even allow the team under manager superior Myung Rye Hyun to enter the country. Since the Korean War of the early 1950s, the UK had no diplomatic relations to the northern Democratic People's Republic. However, visas were granted at the last minute, despite the objection of the South Korean ambassador. In the end, the British authorities even flew the North Korean flag, which was technically illegal.

In the first game against the comrades from the USSR, the North Koreans proved to be loyal proletarians and lost 0-3. The arrogant Chileans, however, were confused by this cooperative of long-distance runners. Had the replacement of English beds with military cots been the right move after all? Two minutes from time, Pak Seung Zin scored with an irresistible shot from twenty meters, tying the game at 1-1. The ants from Chosŏn Minjujuŭi Inmin Konghwaguk—so the correct name of North Korea—managed to keep their rice chamber shut until the final whistle. As goalkeeper Lee Chang Myung reported: "After we had managed to draw against Chile, the masses celebrated so hard that lamps fell from ceilings." Animal names remained popular when describing the North Korean side. While the fans called them "cats" because of their speed and their offensive game, a number of journalists opted for "red mosquitoes."

Real rice was served in the last game of the group stage against the mighty favorite Italy. The game was played at Middlesbrough's Ayresome Park. On the day of the game, Middlesbrough spelled Pyongyang. The workers' town's club had just been relegated to the third league and its jerseys' color matched that of the North Koreans: red. The people of Middlesbrough were used to supporting the underdog and embracing the visitors from the Far East as theirs came easily. Early on in the game, the team with the shortest average height to ever play at a World Cup earned yet another animal nickname due to their jumping power and the skillful evasion of the Italians' tackles: reporters now called them "jumping mice." The English 1966 Sports Photograph of the Year looked like a flip book: it seemingly shows a Korean winning a heading duel—however, upon closer inspection it shows no less than five jumping mice becoming one, demonstrating the union of communist spirits. The picture gave a hint of the "new human being" in the ascetic triumph of a football collective expanding people's consciousness.

The first half was not over yet when comrade Pak Doo-Ik turned into a legend by forcing the ball into the net: flat, fearless, and of course to the left. The Italian offensive that followed could not impress keeper Lee Chang Myung. Conceding a goal was simply no option: "Otherwise we would have not fulfilled the orders of the Great Leader. I guarded the goal with my life." When Pak Doo-Ik was asked about the "professional," hidden fouls of the Italians that followed his goal, he responded matter-of-factly: "We didn't even know what 'professional' fouls were, so we just kept on playing."

In the end, on this memorable day of July 19, 1966, the sensational 1-0 held against the best-paid football professionals on the planet. Italy was out. The team traveled home incognito, but was still greeted by a crowd of supporters throwing fruits and vegetables. The manager, Edmondo Fabbri, was even beaten up. When the political opposition asked in parliament how the football giant Italy could have lost against the communist dwarf from the Far East, a government spokesperson responded: "Ask a dentist called Pak Doo-Ik!"

Pak was indeed registered as a dentistry student. Even before finishing his studies, he had instilled the fear of a dental visit upon an entire country, framed in football terms: "The Fall of the Roman Empire Is Nothing Against This," read one of the Italian headlines. Ever since that day, Italian journalists and fans alike plead during a shaky performance of the *squadra azurra*: "Please, not a second Korea!" The Italian defeat to South Korea at the 2002 Men's World Cup has added yet another dimension to the phrase . . .

While the Italian players washed foul tomatoes off their bodies in 1966, the "Cinderella Team" of North Korea traveled to their quarterfinal game against Portugal in Everton. They were accompanied by three thousand fans from Middlesbrough who called them "our lads" and cheered them on with loud "Heya, Heya, Korea!" chants. As a reward, they were treated to twenty-four minutes of football from out of space, filled with communist stars: only the second ever Asian participant in a World Cup, North Korea took an early 3 0 lead! Pak Seung Zin had scored the first goal after just ten seconds, making him the fastest World Cup scorer to this day.

Manager superior Myung Rye Hyun—"Sternly Shining Sun"—had shown no understanding for the journalists' surprise after the victory against Italy. He explained that the result was simply the outcome of years of socialist planning. In 1966, football was not a very fast game—the tactics of the day called for a slow and careful style of play. Manager Hyun, however, preached "Chollima Lightning Football," named after a horse that, according to Far East mythology, could gallop at a speed of one thousand miles per hour. The "Great Leader" Kim Il Sung had used the same metaphor for the rapid economic development of Korean socialism. With manager Hyun adopting the motto, the Koreans played aggressively, changing their positions without end, and inventing what later become known as "forechecking."

Alas, there was no happy ending. Portugal had Eusebio who, in the end, ensured a 5-3 victory for his country. An undeserved penalty was given to Portugal at a crucial point in the game. However, the real reason for the late collapse of the jumping mice might have been a different one: confused by their success, FIFA had prohibited the consumption of ginseng before the Portugal game—a root the Koreans had devoured nonstop before. Was this their secret? Doping!?

After the World Cup, the players vanished like phantoms. According to anti-communist propaganda, they ended up in the Gulag. But the football workers and peasants knew they had nothing to fear. With their victory against Italy—which had moved them to tears—they had fulfilled the party's expectations. Stories about the players being sentenced to twenty years of hard labor for celebrating the Italian game with women and alcohol were pure capitalist slander.

In October 2001, Dan Gordon and Nick Bonner traveled to North Korea with a film crew of the BBC—a first for any Western camera team. For their documentary *The Game of Their Lives*, they were allowed to visit with the heroes of Middlesbrough and to interview people on the streets of Pyongyang without restrictions. Seven of the players were still active in football. Pak Doo-Ik had been the national team's manager for some years, goalkeeper Lee Chang Myung was coaching the country's army team, and the left-winger Yang Seung Kook was in charge of the important team of Pyongyang's cigarette factory. The people of Pyongyang could name all the players who were carried around the city and rewarded with medals after their return in 1966.

Their vanishing was part of it all—that's what phantoms do. Since 1966, North Korea has at times been banned from international competition and has at times excluded itself, for example when refusing to compete for a spot in the 2002 Men's World Cup in Japan and South Korea. FIFA President Sepp Blatter had planned to organize two games of the tournament in the Democratic People's Republic. This was not the result of socialist sympathies, however, but part of the "Sunshine Policy," that allowed the South Korean President Kim Dae-Jung and Blatter to eye the Peace Nobel Prize. The North Korean Juche dynasty wanted no part of it and remained pissed. There was hardly any TV coverage of the World Cup; game reports were shown at the most ridiculous hours and with great delays. The images used were all pirated and FIFA regulations bluntly ignored. Along the border, North Korean propaganda broadcasts were blasted from huge speakers, competing with the equally illegal broadcasts of the South Koreans.

Despite all the skirmishes, North Koreans are still passionate about football. This was not only confirmed by the BBC documentary. In 2002, the year of the Japan/South Korea World Cup, North Korea's men's team won the renowned King's Cup in Thailand after a penalty shoot-out against the host nation. The women's team also raised worldwide attention. They beat Singapore 24-0, which was at the time the second highest win of a national team ever, and they replaced the world's second-best women's team, China, as Asia Cup winners.

Cut.

Starting with the year of birth of its eternal leader Kim Il Sung, North Korea officially established a new era. The country's government has been accused of smuggling drugs and cigarettes, of illegal arms trade, of orchestrating terrorist attacks, of developing nuclear weapons, of systematically dispersing millions of dollars in fake notes, and of kidnapping political dissidents abroad. U.S. President Bush declared the country a "rogue state"; a part of the "axis of evil" that allegedly supports terrorism. But thanks to Buddha and sports fans, politics has—at least allegedly—

nothing to do with football. Sometimes the axis of evil is but a four-man defense line.

Gerd Dembowski is an author, performer, and spokesperson for the Bündnis aktiver Fußballfans (BAFF). This article was first published as "Roter Reis in Middlesbrough: Die Achse des Bösen als Viererkette" in his book *Fußball vs. Countrymusik* (Cologne: PapyRossa 2007). Translated by Gabriel Kuhn.

Needless to say, the magic display of North Korea's footballers did not halt football's commercialization. Liverpool introduced sponsored club jerseys in the 1970s. The practice soon engulfed the world of football, although this was far from appreciated by all. In *Soccer in Sun and Shadow*, Eduardo Galeano quotes Afro-Uruguayan midfielder Obdulio Varela, who refused to wear advertising on his shirt: "They used to drag us blacks around by rings in our noses. Those days are gone."[57] The FC Barcelona is the most prominent club among the few that have rejected shirt sponsoring for a long time; since 2006, Barcelona jerseys carry a UNICEF slogan.

There were still pockets of resistance to football's complete commercialization in the 1980s. Only amateur players were allowed at the Olympics until 1984, and Sweden's IFK Göteborg won the 1987 UEFA Cup with a team of semi-professionals. In the last twenty years, however, the process of commercialization has taken on a mind-boggling momentum: sponsorship deals, TV contracts, players' salaries, and transfer sums have skyrocketed. Simultaneously, the class background of the spectators has more and more shifted away from the working classes to the more affluent sections of society. In England, the introduction of the Premier League in 1992 has been described by John Reid as "year zero; previous football history did not happen. The new owners and media would like to forget football's working-class roots."[58]

A few numbers: The income of an average German Bundesliga club has multiplied by over one hundred since the Bundesliga's first season in 1963–64. In England, the cheapest tickets at Manchester United home games are now five times more than they were in 1991. Liverpool FC was sold for 332 million euros in 2007. The Manchester United trademark is estimated at 1.3 billion euros. The Sky and Setanta TV contract for the British Premier League is worth 1.7 billion pounds over three seasons. Real Madrid signed a contract with Adidas in 2005 that guarantees 500 million euros a year and Argentinean star player Lionel Messi receives an annual one million euro by the same company. Sweden's Zlatan Ibrahimović and Brazil's Kaká earn nine million euros per season. Barcelona paid sixty-nine million euros to buy Ibrahimović from Inter in 2009. The FIFA profit estimate for the 2010 Men's World Cup in South Africa was more than three billion U.S. dollars.

The income that clubs draw from match attendance—pretty much the sole income of clubs in professional football's early days—has fallen to less than 20 percent. Transfer sums account for even less of an average professional club's income. The sale of merchandise is roughly at the level of ticket sales. Basically, over half of the money moved in the football industry comes from sources that have nothing to do with the game itself, namely TV and corporate sponsorship.

The high sums involved do not mean that everyone is doing well. The New Football Economy follows neoliberal logics. John Reid observes:

> [The] football renaissance has left the rich clubs richer and the poor almost bankrupt. It is a mirror image of society in general. [. . .] The gulf between the Premiership and the Football League [the lower levels of professional football in England] is widening. The 20 Premier clubs generate [. . .] a total income of [. . .] more than twice the amount of the 72 league clubs combined.[59]

Cornel Sandvoss, author of *A Game of Two Halves*, writes that "there appears to be a 'trickle down' effect, but mirroring the wider development of British society, it is one of percolation of poverty, rather than the distribution of wealth."[60]

Apologists of the New Football Economy like to employ well-known political arguments that tie democracy to capitalism. Turning football clubs into corporations, they say, makes them more democratic since fans can become stakeholders and execute a more direct influence on the club. As John Reid explains, this is little more than cheap rhetoric:

> The flotation of clubs on the stock market conned many fans into thinking their clubs would become a shareholders' democracy, that owning shares in "their" club would give them an element of control and a say in the running of their club. They soon found out at shareholders' meetings that their few hundred, or thousand shares were outvoted by large shareholders or companies holding large blocks of shares. The club's new owners were even more faceless than in the past.[61]

For many observers, organized football's future is at stake, as it becomes increasingly dependent on consumers rather than on a solid, working-class supporter culture. Should organized football go out of fashion with the middle and upper classes, the working classes might be so alienated that it will no longer save the industry from going under. As an *Observer* article already noted in the early 1990s: "The danger is that the new commercial version of the game—made for television and performed by individual stars paid millions—will fail to recruit the next generation of addicted consumers."[62] Malcolm Clarke, Chair of the Football Supporters Association, told the paper that "without affordable mass access, future generations may find that football—the people's game—has become a minority sport."[63]

So far, however, the football industry keeps booming. The main movers and shakers have presented various schemes to secure even more income for the top clubs—hereby also creating an even higher gap to the lower tiers of professional football. General managers of European powerhouses, most notably Bayern Munich's Uli Hoeneß, have long argued for the creation of a European Super League, in which the best—read: richest—clubs would unite akin to professional sports leagues in the United States. If this happened, the alienation from the working classes would be complete. Teams would lose their local roots, football would become an exclusive spectacle for the rich, and the system of relegation would be abolished. This would imply the end of an integral part of traditional football culture, the dream of smaller clubs to make it to the top thanks to merit and not to money. In short, the rich and famous would shut the doors around themselves and waltz at their own lucrative ball; the conversion from working-class sport to commercial commodity would see its final chapter.

Even today, the working-class character of the game often survives as a mere gimmick. The majority of spectators in big European stadiums are out-of-town tourists who are entertained by a small section of fans responsible for the "original" Anfield or Nou Camp "spirit." Many season tickets also go to corporate sponsors, which prohibits actual fans from attending the games and often leaves seats empty.

In some of the new shopping-plaza-like stadiums, "spirit" (authentic or not) can no longer be found anyway. A characteristic controversy erupted at Bayern Munich's general members' assembly in November 2007. After a longtime supporter complained about the lack of atmosphere in the new *Allianz Arena*, a 340-million-euro stadium with all modern trimmings (restaurants, shops, daycare centers, Lego World, and Bayern Munich and 1860 Munich "megastores"), general manager Uli Hoeneß leapt into a tirade about the "ungratefulness" of the traditional supporters—supposedly an annoying remnant of an anachronistic football culture that stands in the way of new, clean commercialism.

In this context, it often appears short-sighted and hypocritical to focus one's criticism on corporate teams, which have no traditional fan base, such as Germany's Bayer Leverkusen, the major sports outfit of the pharmaceutics giant, or TSG Hoffenheim, a club sponsored by the media mogul Dietmar Hopp and hailing from a town of 3,300 people: after a rapid ascent to the Bundesliga from the lowest amateur leagues, it recently made serious runs for the national title. As disturbing as these examples of corporate football are, neither Leverkusen nor Hoffenheim are run differently from clubs like Bayern Munich or Manchester United—the only difference is that the latter can claim "tradition" as an additional selling point.

Public pressure and national FAs have so far prevented the European Super League from forming. However, the Champions League introduced by the UEFA in 1992 has already been a step in its direction. Replacing the open draw and the knock-out format of the old European Cup, the Champions League guarantees Europe's top clubs a certain amount of games each year, thereby further increasing the economic gap between them and their financially less fortunate competitors. More games mean more money—unpredictability, crucial ingredient of an exciting soccer world, is of little concern in comparison. It is not surprising that the most recent moments of European football magic occurred at European Championships, which are beyond the control of commercial club interests. In 1992, Denmark was called in to replace a war-torn Yugoslavia two weeks before the tournament. After a shaky start, the Danes won. In 2004, Greece, a 100-1 outsider, beat the odds with exemplary tactical discipline and, after a series of 1-0 victories, were crowned champion.

Eventually, the moneymakers' greed might backfire. Major competitions have turned so big that even some of the most die-hard football fans become oversaturated. The first European Cup, played in 1955–56 had twenty-nine games; the 2009–10 Champions League had 125. At the 1978 Men's World Cup thirty-eight games were played; today, the count is sixty-four.

The sponsors' interests have begun to impact heavily on the game as well. One of the biggest controversies to date was Ronaldo's inclusion in the Brazil side at the 1998 Men's World Cup final although the team's doctors had declared him unfit to play. Both Brazil and Ronaldo had lucrative contracts with Nike and the sports company allegedly pressured Brazilian officials to field Ronaldo no matter what. The striker appeared unfit and Brazil lost 0-3 to France.

Corporate interests also dominate the sale of merchandise. It is a tradition for football fans to wear their team's jersey. These days, many clubs issue two or three jerseys every year. On top of that, the logo of the club's main sponsor is usually splashed across the chest. Essentially, this means that supporters pay a lot of money to serve as walking billboards for big corporations.

Once again, Ronaldo was at the center of one of the most blatant jersey rip-offs: when Inter Milan signed him in 1997, no jerseys with the Brazilian's usual number 9 were ready. After thousands of counterfeit jerseys had been sold, the club decided to play Ronaldo with a number 10 jersey, so it could still profit from selling his shirt.

Television has had an even heavier impact. The fact that some games at the 1986 World Cup in Mexico were played in soaring midday heat so that Europeans could comfortably enjoy a World Cup game after work appears relatively harmless compared to the radical change in league schedules around the world. Up until the 1990s, many leagues played their games on a strict Saturday or Sunday schedule; all the games would start and end at the same time. Today, matches are spread out over several days and hours for no other reason than to satisfy television's demand. This significantly lessens the excitement of former match days and can have serious impacts on fair competition. Most importantly, however, it makes it even harder for working-class folks to attend matches. How do you get from Berlin to Freiburg or from Newcastle to London for a Monday evening game if you are tied into a 9-to-5 schedule at work?

Of course, one has to be careful not to be a mere traditionalist. "Back in the good old days" tirades are as tiresome in football as anywhere else, and slogans like "For Tradition—Against Commerce," commonly seen in European football stadiums today, usually belong to the repertoire of right-wing "anti-capitalists." Innovation is fine, also for the game of soccer. Besides, not all aspects of the commercialization are bad. Arguably, it has contributed to more diversity on the stands in terms of gender and race: there is little to be romanticized about almost exclusively white and male terraces, no matter how working-class they may be. However, the goal must be innovation that challenges bigotry in football culture without delivering the game to corporate interests. Social problems within the working classes are not solved by banning workers, but by giving them opportunities to partake in the management of the sport.

Conservative values are also employed in the fight against commercialization when players are applauded for rating the "honor" of playing for "their country" over the commercial interests of their clubs. Apart from the fact that all-star players earn substantial amounts of money when playing for their national sides, national honor can hardly be seen as a higher virtue than greed. An amusing incident in Austria's football history occurred in 1995: during an entirely lopsided UEFA Cup match between Austria Vienna and Azerbaijan's FK Ganja, the bored Austria Vienna fans soon broke out into chants for Steaua Bucharest—the national competitor Austria Salzburg was to meet the Romanian side the next day. The desperate attempts by Austrian reporters and soccer officials to cover up the obvious disregard of "national unity" were highly entertaining.

A particular challenge for left-wing football supporters was the 1995 "Bosman Ruling." In 1990, the Belgian football professional Jean-Marc Bosman wanted to move from his Belgian club FC Liege to the French USL Dunkerque. According to UEFA regulation, a player could only be transferred abroad if both clubs agreed on a transfer sum. In practice, this meant that a club could prevent a player from moving simply by asking an outrageous amount. This was exactly what Liege did. Bosman, however, took the case to the European court. EU regulations, he argued, granted EU citizens the right to follow their profession in any EU member state of their choosing. The European Court eventually ruled in Bosman's favor. The decision forced European FA's to drop quotas on foreign players overnight. Although the EU ruling only concerned players with EU citizenship, the complications and injustices involved in dividing foreign players into different categories let to a complete opening of the market. This radically changed football internationally, since Europe has long provided the most lucrative market for professionals from all continents. Soon, there were clubs like Belgium's Beveren, which fielded a team consisting almost exclusively of Ivory Coast players, groomed in a club-owned football academy in Abidjan. In England, Chelsea made history on Boxing Day 1999 when it became the first English club to play a league game without a single English player on the pitch. Today, the average amount of non-nationals in European top teams is around 50 percent.

The conflict that arose in this context for leftist football reflected an overall conflict in the face of globalization. Mobility and the coming-together of different nationalities excite progressives, yet globalized commercialism and corporatism repel them.

One of the biggest problems is the unashamed exploitation of Third World football talent, predominantly from Africa. Today, African players as young as thirteen become properties of agents and clubs. While this paves the way for some successful professional careers, many find themselves eventually stranded along the wayside, not to mention the ways in which this practice undermines development on the African continent itself.

Vincent Hanna commented in the *Guardian* in 1996:

> Suppose someone told you there was a regime in Europe where agents scoured the country looking for talented young boys, who are taken from their homes and brought to camps to do menial jobs and train constantly, and for whom, because of the intense competition for places, education is cursory. The lucky ones are kept on, bound under a contract system where they can be bought and sold by employers. The successful and the bright do very well. But many of the second raters will find themselves, in their 30s, on the scrap heap and unemployed. In any other industry this would raise howls of protest. Yet [...] thus does Britain produce "the greatest football league in the world."[64]

The individual despair that the ever-increasing commercialization of the game produces is one of its most overlooked aspects. We see the stars, the Beckhams and the Zidanes, but we do not see the thousands of aspiring young professionals who eventually find their hopes crushed and their future in tatters, often ridiculed and taunted by those who have followed their failed careers with ill intentions. Seventy-five percent of all the players who sign a professional contract in England end their career before they are twenty-one: due to injuries, due to being dropped by their clubs, due to their inability to handle the psychological pressure, and more. If we add the number of players who never even get to sign a professional contract, the ratio between winners and losers becomes clear.

Often enough, the winners are those who best adapt to tough-guy football culture and to club hierarchies. As Chris Bambery states: "The teenagers who become professional footballers are not necessarily the 'best' or most talented players. They are often those most prepared to accept the tight discipline and intensive training demanded of them."[65]

The Bosman Ruling has also helped the rich clubs and leagues to further distinguish themselves by filling their rosters with international stars of whom other clubs could not even afford one. It has also contributed to the ever-increasing income gaps between players. With the possibility of more frequent and bigger deals, significant amounts of the money involved in transfers ends up in the pockets of the big players. While formerly providing infrastructure for clubs, the money now often goes into their mansions, cars, and tropical island trips.

Unfortunately, the players' unions introduced in the 1980s have not been able to sufficiently address the most pressing issues for professional footballers: equity in salaries, protection from exploitation by agents and club owners, a professional transition at the end of their playing careers, and long-term social security. For superstars—who make more than enough for a lifetime during their active years and who can easily secure advertising contracts and lucrative deals with sports companies and media outlets beyond them—this might not matter, but for many unnoticed professionals it does. Many of them fit the newly defined profile of "precarious laborers." The 2005 players' strike in Colombia might serve as a recent example of footballers discovering their strength as a collective labor force. An inspiring historical example was set by the French footballers and their supporters who occupied the headquarters of the French Football Association on May 22, 1968, demanding more rights as players under the motto "Football to the Footballers."

▋Football to the Footballers!

Communiqué by the Footballer's Action Committee

We footballers belonging to the various clubs in the Paris region have today decided to occupy the headquarters of the French Football Federation. Just like the workers are occupying their factories, and the students occupying their faculties. Why?

In order to give back to the 600,000 French footballers and to their thousands of friends what belongs to them: football. Which the pontiffs of the federation have expropriated from them in order to serve their egotistical interests as sports profiteers ...

... Now it's up to you: footballers, trainers, managers of small clubs, countless friends and fans of football, students and workers—to preserve the quality of your sport by joining us to ...

... *Demand the immediate dismissal* (by means of a referendum of the 600,000 footballers, controlled by themselves) of the profiteers of football and the insulters of the footballers.

Free football from the tutelage of the money of the pathetic pretend-patrons who are at the root of the decay of football. And demand from the state the *subsidies* that it accords to all other sports, and which the pontiffs of the Federation have never claimed.

So that football may remain yours, we call on you to *make your way without delay* to the headquarters of the Federation that has again become *your house*, at 60 Avenue d'Iena, Paris.

United, we will make football once again what it ought never to have ceased to be—the sport of joy, the sport of the world of tomorrow which all the workers have started building. *Everyone to 60 Avenue d'Iena!"*

Taken from René Viénet, *Enragés and Situationists in the Occupations Movement, France, May '68* (Autonomedia/Rebel Press, 1992).

Even the internationalist aspects of the global football market enforced by the Bosman Ruling have their flipside. It is not only provincialist narrow-mindedness to wish for a soccer team's connection to a local community. Such a connection enables a club to play an active role in community life and, in turn, motivates supporters to take an active role in the club's management. There remains something special about the fact that Celtic Glasgow won the European Cup Winners' Cup in 1967 with players who were born no further than thirty miles away from the Celtic grounds, or that Malmö FF went to the European Cup Final in 1979 with ten players born in the town itself. These days, big clubs are often at pains to name even one local player, whereby the definition of "local" can be rather stretched: Bayern Munich's Bastian Schweinsteiger, for example, hails from a small Bavarian town about seventy miles south of Munich.

Sports clubs are a part of a local community through personal ties. This has long been the case for football. Restrictions on transfers, as they existed in various countries into the 1960s, contributed to this. It meant that some great players, such as Tom Finney who played for Preston North End, spent their entire careers with small clubs. It has been argued that Tom Finney's last match for the club in 1961 signaled the end of an era in which supporters and players still shared a sense of local belonging and somewhat similar lifestyles.

FIFA has played a big role in the commercialization of football, particularly since the ascent to power by the Brazilian João Havelange in 1974; Havelange presided over the organization for twenty-four years, which should set off alarm-bells in every democracy-conscious mind. Havelange saw the future of the game in generating money, and today's interrelations of FIFA and corporate interests bear witness to this. They became blatantly obvious once again at the recent 2010 Men's World Cup in South Africa—a case that also illustrated how, in a globalized neoliberal world, profits are reaped by multinational corporate powers, not local communities. Andrew Feinstein wrote in the *New Statesman*:

> FIFA has hardly endeared itself to those living on South Africa's margins by creating exclusion zones around the stadiums and parks where the games will be held, thus preventing informal traders from plying their wares anywhere near the showpiece event. Initially excluding local artists from the cultural events that will open and close the tournament was hardly a recipe for local support, either. [. . .] With the World Cup mascots manufactured in China and McDonald's the official restaurant of the tournament, many are questioning whether South Africa will reap adequate economic return on its estimated £3bn investment. [. . .] The temporary, low-skilled and poorly paid jobs that preparations for the tournament have generated will not constitute a solution to South Africa's unemployment rate, which is calculated at between 27 and 37 percent. There are already mutterings of contracts going to politically connected tenderpreneurs.[66]

In a *Counterpunch* article, Patrick Bond focused on FIFA's corporate partners:

> Who are these partners? The Khulumani Support Group joined Jubilee South Africa to demand reparations payments from firms which supported apartheid, a matter currently in the U.S. courts through the Alien Tort Claims Act. Khulumani has begun its own red card campaign against corporate sponsors of the German and U.S. teams who show up on the defendant docket: Daimler, Rheinmettal, Ford, IBM and General Motors. FIFA "partners" who bought exclusive rights to monopolize commerce in SA's cities these next four weeks are Adidas, Coca-Cola, Air Emirates, Hyundai, Sony and Visa, while "official sponsors" include Budweiser, McDonalds and Castrol.[67]

In a *Red Pepper* article, Bond adds with Ashwin Desai:

> Expensive imported German marquee tents apparently require erection by a German construction company. [. . .] Recent national laws provide Blatter [the FIFA president] guarantees in terms of "ambush market-

ing," logistical support, access control and protection for FIFA's corporate partners [. . .]. Only FIFA-endorsed items can be advertised within a one-kilometer radius of the stadium and along major roads. All profits go to FIFA, whose 2010 take is estimated at £2.2 billion. Little will trickle down. Aside from ear-splitting vuvuzela plastic trumpets, the much-vaunted "African" feel to the World Cup will be muted. Even the women who typically sell *pap* (corn meal) and *vleis* (inexpensive meat) just outside soccer stadiums will be shunted off at least a kilometer away.[68]

At least FIFA officials made few efforts to hide their motivations. When asked why a new multi-billion-dollar stadium was built in Cape Town instead of using the stadium in the Athlone township, a FIFA report stated that "a billion television viewers don't want to see shacks and poverty on this scale."[69]

Another disturbing example of the South African World Cup hypocrisy was pointed out by columnist Jabulani Sikhakhane, who explained that within a two-week period, the death of seventeen infants across South Africa could be blamed on a lack of basic medical equipment, while FIFA had demanded an investment of 180 million dollars to ensure medical facilities that are up to par for World Cup players, officials, and visitors. "It's a shame," Sikhakhane wrote, "that a country that invests more than R1bn in order to meet the [health] requirements set by the gods of world soccer is incapable of preventing the deaths of its babies."[70]

▉ All in the Name of the Beautiful Gain

A Zabalaza Anarchist Communist Front (ZACF) statement on the 2010 Soccer World Cup in South Africa
June 2010

The 2010 Soccer World Cup must be exposed for the utter sham that it is. The ZACF strongly condemns the audacity and hypocrisy of the government in presenting the occasion as a "once-in-a-lifetime" opportunity for the economic and social upliftment of those living in South Africa (and the rest of the continent). What is glaringly clear is that the "opportunity" has and continues to be that of a feeding-frenzy for global and domestic capital and the South African ruling elite. In fact, if anything, the event is more likely to have devastating consequences for South Africa's poor and working class—a process that is already underway.

In preparing to host the world cup the government has spent close to R800 billion (R757 billion on infrastructure development and R30 billion on stadiums that will never be filled again), a massive slap in the face for those living in a country characterized by desperate poverty and close to 40 percent unemployment. Over the past five years the working poor have expressed their outrage and disappointment at the government's failure to redress the massive social inequality in over 8000 service delivery protests for basic services and housing countrywide. This pattern of spending is further evidence of the maintenance of the failed neoliberal capitalist model and its "trickle down" economics, which have done nothing but deepen inequality and poverty globally. Despite previous claims to the contrary, the government has recently admitted this by doing an about turn, and now pretends that the project was "never intended" to be a profit making exercise. [A]

South Africa desperately needs large-scale public infrastructure, especially in the area of public transport, which in some cities, including Johannesburg, is almost entirely absent. The Gautrain, which was launched on Tuesday the 8th June (just in time for the big event) is probably the biggest irony here: in a country where the large majority rely on unsafe private mini-bus taxis to travel long distances on a daily basis, the Gautrain offers high speed, luxury transport for tourists and those travelling between Johannesburg and Pretoria . . . who can afford it if a single trip between the airport and Sandton will set you back a massive R100. The same picture reveals itself everywhere: the Airports company of South Africa (ACSA) has spent over R16 billion on upgrading the airports, the commercialised South African National Road Agency Ltd (SANRAL) has spent over R23 billion on a new network of toll roads—all of which will implement strict cost-recovery measures to recoup the billions spent, and most of which will be of little benefit to poor South Africans. All over the country, municipalities have embarked on urban regeneration schemes . . . accompanied by corresponding gentrification schemes, as the government attempts to hastily paper over the harsh South African reality. Over 15,000 homeless people and street children have been rounded up and dumped in shelters in Johannesburg alone, in Cape Town the municipality has evicted thousands of people from poor areas and squatter camps as part of the World Cup vanity project. The City of Cape Town (unsuccessfully) attempted to evict 10,000 Joe Slovo residents from their homes in order to hide them from the tourists travelling along the N2 highway, and elsewhere they are being removed to make space for stadiums, fan parks or train stations. [B] In Soweto, roads are being beautified along main tourist and FIFA routes, while adjacent schools sport broken windows and crumbling buildings.

Although many South Africans remain unconvinced, others are inundated and swept along by the deluge of nationalist propaganda aimed at diverting attention from the circus that is the World Cup. Every Friday has been deemed "soccer Friday," in which the "nation" is encouraged (and school children forced) to sport Bafana-Bafana t-shirts. Cars are kitted out in flags, people learn the "Diski-dance" which is performed regularly at every tourist restaurant, and buy Zakumi mascot dolls. Anyone sceptical of the hype is denigrated unpatriotic, the prime example being when appeals were made to striking South African Transport and Allied Workers Union (SATAWU) workers to shelve their concerns "in the national interest." [**C**] In a context where close to a million jobs have been lost over the course of the past year, government celebrations that the world cup has created over 400, 000 jobs are empty and insulting. The jobs that have been created in the run up have been mostly casual or "Limited Duration Contracts (LCD's)," taken by workers that are not unionised and paid well below the minimum wage.

Apart from the repression of unions, social movements have received similar hostility from the state, which has unofficially put a blanket ban on all protest for the duration of the event. In fact, there is some evidence that this has been in place since as early as the 1st March. According to Jane Duncan:

> A snap survey conducted at the end of last week of other municipalities hosting World Cup matches revealed that a blanket ban on gatherings is in operation. According to the Rustenberg municipality, "gatherings are closed for the World Cup." The Mbombela municipality was told by the SAPS that they were not going to allow gatherings during the World Cup. The Cape Town City Council claimed that it continues to accept applications for marches, but indicated that it "may be a problem" during the World Cup period. According to the Nelson Mandela Bay and Ethekwini municipalities, the police will not allow gatherings over the World Cup period. [**D**]

Although it is clear that the constitution, often hailed for its "progressiveness," is far from the guarantor of freedom and equality that government claims it to be, this new form of repression is clearly in contradiction with the constitutional right to freedoms of expression and gathering. However, social movements in Johannesburg including the Anti-Privatisation Forum and several others have not given up so easily, having managed to get authorization for a protest march on the day of the opening with the help of the Freedom of Expression Institute. However, the march is being forced to be held three kilometres from the stadium where it will not attract the sort of media attention the government is worried about.

Not only has the state been repressively severe on the poor and any anti-World Cup demonstration or activity, all within the guise of painting South Africa as a host flinging its arms open in invitation to those flock-

ing to its upmarket hotels, bed-and-breakfasts and cocktail lounges, but
it does so under the guidance of Sepp Blatter and Friends' legal criminal
empire called FIFA (wonderfully referred to as THIEFA by the Durban Social
Forum). Not only are they expected to benefit from a 2010 windfall of nearly
€ 1.2 billion, but have already gained over € 1 billion from media rights alone.

The stadia, and areas around the stadia, which were handed over to
FIFA for the duration of the tournament ("tax free cocoons" literally creating FIFA-controlled and monitored areas exempt from normal taxation
and other state laws), and all routes to and from the stadia have been
forcibly cleared of anyone selling non-sanctioned FIFA products and those
eking out an existence in squatter camps along airport roads. As such,
people who would have banked on World Cup sales to boost their survival
incomes are left out in the "trickle down" cold.

FIFA, as sole owner of the World Cup brand and its spin-off products,
also has a team of approximately 100 lawyers scouring the country for
any unauthorised selling of these products and marketing of the brand.
These products are seized and sellers are arrested despite the fact that
most in South Africa and on the continent purchase their products from
the informal trading sector, and very few have R400 to dole out on team
t-shirts and other gear. It has also effectively gagged journalists with an
accreditation clause that prevents media organisations from bringing FIFA
into disrepute, clearly compromising freedom of press. [E]

The major irony is that soccer was once truly the game of the working class. Viewing games live at stadia was cheap and easily accessible
to people who chose to spend 90 minutes forgetting about the daily
drudgery of their lives under the boot of the boss and the state. Today
professional football and the World Cup bring exorbitant profits to a small
cabal of a global and domestic elite (with billions spent unnecessarily
and in a time of a global capitalist crisis) who charge patrons thousands
of rands, pounds, euros, etc. every season to watch disgustingly overpaid
footballers fall and dive all over manicured pitches at the slightest tug and
who squabble, via parasitic agents, over whether or not they are deserv-
ing of their huge salaries. A game, which in many respects maintains its
aesthetic beauty, has lost its working class soul and has been reduced to
just another set of commodities to be exploited.

Bakunin once said that "people go to church for the same reasons
they go to a tavern: to stupefy themselves, to forget their misery, to
imagine themselves, for a few minutes anyway, free and happy." Perhaps,
amongst all the blindly nationalistic flag waving and vuvuzela-blowing, we
can add sport to his equation and that it might seem easier to forget than
to actively partake in combating injustice and inequality. There are many
who do though, and the working class and poor and their organisations
are not as malleable to illusion as government would want to believe. From

temporary squatter camp constructions at the doors of the stadia, to mass protest and demonstrations, to countrywide strike action, unsanctioned or not, despite the taunts and jeers and the labels of being "unpatriotic," or blanket bans on freedom of speech, we will defiantly make our voices heard to expose the terrible inequalities characterising our society and the global games played at the expense of the lives of those upon whom empires are built and will be, ultimately, destroyed.

Down with the World Cup!

Phansi state repression and divisive nationalism!

Phambili the people's struggle against exploitation and profiteering!

A See *Star Business Report*, June 7, 2010.

B http://antieviction.org.za/2010/03/25/telling-the-world-that-neither-this-city-nor-the-world-cup-works-for-us.

C http://www.politicsweb.co.za/politicsweb/view/politicsweb/en/page71654?oid=178399&sn=Detail.

D For article see http://www.sacsis.org.za/site/article/489.1.

E http://www.sportsjournalists.co.uk/blog/?p=2336.

Some courageous protests were staged in South Africa, for example by the Anti-Privatisation Forum (APF) on the day of the opening game.

Call to Action by the South African Anti-Privatisation Forum (APF)

June 2010

The Anti-Privatisation Forum (APF) and allies will be embarking on a march tomorrow (11th June) to coincide with the opening of the 2010 Soccer World Cup. The march will start at 09h00 from Ben Naude Drive, opposite Fons Luminous Combined School Assembly Area and will proceed along the Rand Show Road/Aerodrome Drive towards Soccer City. The APF urges all community and other civil society organisations who share our concerns and who wish to add their voices, to join us. We have no intention of disrupting the World Cup but simply to voice our discontent/concerns.

Despite the APF's attempts to overturn them, conditions have been imposed by the Johannesburg Metro Police (in the name of 'national security') such that the march will not be allowed to proceed to Soccer City itself but will end at a designated 'speakers corner' some 1,5 kms away from the stadium. A memorandum of grievances and demands from communities that make up the APF has been drawn up and all the main local, provincial and national government offices have been contacted to come and receive this memorandum.

The Soccer World Cup is here and the official theme is "feel it, it is here." However, despite the fact that most people love the game of soccer, poor communities are only feeling the hardship of South Africa's hosting of the World Cup and the neoliberal policies which continue to ensure that poor people remain poor.

The massive amounts of public funds used to build new stadiums and related infrastructure for this World Cup have only served to further deny poor people the development and services they have been struggling for over many years. Millions remain homeless, unemployed and in deep poverty, thousands in poor communities across South Africa continue to be brutally evicted and those struggling to survive (like street vendors) are being denied basic trading rights and are criminalised.

Yet, our government has managed, in a fairly short period of time, to deliver "world class" facilities and infrastructure that the majority of South Africans will never benefit from or be able to enjoy. The APF feels that those who have been so denied, need to show all South Africans as well as the rest of the world who will be tuning into the World Cup, that all is not well in this country, that a month long sporting event cannot and will not be the panacea for our problems. This World Cup is not for the poor—it is the soccer elites of FIFA, the elites of domestic and international corporate capital and the political elites who are making billions and who will be benefiting at the expense of the poor.

For the past fifteen years the majority of South Africans have continued to suffer the inheritances of the apartheid regime and neoliberal macro-economic policies. General living conditions, largely due to a lack of basic services and employment opportunities, have gone from bad to worse to bad. These problems are very real and they range from:

- the huge backlog in formal housing (parallel to the increased growth in shack settlements in all main urban and peri-urban areas)
- lack of access to electrification in many poor areas (upwards of 30 percent of South Africans—most of whom are poor—remain unelectrified and are forced to use dangerous substitutes such as paraffin and candles)
- a poor quality public education system (in which educational resources are scarce and a serious crisis in the provision of basic services at public schools continues)
- a dire lack of proper recreational facilities and programmes in poor communities (contributing to a range of serious social problems, especially amongst the youth)
- the immense number of impoverished, unemployed people across the country (despite the promises of job creation through the World Cup, over 1 million have lost their jobs over the past two years—including those workers casually employed to build the new stadiums—and the real unemployment rate is around 40 percent—a national crisis!).

The APF wants to make it clear that we love the game of soccer. Soccer is a predominately working class sport that is enjoyed by billions around the globe. But this World Cup does not represent those billions but rather the interests of a small elite who have manipulated the beautiful game and have used this World Cup to make massive profits at the expense of poor ordinary South Africans who, after all, are the ones who have paid—through the public purse—for what so few will enjoy.

South Africa is the most unequal society in the world and we believe that addressing this socio-economic inequality must be the top priority of our country, our government is addressed. One World Cup—no matter how much we enjoy watching soccer—is not going to address or solve our fundamental problems. The more we continue to allow the elites to hide the realities of our country, to falsely claim that this World Cup will provide lasting social unity and leave a positive developmental "legacy" and to spend public funds to do so, the farther we move from confronting the real problems that the majority in our country experience every day of their lives.

Given all the money involved, it is not surprising that football is repeatedly shaken by bribery and match-rigging scandals. As always, the industrialized nations like to cite "Third World" corruption—as always, it is a pathetic gesture of chauvinism and distraction.

A 1971 match-rigging scandal in the German Bundesliga involved some of the country's most prominent clubs and national team players. In Italy, widespread fixing of results was revealed twice on the highest level, in 1982 and 2006. Among the clubs punished with relegation were European powerhouses like AC Milan and Juventus Turin. Many referees, from Switzerland's FIFA representative Karl Röthlisberger to Germany's low-tier Robert Hoyzer, were involved in match-rigging scams. Some crucial games in soccer history were almost certainly rigged, like Argentina's 6-0 thumping of Peru at the 1978 Men's World Cup, which secured a spot in the final for the host nation. No wrongdoing has ever been proven in the highly contested South Korean victory over Italy at the 2002 Men's World Cup, but the game's referee Byron Moreno was suspended some months later in Ecuador after helping Deportivo Quito to a 3-2 win over rival Barcelona Guayaquil with two penalties, two red cards, and thirteen minutes of overtime—coincidentally, he was running for mayor of Quito. In Colombia, drug barons have repeatedly been accused of controlling the national league and they were almost certainly involved in the infamous

Medellín killing of Andrés Escobar, who had scored an own goal in the 1994 Men's World Cup encounter with the United States.

The commercialization of football cannot be opposed by referring to "tradition"—at least not in a progressive manner. With respect to the Bosman Ruling the answer is not to prohibit "foreign" players from joining "local" teams. The answer is to decommercialize the game *while supporting integrative politics at the same time*. The opening of borders demands the creation of new communities. This is an exciting project and football can play an important role in it. Our future favorite football club might play its home games in a small town in France, have not a single French-born player on its team, yet will still be an integrated part of the local community. To make such a vision come true, the fight against bigotry in football culture is mandatory.

Bigotry in Football Culture

Arthur Wharton, a goalkeeper for Preston North End, was the first professional black football player. This was in the 1880s. Although he was a reputed athlete in his time—also excelling in cricket and running—he died in poverty in 1930 and was buried in an unmarked grave in Edlington, South Yorkshire. In 1997, his grave was given a headstone after a campaign by anti-racist activists.

Despite Wharton's achievements, the path to acceptance and respect was a tough one to follow for black players. Jack Leslie, who played for Plymouth Argyle in the 1920s and '30s was never selected for the English team despite being one of the country's leading goalscorers—he was convinced that the reason was racial prejudice.[71]

The first ever black player to represent England was Viv Anderson in 1978. Still, this meant no end to racist abuse in English football. The famous photograph of the black Liverpool striker John Barnes casually kicking away a banana in mid-match dates from the late 1980s. Dutch player Ruud Gullit was subjected to a torrent of racist abuse when Holland played England at Wembley in 1988. Three years later, the entire Cameroon squad had to go through the same experience. Still in 2004, in a well-publicized incident, renowned English manager Ron Atkinson referred to Chelsea player Marcel Desailly as "what is known in some schools as a fucking lazy thick nigger" on the BBC. Atkinson had wrongly believed that the microphones had been turned off. Ironically, Atkinson managed West Bromwich Albion in the 1970s, when the club was regarded as one of the first to actively support black players. A DVD issued by England's FA in 2005, presenting the "seventeen greatest England players of all time" to new members, included only white footballers.

In 2005, every single member of the fourteen-member FA ruling board was white, and so were all of the ninety-two members of the FA Council.

In 2008, Paul Ince became the first black manager in the Premier League. Black referees remain rare as well. Uriah Rennie was the first in the Premier League in 1997. He was exposed to constant racist taunts.

Racism in British football is also reflected in the exclusion of black fans: although about 25 percent of all professional players are black, only about 3 percent of the supporters on the stands are. For a long time, the main difference between a black player and a black fan was that the former was at least somewhat protected from crowd abuse. In the New Football Economy, many non-whites are excluded for economic reasons. This includes members of England's large Asian communities, who have long been almost entirely absent from soccer, battling stereotypes of being "too frail" for the physical game. Zesh Rehman was the first English-born Asian to play in the Premier League when he represented Fulham in 2004.

Racism is in no way limited to English football, nor is bigotry in football culture reduced to racism. Sexist, homophobic, and anti-Semitic sentiments mar the game in many countries. "Cunt" and "fairy" are regularly used as insults, and anti-Semitic taunts—including hissing to recall Nazi gas chambers—are frequently used, especially against teams with historical links to Jewish communities, like Ajax Amsterdam, Tottenham Hotspur, and Argentina's Atlanta. In Italy, Serie A team Udine had to abstain from signing Israeli player Ronny Rosenthal in 1989 after a series of anti-Semitic attacks against the club house.  Claude LeRoy, a Jewish manager at Racing Strasbourg, had to leave the club after repeated anti-Semitic campaigns. True or supposed "Gypsies" are similar targets of right-wing bigots in European football stadiums.

Racism remains an urgent subject in many ways. When Edgar Davids suggested at the 1996 European Championship that black Dutch players were excluded from tactical meetings, he was sent home by the Netherlands' FA—reputedly one of Europe's most progressive. In 2004, at a home game of the current Men's World Champion Spain against England, the "monkey chanting," a regular among racist football crowds, was so relentless that it caused an international outcry. The incident was downplayed by officials and reporters. The journalist Juan Castro, writing for the sports daily *Marca*, went as far as to claim: "Monkey chanting does not have a racist cause. It is a way of insulting the enemy team. It has a football cause, not a racial motivation. The Bernabéu was a cultural thing. It was a joke. It wasn't racist." The Spanish FA reacted similarly when the former national team manager

Luis Aragonés referred to Thierry Henry as a *negro de mierda* while being wired during a training session. A spokesman declared that "there is no racism in our football [. . .] we are sure about it," while president Angel María Villar added angrily that "everyone knows Aragonés is not a racist!"[72] These were high-profile cases. Similar incidents happen regularly all across Europe, mostly without receiving any attention at all.

However, there have been changes, also on the official level. Most FAs have introduced punitive measures for hate speech, both by players and supporters. In October 2004, Rene Temmink was the first Dutch referee to break off a game when the sexist and anti-Semitic chants at a The Hague vs. PSV Eindhoven encounter did not subside despite crowd warnings. In Brazil, Leandro Desabato got arrested on the pitch in 2005 for calling FC São Paulo forward Grafite a "fucking nigger." In 2007, Dortmund keeper Roman Weidenfeller was suspended for three games after insulting the German Ghanaian striker Gerald Asamoah.

General standards among football players are illustrated by the abuse directed at England's Graeme le Saux throughout the 1990s, for no other reason than him reading the *Guardian* and rejecting tough-guy attitudes. "Homo jokes" about le Saux were rife.

There are some particularly dubious characters among football professionals. The Polish goalkeeper Arkadiusz Onyszko is one example. In 2009, he was sacked by the Danish side Odense BK after a court had convicted him for assaulting his wife. He then played for the Danish competitor FC Midtjylland with an ankle monitor for a couple of months, only to be fired again; this time for declaring in his autobiography that he "hates gays" and that he "cannot be in one room with them." Since January 2010, Onyszko has been playing with the Polish side Odra Wodzisław.

Soccer culture has largely been dominated by patriarchal values. Once the football authorities had put an end to the remarkable early history of women's soccer, women were excluded from the sport for large parts of the 20th century. It is therefore encouraging to witness a re-emergence of women's football today.

▌ F_in–"Women in Football"

Interview with Annika Hoffmann
and Nicole Selmer

While football has often been seen as an exclusively male sport, women's football has become increasingly popular over the last twenty years. How do you see these developments?
Nicole: I think in Germany the increasing popularity of women's football has a lot to do with the fact that the women's national team was quite

successful—also at a time when things didn't go particularly well for the men's team. Since the vast majority of female players are amateurs, women also represent a kind of "more honest" football in comparison to the spoiled millionaires of the men's game. Furthermore, Theo Zwanziger, the current President of the German Football Association (DFB), has done a lot for women's football—he has made sure that there are better facilities, better organization etc. At the same time, football remains mainly a male sport, and I don't think that this will change anytime soon. Unless the entire professional system of the Bundesliga and the international competitions collapse economically. But I don't know if this is anything we should wish for.

Speaking of a "more honest" form of football: does a lot of women's football happen apart from the competitive game? That is to say, in hobby teams, weekend tournaments, informal games in the park? Do you think that there are more women than men who are interested in "non-commercial," "alternative" football?
Nicole: Interesting question, especially since common cultural stereotypes would suggest the opposite: usually, femininity is associated with consumerism, superficiality, entertainment, event culture. This is also used as an explanation for why there are more women in stadiums these days: football is no longer football but entertainment. Personally, I believe that gender is not the decisive factor. The said developments are much more complex.

As far as professionalism goes, I believe that female players would like to see more professional infrastructure, more recognition, and larger audiences. I do not get the sense that female players necessarily wish for more professionalism in terms of money. I don't think that the goal is to be like the men.

You are both active in the network F_in—Frauen im Fussball, which translates as "Women in Football." Can you tell us about the project?
Nicole: F_in was founded in 2004, when some of us organized a workshop on women and football, sponsored by the *Koordinationsstelle Fanprojekte* [Coordination Group for Fan Projects], an organization that provides educational programs for football supporters' groups. The original idea came from Antje Hagel in Offenbach who had worked on sexism in football within the *Bündnis antifaschistischer/aktiver Fußballfans* [Alliance of Antifascist/Active Football Fans] (BAFF). I met Antje because of a book on female football fans I was working on, and she had the idea to gather all the women who were active in the world of football. The workshop turned into an informal network, a mailing list, more meetings, a book, our website etc. More and more women joined, and now there are about seventy on our list. Some only read the posts, and not all of them come to the workshops, but the activities are definitely increasing.

F_in has a strong focus on women as football fans. It seems that there are increasing numbers of both women's fan clubs and of mixed fan clubs that become increasingly active against sexism.

Nicole: Yes, that is probably true, whereby it is difficult to say whether there really are more female fan clubs today. Maybe there were as many before but they didn't receive any attention. Hard to say. It is encouraging of course that sexism is slowly becoming a general issue. Just before doing this interview, I listened to a radio program by Nuremberg's Ultras. They insisted that the times of "No Politics in Football" are pretty much over, also within the German Ultra community. I believe that actions of mixed fan clubs are a great way to illustrate that sexism is not a women's problem and that it is not up to women alone to solve it. While F_in is a women-only organization, we engage with men through different forums: our website and the book *gender kicks* as well as direct actions, for example during the Football Against Racism in Europe (FARE) Action Week.

Annika: Activism against sexism has certainly increased over the last few years. I would say that this really kicked off around 2005, although there are many scenes that have their specific discussions, and it is basically impossible to say how each one of them developed. In any case, there are many female fans today who clearly demand their space within the fan scene. And there are more and more groups that make sexism a public issue instead of leaving it only to women's groups. Personally, I'm very happy about that.

When we began to collect "Fan Actions Against Sexism" on our website in 2008, we thought that we would only hear of isolated incidents. Today, we have a huge collection of stickers, statements, and choreographies in stadiums. In the 1990s, there were still many groups within BAFF that exclusively wanted to focus on racism and were worried that they would "overbear" fans with too many issues otherwise. A lot has changed since then. However, a certain "hierarchization of oppressions" remains: racism is still considered a more important issue than homophobia and sexism, and there are some forms of oppression that are hardly addressed at all: anti-Ziganism, anti-Semitism, ableism etc. I think that an overarching perspective is still missing.

Do you know about networks similar to F_in in other countries?

Nicole: Not really. There are definitely female fan clubs or women's Ultra groups in other countries, but I don't think that they are as widespread.

It is important to note, though, that F_in has always included women from Austria and Switzerland. At our last workshop, we had a participant from Sweden who is active in the country's fan network *Fotbollsalliansen*, and at the Football Supporters Europe (FSE) Congress in Barcelona in 2010 we've made some more international contacts.

What are your future plans with F_in?

Nicole: We have a few ideas for different projects. A new book, actions during the Women's World Cup in Germany in 2011, and others.

Annika: So far, we have consciously avoided planning too far ahead. I am just happy that an increasing number of people—especially young people—are discovering antisexism, that it is becoming more and more normal for women to be in the fan sections of the stadiums, and that women have become more accepted as a part of fan culture. I believe that F_in can help to strengthen this process, both as a forum for discussion and as a source of inspiration.

Right now, F_in is involved in the second installment of the traveling exhibition *Tatort Stadion—Diskriminierung im Fußball* [Crime Scene Stadium—Discrimination in Football], organized by BAFF. Compared to the first installment, antisexism plays a much bigger role, and hopefully the exhibition will inspire more discussion and action.

Who will win the Women's World Cup in Germany?

Nicole: No idea. And, to be honest, I don't really care much either. The same goes for the Men's World Cup. The only thing that is important to me is that Schalke doesn't win the Bundesliga.

Annika: World Cups don't matter much to me either. I'm mainly happy that Fortuna Düsseldorf is back in the Second Bundesliga. I am curious, though, about the social impact of the 2011 Women's World Cup in Germany. I wonder if the "party patriotism" will be comparable to what happened during the Men's World Cup in 2006.

Annika Hoffmann is a historian who lives in Hamburg and maintains a long-distance relationship with Fortuna Düsseldorf. Nicole Selmer works as a freelance journalist and translator in Hamburg, writing on football, fan culture, and gender; she is the author of *Watching the Boys Play. Frauen als Fußballfans* [Watching the Boys Play: Women as Football Supporters] (2004). Both are active in the fan networks F_in and BAFF and have been co-organizers of the traveling exhibition *Tatort Stadion—Diskriminierung im Fußball*.

To this day, hardly any gay professional football players have come out publicly. Norwich striker Justin Fashanu was the first in 1990. He took his life eight years later. John Reid stated that "the tragic suicide of former Norwich striker Justin Fashanu was a result of the torrent of abuse he received from fans, players and managers."[73]

Given the homophobia ingrained in football culture, even small gestures can make a big difference, such as the appearance of Italian international Alberto Gilardino on a *gay.it* program. Similarly, the 2002 to 2010 FC St. Pauli presidency of Corny Littmann, a gay entrepreneur and entertainer, had important symbolic value.

One of the most active campaigners against homophobia in football was the Dutch FIFA referee John Blankenstein.

■ The Most Important Referee in the World: Remembering John Blankenstein

Gerd Dembowski

"He would still have so much to say." Those were the words of my friend Thomas Ernst when I told him about the death of our colleague, the international referee John Blankenstein. In 2003, John, Thomas, and I traveled together for the BAFF campaign "Zeigt dem Fußball die Rosa Karte" [Show Football the Pink Card], which was a highlight of the exhibition *Tatort Stadion—Diskriminierung im Fußball* [Crime Scene Stadium—Discrimination in Football].

John turned the presentations into a live autobiography with a unique sense of humor. He came out at a young age. Humor was his means to counter the challenges he met as a gay referee in a heterosexual world, and humor helped him to communicate with his audience. Thomas and I were never sure how to react. Sharing the stage with him, moments of pain became obvious—but he always just took a sip of water and jumped to the next anecdote.

Gentleman John was a master of witty responses. He often answered questions with questions, challenging the audience to investigate their assumptions. "As a referee, you have to do the same on the pitch," he once explained, "you have to let people know very quickly where the journey is going." I will never forget how my mother, who never thought much about homosexuality, hugged John with tears in her eyes and applauded him for his activism.

John Blankenstein was a tireless agitator for the European Gay and Lesbian Sport Federation. He would have loved to show a few FIFA bureaucrats a red card. There were those, for example, who had sent a prostitute with a bottle of champagne to his room—she was to test whether the "fag" could not be bent "straight" after all. There were also those who liked to say, "Congratulations! I mean, just think of it: I am not allowed to join the girls in the shower!"

I have heard similar phrases from a professor in Copenhagen who does not deserve to be mentioned by name. He sweepingly projects the causes of discrimination onto the victims; of course only "to get a discussion going and to be provocative." It goes something like this: there is no real need for homosexuals to come out; rather, "they should be happy that they can shower with all the beautiful men in the sports club without being detected." And: "You know, I am a wrestler, and sometimes, when I wrestle with a woman, I get a hard-on." Great. The sexual organs of those exposed to such verbal garbage certainly remain non-aroused. Talking to such a mad scientist, it needed a lot of missionary drive not to turn into Hulk.

It was incredible how thoughtfully and patiently John answered questions revealing latent homophobia. Of course, he had been through much worse. He talked about how his outing had cost him a place among the 1990 Men's World Cup referees. In 1987, he had apparently been spotted at a gay bar in Canada in a FIFA suit, which enraged FIFA officials. "They said that it didn't matter that I was gay. But to be seen in a FIFA suit in gay surroundings? That was unacceptable!" At the time, John answered: "I have never been interested in bars, and even if I went there I would not wear a FIFA suit. It is hardly a turn-on. I doubt that I'd be able to pick anyone up. By the way: who was the FIFA representative who recognized me?" He never got a response.

In 1994, the UEFA selected John to referee the Champions League final between Barcelona and AC Milan. Berlusconi objected to Blankenstein being Dutch, since Barcelona was coached by Johan Cruyff and had a number of Dutch players. The *Gazzetta dello Sport*, Italy's famous sports paper, brought it all to a boil: a Barca-friendly Dutchman, and *even gay*!? John received death threats. He wanted to referee nonetheless, but the UEFA replaced him with Philip Don. "Allegedly, for my own safety. In any case, rest assured: my nationality was not the issue." He then added with a smile: "I even had to return the advance fee they had paid me . . ."

Something similar happened before the national team encounter between England and Denmark in 1992. During our presentations, John showed the audience an old *Daily Mirror* copy. Its headline read: "Tonight's Ref is Gay!" The following article included "Tips of Conduct" for the English players.

"I know five Dutch professionals who are gay. They have alibi lives with wife and kids, just out of fear," John explained to Gelsenkirchen's *Buersche Zeitung* after his first BAFF talk in 2003. For some years, John was a kind of fatherly adviser for these players living double lives.

John and I had planned to meet in The Hague in November 2006 to chat and to discuss a biography that Thomas Ernst and I wanted to write. But John Blankenstein, the world's most important referee, was taken from us on August 25, 2006. He had long suffered from a serious kidney disease. He was fifty-seven years old. He died the same year that the UEFA finally broke its silence about homophobia. John had been invited as a speaker to the UEFA-sponsored "Unite Against Racism" conference in Barcelona. When I met John Blankenstein there for the last time, in the Nou Camp Stadium, he strongly believed that open homosexuality in football was possible. Dear UEFA, please do not disappoint him!

The article originally appeared in Gerd Dembowski's book *Fußball vs. Countrymusik* (Cologne: PapyRossa, 2007) as "Der wichtigste Schiedsrichter der Welt: Erinnerungen an John Blankenstein." Translated by Gabriel Kuhn.

Lesbian professional footballers have also been hesitant to come out publicly, although there are some celebrities who have been open about their relationships with women. These include the current U.S. team manager Pia Sundhage and Sky Blue FC and U.S. national team striker Natasha Kai.

Homophobia and Football Culture

Interview with Tanja Walther-Ahrens

You are active in the European Gay and Lesbian Sport Federation and your focus is football. Can you tell us about your activities?
I mainly focus on football, because it is the sport I grew up with. I still play, but no longer on the highest level. Besides, football is a great medium to reach people with many different backgrounds; it is almost impossible to ignore. The recent Men's World Cup in South Africa has shown this once again.

Since 2006, I have been trying to raise attention about the issues of homosexuality and homophobia in football. I've been doing this in different ways. It began with a workshop at the 2006 UEFA-sponsored conference "Unite Against Racism" in Barcelona. In 2007, I held a workshop at the first Fan Congress sponsored by the German Football Association (DFB) in Leipzig. The contacts with the DFB have proven valuable since. For example, I got the association's support in producing leaflets for Christopher Street Day events; in Cologne they even sponsored a truck in the parade. They also financed a brochure for the Football Against Racism in Europe (FARE) Action Week in 2009.

There are still hardly any male professionals who have come out. The life of Justin Fashanu ended tragically. Why is it so difficult to accept homosexuality in male football?
Homosexuality in football is a tricky subject. Women's football has a different social status and it is often assumed that "only lesbians" can play the game, as if it was the "lesbian gene" that makes women play football. This illustrates one of the main problems: "femininity" remains excluded from the game and there is acceptance neither for heterosexual women nor for gay men. These prejudices and stereotypes are deeply entrenched in our society. We must not forget that homosexuality was long considered a disease and remains a very sensitive subject to many people.

You mentioned collaborating with UEFA and the DFB. Do you think that the anti-homophobia campaigns sponsored by these institutions can help?
In the long run, certainly. We must all be aware, though, that we do have a long way ahead of us. It will take its time before our message reaches everyone and it will take even longer before it will really change people's minds. Deeply-rooted notions cannot be altered from one day to the next. In addition, there will always be some reactionaries who try to prevent changes altogether.

What needs to be done apart from the official campaigns? How can we as political activists contribute to a less homophobic football culture?
Values like tolerance, respect, and solidarity have to be demonstrated in everyday life and communicated on all sorts of levels. Fighting homophobia cannot be reduced to fighting one particular form of discrimination. It is a part of fighting discrimination in general. To me, the most important aspect is to continuously put the topic of discrimination on the table, so that the discussion reaches everyone and that everyone perceives discrimination as a problem. You cannot expect people to out themselves as long as it is not a safe thing to do. At the same time, coming out is important as others need to realize how long they have known gays and lesbians if we want to change their attitudes.

You have mentioned differences between men's football and women's football. It does appear that homosexuality is less of a taboo in the women's game.

That is true. However, I would say that it is mainly true for your team and your circle of family and friends. In these environments, players can be open about their sexuality. However, there is not a single German player in the highest league or on the national team who is openly lesbian. Meanwhile, all the players—no matter their sexual orientation—are confronted with the stereotype that women footballers are lesbians.

Over the past few years, there have been an increasing number of gay, lesbian, and queer fan clubs. Where are these initiatives particularly strong?

Most gay and lesbian fan clubs exist in Germany. They are very well connected through the Queer Football Fans network, which also includes groups in Switzerland. Apart from these countries, there is only one gay and lesbian fan club in Barcelona. However, this also has to do with different forms of football fan culture. In England, for example, the German "fan club" culture does not exist in the same way. However, there exists a Gay Football Supporters Network (GFSN) in Britain, which does great work.

There are also some gay and lesbian clubs that play in so-called Sunday Leagues, and sometimes even in the official amateur leagues of national football federations. Are there any examples that are particularly significant?

In bigger German cities like Berlin, Cologne, and Munich it is not uncommon for gay and lesbian teams to play in official leagues. My team, for example, Seitenwechsel [Switching Sides], plays in Berlin's Landesliga. We simply wanted to play more often. Gay and lesbian tournaments are only organized once or twice a year.

There are a few things that are special about our team: our players are almost twice as old as all the others in the league, many of us have a strong background in competitive sports (boxing, athletics, team handball, football), and we don't practice.

With the reputation of *Seitenwechsel* as a "lesbian team," did you ever encounter problems?

No, not really. Of course you might get curious looks or you might overhear someone whisper, "They are all lesbians!" But usually sexism is the bigger problem—for example, when young men play nearby and greet you with, "What are you doing here? You want to play football!?" These

men usually don't know that we are lesbians—they just focus on us being women who, supposedly, can't play.

If we look five years into the future: ideally, what will have changed for gays and lesbians in football?
Ideally, gays and lesbians can be open about their sexuality, and their love life will be as exciting—or as boring—as the love life of any heterosexual player. In other words, I hope that sexual orientation will be seen as what it is: one aspect of many in life.

In the 1990s, Tanja Walther-Ahrens played football in Germany's Bundesliga for Tennis Borussia Berlin and Turbine Potsdam, the 2010 European Champions League winner. Today, she lives in Berlin and works as a teacher.

Radical Interventions in the Professional Game

A Stage for Protests

Professional football has been used as a stage for political protests in various ways. To name but a few examples: in the 1970s, streakers regularly disrupted Premier Division football games in England; during the West Germany vs. Chile match at the 1974 Men's World Cup, activists stormed the pitch and waved flags with the slogan *Chile sí, Junta no* in protest against the military dictatorship; at the 1982 Men's World Cup game between Poland and the Soviet Union, banners

reading *Solidarność* were unrolled in support of the Polish trade union movement; in 2006, a protester wrapped in a Palestinian flag ran onto the field during a Glasgow Rangers vs. Maccabi Haifa match, trying to chain himself to a goalpost; in 2009, activists in Sweden hoisted a banner at Gothenburg's

Ullevi Stadium demanding the release of the Eritrean-Swedish journalist Dawit Isaak, imprisoned in Eritrea since 2001. Sometimes, the political messages at football games can be government-sponsored. In Iranian stadiums, teams have been welcomed with slogans like *Down with the USA!* or *Israel must be destroyed!*. That football supporters also have a sense of humor was proven by Scotland's infamous supporter community, the Tartan Army: when Scotland played the Soviet Union at the 1982 Men's World Cup, a banner proclaimed *Alcoholism v Communism*.

Football stadiums have also been sites of coded political protest. During the Third Reich, the hostile reception of German sides at Viennese football grounds were hardly concealed protests against the Nazis' annexation of the country. Under Franco's regime in Spain, forbidden songs were intoned in Catalonian and Basque stadiums.

Football victories have served as catalysts for public rebellion. When the Iranian men's team beat Australia for the final spot at the 1998 World Cup tournament, thousands of Iranian women stormed the stadium, defying clerical orders that ban them from stadiums when men are present. During the team's qualification campaign for the 2002 World Cup, banks and public offices were attacked and anti-government slogans shouted. When Iran lost their final game to underdog Bahrain, rumors abounded that the loss had been ordered by the regime in fear of further disturbances in the case of victory.

In such a political climate, the tiniest gestures can become acts of political resistance, for example when staff members of Esteghlal Tehran allowed one of their men's youth teams to meet the women's side in January 2009—as a result, three club officials were suspended.

Iranian Women Barred From Soccer Games

A Review of the Movie *Offside* by Jafar Panahi
AlterNet, April 26, 2007
Chuleenan Svetvilas

What happens when six Iranian young women disguise themselves as men so they can watch a World Cup qualifying match in Tehran? This is the situation in which director Jafar Panahi places his talented actors (all nonprofessionals) who play their fictional roles in the very real setting of a soccer stadium in Iran, where the national team faces Bahrain.

Women are not allowed in sports stadiums in Iran. So when Panahi went to get permission to make his film, he told the authorities that it was about boys who go to a soccer game. He got approval and promptly made *Offside*, a humorous and engaging film that defies easy categorization. It's not quite a sports movie—we only get a few distant glimpses of the soccer match—and it's not a purely fictional film. But one thing is certain: It is a film worth seeing.

Panahi got the idea for the film several years ago when his daughter wanted to accompany him to a soccer stadium. He didn't think she would be allowed in, but he decided to take her anyway. She was indeed turned away, but to his amazement, found a way in and joined him in the stands.

Winner of the Silver Bear at the Berlin Film Festival, *Offside* captures the plight of women soccer fans who try—often unsuccessfully—to bluff their way into the stadium.

In an early scene, we see a young woman trying to pass as a man on a stadium-bound bus full of men. One passenger points her out to his friend who remarks that women know how to get into the stadium. Instead of reporting her to the authorities, they let her continue her quest to get in. Panahi makes it clear at the outset that people do find ways to get around the rules, and not everyone agrees with enforcing them.

Besides providing lively, character-driven entertainment, the film comments on the political and social contradictions in Iranian society, where, for example, custom prevents women from attending soccer games (to shield them from profanity) but allows them access to movie theaters.

Much of the film takes place in the holding area on the upper level of the stadium where women are forced to stay until the vice squad picks them up and takes them away. The women can hear the crowd but can't see anything, so they plead with the soldiers to let them inside the stadium, saying that they can blend in with the crowd. One woman points out that Japanese women were in the stadium when Japan played Iran. "Well, they couldn't understand the swear words," says one soldier. "So my problem is that I was born in Iran?" she retorts.

The camera often takes a vérité documentary approach, blurring the line between fact and fiction. Some of the soldiers are not just playing a role; they are real soldiers serving in the Iranian army. And Panahi's direction is so self-assured and the acting so natural that you forget that you are watching actors. He captures the fervor of soccer fans—male and female—and their intense desire for their country to qualify for the World Cup.

The script, written by Panahi and Shadmehr Rastin, is filled with unexpected humor, particularly from the women who have the best lines. Upon seeing a tomboy smoking a cigarette, one of the soldiers asks if she's a girl or a boy. "Which do you prefer?" she replies.

Another laugh-out-loud scene occurs when one of the women must use the bathroom, which is, of course, for men only, and we see how one soldier struggles with the task of taking her there and "protecting" her from the graffiti on the walls. Here, Panahi shows the perspective of the soldiers, who are not comfortable with confining the women but also don't want to get in trouble with their superiors and risk having more time added to their mandatory military service.

According to press notes, none of Panahi's films have been released in Iran; however, *Offside* did have at least one screening in Tehran at the Fajr International Film Festival last year.

Panahi's previous films have been described as neo-realist and dealt with poverty-stricken men and the struggle of women in Tehran, apparently subjects the Iranian government doesn't wants its people to be reminded of. Panahi says that he makes his films for Iranians, but so far, his main audience has been people outside of Iran who have seen his work at film festivals and in art house theaters.

Offside has been a darling of the film festival circuit, and deservedly so. It is now making the art house cinema-rounds in the U.S.

In Libya as well, football has served as a site for coded political protest, mainly in the fierce opposition to Alahly Tripoli, a club that enjoys the backing of Muamar El-Gadaffi and his sons. Clashes during a derby against city rival Al-Ittihad in 1996 reportedly left fifty people dead.[74]

In Saudi Arabia, football was the background to a politically charged incident in 2009, when, during a live TV program, Prince Sultan bin Fahd, head of the FA, lashed out at reporters who had dared criticize the performance of the Saudi Arabian team. When the prince suggested that they "had not been raised well," a deep insult in Saudi culture, the former national team player Faisal Abu Thnain objected—it was the first time that a Saudi citizen questioned a member of the royal family in public.

On rare occasions, football associations themselves have played a role in political resistance. The Football Association of Indonesia (*Persatuan Sepak bola Seluruh Indonesia,* PSSI), founded in 1930, was active in the anti-colonial struggle against the Dutch. Similarly, the South African Soccer Federation (SASF), founded in 1951 as an integrated opponent to the all-white Football Association of South Africa (FASA), took on an active role in the anti-apartheid struggle. In 1991, at the eve of apartheid's defeat, the SASF merged with other South African football organizations to form today's South African Football Association (SAFA).

On a humorous note, football was used to express a community's overall frustration with the political system in the British town of Hartlepool in 2002, when the local team's mascot, a monkey, was elected mayor.

Social Justice Campaigns

A number of social justice campaigns have touched on soccer, mainly connected to labor rights and anti-sweatshop activism. The best known of these might be the FoulBall Campaign, launched by labor rights organizations in 1996 after a *Life* magazine article had addressed the production of soccer

balls in Pakistan's Sialkot region, where 75 percent of the world's hand-stitched soccer balls are made. The article revealed that twelve-year-old kids received sixty cents for stitching balls that Nike, Adidas, Umbro, and other companies sold for up to fifty dollars in the United States. The maximum number of balls that these kids were able to finish in a day was two.

The FoulBall Campaign made the sports company giants react, but mainly on a public relations level. Labels like *Guarantee: Manufactured Without Child Labor*, *Certified: No Child or Slave Labor Used on this Ball*, and *Adult Sewn Product* appeared. Puma introduced a *FairTrade* ball in 2008.

FIFA has supported the campaign by making star players' hold hands with children while entering the field. Meanwhile, little has changed on the ground. The following is the summary of a 2010 report by the International Labor Rights Forum (ILRF):

> More than half of the 218 surveyed workers in Pakistan reported that they did not make the legal minimum wage per month. In one Pakistani manufacturer, ILRF researchers found that all interviewed stitching center or home based workers were temporarily employed resulting [in] workers not having access to healthcare or social security. In the same Pakistani manufacturer's supply chain, female home-based workers faced discrimination based on their gender. They were paid the least and faced the possibility of losing their jobs permanently due to pregnancy. In one Chinese factory, workers were found to work up to 21 hours a day during high seasons and without one day off in an entire month. Indian stitching centers were described as "pathetic." Proper drinking water or medical care facilities, and even toilets were often absent. Child labor was identified by workers producing for three different factories in Pakistan.[75]

Personalities

Very few prominent football personalities have used the platforms provided by their popularity for sound political intervention. Arguably, people with strong political principles often do not make it to the top-level because they cannot deal with the authoritarian and corporate structures, or because they are weeded out as troublesome players. Barney Ronay wrote in a 2007 *Guardian* article, "At the top level at least, footballing socialists are an almost extinct breed." He quotes former Scotland international Gordon McQueen, who states that "I'd say 99 percent [of all footballers] are totally uninterested in politics."[76]

Most players who dabble in political affairs lend support to conservative parties, like England's Kevin Keegan, or they run for office based on their fame: Pelé has acted as the Minister of Sports for the Brazilian government, and former AC Milan striker George Weah ran as a candidate in

Liberia's presidential elections of 2005. Others, like Michel Platini, the current UEFA president, have worked their way up in the ranks of international football bureaucracy.

There are even footballers with well-established links to loyalist paramilitaries, like Scotland's Andy Goram, and self-professed fascists, like Italy's Paolo di Canio, who sports a *Duce* tattoo and enjoyed greeting Lazio Roma's right-wing fan groups with the fascist salute. The fact that the Italian keeper Gianluigi Buffon has sported a fascist slogan on a T-shirt (*Boia chi molla*—roughly, "Death to Deserters") and that he chose the unfortunate number 88 at Parma (a code for *Heil Hitler!* in white supremacist circles) was probably based on ignorance rather than neo-Nazi conviction, but still leaves a bad aftertaste. Speaking of ignorance, it is hard to beat the answer of Berti Vogts, captain of the German team at the 1978 Men's World Cup in Argentina, to a journalist who inquired if Vogts was worried about playing in a country full of torture chambers: "Not at all," he said, "I don't think that anything will happen to us."[77] In comparison, it is refreshing to see Thierry Henry in a Che Guevara shirt or Juan Verón with a Che tattoo—even if these choices might be based on political ignorance as well. Verón has stated that his Che tattoo was not a political statement but a way to honor an "Argentinean hero."[78] So much for Che's internationalism!

There are some more encouraging examples, though.

Matthias Sindelar was a legendary Austrian player in the 1930s. Due to his frailness he was known as *der Papierane* (Austrian for "made of paper"), but he made up for physical weakness with exquisite technical skills. In 1938, after the Nazi annexation of Austria, he refused to play in the new "pan-Germanic" team and ran a café in Vienna instead. He was found dead in an apartment in January 1939, together with an Italian woman whom he had met a few days earlier. The official cause of death was carbon monoxide poisoning, but the exact circumstances were never clarified. The police reports of the case went mysteriously missing.

Gusztáv Sebes was the manager of the Hungarian side that dominated world football in the early 1950s before sensationally losing to Germany in the 1954 Men's World Cup final. The Hungarians staged their probably biggest upset when beating England 6-3 in a game at London's Wembley Stadium in November 1953. It was the first time that England was beaten on home turf. Sebes was considered the mastermind of these glorious years of Hungarian football. He stressed permanent fluctuation on the pitch over strictly assigned individual roles, conceiving an early form of what became known as "total football" in the 1970s, a tactical approach defined by the Dutch coach Rinus Michels. England's Tom Finney, who watched the game from the stands due to an injury, confirmed the approach's effectiveness: "It was like carthorses playing racehorses. They were wonderful to watch, with tactics we'd never seen before."[79] For Sebes, a dedicated communist, this represented "communist football." Gyula Grosics, the era's Hungarian goalkeeper, has stated: "Sebes was very committed to socialist ideology, and you could sense that in everything he said. He made a political issue of every important match or competition, and he often talked about how the struggle between capitalism and socialism takes place on the football field just as it does anywhere else."[80]

The best-known British socialist manager was William "Bill" Shankly. Born in Scotland, he rose to fame as the manager of the hugely successful Liverpool side of the 1960s and '70s. He has been quoted as saying: "The socialism I believe in is everyone working for each other—everyone having a share of the rewards. It's the way I see football, it's the way I see life."[81]

Brian Clough, who celebrated sensational successes with Nottingham Forest in the 1970s, including back-to-back European Cup victories, also counts as a socialist manager. He used to join picket lines at miners' strikes and he has sponsored the Anti-Nazi League during its campaigns against right-wing supporters' groups in the stadiums. Clough allegedly stated: "For me, socialism comes from the heart. I don't see why certain sections of the community should have the franchise on champagne and big houses."[82]

In Italy, Osvaldo Bagnoldi, who sensationally led Hellas Verona to its only Italian title in 1985, had socialist leanings and was a harsh opponent of the modern football industry.

In South America, the Brazilian manager João Saldanha was a reputed communist. After leading Brazil to qualification for the 1970 Men's World Cup in Mexico, he was replaced by the military dictatorship shortly before the tournament started.

César Luis Menotti, who coined the term "left-wing football" has already been mentioned. Menotti was a successful player but rose to fame as Argentina's manager during the victorious 1978 World Cup campaign of the men's team. After Argentina's victory, he refused to shake hands with junta leader Jorge Rafael Videla. Menotti went on to become one of the most outspoken critics of football's commercialization. In the late 1990s, he stated in an interview that "a country has no future without an organized left. Who would otherwise stand up for a life in dignity and justice, for respect and solidarity with the poor?"[83]

In the 1970s, a few professional players openly embraced left-wing ideals. The Brazilian Afonsinho was active in the struggles against the military dictatorship and for players' rights. In Sweden, Ruben "The Red" Svensson wrote columns for the communist journal *Proletären*. In Germany, Paul Breitner brought Mao books to training sessions, while Ewald Lienen wore long black hair, was nicknamed "Lenin," refused to sign autographs, propagated vegetarianism, supported the peace movement, and co-initiated the first German players' union. In the Basque country, José Iribar, the Athletic Bilbao keeper, and Inaxio Kortabarria, a defender for San Sebastián, brought out the Ikurriña, the Basque flag, in December 1975 before the great Basque derby—it was the first open display of the Ikurriña in forty years, and still prohibited.

One of the most impressive political campaigns of footballers ever was set in motion in São Paulo by Corinthians' players in 1982, the famed Sócrates being the most prominent. The initiative became known as "Corinthians Democracy" and aimed at greater self-determination and increased players' rights within the club. However, the campaign's political significance went far beyond these aspects, since Brazil was still a military dictatorship. Sócrates explained: "I'm struggling for freedom, for respect for human beings, for ample and unrestricted discussions, for a professional democratization of unforeseen limits, and all of this as a soccer player preserving the ludic, joyous, and pleasurable nature of this activity."[84]

The 1980s also saw the rise of the perhaps most legendary of all radical football players, the FC St. Pauli goalkeeper Volker Ippig. At times, Ippig interrupted his career to do social work or to join workers' brigades in Nicaragua. He had close contacts to Hamburg's squatting scene and was involved in defending the houses of the legendary Hafenstraße. He always greeted St. Pauli supporters with a raised fist. Today, he is an amateur football coach and a dock worker.

▌Remaining Flexible: Volker Ippig, the St. Pauli Legend

Rainer Schäfer

Volker Ippig

"It is good to have distance." These days, Volker Ippig does not talk much about the FC St. Pauli. It is obvious that the end of a long and intensive relationship has left its wounds. Things need time to heal, and acting has never been one of Ippig's virtues. Eventually, he says: "The mechanisms that have brought the club down still continue today—on an athletic as well as on a personal level."

Ippig was involved in the "Project St. Pauli" for almost fifteen years. With short breaks, he was the first team's goalkeeper from 1981 to 1991, and in 1999 he returned as a goalkeeping coach, first for youth teams and the reserves, then for the professional squad. Ippig contributed to St. Pauli's 2001 return to the Bundesliga under manager Dietmar Demuth. Later, he was fired by Demuth, but reinstated by the successor Franz Gerber. When St. Pauli was relegated two times in a row and ended up in Germany's third league in 2003, Ippig left the club for good.

This is not to say that he will never return. For one and a half decades, Ippig and the FC St. Pauli seemed like they were made for one another and they could hardly be imagined apart. No other player has formed the FC St. Pauli identity in the same way that Voker Ippig has. In the late 1980s, the St. Pauli supporters' dream of a different, leftist football focused primarily on him. Greeting the back straight at the Millerntor with the raised fist, the workers' salute, he made the FC St. Pauli, in the eyes of many, a model for a better future of a sport alienated from its roots.

Ippig was a non-conformist who did not fit the clichés of a professional athlete. His enormous talent and ambition as a goalkeeper collided with his desire to realize himself, ideally in a politically correct manner. He lived in the Hafenstraße, one of Germany's most legendary squats, and occasionally left the confines of the penalty box to work in a school for disabled children or to join a workers' brigade in Nicaragua. Today, Ippig states: "I still stand by those decisions, but I was never the big political ideologue I was made out to be. I was always more of a freethinker."

Up in the *Winkel*, as the hilly landscape around Lensahn in Schleswig-Holstein is called, there lives a particular kind of people. When they decide to do something, they will do it. Lensahn has a population of six thousand. It is the town where Ippig grew up and where he always returned. It is his refuge. There, he finds energy and inspiration. It is also the place where everything started: football in an old gravel-pit, and then the relationship with the FC St. Pauli when he was called up to play for their Under-18 side. In 1983, under manager Michael Lorkowski in the Oberliga, Ippig took his first time-out. "I was tired of doing nothing but playing football." For one year, he worked in a kindergarten for disabled children in Oldenburg. He also built a cottage in the Lensahner Wald and spent many weekends there. "It was a spiritual place. Every night, I lit a fire, the oldest form of television." Ippig read Carlos Castaneda and tried to find his inner worlds. "Asceticism in bizarre brush, with wild colors: if you read Castaneda, you become light as a feather." Later, Ippig went to Nicaragua. Finally, he returned to the Millerntor, the infamous St. Pauli stadium.

When Ippig was forced to end his professional career in 1992 after sixty-five games in the Bundesliga, he was at a dead end. Not only was his back too weak to carry on playing, it was also burdened by a huge myth. Did he have any ideas about how to carry on? "No, I was never a plan-maker."

Ippig had been the romantic epitome of alternative football, but reality was catching up fast. Now he was a disabled twenty-nine-year-old ex-footballer who was "no longer needed." Even social utopias no longer seemed to "make much sense." Ippig left Hamburg in 1993 and returned to Lensahn as a bitter hermit with a long beard and a buckskin jacket, at times "losing the sense for human connection" and "isolating myself." Visitors were shown the door. "I spent a lot of time reflecting on the ills of the world. But you go crazy over that."

The thinker Ippig never turned into a late-night entertainer at the bar, but he started to embrace life. In his words, he realized that he "needed to receive and to give positive energies: life is now, here, everywhere." His interest in natural healing never led to a diploma, however. "I was probably too lazy to pass the exams."

Ippig was past his search for the meaning of life when he returned to the Millerntor in 1999. He had also cleared up his relationship to football and to the FC St. Pauli. When he was received as a goalkeeping coach, he evoked old principles and ideals: "Everything I am, I am because of football. My heart beats left. I cherish social and communal values—and this is still the big asset of the FC St. Pauli."

On the training grounds, Ippig eschewed beaten paths. He used unconventional methods to lead the Millerntor keepers to success. "What are we doing today?" Ippig added handstands and cartwheels to the routine. The keepers greeted him in the same way that kindergarten kids greet a magician: with a mixture of joy, curiosity, and skepticism. "Remaining flexible," was how Ippig described the purpose of such exercises, "also in the head." Those who watched the training sessions had fun when Ippig's keepers battled it out with plastic dolls from porn catalogs. The "small leather bag ritual" was also renowned: the hobby healer liked to summon players with minor injuries to give them homeopathic medicine from his leather pouch.

It seemed inevitable that the innovative Ippig would run into problems with a club whose structure often resembled that of an old, boring party. A particular conflict arose when he supported Carsten Wehlmann, one of St. Pauli's keepers, in his plans to transfer to the local rival Hamburger Sportverein (HSV). The dogmatic wing of the St. Pauli fans accused Ippig of high treason. He was not impressed: "Each cow changes its meadows, but someone from St. Pauli should never be allowed to play for the HSV? There was a time when I was that stubborn too. But myths have to burst like bubbles." Maybe especially, when they are your own . . .

Volker Ippig has gone through significant personal changes, but one thing has always remained the same: he follows his ambitions with enormous dedication and creativity. Didi Demuth had little understanding for Ippig's "holistic" training methods, which added the abovementioned "mental flexibility" to physical strength, coordination, and technique. In the end, he got Ippig fired. For Ippig, Demuth was one of those who lost touch with reality after the unexpected Bundesliga return of St. Pauli in 2001; one of those who rendered the notion of a "different" football club absurd in light of nepotism and narrow-mindedness.

Ippig gets irritated when the management tries to evoke the St. Pauli myth today to distract from the team's dismal performances: "The Millerntor was once an outdoor laboratory for German football, and the close relationship between fans, players, and management was successful. At the time, this relationship was real. Today, it is orchestrated. Today, only the myth remains, a lot of fog, and a lot of blabber."

Ippig once again goes novel ways with Germany's first "Mobile Goalkeepers School," which he offers to support the development of keepers from the youth to the professional level. "The technical standard of goalkeepers' practice is still low, even in the Bundesliga."

In July 2004, Ippig will start his courses for a coaching diploma at the German Sport University in Cologne. The world of football can look forward to a coach who will not do anything just because it has always been done!

This text was published in 2005 as "Gelenkig Bleiben" in Christoph Ruf, ed., *Die Untoten vom Millerntor: Der Selbstmord des FC St. Pauli und dessen lebendige Fans* [The Undead of the Millerntor: The Suicide of the FC St. Pauli, and the Story of Its Lively Fans] (Cologne: PapyRossa 2005). Translated by Gabriel Kuhn. *Postscript (GK)*: Ippig received his coaching diploma in 2005. In 2008, he led the TSV Lensahn into the Verbandsliga, a medium-level amateur league. He described winning the decisive game as his "happiest moment in football." Ippig still maintains his Mobile Goalkeepers School and has worked as a goalkeeping coach for the Bundesliga side VFL Wolfsburg in 2007. Since 2008, he has supplemented his income as a dock worker at Hamburg's port. In May 2010, he played with the "FC St. Pauli All-Stars" against the FC United of Manchester to celebrate St. Pauli's 100th anniversary. He lives with his partner and two children in Lensahn.

In the 1990s, the Norwegian striker Jan Åge Fjørtoft was one of the few white players who took supporters to task for racist abuse of opponents, even if this meant confronting his own team's fans. The Swiss midfielder Alain Sutter objected to football players being treated as "commodities" and challenged masculine stereotypes with Buddhist concepts. In France, the New Caledonian Christian Karembeu refused to sing the Marseillaise as a member of the national team. The new hero for radical football fans, however, was Cristiano Lucarelli: a communist striker from Livorno, a dock workers' town with a long radical tradition and fan culture, who rejected many lucrative offers and played for the side of his home town, the AS

Livorno, instead. Like Ippig, he saluted supporters with the raised fist. He also actively supported left-wing Ultra groups and even chose the number 99 to honor the 1999 foundation of the radical Brigate Autonome Livornese.

Cristiano Lucarelli

Erik Niva

He rejected 500,000 euros, founded a daily newspaper, and moved to Ukraine to learn something new about the world. In the process, Cristiano Lucarelli also became one of Europe's most successful goal scorers.

Soon, I will have no heroes left. Maybe because I am getting older, maybe because my job has brought me too close to the players, maybe because modern football has changed too much. I am not sure. I only know that I no longer look up to successful football players. In the best case, they are simply regular folks. In the worst case, they are spoilt, untrustworthy, and arrogant jerks who have lost touch with reality.

However, there are still exceptions. There is one fellow who can make me send my credit card number to a mysterious server in Ukraine the very same day that the computer world is warning us of rising Internet fraud in Eastern Europe. Some of you have certainly heard the story of Cristiano Lucarelli before, but it is time for an update.

In the fall of 1992, Cuoipelli played against Livorno in one of Italy's amateur leagues. Livorno scored an equalizer in overtime, and the dock worker Maurizio Lucarelli celebrated on the stands. He taunted Cuoipelli's supporters, he insulted them, he provoked them with obscene gestures. All the while, his own seventeen-year-old son Cristiano played for Cuoipelli. Today, Maurizio Lucarelli shrugs and smiles innocently: "If it comes to Livorno, then—well, then there is nothing else to do. I have always said that Livorno was my fourth son."

This was the spirit in which Cristiano Lucarelli was raised. Although Livorno was a weak club in the lower leagues, Cristiano developed an almost neurotic loyalty to the team and to the town.

He has called the day when he started his professional career "the saddest day of my life." "I managed to say goodbye to my family without crying, but when I sat on the train and saw the Livorno sign disappear, I could no longer control myself."

It would take an entire decade before the lost son came home. An early summer day in Treviso changed everything. Livorno won against the home team and was promoted to Serie B. After the final whistle, the team's ecstatic supporters stormed the field in celebration. One of them was Cristiano Lucarelli.

Lucarelli was a well-established Serie A striker at the time and his own team Torino played that same afternoon. However, it was more important for him to watch Livorno. In official terms, he was "slightly injured."

With Livorno advancing to Serie B, everything seemed crystal-clear. Cristiano Lucarelli would go home. He wanted it, he demanded it, and he was ready to sacrifice both money and career for it. After all, he did not only say goodbye to Serie A—in order for Livorno being able to afford him, he accepted a salary cut of 50 percent. In other terms, he rejected one billion lira—about 500,000 euros—in order to play for Livorno. A football world ruled by economics was stunned. What Lucarelli did seemed incomprehensible, and his explanation did not clarify things either: "I placed high bets on Livorno's roulette. But my number, 99, was not on the wheel, and so I knew I couldn't win." This was followed by his most famous quote, the words that define Cristiano Lucarelli: "Some players buy themselves a Ferrari or a yacht. I bought myself a Livorno shirt."

Livorno is a special town. It is a town of dock workers. It is a left-wing town. The Italian Communist Party was founded here in 1921. Children are sung to sleep with old party songs instead of lullabies. The ringtone on Cristiano Lucarelli's mobile phone is the socialist anthem "Bandiera

Rossa." We could use this whole article trying to define how far left Lucarelli really is, what the clenched fist means when he celebrates his goals, and whether it is true that he votes for the Rifondazione Communista, the "Communist Refoundation Party"—but all that would miss the point. Lucarelli is an unconventional football player. He has opinions. He is active. He does things. The number of his shirt, 99, is a tribute to the year when the (now defunct) supporter network Brigate Autonome Livornese was founded. He personally went to Livorno's police station to have stadium bans for supporters lifted, guaranteeing that they would behave. In football terms, this meant that Lucarelli cared about supporters. In social terms, this meant much more.

Last summer, Cristiano Lucarelli and Livorno parted ways again. He had just shot the club into Serie A for the first time in fifty-five years and into European club competition for the first time ever. In four years, he had scored more than one hundred goals and won the crown of Italy's top scorer. Still he had problems with the club's president and there were supporters who thought that he was not always giving his best. Lucarelli decided to leave his club and his city—but he was very careful about where to go and he would not leave without a goodbye present. First, he made yet another stunning decision. Rather than signing for a glamorous team, the top scorer joined Shakhtar Donetsk, a club of miners in Eastern Ukraine. Then, instead of opening a restaurant in Livorno, he founded a daily newspaper. In his own words: "Out of respect for Livorno, I did not want to go to another Italian club. And if I already moved abroad, I wanted a challenge that allowed me to learn something new." Okay, this part might be fairly easy to grasp—but how about that newspaper? "Livorno is one of the very few Italian towns that only have one daily paper. I think that another one would contribute to the diversity of opinions and to the freedom of expression."

It only took a few weeks for Lucarelli to realize all the implications of increased freedom of expression. After coming on as a substitute for Italy in a European Championship qualifier against France he got a mediocre 5.5 rating in his own *Corriere di Livorno*. His reaction? "Haha, this is something I am really happy for. I wanted to have an independent paper—now I have to pay for it!"

In Lucarelli's career, it is hard to distinguish the steps that made him progress from the ones that held him back—it was a winding path. In any case, this week Cristiano Lucarelli, 32, draws more attention than ever. Last Wednesday he was back in Tuscany, scoring both goals in an Italian win over South Africa in Siena. "Despite all the scoring, I hardly ever got a chance to play in the national team. Maybe because I played for a club that was too small, maybe because I said too many things that were controversial. But now I hope that my time has come!"

This Wednesday, Lucarelli will enter the epicenter of Italy's football, Milan's San Siro Stadium. The set-up is thrilling: a hungry Shakhtar side has won its first two Champion League games and has a good chance of making it past the group stage for the first time, while a slow-starting Milan is coming from a defeat in Glasgow and risks ending up in a very difficult spot. In a nutshell, Cristiano Lucarelli has the chance to step on the toes of Milan owner Silvio Berlusconi, who he believes "has hurt today's Italy more than anyone else." Lucarelli adds: "To claim that an important goal against Berlusconi's team doesn't mean more than other goals would be as dumb as claiming that football is only a sport."

A few weeks ago, I got a call from a customs officer in the Swedish port town of Helsingborg. A strange package had arrived for me—it had been picked up at Pushkin Avenue in Donetsk before being shipped to Sweden via Kiev and the Belgian port of Liège. The officer asked whether I know anything about the contents. I did. It contained an orange Shakhtar Donetsk shirt with the number 99 and "Lucarelli" in Cyrillic letters written on it.

Shakhtar Donetsk lost the Champions League game against Milan 4-1. Cristiano Lucarelli scored Shakhtar's goal. Since then, he has zigzagged through his career, in the end always returning to Livorno. Throughout all the changes, certain things remained the same. When Livorno stole points from Berlusconi's Milan in the spring of 2010 at San Siro, Lucarelli scored again.

Erik Niva is an award-winning Swedish soccer writer whose work mainly appears in the daily *Aftonbladet*. Many of his articles and columns—praised for skillfully blending reflections on soccer with social, political, and cultural analyses—have been collected in the books *Den nya världsfotbollen* [The New World Football] (2008) and *Liven längs linjen* [The Lives along the Line] (2010). This article on Cristiano Lucarelli is included in the latter. Translated by Gabriel Kuhn. *Postscript (GK):* In the summer of 2010, Lucarelli moved to Napoli, a longtime Southern rival to the football powerhouses and financial centers in Italy's north.

Currently, another Italian striker draws a lot of leftist sympathies: Fabrizio Miccoli, who has been playing professional football in Italy and Portugal for fifteen years, openly supports the Trotskyist *Partito Comunista dei Lavoratori* [Workers' Communist Party]. Like his idol, Diego Maradona, he wears a tattoo of Che Guevara.

Maradona, widely regarded as one of the best players the game has ever seen, is an illustrious and controversial figure, regarding politics as much as anything else. Sporting not only a Che Guevara tattoo but also one of Fidel Castro, and participating in anti-neoliberal and anti-imperialist protests, he has been embraced by many as a man of the left. Others point to the numerous contradictions in Maradona's life, which include erratic and authoritarian personal behavior and a lavish lifestyle. Be that as it may, Maradona is a breath of fresh air in an obedient, corporate football world. It is of little wonder that he has had many run-ins with FIFA, not least after his exclusion from the 1994 Men's World Cup due to a failed drug test.

The career of another controversial South American footballer, Colombian goalkeeper René Higuita, reveals some of the more tricky aspects of the role that some football celebrities play for impoverished communities. In 1993, Higuita was sentenced to several months in prison due to connections to Medellín drug cartels. In the Western media, the links between football and organized crime in Latin America are generally exploited to confirm Latinos' alleged criminal-mindedness and corruption. Apart from the fact that many Western football associations act like crime syndicates, such stereotypes ignore the fact that neighborhoods bereft of social services often depend on the few among them who have made it—usually in sports or in the entertainment industry—to return money to their communities. The involvement of organized crime in these cases is often a consequence of sociopolitical realities and something the athletes have only limited control over. While Higuita went to prison, he was hailed as a folk hero in the neighborhood he had grown up in. Liberal analysts have to come to terms with these apparent "contradictions."

This is not to deny that there are safer ways for footballers to show social responsibility. The Brazilian striker Romario is a high-profile supporter of the progressive President Lula and has assisted with projects to relieve poverty in the favelas. Manchester United's Gary Neville has earned the nickname "Red Nev" by speaking up against football officials and contributing regularly to social causes. Players like France's Robert Pires and Italy's Damiano Tommasi were outspoken critics of the war in Iraq and have voiced their opinions on a number of social and political issues. The French international Lilian Thuram publicly criticized President Nicolas Sarkozy over his immigration policies and his inflammatory remarks during the 2005 French suburban riots. In September 2006, Thuram ostentatiously invited eighty people who had been expelled from an illegal flat on the outskirts of Paris to a France vs. Italy game. The English international Ian Wright also became an important voice in antiracism activism.

Some players have sported political messages on T-shirts after lifting their jerseys following a goal. The best-known example is probably Robbie Fowler declaring his support for striking Liverpool dock workers in 1997.

More recently, the Malian international Frédéric Kanouté revealed a shirt in support of the Palestinian struggle for independence after scoring for Sevilla in January 2009.

In a relatively well-known incident, the Inter Milan captain and Argentinean international Javier Zanetti convinced his teammates to donate a substantial amount of money, an ambulance, and football gear to the Zapatista rebels. Zanetti declared in a letter: "We believe in a better world, in a non-globalized world, enriched by the cultural differences and customs of all people. This is why we want to support you in this struggle to maintain your roots and fight for your ideals."[85] In response, the media-savvy Subcomandante Marcos challenged Inter president Massimo Moratti to a game against his team in Chiapas.

■ Letter by Subcomandante Insurgente Marcos to Massimo Moratti, President of the Milan International F.C.

May 25, 2005

Don Massimo,
We have received the letter in which you inform us that your football team, the International F.C., has accepted the fraternal challenge we made to you. We appreciate the kindness and honesty of your response. We have learned through the media of statements by the Inter's management, coaching staff and players. They are all simply more examples of the nobility of your hearts. Know that we are delighted to have met you along our now long path and that it is an honor for us to be a part of the bridge which unites two dignified lands: Italy and Mexico.

I am letting you know that, in addition to being spokesperson for the EZLN, I have been unanimously designated Head Coach and put in charge of Intergalactic Relations for the zapatista football team (well, in truth no one else wanted to accept the job). In this role I should, perhaps, make use of this letter to move forward in fixing details about the match.

Perhaps, for example, I might suggest that, instead of the football game being limited to one match, there could be 2. One in Mexico and another in Italy. Or one going and one on return. And the trophy known the world over as "The Pozol of Mud" would be fought for.

And perhaps I might propose to you that the game in Mexico would be played, with you as visitors, in the Mexican 68 Olympic Stadium, in CU, in DF, and the stadium receipts would be for the indigenous displaced by paramilitaries in Los Altos of Chiapas. Although then, obviously, I would have to send a letter to the UNAM university community (students, teachers, researchers, manual and administrative workers) asking them to lend us the stadium, not without previously solemnly promising them that

we wouldn't ask them to remain silent . . . and then imposing Don Porfirio's word on them. And perhaps we might agree, given that you would already be in Mexico, that we would hold another game in Guadalajara, Jalisco, and that the proceeds would go to provide legal help for the young *alter-mundistas* unjustly imprisoned in the jails of that Mexican province and to all the political prisoners throughout the country. Transportation would not be a problem, because I have read that someone here in Mexico, generous as before, has offered his help.

And perhaps, if you are in agreement, for the games in Mexico the EZLN would turn to Diego Armando Maradona and ask him to be referee; to Javier El Vasco Aguirre and to Jorge Valdano and ask them to act as assistant referees (or linesmen); and to Sócrates, midfielder who was from Brazil, to be 4th referee. And perhaps we might invite those two intergalactics who travel with Uruguayan passports: Eduardo Galeano and Mario Benedetti to do the play by play of the game for the Zapatista System of Intergalactic Television ("the only television which is read"). In Italy, Gianni Mina and Pedro Luis Sullo could be the commentators.

And, perhaps, in order to differentiate ourselves from the objectification of women which is promoted at football games and in commercials, the EZLN would ask the national lesbian-gay community, especially transvestites and transsexuals, to organize themselves and to amuse the respectable with ingenious pirouettes during the games in Mexico. That way, in addition to prompting TV censorship, scandalizing the ultra-right and disconcerting the Inter ranks, they would raise the morale and spirits of our team. There are not just 2 sexes, and there is not just one world, and it is always advisable for those who are persecuted for their differences to share happiness and support without ceasing to be different.

Rushing headlong now, we might play another game in Los Angeles, in California, the U.S., where their governor (who substitutes steroids for his lack of neurons) is carrying out a criminal policy against Latin migrants. All the receipts from that match would be earmarked for legal advice for the undocumented in the USA and to jail the thugs from the "Minuteman Project." In addition, the zapatista "dream team" would carry a large banner saying "Freedom for Mumia Abu Jamal and Leonard Peltier."

It is quite likely that Bush would not allow our spring-summer model ski masks to create a sensation in Hollywood, so the meeting could be moved to the dignified Cuban soil, in front of the military base which the U.S. government maintains, illegally and illegitimately, in Guantánamo. In this case each delegation (from the Inter and from the Ezeta) would commit themselves to taking at least one kilo of food and medicines for each of their members, as a symbol of protest against the blockade the Cuban people are suffering.

And perhaps I might propose to you that the return games would be in Italy, with you as the home team (and us as well, since it is known that Italian sentiment is primarily pro-zapatista). One could be in Milan, in your stadium, and the other wherever you decide (it could be in Rome, because "all games lead to Rome" . . . or is it "all roads lead to Rome?" . . . ah well, it's the same). Some of the receipts would be to help migrants of different nationalities who are being criminalized by the governments of the European Union and the rest for whatever you decide. But we would certainly need at least one day in order to go to Genoa to paint *caracolitos* on the statue of Christopher Columbus (note: the likely fine for damages to monuments would be covered by Inter) and in order to take a flower of remembrance to the place where the young *altermundist* Carlo Giuliani fell (note: we would take care of the flower).

And, if we are already in the Europes, we could play a game in Euzkal Herria in the Basque Country. If "An Opportunity for the Word "couldn't happen, then we'd try for "An Opportunity for the Kick." We would demonstrate in front of the head office of the racists from the BBVA-Bancomer who are trying to criminalize the humanitarian aid received by the indigenous communities (perhaps in order to divert attention from the criminal proceedings against them for "tax evasion, secret accounts, illegal pension funds, secret contributions to political campaigns, bribes in order to buy banks in Latin America and wrongful appropriation of goods"—Carlos Fernández-Vega, "Mexico, S.A.," in *La Jornada* 2S/V/o5). Hmm . . . It looks like there's going to be 7 games now (which isn't bad, because that way we can compete for the audience for the European Cup, the Liberators and the qualifiers for the World Cup). The one which wins 4 of the 7 games will win "The Pozol of Mud" (note: if the zapatista team loses more than 3 games, the tournament will be canceled).

Too many? Fine, Don Massimo, you're right, perhaps it's better to leave it at 2 games (one in Mexico and the other in Italy), because we don't want to tarnish the Inter's record too badly with the certain defeats we're proposing.

Perhaps, in order to balance your evident disadvantage a bit, I might pass on to you some secret information. For example, the zapatista team is mixed (that is, there are men and women); we play with so-called "miner's" boots (they have steel toes, which is why they puncture balls); according to our uses and customs, the game is only over when none of the players of either team is left standing (that is, they are high resistance); the EZLN can reinforce itself at its discretion (that is, the Mexicans "Bofo" Bautista and Maribel "Marigol" Dominguez can appear in the lineup . . . if they accept). And we have designed a chameleon-like uniform (if we're losing, black and blue stripes appear on our shirts, confusing our rivals, the referee . . . and the public). And also we've been practicing, with relative success, two new plays: the "marquiña avanti fortiori" (note: translated into gastronomical terms it would be something like a pizza and guacamole sandwich) and the "marquiña caracoliña con variante inversa" (note: the equivalent of spaghetti with stewed beans, but spoiled).

With all this (and a few other surprises), we might, perhaps, revolutionize world football, and then, perhaps, football would no longer be just a business, and once again it would be an entertaining game. A game made, as you put it so well, of true feelings.

Perhaps . . . Nonetheless, this is just to reiterate to you and to your family, to all the men and women of the Inter and the nerazzurro fans, our appreciation and admiration for you (although I'm warning you that, in front of the goalposts, there will be neither mercy nor compassion). As to all the rest, well . . . perhaps . . . but . . .

Vale. Salud and may the green-white-red that clothes our dignities soon find themselves on both lands.

From the mountains of the Mexican Southeast,

Subcomanadante Insurgente Marcos (D. T. Z.)

(designing plays on a chalkboard and fighting with Durito because he's insisting that, instead of the traditional 4-2-4, we should present 1-1-1-1-1-1-1-1-1-1, which, he says, is confusing)

P.S. for the Mexican Federation of Football, the Real Madrid, the Bayern Munich, the Osasuna, the Ajax, Liverpool and the Ferretería González team—I'm sorry, but I have an exclusive contract with the Ezetaelene.

P.S. in the tone and volume of a sports announcer—The Sup, using the tactics of the Uruguayan Obdulio Varela in the final against Brazil (World Cup, Maracaná Stadium, Rio de Janeiro, 7/16/1950), ball in hand, having traveled as if in slow motion (since May of 2001), from the zapatista goal-post. After complaining to the referee about the illegitimacy of the goal, he puts the ball in the center of the field. He turns around to look at his *compañeros* and they exchange glances and silences. With the scorecard, the bets and the entire system against them, *no one* has any hope for the zapatistas. It starts to rain. A watch reads almost 6. Everything appears ready for the game to resume . . .

This version published by Z-Net.

The most recent radical celebrity among football professionals is the soft-spoken Oleguer, a former Barcelona and current Ajax Amsterdam player who has always embraced left-wing struggles the causes of Catalan and Basque independence.

Presas Oleguer: The Defender of Catalonia

Damiano Valgolio

In Cyprus, the ELF Cup is taking place, a tournament of teams not recognized by FIFA. The giant among the excommunicated is not present: Catalonia. Few individuals represent the region as much as FC Barcelona's Presas Oleguer.

Statements like the following are hardly outrageous: "The EU constitution only serves the ruling class and capital." How about abandoned buildings? "Occupy them! At least if they are owned by speculators." You find a few thousand people in every bigger European city who share these thoughts. In the rebellious Barcelona probably even more. But how many of them have studied national economy? Certainly not a lot. And how many of these radical national economists have kissed the Champions League trophy in the Paris rain in mid-May? Only one.

Joan Oleguer Presas Renom is an autonomous activist, a recently graduated economist, and a defender for what's probably the world's best club team at the moment. His name sets off alarm bells in FC Barcelona's press office. There, Oleguer is more tightly guarded than Ronaldinho. Everything is done to avoid publicity! After all, state prosecutors are investigating his alleged participation in a riot, and many officials in Spain's FA keep a close eye on him. A careless comment about the Spanish national team might ban the 25-year-old to the terraces when the next season starts. The Barca press relations' officer tries to prevent all interviews: "He is on vacation and cannot be reached." Maybe in August, he adds. However, Oleguer can be reached. This probably says more about him than all of his radical quotes. In order to find the towering defender one has to call people who do not answer the telephone with their names and who assume no air of officialdom.

With Catalonia to the World Cup

Eventually, I reach the poet Roc Casagran, a known name in hip circles. He only writes in Catalan and reads in the cafés of Barcelona and Sabadell. Most of his poems are about love, dreams, and politics. He has just published a book—together with Oleguer Presas. He should know where the football rebel can be found. "Of course, he's right next to me, but he is driving. *Espera un momento*, we are pulling over." Then the defender of the Spanish champion is on the line himself. "Congratulations Oleguer, great season—where are you?"—"I am driving to Valencia with Roc, we have an event there tonight." The two want to present their new book in Valencia because of the many Catalans who live in the city's surroundings. "It is important for them to read Catalan so that they don't lose their language."

Soon after the Champions League win, Oleguer is back on a political mission. There is only one team he wants to play for at a World Cup: Catalonia. And this although right now he could experience what millions of his peers dream about: to play at the World Cup in Germany. Is he not sad to miss it? "I wish the Spanish team all the best," he says diplomatically. He has become cautious, but it is obvious that he is not upset about having been left out of the squad. Everyone knows that the kid from a Barcelona suburb only wants to play for Catalonia at such an event. Oleguer is not only a leftist. He is also a fervent Catalan nationalist, many would say: separatist. In his words, he demands "autonomy" for the northern Spanish province and its capital Barcelona.

In November 2005, many held their breath—not only in Barcelona—when Spain's manager Luis Aragonés named Oleguer as one of the possible players for the World Cup. Of course, Aragonés could have hardly made a different decision. It is true that Oleguer only joined Barcelona's A-side in 2004 after playing for the lower league club UEA Gramenet and as a semi-professional for the Barcelona reserves before his twenty-third birthday. But since the beginning of 2005, the 6 ft 1 player has been so imposing that it was impossible for Aragonés to ignore him. For Oleguer this meant a huge dilemma. The campaign "One Nation, One National Team" was in full swing, demanding FIFA's recognition of the unofficial Catalan team. The campaign's most important supporter? The Barca defender with the number 23. Yet, the regulations of the Spanish FA foresee long suspensions for players who refuse to join the national team for political reasons. The supporters at Barcelona's Nou Camp Stadium demanded *No hi vagis*, "Don't Go," on their banners. The "Republican Left of Catalonia" party, ERC (*Esquerra Republicana de Catalunya*), filed a motion in the Spanish parliament to prevent a potential suspension. However, at long last, Oleguer gave in. When even Barca captain Carles Puyol, himself a Catalan and a Spanish international, encouraged him to do so, he reported at the meeting of the thirty-three potential World Cup players. The national team manager Aragonés approached the affair rationally. "I know players who have played for three countries. I don't care whether someone is a communist, a right-winger, or a separatist, I'm only interested in his performance on the field." In the end, Aragonés went to Germany without Oleguer. Maybe because he could not be sure whether the defender would really come along—or was it indeed because Oleguer played a little weaker towards the end of the season?

"The Only Normal Guy"

Instead of representing Spain in Germany, Oleguer Presas drives across the northern parts of the country with Roc Casagran in a Volkswagen van, campaigning for the cause of Catalonia. The poet and the footballer have known each other for a long time. Both were born in Sabadell, twenty kilometers west of Barcelona, and both belong to the editorial collective of the local autonomous paper *Ordint la trama*, "Preparing the Struggle." On training days, the grey van parks between the sports cars and limousines of the other Barca players. Spain's biggest daily, the conservative *El Mundo*, calls Oleguer a "provocateur." Roc Casagran sees things differently: "He is the only normal guy in the mad world of football."

The book promoted by Oleguer and Casagran is a football fairy tale and a political manifesto at the same time. Oleguer calls it "an urban road movie about friendship and utopia." The title, "The Way to Ithaca," makes reference to Greek mythology. It alludes to the hard struggle of the FC Barcelona for the 2005 Spanish Championship. The narrative opens with Oleguer's thoughts after the victory. These are rather special. He compares his team to the antifascists who defended Barcelona in 1939 against Franco's troops. "We were an army of joy and merriment that was finally able to repel those who oppressed our people sixty-six years ago." Oleguer also writes about the commercialization of football, the alterglobalization movement, and the Iraq War: "It was against the will of the people that the Spanish government took part in the invasion—or, let's say, in the massacre."

This is the world of Oleguer Presas: football, Catalan regionalism, and revolution. A mixture that can only exist in Barcelona—and one that needs some getting used to. To be against capitalism and war? Why not? But how does this fit in with Catalan folklore? Nou Camp: terraces as pockets of resistance.

In order to understand Oleguer, one has to know the history of the region, especially the history of the club. During the Spanish Civil War, Catalonia was the stronghold of Franco's enemies and of the CNT, the anarchist labor union. The military dictatorship oppressed everything that appeared in the least Catalan until the 1970s, whether it was language, music, or culture. Oleguer is not the only one who sees antifascism and Catalanism inextricably linked—there are many. And football is part of the equation too. The Nou Camp Stadium was one of the few places where people could speak Catalan under Franco's regime: terraces as pockets of resistance.

Barca, The Other World

"Barca is the symbol of the Catalan people's identity," says the renowned writer Manuel Vázques Montalbán. The former club president Josep Suñol, executed by one of Franco's firing squads in 1936, counts as a martyr. At the time, the entire team was forced to go into exile in Mexico. Allegedly, Barca club members ranked third on the wanted lists of the dictatorship, right behind anarchists and communists. "To support the club meant to reject the regime," explains Oleguer Presas, "and that's why Barca will always be more than just a club." Even the German Bernd Schuster, who played for Barcelona in the 1980s, declared: "To talk about this club is like talking about a different world."

In his writings, Oleguer states: "At its core, football is only a game, but as long as there is oppression it is also a vehicle for people to express dissident opinions, whether we like it or not." We might not share Oleguer's political views, but the relationship between football and revolt has rarely been described as compellingly.

Especially the matches against the rival from the capital city, Real Madrid, retain the aura of political confrontation. "The Royals" are regarded as Franco's favorite club and as a symbol of the despised centralist state. In March 2006, Oleguer arranged a book launch two days before the *derbi clásico*. Even if the date was coincidental, the location certainly was not. The footballer received journalists and guests in the Can Vies, a Social Center in Barcelona's Sants district, occupied since 1997. With a stubble and a black hooded sweatshirt, Oleguer posed for photographs in front of posters reading "Freedom For Political Prisoners" and "Everything for Everyone."

Oleguer has never held back. He has talked at protests against the "neoliberal" EU constitution and at a huge rally against the war in Iraq with a keffiyeh around his neck. He dedicated his first goal in the Primera División to a kid called David, a fourteen-year-old youth from Sabadell. David had been arrested for putting up left-wing posters. Oleguer figured that he "must be going through a hard time." Last year, the defender covered the costs of a free Manu Chao concert, an icon for globalization critics. Allegedly, Oleguer is also good friends with Subcomandante Marcos, the football-crazy Zapatist leader in Mexico.

Particularly tight are his relations with the squatting scene. The "Bemba affair," as it is called by Spain's press, dates back to an incident on September 27, 2003. It remains unclear what exactly happened. Oleguer speaks of "police brutality." The illegal youth club *Bemba* in Sabadell was to be evicted. Six police officers and twenty youth ended up injured. Eleven protesters spent the night in prison, among them Oleguer. The case against him is still pending, the indictment speaks of assault against a police officer and of inflicting bodily harm. Joan Laporta, Barca's president and a lawyer himself, declared at a press conference: "We fully support Oleguer in this case!"

Red and Yellow, Catalonia's Colors

There are a few more special aspects to the FC Barcelona. While other European top clubs like Juventus or Manchester United have registered at the stock market, Barca remains a simple association, the property of about 160,000 members. As long as the Catalan national team is not officially recognized, the FC Barcelona will also serve as the region's de facto football representative. Red and yellow, the colors of Catalonia, are part of the club's crest. And, like all national teams, Barca has no sponsor on its jersey, even though companies are offering dozens of millions. The only thing that Barcelona does share with other top clubs is the pursuit of the best talents in world football—luckily! Still, about half of the players on the current roster went through the club's own youth program. It is a remarkable defensive trio that covers the backs of international stars like Ronaldinho and Eto'o right now: the young keeper Víctor Valdés was born within earshot of the Nou Camp Stadium in the working-class neighborhood of Hospitalet; Varles Puyol, the team's captain, is the son of a Barcelona baker and became a folk hero by rejecting a Real Madrid offer in 2004; finally, there is Oleguer, the Catalan intellectual.

In contrast to Oleguer, however, Puyol and Valdés do play for Spain. Is the activist too stubborn? After all, Catalonia has far-reaching autonomy rights today. The region around Barcelona is no longer oppressed—in fact, it has become Spain's richest. Some say that Oleguer is abusing his popularity. He objects: "Shall I no longer be allowed to have an opinion only because I'm a professional footballer?" Sometimes, he feels uncomfortable in his role: "I don't like to be adored. Of course it is nice when a fifty-year-old man congratulates me on the street. But I always feel like he has done much more in life than I have."

Oleguer is surprisingly thoughtful for an autonomous activist, and especially for a professional footballer. "I am against injustice and oppression, but I do not adhere to any strict ideology. I want to learn more, that's why I keep on studying." In the fall of 2006, Oleguer will be back at the university. After finishing his studies in economy, he will now pursue philosophy and history. He also wants to continue writing. On the side, he will continue to play football as well. After the triumph in the Champions League, the FC Barcelona will compete in the FIFA Club World Cup. The chances to win are good. And maybe Catalonia will one day become World Champion too—maybe even sooner than Oleguer dares to dream.

The article originally appeared as "Presas Oleguer: Der Verteidiger Kataloniens" in *11Freunde*, no. 56 (July 2006). Damiano Valgolio is a lawyer and journalist who lives in Berlin. He acts as the deputy chairperson for Germany's left-wing party DIE LINKE in the district of Friedrichshain-Kreuzberg and plays as a midfielder for the VfB Berlin Friedrichshain. Translated by Gabriel Kuhn.
Postscript (GK): Barcelona lost the 2006 FIFA Club World Cup final to Brazil's Internacional 0-1. In July 2008, Oleguer moved to Ajax Amsterdam. He has played six games for the still unofficial Catalan national team. He has never played for Spain.

There are also football players who have attracted attention as "libertines" or "rebels," rejecting conformity and authority, but not necessarily embracing left-wing ideals or principles. Therefore, the list includes cholerics like the Bulgarian Hristo Stoichkov or Paul Gascoigne, who enjoyed provoking Celtic Glasgow fans with loyalist gestures. It also includes players whose "rebel" identities are mainly based on fashion—the Dennis Rodmans of football—like Djibril Cissé of France and Hidetoshi Nakata of Japan. The best-known examples, however, are George Best, Johan Cruyff, and Eric Cantona.

George Best, born in Northern Ireland and rising to fame with Manchester United, was dubbed the "fifth Beatle" in the 1960s for his good looks, long hair, and off-field escapades. Best was known for drinking, gambling, and skipping practice. He became an idol to football fans who were looking for someone "not playing by the rules."

Johann Cruyff, hailed as the Netherlands' best player ever and as one of the game's global stars in the 1970s, has always been known for speaking his mind, even if it caused him trouble. He remained a controversial figure in the international football world when, after the end of his playing career, he managed clubs like Ajax Amsterdam and FC Barcelona. His clashes with another Dutch manager, Louis van Gaal, have become legendary; Cruyff has relentlessly criticized van Gaal's emphasis on efficiency at the cost of the game's aesthetic dimensions.

Eric Cantona was the darling of those looking for a player who would "take no shit." Despite being one of the best players of his generation, Cantona was repeatedly excluded from the French national team after run-ins with the country's football officials. He was banned from club soccer for eight months after kicking a fan, and journalists never knew what to expect when asking a question he did not like. Cantona retired from football at the age of twenty-nine. Apart from registering three names as trademarks—*Cantona*, *Cantona 7*, and *Oh, ah, Cantona*—he had advertisement deals with companies like Nike way beyond the end of his career.

Luther Blissett, an English striker who played a rather unadorned season for AC Milan in the early 1980s, regularly appears in connection with radical football. However, this has little to do with him and is merely the result of a mid-1990s Situationist group adopting his name.

Hardly any of the mentioned individuals—with the possible exception of Sócrates, Ippig, and Lucarelli—can pass as leftist role models. Brian Clough, for example, was not above racist remarks. He commented in the 1970s: "If the African nations get their way, and only one British team plays in tournaments in the future, I think I'll vote Conservative. Think about it, a bunch of spear-throwers who want to dictate our role in football. They still eat each other up."[86] The Viennese café run by Mattias Sindelar during the Third Reich was an expropriated Jewish business. And Robbie Fowler, the dock workers' supporter, was involved in blatant homophobic taunts of Graeme le Saux in a 1999 Liverpool vs. Chelsea match.

A lot remains to be done on one of the most basic levels of football politics, namely the democratization of clubs and associations. It is embarrassing that the only reason for players to oppose the activities of football bureaucrats is money. National team players threaten with strike if they do not get paid, yet they never even attempt to put pressure on the government to change offensive laws and policies. This reconfirms their roles as mere pawns in a commercial enterprise. It is the behavior that is expected from them. It was interesting to observe the reactions to the French team's boycott of a single training session at the 2010 Men's World Cup in South Africa in solidarity with striker Nicolas Anelka who had been suspended for insulting the manager. The incident turned into a state affair. President Nicolas Sarkozy got involved and ordered Sports Minister Roselyne Bachelot to personally settle the matter.

In short, footballers are expected to entertain—and to keep their mouths shut. If they do not, they are demonized as ungrateful and greedy—as if they were responsible for the modern football industry. The French incident shows the potential that lies in footballers' collective political action because it is not expected of them.

Teams

Sometimes, entire teams—both on the club and on the national level—have made sound political statements.

The Soviet Union refused to play its final qualifying match for the 1974 Men's World Cup in Chile because the stadium had been used to imprison and torture political dissidents only weeks earlier. In 1978, the Dutch team refused to shake hands with junta leader Jorge Videla after the Men's World Cup final. In the 1990s, Turkish football teams regularly displayed banners pledging allegiance to the country's secular constitution in light of increasing religious fundamentalism. Before an international encounter in 1996, the Swiss team carried a banner against nuclear testing in the Pacific. A rather unique action was taken by Italy's ASD Treviso when, during a game in 2001, all players wore black shoe polish on their faces in solidarity with their Nigerian teammate Akeem Omolade, a regular victim of racial abuse.

The reasons for obsessively and passionately supporting particular teams are often hard to explain. Even for the radical fan, they are not always related to politics. Renato Ramos, a member of the Rio de Janeiro Anarchist Federation, admitted in a 2004 interview that he is a fan of Fluminese, Rio's "club of the rich."[87] The left-leaning Turkish author Orhan Pamuk is a fan of Fenerbahçe, Istanbul's "club of the bourgeoisie." The famous revolutionary theorist Antonio Negri remains an AC Milan fan despite the club being owned by Silvio Berlusconi. As Pamuk explains, "It's like religion. There is no 'why.'"[88]

Still, there are radical soccer fans who base their fan affiliations on political grounds.

On the national team level, common choices are outsider teams from Africa, Asia, or Central America. The teams are often seen as representatives of the colonized and underprivileged world, though things become a bit more difficult when the countries are governed by a right-wing regime.

Among teams that might actually win a World Cup, Argentina has been a favorite among radicals, mainly due to figures like César Luis Menotti and Diego Maradona.

Brazil also remains a favorite among radicals who still embrace the *futebol arte* notion, no matter how far the contemporary Brazilian game is removed from it.

During the Women's World Cup, the Swedish team often attracts the sympathy of those embracing and propagating liberal and progressive values.

Once again, none of these affiliations are clear-cut. There is no "left-wing national team." In 1998, for example, Argentina competed at the Men's World Cup under former national team player Daniel Passarella, who would not allow players to wear long hair or earrings. Fernandeo Redondo, who refused to obey, was left out of the squad.

In Europe, it is the Dutch men's team that has probably drawn most left-wing sympathies over the last decades for a number of reasons: Johann Cruyff, "total football," the reputation of Dutch liberalism, the integration of black players in the 1990s. Arguably, the reputation of the Dutch side has suffered in recent years due to repeated internal strife and an overly aggressive display during the 2010 World Cup Final against Spain.

On the club level, the most common choices for radical fans in Europe are the FC Barcelona, Celtic Glasgow, Athletic Bilbao, and Ajax Amsterdam. Lesser known clubs like AS Livorno, Omonia Nicosia, and Rayo Vallecano also draw widespread radical support. Hamburg's modern-day radical soccer legend, the FC St. Pauli, of course, has special status.

The FC Barcelona is one of the main symbols of Catalan independence. This was particularly pronounced during the Franco regime when Real Madrid represented the authoritarian, capital-

centered Spain, while the FC Barcelona stood for
the independent, internationalist, and socialist
Catalonia. During the civil war, the FC Barcelona
president Josep Suñol was murdered by Franco's soldiers and the club was forced to change its name (to
Club de Fútbol Barcelona) and to remove the Catalan
symbols from its crest. This only strengthened the
significance of Barcelona games as sites of political
protest: the display of Catalan flags and the singing
of Catalan songs could never be fully oppressed. The
Barcelona slogan of being "more than a club" is also
reflected in organizational aspects: the club is owned

by its members who directly elect the president, and it is the only top club
in professional European football that rejects corporate sponsorship on its
shirts—since 2006, it has been advertising UNICEF.

Celtic Glasgow's support among radical football fans comes almost
exclusively from the club's symbolic significance for Irish republican pride
and its roots in Glasgow's impoverished Catholic neighborhoods. The
Marist brother who founded Celtic in 1887 stated as its purpose "to alle-
viate poverty in Glasgow's East End parishes."[89] The question of whether
Irish republicanism can really be considered radical cannot be discussed in
this book. Fact is that Celtic is held in high regard among many progressive
supporters and that the Green Brigade group or the TÁL fanzine are integral parts of Europe's antifascist supporter culture.

Athletic Bilbao is to the Basque Country what the FC Barcelona is to
Catalonia. However, while the Catalan side embraces internationalism as
a part of its identity, Athletic Bilbao is decidedly Basque; in 1912, it adopted
the unofficial policy of *cantera*, which means that only players with Basque
heritage are allowed to play for the club. Real Sociedad had a similar policy
until 1989, but eventually abandoned it. This has only increased the significance of Athletic Bilbao for Basque pride. The club was also the last in
professional Spanish football to allow corporate stadium advertisement, it
rejects corporate logos on its shirts, and it is one of the very last clubs in
Spanish professional football that has not turned into a joint stock company.
Once again, how Basque nationalism fits into radical politics is a complex
issue, but as long as the Basque demand for independence is embraced by
many activists as an anti-colonial struggle, Athletic Bilbao will remain in
good standing with radical football supporters.

Ajax Amsterdam's high reputation among radical football fans derives
from a few aspects: Ajax is seen as a representative of a liberal and cosmopolitan city; given its Jewish roots, it is subjected to a lot of anti-Semitic
abuse by right-wingers; and its successes are largely built on talent from
its football schools, not on big money. In 1995, Ajax won the Champions

League with players of whom the majority had already played in its youth teams—a feat that might not be repeated for a long time.

The AS Livorno represents a dock workers' town and communist stronghold in Italy. Omonia Nicosia was founded by socialist internationalists on the divided island of Cyprus in 1948. Rayo Vallecano hails from the poor working-class quarters of Madrid. In the Czech Republic, Bohemians 1905 have always had a dissident image; in 2005, the club was saved from bankruptcy by its supporters, who turned it into a cooperative. Eastern European clubs with strong antifascist support include the FC Partizan Minsk in Belarus and the FK Admira Prague in the Czech Republic. Red Star Belgrade, Partizan Belgrad, and Hajduk Split carry proud names, but their left-wing implications have faded in the intricacies of Balkan politics.

Milan provides an interesting example for how radical support can shift over time. In 1908, a group of disgruntled internationalists split from the Milan Cricket and Football Club (CFC) and its nationalist policies. The renegades founded Inter Milan; the Milan CFC turned into the Associazone Calcio (AC) Milan. While Inter always received left-wing recognition for its cosmopolitanism (under Mussolini, it was forced to carry the name Ambrosiana), AC increasingly represented Milan's working-class. Radical fan allegiances shifted according to the political climate. In the 1960s, with workers' rights high on the agenda, AC was popular among radicals. Antonio Negri: "I participated in the creation of the Brigate Rossonere, which have nothing to do with the Brigate Rossi; it was before, in the 1960s. We were followers of the left and we installed ourselves in the south end of the [AC Milan] stadium." In the 1980s, AC challenged Inter even on the cosmopolitan level by signing the charismatic Dutchmen Ruud Gullit and Frank Rijkaard. However, with Silvio Berlusconi's ownership of AC and Inter's contacts to the Zapatistas, the tide has once again changed.

The one team that has captured the imagination of every radical soccer fan in the last twenty years is Hamburg's FC St. Pauli. Based in the harbor district of the city, where lumpen proletarians, petty criminals, and prostitutes mingle, the club's radical image derived from the 1980s squatting battles, when many of the black-bloc-prone activists made the FC St. Pauli their football club. They frequented the old, charming Millerntor Stadium in increasing numbers and soon the terraces were filled with punk hairdos, torn clothes, and revolutionary slogans. Meanwhile, the fanzine *Millerntor Roar* provided football information in true DIY fashion. The team's promotion to the Bundesliga in 1988 gave the St. Pauli phenomenon yet another boost. While there was nothing particularly radical about the club per se, left-wing folk heroes like goalkeeper Volker Ippig added to the St. Pauli mystique.

The fan culture that developed around St. Pauli was certainly unique: the fashion, the political sloganeering ("No More War, No More Fascism,

No More Relegation!"), the skull and crossbones as the unofficial club logo. The fact that St. Pauli was one of the poorest Bundesliga clubs also prompted class-war style rhetoric around games against corporate giants like Bayern Munich. The phenomenon attracted radical fans across Germany and, soon, across the world. Within a few years, the FC St. Pauli turned from a football club into a radical myth, its name adorning T-shirts, subway cars, and squats from Hamburg to Sydney.

One reason why the term "myth" seems commonly accepted in connection with the St. Pauli phenomenon, even by its fans, is that the club's radical image was never reflected by the management. Traditionally, nothing distinguished the club policies of St. Pauli from those of other professional clubs in Germany. From 1970 to 1997, the stadium carried the name of a former president and Nazi Party member, Wilhelm Koch. Over the last twenty years, many officials have gone through pains to separate the image of the club from radical politics. Among the players, too, few radicals can be found. Some have even been accused of insulting black opponents. However, the radical fan base has impacted the club itself over the years, with some fans becoming official members to directly influence management decisions. The change of the stadium's name back to Millerntor is one example. Others are social campaigns run in the club's name, such as *Viva con Agua de Sankt Pauli*, which collects funds for water dispensers in countries of need.

In any case, St. Pauli's radical fan culture spearheaded a radical football supporters' movement that spread across Europe, and beyond. FC St. Pauli fans have been driving forces behind the formation of Germany's *Bündnis antifaschistischer Fußballfans* [Association of Antifascist Football Fans] (BAFF) in 1993 and remain to a large degree responsible for the country's unique political supporters' culture, which also includes initiatives like *F_in—Frauen im Fußball* and *Queer Football Fanclubs*.

▮ The FC St. Pauli and Its Radical Reputation

Interview with Mike Glindmeier

These days, it is hard to visit any place with a fairly intact left-wing culture without coming across an FC St. Pauli sticker or graffiti—and that means worldwide. What's the history behind the association of the club with radical politics?
It all goes back to the 1980s when the squatting movement in Germany was very strong and a particularly important battle was fought over a few houses in Hamburg's Hafenstraße—that battle was won and a significant radical culture developed around the site. The Hafenstraße is in St. Pauli, which is basically the area around Hamburg's port. The St. Pauli stadium was right there, and so people who lived and hung out in the houses

started going to see games. St. Pauli was not a particularly great team at the time—or ever, for that matter—and there were never more than a few thousand people at

the stadium. So the new supporters had a strong impact early on, and the image of soccer fans with studded leather jackets, mohawks, and Che Guevara flags traveled far. It attracted more and more like-minded supporters—also from places far from Hamburg—and eventually the radical fans dominated the stands, the skull and crossbones logo became hugely popular, and the FC St. Pauli and its supporters gained notoriety beyond Germany's borders. I guess that's how the international myth of St. Pauli developed in a nutshell.

As you said, the squatting movement in Germany was generally strong in the 1980s. Yet, St. Pauli was the only place where such a phenomenon developed. It has been argued that this had a lot to do with the character of St. Pauli itself: the port, a strong working class history, and an infamous red light district.
Certainly. Without the special characteristics of St. Pauli, I don't think the phenomenon could have developed the way it did. If the stadium had been in any other part of the city, for example, I don't think that this could have happened. It was the blend of dock workers, junkies, prostitutes, small-time crooks, and political radicals, which provided very unique conditions.

I guess it also made it possible to follow a "guilty pleasure" like soccer in an environment that appeared politically sound.
That was definitely a big factor too. In the 1970s and early 1980s, soccer wasn't particularly fashionable among left-wing activists. The St. Pauli story changed that.

Let me confront you with a quote from a 1997 article in the left-wing German weekly *Jungle World*: "The FC St. Pauli has united soccer and revolution, with results that had to be expected: adolescent hero

worshipping, beer hall stupidity, bourgeois self-satisfaction, and pathetic notions of brotherhood." What's your response?

Well, I think that it works as a sarcastic comment, except for the "pathetic notions of brotherhood" part. I mean, sure, the old saying that ten Germans are worse than five still holds true. However, a couple of weeks ago, the one hundredth anniversary of the club was celebrated with a big concert, and Slime, a legendary Hamburg punk band, opened with "Deutschland muss sterben," which translates as "Germany must die," in front of twenty thousand people. That's pretty special, and I don't think you'd find that anywhere else in Germany.

Has the commitment to political activism always been strong among the fans or was the rebellious attitude on the stands largely symbolic?

You had all sorts of groups. There have always been factions who took their political work very seriously—and there were those who adopted the symbols and were at the games, but having fun was the priority. However,

I think that this overlap was important too, and it went both ways: the political activists kept the St. Pauli rebellion from becoming a mere show, and the fun-oriented folks kept St. Pauli blocs at demonstrations from being boring. So it paid off for everyone . . .

Does the political activism continue?
In the mid-1990s, there occurred a bit of a rupture in connection with a general conflict among Hamburg's radical left; it concerned the member of a popular German punk band being accused of rape. It all turned pretty nasty, and some of the most active representatives of the St. Pauli fans were targeted because they felt it was wrong to condemn the accused without proof. Butyric acid was thrown into their store, the well-known *St. Pauli Fanladen*, an institution for St. Pauli fans. This hampered common political activism for a while. But, again, it was mainly a reflection of a general problem within Hamburg's scene, and many fans remain politically very active to this day. It's not by coincidence that the St. Pauli fan crowd at away games in neo-Nazi strongholds is particularly big!

So far, we've mainly talked about the fan culture. How about the club itself? It has sometimes been argued that it's an irony that a radical fan culture developed around a club that, in the end, is just like any other, has no particularly radical history, and, in fact, sometimes rather conservative figures in its management.
On a basic level, that is true. However, I would argue that the fans have had an impact on the club since the 1980s. I don't think you have any other club in Germany where fans are so actively involved and where they are able to force the management to make certain decisions or drop certain measures. For example, during the long debate about why the stadium was named after a former St. Pauli president who had profited from the Nazi expropriation of Jews, Wilhelm Koch, many fans became official club members so they could influence the management decisions in the general members' assembly. This has brought a number of tangible results; a

recent example was the cancellation of an advertising campaign for a drink called "Kalte Muschi"—in English, "Cold Pussy."

It is true that throughout the last twenty-five years you've always had individuals within the management trying really hard to detach the club from the fans' politics. And this is true today as well. It got to the point where they tried to forbid people wearing fan colors at political events. But this just doesn't work at St. Pauli. If you will, there's a constant struggle between commercially oriented forces and politically oriented forces. It is true that the latter sometimes have to accept compromises—but so do the former. I believe that a certain balance has been kept to this day that still distinguishes St. Pauli from other clubs.

For international visitors: what should a proper St. Pauli weekend in Hamburg look like?
To begin with, you have to spend time in the *Jolly Roger*, the bar across the stadium, an essential gathering place for St. Pauli fans. Not only is it filled with all sorts of soccer memorabilia, but you are bound to find people who have got many stories to tell. Conveniently, you can just stay upstairs, in the so-called *Jollyday Inn*—after a long night at the Jolly's you might not make it much further.

Then you need to walk around the neighborhood. If you've spent the night before at the Jolly's, you are destined to have a guide. Peek in the club's headquarters, called *Klubheim* in German—there are no trophies, but interesting tidbits from St. Pauli's history. You might also wanna tour the stadium apart from your visit to the game. It's recently been rebuilt but retains a lot of the old flavor. And then there is the *Fanladen* of course!

For some more drinking, you should pay a visit to the *AFM Container*, which opens on match days right behind the back straight, and to the *Weinbar St. Pauli*, a new local favorite—I know that the step from beer to wine can be a daring one, but this place is run by avid St. Pauli fans and it is well worth to stop by. If drinking alone won't get you through the day, you can try *Labskaus*, a very non-vegetarian Hamburg special (think corned beef and lard), at the *Brasserie Raval*—it's popular with St. Pauli Ultras, and one of the few places where you are still allowed to smoke!

Mike Glindmeier is a Hamburg native, sports journalist, and longtime St. Pauli fan. He was active in the fans' movement for many years, and, together with Folke Havekost and Sven Klein, wrote the "Fan Triography" *St. Pauli ist die einzige Möglichkeit* [St. Pauli Is the Only Option], published by left-wing Papyrossa Verlag in 2009.

In South America, left-wing support is divided among a number of clubs. In Brazil, Corinthians remains a common choice for many leftists, Vasco da Gama draws from the legacy of first fielding black players in the early 1900s, and Flamengo is considered the "club of the poor." In Argentina, a few prominent clubs have radical roots: the Argentinos Juniors (Diego

Maradona's first professional club) were once called the Chicago Martyrs, El Porvenir has utopian roots, and the Chacarita Juniors were founded by libertarian socialists. Platense was popular with communists and anarchists in the 1930s, and Rosario Central was supported by Che Guevara. Boca Juniors and Independiente often count as the country's main working-class teams, while Racing was the favorite of the populist leader Juan Perón. San Lorenzo was supported by some left-wing radicals in the 1970s. Today, however, most of these connections have been lost.

Other Latin American teams with working-class or left-wing credentials include Universidad de Chile, the main rival of the Pinochet-supported Colo-Colo during the dictatorship; Independiente Medellín, Colombia's "club of the poor"; and the Mexican Pumas, club of the left-leaning *Universidad Nacional Autónomia de México* (UNAM).

In North America and most Asian countries, professional soccer teams have often been short lived and/or tied to corporations, radical fan cultures have hardly developed. A possible exception is Iran's Persepolis FC, which has traditionally been supported by Persia's poor.

In Australia, the fan base of clubs has mostly been defined by the affiliation with different immigrant communities.

In Northern Africa, some of the first clubs founded by nationals remain symbols of anti-colonialist resistance, among them Al-Ahly in Cairo and both Raja and Wydad in Casablanca.

In Sub-Saharan Africa, political affiliations of clubs are more based on patron politicians than ideologies, although many South African clubs have a strong anti-apartheid legacy.

In the Middle East, an Israeli-Arab team captured the minds and hearts of progressively-minded football fans in 2004: Hapoel Bnei Sakhnin, hailing from a small Arab town in the country's north, staged a huge upset by winning the Israeli Cup.

▮ Sakhnin's Success Brings Cheers and Jeers

August 13, 2004, BBC
James Reynolds

They have qualified to play in the UEFA Cup—it is the first time an Arab team from Israel has ever gotten this far.

"It's important for me and for all the Arabs in Israel and all the people who believe in peace and co-existence," says Shuwan Abbas, the team captain.

"I think it's very important for the whole country to know how to practice co-existence."

For the fans watching the team in training, Sakhnin's victories have had a tremendous effect. The million Arab citizens living inside the Jewish state have long felt ignored. But now they feel they have something to be proud of.

"Sakhnin is a symbol for all the Arab minority inside Israel," says one fan. "It has 1.25 million people cheering for it. If the team wins, it's as if all the Arabs in this country win."

Many officials are happy as well. They see the team's success as a sign of Israel's strength as a multi-ethnic democracy.

"They are an Israeli team representing Israel," says Ronnie Bar-On, who represents the right-wing Likud party in the Israeli parliament.

"Nevertheless they are from an Arab town. In the team there are Jews, Muslims, Christians—terrific!"

But those who cover the team every day see a different story.

Yoav Goren, who reports on Sakhnin for Israel's *Haaretz* newspaper, has watched over the past year as the Arab team's success has been met with curiosity, indifference, and sometimes even hostility among Israel's Jewish majority.

He remembers one recent match against a team from Tel Aviv. "It wasn't football, it was war," he says.

"There were helicopters in the sky. When I got to the game, it was like being in Lebanon. You felt like you were in the army on operation. Didn't like it."

The Jewish state watched in surprise in May as Sakhnin won the Israeli cup.

Sharon Mashdi has kept a close eye on Israel's reaction. He monitors racism in Israeli football for the New Israel Fund. The Arab team's victory, he says, went down particularly badly with fans of Beitar Jerusalem, a team known for its ties to Israel's right wing.

"After the cup final the Beitar Jerusalem fans put an ad on the Internet about the death of Israeli football," he says.

"I think it's like what's happened in Israeli society: some percentage of the Jews don't like Arabs at all and don't want them here in this country."

Such is the political climate right now that few in Israel want to go all that far in backing the Arab team.

Sakhnin does not have its own stadium. And it has found it tough to get sponsors.

"This is the biggest problem of Sakhnin," says Goren of *Haaretz*.

"Jewish companies don't sponsor Sakhnin. No one from the Jewish business community said: let's take Sakhnin and make it a symbol for peace, for living together.'

"Sakhnin has succeeded in a professional way, but in a social way it's been a failure."

For many that is no great surprise. One football team cannot in itself change the make-up of a divided society.

> And this Thursday night, most in Israel will have other plans. But the Arabs of this country will watch as their team walks out to play in Europe, representing the flag of the Star of David.

Like the abovementioned football personalities, none of the listed clubs can live up to radical, or even progressive, standards as a whole. Contradictions in the FC St. Pauli identity have already been pointed out. The FC Barcelona, with all its unique features, is one of football's biggest moneymakers. Vasco da Gama first signed black players in Brazil, but has always been run by rich Portuguese merchants and their descendants. Celtic signed the self-described fascist Paolo Di Canio, and since the mid-1990s the club officials have been trying hard to shed the club's strict Irish-Catholic identity. Ajax Amsterdam supporters are not beyond yelling racist abuse at non-white players from opposing teams, and homophobic chants are common at Athletic Bilbao's stadium. Luckily, an impressive number of radical and progressive fan initiatives have emerged in the last twenty years, committed to tackling these issues.

Supporters

The first wave of radical supporters' initiatives was tied to the increased presence of right-wingers at British football grounds in the late 1970s. National Front (NF) activists started campaigning outside a number of stadiums, particularly in London at the Chelsea, Millwall, and West Ham venues. In their youth paper *Bulldog*, they ran a column entitled "On The Football Front," instigating fans "to join the fight for race and nation." Left-wing groups first started to organize resistance by confronting National Front members. It soon became clear, however, that the most effective way to diminish their influence was to get a left-wing hold within the supporters themselves. The Anti-Nazi League (ANL) and Anti-Fascist Action (AFA) took on prominent roles in a struggle that, after a couple of years, proved very effective.

■ The Hard Left

The Guardian, November 25, 1994
David Eimer

White working class football supporters have always been targeted by the racist right. But now an anti-fascist group is attracting support on the terraces and it's ready to fight fire with fire. David Eimer meets the men and women prepared to put the boot in for the left cause.
When Beackon won a council seat in London's Isle of Dogs on September 16, 1993, not everyone was surprised by the British National Party's success. For the past two years, Anti-Fascist Action had been warning that

the far right was organised—and winning. And now AFA is preaching a militant form of protest.

Formed in 1985 by veterans of the Anti-Nazi League (ANL), it is a nationwide organisation which promotes a dual policy of confronting the far right ideologically—and physically. The group makes no apologies about what that kind of work can entail.

"It's political violence," says AFA activist Danny. "The fascists use it because they think it works and if [they] think it works, you can't do any better than doing it on them, only a lot harder. Whatever's necessary to cause them to desist from what they're doing."

Danny should know: he's been involved in combating the far right since the seventies, when he ran with Reds Against The Nazis, a group of Manchester United fans who fought the National Front. Now he's one of the top men (or what AFA calls "fighting stewards"), responsible for controlling what they claim is anything from 20 to 150 people in street confrontations. Danny sees the use of violence as a necessary antidote to what he sees as the far right's increasing influence and the corresponding rise in racial incidents recorded by the police: 9,762 in England and Wales last year.

"The whole reason for the violence is that they want people to stay away, to let them do what they want to do," Danny explains. "If you don't attack them, they're free to organise politically. But if you attack them, they can't do that ... that's the relevance of violence, it's not something you want to do."

Like most AFA members, Danny comes from the constituency that the British National Party (BNP) tries to recruit from: white working class youths from depressed areas with a high proportion of ethnic minorities; and it's their opinions that dominate the organisation. That, in itself, sets AFA apart from the ANL or Youth Against Racism In Europe (YRE); AFA is openly contemptuous of the students and "smellies" who go on marches and then return to their homes in areas where the BNP tends not to be active.

The ANL and the black-led Anti-Racist Alliance (ARA) were seen as the voice of the antiracists. With celebrities like Lenny Henry and Stephen Fry backing them, and with frequent references to their successful campaign against the National Front in the late seventies, the ANL claimed that the subsequent defeat of the BNP in Millwall showed that its policy of rallies, marches and gigs was working. But although the BNP lost its seat, its share of the vote was 30 percent up on the previous council election, even though the turnout was 70 percent, the highest ever recorded. It is statistics like these that appear to be prompting increasing numbers of people to question whether the ANL's tactics are effective. Also, the ANL is controlled by the Socialist Workers Party—they share the same leadership—while the YRE has close links with Militant. In contrast, AFA purport to push no political line beyond the defeat of fascism, although there is nothing to stop individual members joining other groups.

Instead, AFA challenges the BNP on territory that is closed to the ANL, the ARA and YRE. So, just as the BNP has always seen football fans as a fertile source of recruits, AFA is particularly active in and around soccer grounds.

"Our attitude has been that most people aren't fascists or anti-fascists," points out John from Manchester AFA. "They're in the middle and sometimes open to persuasion from both. With football it tends to come from the right."

Manchester AFA tries to redress that balance via the United fanzine *Red Attitude*; crucially, though, all such efforts are by AFA members who would be at the football anyway. "We're not like Sky TV—here this week and there next week. There's no point turning up at a club you don't support just to peddle politics," Danny says.

Football is also where AFA finds most of its so-called "street fighters." "The thing is you get people ready-made," explains Jo, another AFA leader. "If they come from football, they know how to deal with the police, they understand the gang mentality, they know how to fight and understand the psychology of the other mob."

This is particularly relevant in Scotland, where the far right are closely tied to Ulster Loyalism; Celtic and Hibernian supporters lead the battle against the BNP, who in turn have a heavy presence amongst Rangers fans. "It's been a straight physical war," admits Sean from Glasgow AFA. "If they hit one of ours, we hit three of them. We're making it clear that the anti-fascists are setting the agenda."

But AFA is more than just a sophisticated football firm. It produces its own magazine, *Fighting Talk*, and has links with similar groups elsewhere in Europe, like Reflex in France and the German Autonome Antifa (M).

Many AFA members are women. Marion, for instance, is a regional organiser based in the Home Counties. A former skinhead who flirted with the far right in the early eighties ("I went through a stage of being a complete racist"), she now runs one of the numerous AFA branches around the country, gathering and collating intelligence about the far right in her area, as well as organising meetings and fundraising events.

Marion dismisses criticisms that the use of violence, for whatever cause, is insupportable. "Violence isn't the issue, it's a tactic. It's about disillusioning and intimidating the fascists," she says. "You don't feel guilty about it; politically it was the right thing to do."

Their willingness to use violence makes the AFA a clandestine organisation. Breaking up BNP meetings, kicking its paper sales off the streets and preventing its bands from holding money-making gigs have brought AFA into conflict with the law, and at least three AFA members have served prison terms for their part in such events.

But they claim precedents for what they do. In the thirties, Mosley's British Union of Fascists (BUF) frequently encountered physical opposition, most notably at the Battle of Cable Street in 1936 when thousands of people turned out on the streets to prevent them marching through the East End.

And immediately after the Second World War, the 43 Group—a collection of mainly Jewish ex-servicemen—used its military training to play a major part in destroying the BUF's short-lived successor, the Union Movement.

As its name suggests, AFA is a negative reaction to the resurgence of the far right in the UK. The BNP sensed in the Isle of Dogs that a vacuum had been created which it could fill. Yet the ARA is in the throes of an internal power struggle that saw its chair, Diane Abbott MP, walk out at the beginning of November after just two weeks in charge. AFA's approach has been heavily criticised by other anti-racist organisations and targeted by the police, but some credit it with disrupting the BNP's ability to operate and organise.

Occasionally AFA's activities reach a nationwide audience, as at Waterloo in September 1992, when it prevented hundreds of skinheads from attending a gig by neo-Nazi band Skrewdriver, and in the process closed down the station. But more often than not, its work goes unreported and any credits often claimed by the ANL. AFA sees itself as offering an alternative to the type of people who might consider joining the BNP, which sets them apart from other anti-racist groups, and in so doing, has attracted great criticism from many of them. Some of the other anti-racist groups would like to see them disband. But this is unlikely. With Derek Beackon planning to stand in a by-election in the Lansbury ward in Tower Hamlets next month, it seems that Anti-Fascist Action is certain to be around for a while yet.

When more and more politically oriented fanzines emerged and the fight against racist and fascist organizing on the terraces was joined by some local trade unions, the right-wing extremists were forced to retreat. By the late 1990s, they were practically gone from British football grounds. This must count as one of the most tangible successes of radical football activism. The collaboration of radical activists and football supporters opposed to racist ideas established the basis for a number of important progressive projects. Among the best-known are *Football Unites, Racism Divides, Show Racism the Red Card*, and *Kick It Out*.

◼ Ten Point Plan for Actions by Clubs

Kick It Out Campaign by The Advisory Group
Against Racism and Intimidation

1. To issue a statement saying the club will not tolerate racism, spelling out the action it will take against those engaged in racist chanting and individual racist abuse. The statement should be printed in all match programs and displayed permanently and prominently around the ground.
2. Make public address announcements condemning racist chanting and individual racist abuse at matches.
3. Make it a condition for season ticket holders that they do not take part in racist abuse.
4. Take action to prevent the sale of racist literature inside and outside the ground.
5. Take disciplinary action against players who engage in racial abuse.
6. Contact other clubs to make sure they understand the club's policy on racism.
7. Encourage a common strategy between stewards and police for dealing with racist abuse.
8. Remove all racist graffiti from the ground as a matter of urgency.
9. Adopt an equal opportunities policy in relation to employment and service provision.
10. Work with all other groups and agencies, such as the Professional Footballers association, supporters, schools, voluntary organisations, youth clubs, sponsors, local authorities, local businesses and police, to develop pro-active programs and make progress to raise awareness of campaigning to eliminate racial abuse and discrimination.

In Germany, the *Bündnis antifaschistischer Fußballfans* [Association of Antifascist Football Fans] (BAFF) was founded in 1993 as a means to unite fan initiatives fighting both against bigotry on the terraces and the ever-increasing commercialization of the game. BAFF was renamed *Bündnis aktiver Fußballfans* [Association of Active Football Fans] in 1998 and has grown into a widespread and very effective network, exemplary for progressive and radical organizing around football.

■ Football, BAFF, and Political Activism

Interview with Gerd Dembowski

I once heard you say that one of the main reasons for football's political significance was the fact that it brings more people together on a regular basis than anything else. Tell me about political activism in football ...
Football is a focal point of social relationships. For many, it is a valve that allows suppressed desires to come to the fore. It reveals people's feelings. In an anonymous mass it is easier to express yourself, sometimes also violently. Football stadiums make social developments visible.

In the fight against discrimination, football is an important field because it constantly reproduces traditional masculinity, nationalism, and different forms of oppression and exclusion. It is also an important field to address issues like surveillance, police brutality, and the undermining of civil rights.

After the brutal attack of German hooligans—some of them neo-Nazis—on the French policeman Daniel Nivel in Lens in 1998, the Ministry of the Interior suspended the Schengen Agreement and temporarily closed the borders. I.D. controls and the obligation to register with the police were introduced for certain football supporters. Since then, these means have affected left-wing protesters and activists as well. The same goes for the database *Gewalttäter Sport* [Violent Sports Supporters] which became a direct model for the database *Gewalttäter Links* [Violent Left-Wing Activists].

The 2006 Men's World Cup in Germany became a testing ground for the domestic employment of military forces. The event also lifted the "soft" privatization of public space to new levels with the so-called "Fan Miles." For "marketing research" purposes, Coca-Cola filmed the temporarily privatized zone between the Victory Column and the Brandenburg Gate in Berlin during the entire tournament. It is no problem for the police to access the recordings.

In short, football allows for seismographic readings of social tendencies. It is no flying saucer traveling in outer space—quite the opposite. That makes it so unfortunate that some leftists still look down on it. Other leftists might watch football, but they reduce it to a leisure activity: "Well, it is only football!" No. It isn't.

For example, it would be a grave sin for the left to ignore the Ultras as an important new form of youth culture. The impact of Ultra groups goes way beyond football. It is essential to have a left-wing presence within groups that are instinctively against commercialization, consumerism, discrimination, and repression; especially, when these groups are very attractive to a lot of young people! Here it is important to develop mutual relationships, share political experiences, and have an impact on how this culture develops further.

You also said once that football "can create moments of utopia." What does that mean?
Utopia means hope. Football reflects this in the sense that even a bad player can beat a world-class goalkeeper with a perfect shot.

Otherwise, there is nothing utopian about today's professional game, although we could toy with some ideas: annual budgets could be the same for all clubs; teams that end the season in the lower half of the table should be allowed to choose on the transfer market first, etc. A utopian element might also be implied in the hopes of players from marginalized communities to use football as a vehicle for social and economic success that is independent from education. In fact, this even goes for supporters, who project a lot of their dreams into football. Many football supporters are masochists. They travel in trains with clogged toilets, are treated like shit by the stadiums' security staff, and when things go really bad, their team loses in the ninetieth minute while they are standing in the pouring rain. To romanticize such experiences and to relive them over and over again can only be characterized as masochistic; what we are witnessing is a kind of ersatz freedom.

The sociologist Dieter Bott, who has done a lot of work on football fan culture, once called the football supporter the "prototype of the ideal citizen," referencing the analysis of the authoritarian character by Erich Fromm and Theodor Adorno. Football is for many supporters a binary concept that reassures them in their own identity: "us" vs. "them." In this sense, the game is about exclusion, it follows the logic of nationalism. This is why political activists can learn a lot about the current state of capitalist society and its rituals of symbolic self-preservation through football, in a very concrete sense. Football illustrates how concepts like nationalism and heteronormativity "modernize," meaning that they take on apparently less harmless forms. Today, a "soft" nationalism or an "open" masculinity is used to secure domination—but the traditional forms are only dormant and can reappear at any time. Often, this is only about economic target groups; it's like vegan products in supermarkets: you can buy them now, but not a single animal product has disappeared. Real change can only come from permanently dismantling and deconstructing these conditions and from sharing reflections with football fans while becoming a fan yourself. This is what can alter people's behavior in many ways, not only in relation to football.

Since my first meetings with Dieter Bott and my decision to join BAFF in 1995, I am somewhere between a fan and a sociologist/anthropologist. It is important for me to reflect on my behavior as a fan and not to romanticize myself as an object of oppression—after all, a voluntary choice for a white male German. Nor do I want to join the hipsters who read "high-brow" football magazines like *11Freunde* and whose interest in the game is part of a trendy identity package. My ambition is to free the dreams projected into football from the claws of conformism, step by step. At least football still makes the masses dream! Of course I fail with my ambition every time I go to the stadium—but every time I fail a little better . . .

You speak a lot about projection—can you explain this?
People project many things into football that have become impossible in their daily lives. In football, a lot remains possible in a very short amount of time. That is the fascination of the game. Each generation looks for valves to release pressure, to find a social field that allows for projections of freedom, moments of excitement, and temporary catharsis. People will always find excuses to go watch football. Football is, paraphrasing Heiner Müller, an omnivore, like parliamentary democracy, which always finds a way to continue but never creates democracy. We must not forget that professional football in Spain, Italy, and England is essentially broke but still lives beyond its possibilities. The question is: can capitalism run on credit forever?

What are the options for political activists to interfere?
This is a question that all activists have to answer themselves, depending on the focus of their activities. Sometimes, I feel that I am asked as a "football expert," so that others don't have to ask themselves. I am being facetious, of course, but domination and authority cannot be toppled by football. We have succeeded in forcing changes over the last fifteen years, but they were all reforms within the system. In the end, today's football remains caught in the triangle of performance, capital, and identity. Do projects like BAFF only modernize capitalism? Well, this takes us back to the old question about "the right in the wrong." There is no outside of the system.

Essentially, the political struggle in football is a human struggle. In a society without domination, sport might indeed become play again, reflecting the social conditions. Many ideas and concepts can be derived from this.

Can you give us examples for some of the successes of football activists in Germany?

The foundation of BAFF in 1993 established a nation-wide, self-organized network of fans from different clubs. This was necessary at the time to change the overall atmosphere in the stadiums. There was a strong

neo-Nazi presence. Fanzines played a major role in this. In 1997, there were eighty alternative, often humorous, fanzines in Germany. In addition, innumerable flyers, stickers, and banners were produced, concerts were organized, and direct actions happened in stadiums and at club meetings. A big early success—a collaboration between BAFF and autonomous activists—was the prevention of a 1994 game between Germany and England in Berlin on April 20, Hitler's birthday. BAFF felt that neither the date nor the place was chosen wisely, especially since neo-Nazis were already mobilizing. During the campaign, BAFF discovered the powers of guerrilla communication: seven thousand red cards were shown during a game of the German B-side at the St. Pauli stadium. In the end, the English FA canceled the game.

Is antifascism the dominant theme in BAFF?

BAFF is not run by leftists who went into football from the outside, but by people who became politicized as fans. Hence, BAFF was never just about anti-discrimination; it always dealt with all sorts of issues relevant for football supporters, for example resisting all-seating stadiums, commercialization, and kick-off times that were inconvenient for fans. There was also a lot of activism against the 2006 Men's World Cup in Germany when it was first announced.

I can give some concrete examples of successful campaigns and actions. In 1994, at the headquarters of the German FA in Frankfurt, and in 1995, at the UEFA headquarters in Geneva, BAFF organized demonstrations against the planned seating-only policy in stadiums all over Europe. The main argument of the officials concerned security. With the help of many local initiatives, BAFF managed to turn the debate into a big media issue. In the end, many traditional stands remained in German stadiums, which served as a motivating example for activists in other European countries. Further examples include the Fanzine Festival in 1996; various Fan Congresses; resistance against the plans by the TV station DSF to introduce a "Monday Night Game"; participation in the Fans United Day in Brighton to help secure the survival of the local club; the campaign *Vier*

Wochen WM—ein Leben lang sitzen [Four Weeks World Cup—Sitting for
a Lifetime] against the seating-only policy for the 2006 Men's World Cup
stadiums; the campaign *Ballbesitz ist Diebstahl* [Ball Possession/Property is
Theft] against the pay-TV decoders of the Premiere channel; the campaign *Zeig dem Fußball die Rosa Karte* [Show Football the Pink Card], which
included the first worldwide catalog of demands tackling homophobia in
football; the traveling exhibition *Tatort Stadion* [Crime Scene Stadium];
and the publication of the books *Ballbesitz ist Diebstahl* [Ball Possession/
Property is Theft] and *Die 100 ›schönsten‹ Schikanen gegen Fußballfans* [The
One Hundred Most Beautiful Ways to Harass Football Fans]. Witty slogans and agitprop were strong points in all these campaigns—especially
against the pay-TV stations.

How is BAFF organized?

BAFF is a registered organization but its structure still rather resembles
that of a rhizome. Anyone can do actions in the name of BAFF as long as
basic guidelines are followed. There are no "local BAFF chapters." BAFF
is simply a network that unites many local fan and Ultra groups. It serves
as a useful label, though, and many of the messages it has thrown out in
bottles have been picked up. There are two general meetings every year.
The attendants discuss the development of fan culture and its DIY dimensions. The meetings can be seen as dynamic "Good Practice Guides" and
"Think Tanks." They are also media-effective events where awards like
the *Goldener Schlagstock* [Golden Baton] are announced, a prize bestowed
upon the most violent security services and police units.

In 1995, BAFF changed its name from *Bündnis
antifaschistischer Fußballfans* [Association of
Antifascist Football Fans] to *Bündnis aktiver
Fußballfans* [Association of Active Football Fans].
This was not to indicate a turn to social democracy,
but to make it clear that the organization was not
just about antifascism. It was a compromising concession to fans that
were interested in BAFF but scared of its "radical left-wing" reputation.
To this day, there are discussions about how helpful changing the name
was. In hindsight, some saw this as the end of purely autonomous politics.
For others, the situation at the time made it practically impossible to be
openly autonomous and to do effective fan culture work at the same time.
When antisexist demands were discussed in BAFF in 1994, a strong male
lobby reproduced the imaginary hierarchy of discrimination in the stadiums. The result was a list of demands addressing racism only. "The fans
are not ready for anything else yet," was the argument.

The work against sexism only really took off with the foundation
of *F_in—Frauen im Fußball* [Women in Football] in 2004. A big success

was also the award-winning DSF documentary *Das große Tabu* [The Great Taboo] by Aljoscha Pause, finished in 2008, which really turned homophobia and sexism into widely discussed topics. We can say that BAFF once again was the ice pick coming down on twisted social conditions.

In general, I would say that BAFF has opened up possibilities for anti-discrimination activities in football that many fan groups and organizations now make use of. Today, I would call BAFF a pluralistic left-wing mix with Ultra participation that still doesn't shy away from militancy. Of course the danger of a "Green Party Effect" is always there, i.e., having a big mouth at first and then adapting to the system. We always need to be alert: at a certain point, the embrace of big institutions leaves you squashed.

Within BAFF, you often hear people say, "Five years ago we would not have said/done this." I think this is both good and bad. There is still a need to be loud and confrontational—but today, we also have different means. For example, BAFF has its own pool of speakers who are consulted regularly by the media. In 2009, BAFF was a founding member of Football Supporters Europe (FSE), a continent-wide fan network. BAFF consciously does not send any elected representatives there, but it is involved in certain committees. In any case—and this is where we are really different from the Greens—our concerns are never the distribution of paid positions. On this level, I still believe in the independence of BAFF and in its permanent self-renewal.

Gerd Dembowski has been a BAFF spokesperson since 1997. This interview first appeared as "Interview mit Gerd Dembowski zu Politik und Fußball" in *Perspektiven autonomer Politik* [Perspectives of Autonomous Politics], edited by ak wantok (Münster: Unrast, 2010). Translated by Gabriel Kuhn.

The Golden Baton

Press Release by the *Bündnis aktiver Fußballfans* (BAFF), January 2009

It looks like neither Bremen nor Schalke will celebrate a championship this year, but both will be honored with a Golden Baton, awarded by the *Bündnis aktiver Fußballfans* (BAFF). BAFF awards this prize every year for the most ludicrous treatment of fans by German security forces. This year, Bremen tops the category "Police," while Schalke triumphs in the category "Security Staff."

Bremen's police force earned the Golden Baton by detaining 232 visiting fans of Eintracht Frankfurt on November 29, 2008. Although nothing had happened other than slogans being chanted and one firecracker lit, the police detained the fans in the morning and kept them in overcrowded

cells until the end of the game.
Apparently, this was the only
way to guarantee public safety.
In the stadium itself, eyewit-

nesses reported police attacks on Frankfurt supporters who had to be
protected by Werder Bremen's own security staff.

At Schalke, on the other hand, it was the security staff that treated
visiting fans like hardened criminals when Paris Saint-Germain came to
play a UEFA Cup match. Up to 150 French fans were strip-searched in con-
tainers placed at the stadium entrance for this specific purpose. Despite
the nakedness, the search for flares, firecrackers, and smoke bombs was
in vain. Among German fans, the Schalke stadium is known as one of
the least welcoming football arenas—it appears that the club is eager to
spread the reputation all across the continent.

Both incidents indicate a troubling lack of respect for the basic rights
of football fans. Based on dubious intelligence and the rationale that "the
ends justify the means," the dignity of fans was disregarded. This fits a
society that increasingly pits civil rights against security. But those who
treat young football fans like criminals will only contribute to more antagonism and jeopardize peaceful coexistence—and not only on match days.

BAFF has existed since 1993 and is a network of fan clubs, fan initiatives, fan journals, fan projects, and individual members. The organization
works for a lively fan culture, free of racism and discrimination, free of
gung-ho commercialism, and free of criminalization.

The Golden Baton has been awarded since the early 1990s. Last
year, the Operational Command of Ahlen's Police won the race, with the
Bavarian Anti-Riot Unit coming in as a close second.

Translated by Gabriel Kuhn

While antifascist and antiracist struggles and the resistance to police repression and all-seating stadiums defined the focus of early BAFF campaigns,
homophobia and sexism have received increased attention in recent years.
Female football fans have begun to organize in *F_in—Frauen im Fußball* and
have issued a number of antisexist declarations directed at fans and football officials alike.

If I Were a Boy . . .

SenoritHAs Jena

If I were a boy I would wear what I want, drink beer with my friends, and
then go to the stadium. I would watch the game and scream until I lost my
voice. I would express my emotions freely and I would curse if something

rubbed me the wrong way. If I were a boy I would challenge whoever I want, I would give everything for ninety minutes, and then I would finish the night in a bar. But I am not a boy.

Do I still have the right to do all these things? One would think that in a liberal and emancipated world, this should not be a problem. But it often enough is. The media provides the best example. While men comfortably watch a game, women appear in beer ads and supply drinks—the division of gender roles could not be clearer. Society as a whole reflects these images. Stadium owners try to help poor females by lowering the prices for them—which only reaffirms stereotypes of them being inferior. Women are pigeonholed although they have done nothing wrong.

We do not want reduced tickets or any kind of special treatment! We do not want pity and condescension, nor do we want to justify ourselves for what we do! We want to be accepted! We, and many other girls, live for soccer. We give one hundred percent during the entire game, and we try to support our club in any way we can. Is all this worth less, just because we are women? Do we really have to disguise ourselves and leave behind the last bit of femininity in order to get some recognition?

Racism is seen as antiquated, but why is it okay if women are treated differently because of their gender? Is this not discrimination? Do we have to stand by when others throw dirt on our name just to provoke us? Are we supposed to ignore all this just to be accepted in a man's world?

We no longer want our intelligence, our knowledge, our thoughts, and our experiences belittled just because we have entered the apparently last male domain. Is it not sad that men feel so threatened by the mere presence of women? Men cover their insecurities through particularly tough behavior, at times making stadium visits for women unbearable. Is that really how it should be? Would it not be much more beautiful if we all worked together? After all, we are driven by the same thing: a boundless love and dedication for our club.

Together, we have managed to drive racism out of the stadiums. Now it is time to take the next step: we must not close our eyes. Let us fight sexism! Together we will manage, in football and everywhere!

The SenhoritHAs Jena are a part of the Ultra group Horda Azzuro, supporting FC Carl Zeiss Jena in Thuringia, Germany. "If I Were a Boy" was written and distributed in early 2009. Translated by Gabriel Kuhn.

Progressive supporters' organizations have also been founded on the European level, like Football Supporters Europe (FSE), which assists fans during international tournaments and coordinates the efforts of national and local fan initiatives. Of particular importance is the network Football Against Racism in Europe (FARE), which developed out of the Austrian

FairPlay initiative in 1999; the initiators invited players unions and migrant organizations to Vienna with the aim of developing a common strategy against racism and xenophobia in European football. In its monthly bulletin, FARE lists racist incidents from around the continent and informs readers about antiracist activities. Every year, a FARE Action Week is organized, with football-related antiracism events all across the continent.

Today, FARE receives funding from bodies like the European Union. The institutionalization of the antiracist struggle is a double-edged sword. On the one hand, it is without doubt important that even FIFA gets behind the antiracist message and has teams carry "Say No to Racism" banners before World Cup games. On the other hand, it raises the usual problems of institutional politics, namely empty moralism, sloganeering, and hypocrisy.

As early as 1992, Bundesliga teams in Germany played a round of games in jerseys with the slogan *Mein Freund ist Ausländer* ("My Friend is

a Foreigner") on their shirts instead of the logo of their corporate sponsors. The same year, players of Italy's Serie A and B participated in a similar action, when their jerseys carried the slogan *No al razzismo!* ("No To Racism"). However, as a group of British football scholars has stated: "Anti-racist initiatives are designed to create positive publicity but generally consist of little more than token gestures, such as

rock concerts and short term advertising campaigns."[90] Manchester United's Gary Neville
is on record saying: "We've got to make sure
it's done in the right manner, and not just as a
public relations exercise as sports companies
seem to be doing at the moment. We've got to
be aware that it's not cheapened by companies
like Nike who are making a lot of PR by doing
nothing really."[91]

The importance of PR in today's football
relates to the second main agenda of most contemporary fan initiatives: the fight against the
New Football Economy—against all-seating stadiums, the rise in ticket
prices, the influence of television and corporate sponsors, and club-related
merchandise.

The fight against all-seating stadiums derives its importance from the
desire to keep terrace culture alive. This is not a mere romanticization of
"the good old times," as most fan initiatives actively combat bigotry on the
terraces as well; but it is a means to retain the potential of an active grassroots fan culture instead of leaving the entire stadium to middle-class and
upper-class consumers. Standing terraces also fulfill an important social
function: people can move around freely, meet friends, and converse. In
traditional football culture, people would show up hours early for a game
only for this reason.

The officials' interest in all-seating stadiums lies in higher ticket prices,
more control over the audience, and a "more reputable" football image that
is less proletarian and more sellable. The security argument, also employed
here, is a mere token: all-seating stadiums do not prevent fatalities due to
clashes between supporters, nor do they prevent deadly mass panics, as
the tragic death of eight-six spectators in a stampede during a 1996 Men's
World Cup qualifier in an all-seating Guatemala City stadium proved.

One of the biggest anti-corporate campaigns of football supporters
followed the 2005 takeover of Austria Salzburg by Red Bull. The Austrian

energy-drink giant not only renamed
the club FC Red Bull Salzburg, but
also changed its traditional colors,
white-purple, to white-red-and-blue.
When Red Bull stuck to its decision despite fan protests that went
far beyond Austria's borders, a section of Salzburg fans founded a new
amateur club keeping the name of
the traditional FC Austria. The club

now plays—in the traditional white-and-purple jerseys—in Austria's third league. Since its foundation, it has been promoted every single year. In a similar sort of defiance, a section of 1860 Munich supporters refused to attend the A-side's games when club officials moved them to the stadium of city rival Bayern Munich where higher profits could be expected. The rene-

gade fans remained at the traditional Grünwalder Stadium to cheer for the B-side in Bavaria's highest amateur league. In Argentina, mass protests first stopped the closure of Racing in 2000, and then the club's corporatization in 2009.

It is not an exaggeration to say that some of the political struggles fought around football

over the last twenty years belong to the most successful examples of radical ideas and actions blending with wider social movements and changing everyday life for the better. To quote Tamir Bar-On: "These 'micro' struggles through the medium of football may . . . be more fruitful than larger 'universal' struggles in the names of vague slogans like 'social justice, peace, and human rights' because they may galvanize a greater cross-section of supporters divided by different material interests and political ideologies."[92]

▌Against Racism in the Stadiums

Press release by the Never Again Association, Warsaw, Poland, 2002

The Never Again Association from Poland is launching a new CD with an antiracist message. This time it is focused on the fight against racism in the sport field—the CD's title is *Let's Kick Racism Out of the Stadiums*, it is released in co-operation with Jimmy Jazz Records. Well-known Polish, German, and Italian bands contributed their songs.

The CD is one of initiatives undertaken during the Action Week of Football Against Racism in Europe (FARE) that lasted from April 12–20, 2002. This season's extended week of activities and events in and around football stadiums across Europe looks set to be the biggest demonstration to date by the football family against racism and xenophobia in the world's most popular game.

In addition, Never Again in cooperation with Polish Humanitarian Action is distributing antiracist info leaflets and posters featuring the first

Polish black player in the national team, Emmanuel Olisadebe, to over 2,000 schools as well as fans during the Action Week. The Association is also collecting signatures supporting a petition to Polish sports authorities demanding action against racism and anti-Semitism in stadiums.

The Never Again Association is an independent antiracist organization, not linked to any political party. One of its campaigns, "Let's kick racism out of the stadiums," aims at raising the level of antiracist sensitivity among football fans. Never Again is the Polish partner of the International network Football Against Racism in Europe.

The most significant development in football supporters' culture in the last fifteen years has been the spread of the Ultra movement. The movement remained long confined to Italy but nowadays it counts groups in almost all European countries.[93]

It has been argued that the emergence of the Ultra movement in the late 1960s was tied to Italian protest culture; the widespread use of banners, chants, and megaphones would attest to this. However, the political affiliations of Ultras have always been ambivalent. While most have maintained a decidedly "apolitical" stance, there have been explicitly right-wing as well as explicitly left-wing adaptations. Practically all Ultra groups, however, are united in the struggle against "Modern Football": the over-commercialization of the game and the repression of football supporters.

Ultras

Interview with Christophe Huette

In the media, Ultra groups are often presented as violent hooligans—this seems far too simple, though. Can you tell us a little about the history of the Ultra movement?
First of all, you are right: presenting the Ultras as little more than violent hooligans is indeed a simplification, a downright confusion too. Hooliganism and the Ultra movement have little in common except that they both refer to football supporters. Oktoberfest beer-drinkers and Rio Carnival drag queens are both festival-goers, but try to call a Lederhosen-clad beer-drinker ... Priscilla. You see what I mean.

Hooliganism and the Ultra movement don't share the same history. The former was born in the UK at the end of the 19th century and reborn in the 1960s when mods, rockers, and—slightly later—skinheads decided to take their animosities to the football terraces. The Ultras, on other hand,

received their name in the 1960s in Italy, where they became a widespread phenomenon before spreading to other countries. There may be relative synchronicity between the two movements, but their motives are diametrically opposed.

I'll stop here with hooliganism. Firstly, I have the impression that it is better-known to the general public than the Ultra movement, probably because it has been extensively covered—or promoted?—by the British and European media in the 1980s. Secondly, your question is about the history of the Ultra movement.

The origins of the Ultra movement are to be found in the 1950s in Yugoslavia. During the 1950 World Cup in Brazil, which Yugoslavia took part in, the Yugoslavian state television showed extensive footage of the games, including Brazil vs. Yugoslavia. Brazil won 2-0, which may explain why some TV watchers paid more attention to what was going on in the stands than to the action on the field. Maybe or maybe not, the fact is that just after that World Cup, a group of supporters appeared in Split's Stari plac Stadium for a game between Hajduk Split and Red Star Belgrade with "Torcida" banners. Torcida—which comes from the Portuguese verb *torcer*, to support—is the generic name used in Brazil for supporters' groups. Apparently, the name hadn't escaped the eyes of some Hajduk-mad viewers during the 1950 World Cup. So was born, on October 28, 1950, the first organised group of supporters in Europe. When the Communist Party expressed worries about the behaviour of Torcida members, Hajduk's chairman took their defense, explaining that they were doing nothing but "intentionally supporting their club." I can't think of a better definition of what the Ultra movement is all about. Or maybe I would add just one word: being an Ultra is a way of intentionally and *conspicuously* supporting your club.

Given the visual (as well as vocal) impact of the Torcida at every game, it didn't take long for supporters elsewhere to follow suit, particularly in Italy, where the first such group was founded in 1951 by a bunch of Torino FC followers. They called themselves the Fedelissimi Granata—*granata* (claret) being the club's color and nickname, *fedelissimi* roughly meaning "extremely loyal." The word "Ultra" itself was coined in 1969, by Sampdoria fans. They founded the group Ultras Tito Cucchiaroni, named after Ernesto "Tito" Cucchiaroni, an Argentinian player who scored quite a few goals for the Sampdoria in the late 1950s. From there, the Ultra movement spread first within Italy (partly thanks to a new policy, whereby football clubs reduced ticket prices in certain areas of the stadiums), and then, from the late 1970s until the early 1990s, to the rest of Europe (with the notable exception of England as far as big clubs are concerned). Where I come from, in Marseille, the first supporters' group, Commando Ultra, was created in 1984, and the most recent one, Cosa Ultra, in 2009—however, the latter made the fatal mistake of covering a Commando Ultra banner before a game, got their arses kicked for it, and seem to have disappeared. They may still be there—I can't really tell from where I sit—but they are definitely bannerless.

Now you'll tell me, "But you said the Ultras were not violent!" Point taken, but at the same time, is there such a thing as a supporter without violent impulses? Last home game I went to—Olympique de Marseille (OM) vs. Lens—I threw my lighter on the pitch out of sheer anger when the referee gave a straight red card to M'Bia, supposedly for elbowing an opponent. I later saw the replay on TV and was vindicated—not for throwing my lighter, but for thinking that M'Bia hadn't even touched the Lens player. Anyway, to come back to what you were saying about the Ultras being shown or perceived as violent, I'll tell you what my stance on the matter is. I've seen live games at all levels of football and in many European countries, from Glasgow to Tirana, and have always noticed the same thing, namely that the main criticism of Ultras by other spectators is a basic and practical one: Ultras are a nuisance because they make it difficult to watch the game. They never sit, they use smoky pyrotechnics, they unroll huge banners, and they wave gigantic flags, hence disrupting what most spectators expect: visual comfort. When I took my older daughter to an OM game at the age of three, there was so much fire and smoke in the "Virage Sud," the southern end of the Stade Vélodrome, that she asked me if there was a dragon somewhere. My second daughter holds something else against the Ultras: they're too noisy. Then again, she always makes a visual nuisance of herself, throwing five kilos worth of *papelitos* at every game I take her to . . .

Would you say that Ultras generally veer towards the left politically?
It's a little tricky. Again, I'll take OM as an example—it's the club I know
the best and it happens to be the one with the most supporters' groups
in France. In general, I would say that the only thing the Ultras really are
committed to here in Marseille is their football team. Therefore, their only
sense of organisation revolves around the matches. That involves preparing banners, creating the weekly or fortnightly *tifo*—meaning the way
they present themselves in the stadium: outfit, choreography, fireworks,
etc.—making travel arrangements for away games, and of course spending
time together to discuss anything from football results to new ideas for
songs, slogans, etc.

That said, there is an undisputable libertarian element in many Ultra
groups, which has to do with the very nature of the movement. Like I said
before, the Ultras were born from a will of (mainly) young football lovers
to support their favourite team in a conspicuous way. That often meant
going against the expectations of spectators in modern football. The
established order prefers silence to noise, stillness to motion, uniformity to
diversity, suppression to expression, etc. The Ultras systematically oppose
the established order. For a while, one of OM's supporters' groups, the
South Winners, called themselves the Kaotic Group, and they still display
that banner at every game at the Vélodrome. "Chaos versus order" would
be another good way of summing up what the Ultras stand for.

The intrinsically libertarian nature of the Ultras is at work every time
a new law is passed. Take for example the recent ban on pyrotechnics. At
the Vélodrome, supporters' groups have always used them enthusiastically. When the ban came into force, after a short period where nobody
took any notice of it, OM's president—arguably hard pressed by the
club's accountant and definitely under pressure from the French Football
Association—met with representatives of the supporters' groups. The deal
was: either you abide by the new law, or OM stops subsidising your trips
to away games. Libertarian but not stupid, all the Ultras stopped using
pyrotechnics almost instantly, with one exception: at every game, one
single flare is lit. The honor was bestowed upon the Commando Ultra, the
longest serving group.

Most Ultra groups embrace values like anti-racism, anti-nationalism,
anti-capitalism, anti-all-those-things that took football away from what it
originally was: a simple game for all, regardless of the color of your skin,
the country you live in, or the amount of cash you have in your pocket. I
may be stating the obvious here, but access to football—be it as a player
or as a spectator—has been dramatically reduced throughout the years.

The rural exodus towards concrete jungles saturated with vehicles
has made it increasingly difficult to have a kick-about in urban areas,
where over half of the human population lives. Playing football in the

street at the beginning of the third millennium is little more than one of the options available if you want to take your life. That said, the Ultras may be ultramen, but they are not supermen, so there isn't much they can do to promote access to football for players. Their focus is on defending free access to the game as *spectators*, which they do through exerting or demanding the freedom to stand during the game, the freedom to express themselves on banners, the freedom to drink champagne like those who attend the game on a freebie in the VIP section, the freedom to purchase a ticket no matter what your income is, etc.

How well are Ultras connected?

Since we are already talking about politics, I would say that relations between Ultra groups are very similar to those between political parties. You see it on the local scale as much as on the European one. What I mean by that is that Ultra groups of similar political persuasion do communicate with each other—but in an informal way. The main purpose is to exchange and defend ideas and, more simply, to have a good time together around the same passion.

In Marseille for example, the Commando Ultra has links with the aforementioned Ultras Tito Cucchiaroni of Sampdoria, the Ultrà Sankt Pauli, the Biris Norte of Sevilla FC, the Original 21 of AEK Athens, and many more. Members of these groups visit each other, gather at special events such as the *Mondiali Antirazzisti*, and coordinate demonstrations as part of the "Against Modern Football" campaign that targets the game's ever-increasing commercialisation.

In France—being one of the most bureaucratic countries in the world—there is an organisation of Ultra groups called *Coordination Nationale des Ultras* (CNU), made up of Ultra groups from Marseille, Bordeaux, Saint-Etienne, Lens, Paris, Strasbourg, Gueugnon, and Paris. In 2007, the CNU published a manifesto, which is basically a one-page text stating fundamental supporters' rights and warning against the drift of modern football towards total commercialisation.

There have also been international solidarity campaigns for imprisoned Ultras. One of the biggest concerned Santos Mirasierra, a member of Marseille's Commando Ultra, who was arrested in Madrid minutes before a 2008 UEFA Champions League game against Atlético. Here's what happened: before kick-off, the Guardia Civil asked the Ultras to remove a banner that they deemed offensive; it had a blue and white skull on it wearing a woollen hat. The Ultras pointed out that a much bigger banner had been hoisted by Atlético fans at the other end of the

stadium, sporting a Nazi helmet, complete with swastika. The result was that the police started charging frantically into the Marseille crowd, which included children and even disabled people. I should add that one of the freedoms that Ultras demand

is also the freedom to defend themselves against attacks by ex-Franco henchmen, which is exactly what the Marseille Ultras did. Among them was Santos. To cut a long story short, he received a three-and-a-half year prison sentence after a kangaroo trial, which triggered unprecedented reactions in France and elsewhere in Europe, including a 10,000 people strong demonstration in Marseille asking for his immediate release, letters and petitions to the French President, etc. The sad thing is that after some back and forth, Santos did go to jail and is still serving his sentence as we speak. The French government's position on the matter is that "the less noise we make about the story, the better for the culprit"—I'm not joking.

The opposition to "modern football" seems to unite almost all Ultras, no matter their exact political persuasion. How do you personally see the game's development?
Here things become personal. You see, my grandfather was and my father is football-mad. The former was the chairman of the local football club in the small town of Fécamp, in Normandy, and my father, in his heyday, was the team's goalkeeper. For the two of them, football has always been "better before." Or rather, football has never been what it used to be. I heard that for the first time from my dad during the 1978 World Cup, and I still hear it today.

What I'm trying to say is that it's all too easy to be overly nostalgic about football's past—or to be all doom and gloom about its future. I'm optimistic. Football has proven time and again that it contains a magic, immensely powerful element, not unlike the stuff religions are made of; something that almost compulsively attracts people worldwide and unites them, at least for the duration of a game; something people take part in from the outside (spectators) or the inside (players) with identical passion. Everybody is at a loss to explain why football exerts such fascination on billions of people. Football can give you emotions never felt before. My daughters' births aside, the beautiful game brought me the strongest moments of happiness. Extremely powerful stuff indeed, which is why I believe that football, thanks to its mysterious ingredient, will always take care of its own survival.

Of course, if you look at the dark side of the ball, you'll find reasons to worry. Football could very well become a privilege of the rich, with twenty—or should I say fourteen?—teams competing in the same obscenely advertised competition, preferably on a quarterly basis to generate more money. FIFA could modify the rules indefinitely in order to make football more attractive to the most solvent market. But even if they can change the rules of the game, they cannot change its nature. At least that's what I hope.

Christophe Huette lives in Marseille with his wife Snjezana and his two daughters, Ana and Iva. He works as a freelance sports translator, relaxes with music, and holidays in Sebišina (a no-man's-land). He is a co-founder of the charity organization The Serious Road Trip as well as a self-declared Olympique de Marseille fanatic.

Manifesto by the French Coordination Nationale des Ultras (August 2007)

Purpose of the Manifesto

C.N.U

This manifesto intends to initiate a union of supporters' groups from different clubs, which unite for no other purpose than to defend their common interests. It addresses both the recent attention and repression that we have experienced, and our vision of football.

Supporters' Rights

- The right to use material for choreography on the stands: flagpoles, megaphones, sound systems, etc.
- The right to facilitate our choreographic efforts: permission to enter the stands early and to store material conveniently. We demand to be acknowledged for our contributions by the clubs.
- The right to direct communication with the club's management, which is expected to consult the supporters on all matters that concern them directly or indirectly.
- The right to partake in management meetings.
- The right to freedom of expression as long as it is not offensive, political, or discriminating.
- The right to be considered football *activists* and not *clients*; this includes respecting the five percent ticket quota for visiting supporters as foreseen in Article 362 of the *Ligue de Football Professionel* (LFP) regulations.
- The right to proper conditions when traveling to away games: reasonable visitor parking; access to eateries, toilets, and stands with decent visibility; respectful reception by the security staff; presentation of a list

of authorized materials, clearly issued in advance, and not randomly changing from one stadium to the next.

Repression

- Condemnation of abusive and unprovoked attacks on supporters by security staff in the stadiums.
- Condemnation of the disproportionately high sentences for football supporters; we demand to be treated like all other citizens.
- Condemnation of preventive searches by security staff, which violate the principle of presumed innocence; if a supporter is prevented from entering the stadium as a consequence of preventive searches, we will file a legal complaint.
- Condemnation of the rigid pyrotechnics law implemented by Justice Minister Michèle Alliot-Marie; we demand to respect the accountability of the supporters and a differentiation between *holding* and *throwing* pyrotechnical objects.
- Condemnation of laws that violate the individual freedom of citizens by evoking collective punishment, that request tickets issued by name, that demand the registration of supporters' club members, and that allow security staff to dissolve groups.

Modern Football

- We need to make sure that football stays accessible to the biggest number of supporters; we need to categorically reject a significant rise in ticket prices and to defend a quota for eight-euro tickets.
- We need to fight the obligation to sit; on the people's stands, people have the right to stand!
- We need to ensure that supporters and full stadiums are favored over the interests of television: weekend games need to have priority over weekday games; no Monday games in the Second League; kick-off times on weekdays at 8 p.m.; kick-off times that suit the majority of the spectators, i.e., no weekday games at 4 p.m., no Sunday games at 9 p.m., etc.
- We need to ensure that the logos and the historical colors of our clubs are maintained, and we need to condemn changes that have solely the purpose of selling merchandise: club shirts have to be limited to two, one for home and one for away games; the shirts for away games must only be used if necessary to avoid confusion with the home team.
- We need to reject organizations like the G14.
- We need to fight against the stock market identity of the clubs and against developments that exclusively serve the interests of shareholders; the clubs must prioritize sport over profit; the winter trading period must be abolished.

- We need to strengthen the power of the Football Association's Ethical Council.
- We need to prevent the sale of licenses for club names to be used in non-sports-related contexts.
- We need to ensure that alcohol is not only prohibited on the people's stands, but also in the VIP boxes.
- We need to ensure that players are allowed to celebrate goals with the supporters.
- We need to ensure that TV rights are distributed justly.
- We need to reject the system of seeded teams and return to an open draw.

Translated by Gabriel Kuhn

Among the best known left-wing Ultra groups were/are the Brigate Autonome Livornesi 99, the Ultrà Sankt Pauli, AC Omonia Nicosia's Gate 9, Celtic's Green Brigade, Olympique Marseille's Commando Ultra 84, and Hapoel Tel Aviv's Ultras Hapoel. Many lesser known groups exist, even in towns as remote as Irkutsk, Russia, and Karabük, Turkey. Ultras like Fossa Garrafoni, supporting Real Valladolid in Spain, explicitly reference working-class culture. There are also Ultra-akin groups at the amateur level, for example at SV Babelsberg 03 in Germany. Left-wing Ultra groups at bigger clubs include Bayern Munich's Schickeria, the "arch enemies of general manager Uli Hoeneß."[94] In Latin America, a radical Ultra group supports Ferroviário AC. Left-wing Ultra groups are repeatedly attacked by right-wing extremists. In August 2010, antifascist supporters of the Russian side FC Karelia-Discovery Petrozavodks and the Ukrainian side Arsenal Kiev were attacked by neofascists on consecutive days; several people were left injured.

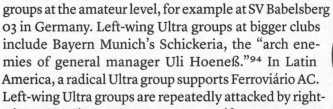

Many of the left-wing Ultra groups are united in the *Alerta* network, founded in 2007. In Italy, there is also the *Fronto di Resistenza Ultras*. Numerous informal connections exist, from prominent alliances like those between St. Pauli and Celtic fans to lesser known bonds between supporters of lower league teams like Wales's Wrexham FC and Italy's Virtus Verona.

Ultras have also operated on the national team level. In 2007, Bosnia's BHFanaticos lit fires during a Men's European Championship qualifier at Oslo's Ullevaal Stadium to protest alleged corruption in Bosnia's FA.

It is difficult to assess the political dimensions of the Ultra movement overall. Most Ultra groups' "apolitical" stance implies both an encouraging resistance to right-wing infiltration and a frustrating bashing of left-wing politics. This was recently exemplified in Germany when members of Rostock's Ultra group Suptras chased a group of neo-fascists from the stadium only to distance themselves from "left-wing extremism" in a communiqué published the following day.

Perhaps the most troubling aspect of Ultra fan culture, no matter the political stance, is the principle of uncompromising "loyalty" to one's club. Uncompromising loyalty to a football club? It is hard to see how this can ever fit progressive ideals. As the German writer and entertainer Christian Gottschalk puts it: "To be honest, I'm suspicious of the entire 'fan concept.' Fan identities of all kinds, whether related to a football club or to a musical genre, are almost always but variations of patriotism: 'You stupid, we great, olé!'"[95]

Tricky issues aside, Ultras have developed an extensive and impressive DIY supporters' culture with many attractive characteristics for radical activists. It will be interesting to see in which way the Ultra movement will develop.

There are also radical supporters' networks that do not align themselves with the Ultra phenomenon. Greece's Radical Fans United is one example.

▌ Radical Fans United

Interview with Supporters from Greece

When was Radical Fans United (RFU) founded?

On March 29, 2007, before a cup semifinal in women's volleyball, fans of Panathinaikos and Olympiakos clashed and a Panathinaikos fan died of multiple stab wounds. The ensuing police repression and media frenzy mobilized fans from different teams to gather, discuss, and organize. The result was the formation of Radical Fans United, a collective of fans from different teams. We struggle against the commercialization of sports, against racial prejudice, and against oppression. We believe that every fan has to take these matters seriously. It is necessary to act against everything trying to turn supporters into mere consumers.

Where do most of the people active in RFU come from?

RFU are based in Athens, and this is where all the participating fans come from. But this doesn't mean that we only act in Athens. We have relations to fans all over Greece, and our fanzine is distributed in more than ten cities and more than fifteen stadiums.

What are the political backgrounds of the people active in RFU?

Every person stands for his or her own political view. There is no need to formulate a kind of "political program." We stand against fascism, racism, and oppression. This is our common political view and that's what we are fighting for. We don't like to see expressions of these ideologies on the terraces. Every fan should be aware.

Are most RFU members active football fans? Do you also organize alternative football events?

Of course we are active fans! And that's exactly why we also organize our own events. So far, we have organized two summer festivals—with sport events, discussions, movies, parties—in order to promote the idea of fans getting in touch, having conversations, and a nice time together, instead of just fighting one another because we support different teams. There are many more things that unite us than things that divide us.

We also show movies about sports and fan culture, and we have discussion nights about fan violence and new sports laws.

So within RFU, supporters from different clubs are able to meet without problems?

Yes, and that's our beauty! We believe that fans should be able to sit around the same table and talk about their common problems without criticizing one another for wearing the wrong scarf. So far, we have achieved this with the events we have organized. They draw many people who feel comfortable speaking about their problems. It has been very encouraging for us to see that we are not alone! It is awesome to hear people who support different teams to discuss legal measures and police oppression, knowing that these are common problems for us all and not just for a single group.

In Germany, there are also radical fans who distance themselves from Ultra culture, for example at the amateur clubs of Altona 93 and Tennis Borussia Berlin (TeBe). TeBe is also an example for active fans gaining a strong influence on the internal structure and decision-making processes of the club—even management positions are held by people coming from the supporters' scene.

In Turkey, the logo of the Beşiktaş Istanbul supporters' network Çarşı includes a circle-A, the common "Anarchy" symbol. This has caused a fair amount of confusion among radical football fans.

Çarşı and Left-Wing Supporters in Turkish Football

Interview with Erden Kosova

A lot of people wonder about the circle-A in the Çarşı symbol. Some claim that it does reflect a political stance, others say that it's mainly provocation. What is your take?

As far as I'm concerned, the leftism attributed to it is a myth. The anarchist sign they use has nothing to do with the real anarchist movements in the country. It simply stands for urban laddishness. I have never seen a tendency among Turkish anarchists to support Beşiktaş because of Çarşı. Çarşı rhetoric is more sexist than that of most other supporters' groups. They make use of leftist references, but they are also borrowing from the ultra-nationalists.

Since I belong to a left-wing supporters' group of Fenerbahçe and since Çarşı cannot stand the idea of a rival in the left-football-conjunction, my relationship with Çarşı is particularly bad. Some friends and I were physically attacked at the last May Day demonstration for no other reason than provocation.

I find it very unfortunate that Çarşı has been copyrighted as an expression for left-wing politics in Turkish football. In particular, they have established a hold on the imagination of the mass media. The socialist newspaper *BirGün* also functions as a Çarşı fanclub, while ignoring the work of all other left-wing fan groups.

But all this indicates that there are at least some left-wing tendencies within Çarşı?
Çarşı had members who tried to establish a left-wing agenda. But the current situation is more complicated. The Çarşı stands are divided into two parts. One has traces of leftist affiliation but evades confrontational politics. The other is outright conservative and feels uncomfortable with all leftist references. Those are the ones who desperately want to remove the circle-A from the logo. But even among the "politically conscious" fans, the activism amounts to little more than adolescent iconophilia and cheap agitprop: banners with witty slogans that rhyme on "karşı," which means "being against." This is how Çarşı has become a media darling—even some intellectuals have fallen into the trap.

Since the substance is so weak, the political sloganeering of Çarşı can sometimes escape the framework of the left entirely and appeal to hardcore nationalism, homophobia, misogyny, and so on. For example, they have been chanting discriminative slogans against Diyarbakırspor, a club from the predominantly Kurdish part of Turkey. The recent tension between Çarşı and the Beşiktaş president, an industrial baron, was settled when he contracted two "mega-transfers," Quaresma and Guti. No one seems to care about the huge amount of money the club owes him . . .

How representative is Çarşı for Beşiktaş fan culture overall?
Çarşı certainly dominates the fan culture of Beşiktaş. Ultraarslan plays a similar role for Galatasaray. In the Fenerbahçe stands, there are more groups and their relationships are more egalitarian.

You have mentioned the main Istanbul clubs: is there a historical difference in terms of left-wing/working-class support?
Beşiktaş, Fenerbahçe, and Galatasaray share more or less the same sociology. In the early 1980s, a professor who was a Marxist Beşiktaş supporter conjured up the myth that Galatasaray represents the aristocracy, Fenerbahçe the bourgeoisie, and Beşiktaş the proletariat. This left a trace in public consciousness, but it is nonsense. Surveys show, for example, that Beşiktaş supporters have stronger economic backgrounds than both Fenerbahçe and Galatasaray supporters. Óscar Córdoba, the Colombian goalkeeper who played for Beşiktaş from 2002 to 2006, said that he never figured out how people in Istanbul pick their team.

Does Galatasaray also have left-wing fan clubs?
There is a small group called Tek Yumruk, or "Single Fist." However, their activities are largely suppressed by Ultraarslan, the dominant supporters' group. There has been some Kurdish support for Galatasaray because

Abdullah Öcalan, the PKK leader, expressed his sympathies for the club since Galatasaray's colors (yellow-and-red) resemble the Kurdish tricolor (yellow-red-and-green).

But that resemblance is pure coincidence, right?
Yes.

Are there any other clubs with significant left-wing support?
There is a club in the second division, Adana Demirspor, that has been associated with the left, mostly because it is a railway workers' club and has a leftist tradition. Last year, they played a friendly with Livorno. Yet, this is also ambivalent. Their current president is from an ultra-nationalist party . . .

Karabükspor is another club with a strong working-class identity since it is tied to the state-owned steel factory. They were recently promoted to the Süper Lig. Their players came to the May Day demonstration in Istanbul this year where they were warmly welcomed.

Erden Kosova is an art critic based in Istanbul. He is a member of Vamos Bien, a left-wing supporters' group of Fenerbahçe.

In recent years, many left-wing activists have stressed the importance of radical projects within contemporary football culture. In 2007, the British Class War Federation interviewed the makers of the Celtic fanzine TÁL for its journal, which regularly includes articles about football.

▌Interview with Editors of the Celtic Fanzine TÁL

Class War, no. 93 (Winter 2007)

Can you give a brief history of TÁL and where it's going now so much is changing at Celtic Park?
The formation of TÁL and *Celtic Fans Against Fascism* was really the culmination of our reaction against the racism of our own supporters towards Rangers' signing of the Black English player Mark Walters in the late 1980s. In the first game that Walters played for Rangers at Celtic Park, many of our fans made monkey chants and threw bananas on to the trackside. That day was one of the most depressing for the militant anti-fascists and republicans among our support. Although it took another couple of years before the fanzine was established, it was our determination to address that kind of racism among our own fans that spurred us on. Our approach was simple. We were supporters of the Irish republican struggle and identified with the militant approach of Anti-Fascist Action (AFA). We also sought to champion the idea of democratising of the club,

campaigning to put the most important people—the fans—in control of the club. It was also important from the anti-racist point of view to highlight the history of the club as a football team that grew out of an immigrant community. The Irish in Scotland were themselves the victims of racism and discrimination. Therefore, it was hypocritical, to say the least, for the second and third generation of that immigrant community to be the perpetrators of racism. Within a short space of time the situation was transformed with the majority of our fans recognising this incongruity and identifying with the victims of racism. This in turn led to large sections of Celtic supporters either drowning out or directly confronting the racists within our own support. Within a relatively short space of time the situation had been completely reversed with the anti-fascists and anti-racists now in the majority and any public displays of racism stamped out quickly and efficiently. The most important aspect of all of that period is that we won the political argument with the majority of fans, as well as any physical confrontations with racists that resulted. In the end, it really became "anti-Celtic" to be a racist, with our fans now taking a pride in their progressive attitudes to politics and struggle. Our reputation grew as a result and we established good relations with like-minded supporters from various clubs such as St Pauli, Athletic Bilbao, Bordeaux, Juventus, Anderlecht and Manchester United.

An equally important issue for us was our support for the Irish republican struggle, which impacted Celtic supporters because of the Irish family backgrounds that so many of us shared. For us, the war in Ireland was a litmus test of political mettle. Some of us had been involved in conservative left-wing groups in the past and had broken from them largely because of the Brit Left's cowardice and inability to take the side of the oppressed people of the Six Counties against the British occupation. It was therefore essential that TÁL clearly expressed its support for the republican people and their struggle to get the Brits out, by any means necessary.

To bring things up to date, we had decided on the publication of our 40th issue in 2005 to call it a day after thirteen years. One reason behind that decision was the changed political situation in Ireland; another was the changing nature of Celtic as a club, with it becoming a global capitalist institution, making it more and more difficult for the politically motivated fans to maintain our identity and organisation. However, after about eighteen months there was such a demand for TÁL to refill the political vacuum that we had left that we felt it our duty to return to the fray. In that short time, however, we had gained allies from a new, younger generation of Celtic fans who had formed the Ultras group Green Brigade. These were young fans who had grown up reading TÁL and whilst maybe not being as militant in every way as ourselves, still identified clearly with the Irish republican and anti-fascist culture that TÁL promoted. In addition, we recruited more people to take part in the editorial group of the fanzine. The fanzine editorial group includes Green Brigaders, anti-fascists, republicans, communists, militant trade unionists and those with no political affiliation. The things that bind us all are the love of our football team, the political culture of the supporters and our commitment to anti-sectarianism, anti-racism and anti-fascism.

So, we decided to republish the fanzine in a smaller thirty-two-page A5 format and have produced two issues in the last six months, moving towards it coming out every eight weeks during the season. The comment in the fanzine is still hard-hitting politically and, from a club and football point of view, we are still the biggest thorn in the side of Celtic PLC and their globalist ambitions.

How have you been able to maintain your group/fanzine when others—such as *Red Attitude* at Manchester United, have collapsed?
I think we were different because we had a bigger political sea in which to swim at Celtic Park. Celtic fans are generally quite liberal, which you'll have witnessed if you've ever been away in Europe with our supporters! TÁL was going through an already open door because there are a lot of our supporters who are politically aware and who have opinions across a range of issues. Politics is part of the club's foundations with the link to Michael Davit and other Irish republicans being there at the start and con-tinuing throughout its history, certainly among the fans, if not among the hierarchy of the club today. To be talking about the future of our club and its heritage alongside articles about the latest moves in republican politi-cal strategy is completely natural to us. We have heated discussions about the last game on our website, where almost no-one agrees. We have Che Guevara articles and posters in our fanzine alongside what many might see as football tittle-tattle, but then we also have serious analysis of our club, its identity, the slow bleeding of the working class base of the sup-port. Plus there are always articles and interviews with anti-fascist Ultras groups from around the world and the occasional hooligan interview like the *Cliftonville Lunatic Fringe* in our current edition. We still play our part in the fan culture at Celtic, politically and socially. TÁL was re-launched last season and so far the response has been great. Our fanzine sales at the ground are usually pretty good.

Gerry Adams sees the peace process as a step towards a united Ireland, whilst Ian Paisley argues it settles the question of the union—perma-nently. How can they both be right?
Well, they can't both be right and that's the dilemma that they will both have to face up to at some point. I don't have any big analysis to offer of

Irish politics. Republicans are in government in the Six Counties. Had they not taken their eye off the ball in the recent Twenty-Six County Election they might also be in government there too. It's important that the working class base of republicanism is maintained and that, in addition to all the grand talk about national consensus and the reunification of the country by 2016, bread and butter issues are put to the fore of republican politics, or the working class composition of the movement will diminish. That aside, Sinn Fein are now in seats of power in Stormont and they'll be judged on what they achieve there.

Ireland is changing so drastically, is it likely to lead to denying its own history and identity or is it a positive? Recent events at Croke Park seemed to suggest that many of the Irish rugby fans were oblivious to what had even happened there in the past, others seemed to prefer to forget and let bygones be bygones.

Father Jack might say, "That would be an ecumenical matter . . ."

Ireland is changing in many ways, but its unfair to describe those changes as drastic, it is a process that has been going on over many years and owes more to its membership of the European Union than it does to any new political thinking on the part [of] Fine Gael or Fianna Fail. The growth of Sinn Fein in both the Six and Twenty-Six Counties is undoubtedly a major factor in that change and a real and welcome challenge to the political status quo on the island of Ireland.

The decision by the GAA to open up Croke Park for use by other sporting bodies such as the Football Association of Ireland and Irish Rugby Football Union along with the implementation of the Good Friday Agreement is seen by many as an example of a 'New Modern Ireland'. However, to use such a term simply panders to negative stereotypical visions of an 'Old Ireland' full of Shamrocks and Shillelaghs.

If the GAA's decision to open up Croker has contributed to the education of those who were unaware of the historical significance of the venue during the war of independence then it is welcome. And those who choose to disregard the events that took place there on 21st November 1920 are as much the enemy of Irish republicanism as British rule in Ireland.

As for the country's history and identity, quite simply, too much was invested by those who fought for an Ireland that they would never live to see, for it to be denied. However, its history and identity can only be truly recognised when the aspiration of a United Ireland has finally been achieved, until then we will continue to honour its past and help in whatever way we can to shape its future.

What groups would you recommend to anti-fascist football fans today?
Well, to our own supporters, we'd obviously recommend Celtic Fans
Against Fascism, which we started ourselves and which has been at the
forefront of anti-fascist, anti-racist and anti-sectarian campaigns at Celtic
for about sixteen years.

The Independent Working Class Association (IWCA); because we
have to rebuild our communities from the bottom up and the IWCA seem
to have an approach to the working class that is unique on the left and
which seeks to politically empower our communities. An organisation like

the IWCA can politically compete with the
fascists for 'hearts and minds' in working
class areas, as well as the obvious benefit that their democratic approach puts
political space between their methods and
those of the old left; fighting for the rights
of all and facilities for the use of all, not for
sectional interests based on the racial seg-
regation of our communities, something
that the left's attachment to the philosophy of multiculturalism
has shamefully encouraged rather than fought against.

I've met some people from Antifa and they were sound. It all depends
on the political circumstances in particular areas, the threat posed by the
fascists and the calibre of the anti-fascist activists available—you have to
tailor your strategy and tactics accordingly. Fight when you can win . . . and
if you can't win, don't fight! There will be other days. It's a simple formula
that brought AFA a lot of success against the fascists.

I don't believe in ghost-hunts or wild goose chases for invisible fash
or NFers that go around with double the numbers of police guarding them.
There's very little street presence of fascists on parade anywhere, so it's
important to be fighting them in working class communities where they
are politically active. That means anti-fascism must learn to politically
adapt.

**There is such an amazing bond between Celtic fans and St. Pauli fans,
why has this happened and can it be replicated elsewhere?**
It started in 1992 very soon after our fanzine was founded. Some of the St.
Pauli fans had contact with less political elements from another fanzine,
but they contacted us and expressed the many things that we shared in
common, from football culture and music to support for anti-fascism and
the Irish struggle. The bond between the fans is unbreakable now. We can
have political disagreements with them and they with us on many issues,
but there remains at root an anti-fascist attitude that has strength in
depth. It's social attitudes, politics and football that is the real affinity. And

it's outside of the control of the football bosses, even though they now try to commercialise it with a merchandising deal between the clubs. Celtic PLC have no understanding of the unbreakable bonds that exist between TÁL and the anti-fascists at St. Pauli.

We also have good links, going back over many years now, with *Herri Norte Taldea* (HNT), the militant anti-fascists from Athletic Bilbao. We went over to Bilbao earlier this year to help celebrate the 25th Anniversary of their group. These are solid working class football fans with militant anti-fascist attitudes combined with a strong support for the independence struggle in the Basque Country.

Do you ever see events like those at Manchester United occurring with sections of fans leaving to set up their own club?
No. A similar situation to that of FC United, where an 'FC Celtic' might be started up by a section of disgruntled fans, just won't happen at our club. The essential belief among our supporters is—regardless of share deals and big business interests—that the club belongs to the fans. That sentiment is still very strong at Celtic; that we are a working class club, founded by Irish immigrants, whose sons, daughters and grandchildren have had to put with a lot of shit just to get on in life. The experience of Celtic supporters is very much tied in with the whole experience of being part of a 'minority community' in Scotland. The club is seen to be an extension of that community. Whatever happens in future with regard to supporters' movements at Celtic Park, I believe it will happen inside the club, not outside of it. It was the commitment of our fans that saved this club in the past and we still want to see *our* club democratised. Ultimately we have the Barcelona model to work towards. It's not a perfect solution, but it does provide an example where its supporters can at least partially democratically control a club; a club that can embrace with pride its Catalan identity and relate to the political and cultural aspirations of its fans. That's what we want to see at Celtic; a club based in Scotland that is at ease with its Irish identity and the working class politics and culture of its fans.

Clubs as Cooperatives, Not as Corporations

In recent years, much of supporters' activism has focused on keeping football clubs from becoming corporations, owned by people with no relations to the local community and alienated from local fans. Particularly in England, this has become a heated issue with legendary clubs like Chelsea, Liverpool, and Manchester United bought by billionaire businessmen. In Manchester, the FC United of Manchester has been founded in protest, in Liverpool the Spirit of Shankly campaign kicked off in 2008, and at several clubs, supporters' trusts and shareholdings have been set up to keep the clubs "in the hands of the people." Some of these initiatives have saved clubs from bankruptcy. The website *myfootballclub.co.uk* has been established to help spread the movement. Club officials, however, have rarely acknowledged the efforts: "All around the country, Supporters Clubs were busy raising money on behalf of their football clubs, and receiving little or nothing in exchange in the way of representation. Whilst the money that they provided was gratefully received, this did not entitle them to recognition, or to any sort of say in the running of their club."[96]

In Scotland, First Division team Stirling Albion FC became the first club fully owned by its members in 2010. In Israel, Hapoel Kiryat Shalom is run directly by its supporters. In Germany, the Internet community *www.deinfussballclub.de* allows its members an active participation in the management of SC Fortuna Köln.

■ Fan-Controlled Football Clubs

Organise! For Revolutionary Anarchism: Magazine of the Anarchist Federation (UK), no. 71 (Winter 2008)
Stuart Saint

There has previously existed a tradition amongst some anarchists and Marxists to perceive sport as an "opium of the masses"; a distraction from the more pressing concerns of the working class—similar to religion. This argument could feasibly be extended to any pastime, from celebrity gossip, art and stamp collecting to poetry, theatre and cinema. The attitude of some anarchists towards sport (and usually any pastime that is not high-brow art, music or poetry) reflects that of the utilitarian philosopher John Stuart Mill, who, despite his belief that all pleasures are intrinsically good unless they result in harm, maintained that there exist "higher" and "lower" pleasures (*On Liberty*, 1859, London: Penguin Books). The opinion that sport, particularly football, is pointless and that enjoying it is a submission to the bourgeoisie smacks of elitism, and also raises the question as to whether sport would still be "permitted" in a future anarchist society. Of course, the answer to this has to be "yes," given our desire to live life for pleasure not profit, and requires us to discuss the issue of sport within an anarchist framework.

Sport provides people of all ages, races, cultures, and genders with an opportunity to interact voluntarily with individuals outside of the workplace in a leisure environment. Like art and music, there are many different ways to take part in sport, either as spectator or player. Rather than look down upon sport, anarchists should view sport as an opportunity to meet other working-class people and to organise amongst ourselves for change. This article will thus document how working-class people have organised independent football clubs in place of corporate-dominated clubs in recent history.

In 1992 the clubs of the Football League First Division set up the FA Premier League to replace the former as the highest echelon of professional English football, bringing the twenty-two founder clubs (reduced to twenty for the 1995–96 season onwards) a huge influx of money due to an unprecedented television rights agreement with Rupert Murdoch's "Sky Sports" station. In the sixteen years since, both the commercial and popular appeal of football, particularly the Premier League, has skyrocketed. Top clubs such as Manchester United, Arsenal, Liverpool and more recently Chelsea can count their fans in the hundreds of millions, United alone boasting a third of a billion fans worldwide ("Man Utd's 333m fans," *Daily Mirror*, January 8, 2008). The Premier League "brand" is now touted as the best league in the world, the result being that each week's round of games are seen as the next chapter in a soap opera, plugged relentlessly on satellite television. Matches are no longer a place to go and meet with friends, but a spectacle to be witnessed, either with potential corporate clients in a VIP suite, or in the safety of your own home on the television. Echoing the gentrification of many city centres, the traditional working-class base of the terraces have been replaced by members of the upper classes, with clubs only too happy to entertain them with luxury bars and expensive restaurants inside stadiums. For many working-class fans, the only option left for any sort of communal solidarity is to go to the pub and watch the game on a big screen TV.

The psychology of the game off the field has also changed drastically, with club executives and chairmen now more inclined to view fans as "customers" of the club, rather than supporters with a right to a say in the club's affairs. This attitude was most starkly demonstrated in the takeover of Manchester United by Malcolm Glazer, an American hedge-fund entrepreneur who left the club in $850m of debt after taking over as owner in spring 2005. In an effort to make back the money, Glazer has subjected season-ticket holders to a series of price increases, and led to a group of fans setting up a "rebel" club, FC United of Manchester (FCUM), in protest at price hikes and the autocratic nature in which the club was being operated. The club's founders drew up a manifesto outlining its opposition to the commercialisation of the Manchester United, the Premier League and the sport in general, and held a democratic vote to decide on the name of the club, with each of the potential names having varying degrees of relevance to the club they broke away from. FCUM's policies of direct democracy and developing links with the local community, as well as remaining a non-profit organisa-

tion and refusing to display a sponsor on club shirts will appeal to anarchists; "members have so far set season ticket prices, decided how much membership will cost, voted on how often the team's playing strip will change and whether it will carry a sponsor or not" (Membership section of the FCUM website).

FCUM were also offered advice and support from AFC Wimbledon, another breakaway club who had formed after Wimbledon FC were taken over and relocated north to Milton Keynes. The plight of the Wimbledon fans was well-publicised, and to this day, the fanzine *'When Saturday Comes'* refuses to acknowledge the existence of the Milton Keynes Dons football club. The decision to move the club was unprecedented in League football (although non-league side Enfield were relocated to Borehamwood in 2001, spawning the formation of Enfield Town), and drew comparisons with the practice of "franchising" that is evident in American sport, where a club can be moved to a new city if there is evidence for a more fertile market in this area. Thus, the NHL ice hockey club Québec Nordiques, sandwiched between two traditional hockey powerhouses, the Toronto Maple Leafs and the Canadiens du Montréal, was moved in the early 1990s to Denver, Colorado, where there was not another major hockey club for hundreds of miles in any direction.

The system of franchising has already extended to rugby league, where from next season clubs will have to meet strict criteria before entering the Super League, and the last decade has seen constant rumours of a breakaway continental Super League for European football based on a similar system. Only the richest and most profitable clubs would enter, severing their ties completely with the established domestic and European club competitions that are so popular with fans. Much of the protests against a Super League and franchising are characterised by a passion to retain what many fans love about the game. An entire culture of banter and rivalry has grown up around football, some unique to clubs, some widespread across the entire game. Outrage was rife when Manchester United chose not to defend the FA Cup in 2000, instead attending a World Club Challenge tournament in Brazil. The FA Cup retains a magic all of its own amongst English fans, and the club owners seemed oblivious to this, preferring to attend a tournament that, whilst sanctioned by FIFA, holds little value amongst fans. Similar protests were voiced against the Premier League's proposed plan for a 39th round of games to take place in a number of locations worldwide. The plans were met with derision from across the British media, and many football federations voiced opposition to the arrogance of the Premier League. Fans have an acute sense of the money talking in football, and many are desperate to keep the traditions and culture of the game despite the ever-tightening grip that global capitalism holds on the game.

It is in this light that independent, fan-controlled clubs have sprung up. While the cases of AFC
Wimbledon and FC United present anarchists with
glamorous, anti-capitalist examples of fan-controlled clubs, other examples, notably AFC Liverpool
and a raft of lower league teams such as Exeter

AFC Liverpool

City, Cambridge City, Notts County and Stockport County provide equally
pragmatic examples. Despite season-long protests against the American
owners at Liverpool football club, the formation of AFC Liverpool in spring
2008 was touted as an "affordable alternative" rather than a new club, and
sought to retain ties with Liverpool. Like FC United, AFC Liverpool oper-
ates according to a democratic vote from the membership and is not-for-
profit, but has sought to distance itself from much of the anti-capitalist
rhetoric of FC United and AFC Wimbledon. Nevertheless, the nature of
the club represents an attempt by fans to organise alternatives to the "Big
Football" of the Premier League that is no longer affordable to the working
classes. This strategy has indeed borne fruit; Exeter City was taken over
by a fans' trust following relegation to the Football Conference (the first
tier of English football below the Football League), and was taken out of
administration two years later, and promoted back to the Football League
in May 2008. Even more remarkable is the rise of FC United, who started
life in the second division of the North West Counties League—the tenth
tier of English football—and will start the 2008/09 season in the seventh
tier Northern Premier League, having being promoted every season since
their inception.

However, it is not just on the field success that drives fan-controlled
clubs. As stated above, FC United's manifesto seeks to develop links with
the local community and the youth of the area. Most notable was a "fan
day" held in 2008 as part of an anti-racist campaign where the club sold
Fair Trade food, and, according to its website, the club emphasized that . . .
"any activity such as 'Kick Out Racism' week has a strong element of being
merely symbolic. However, we wish to stress our anti-racist and inclusive
approach. We are a young club, and aim to ensure that our day will be the
springboard to further activity."

On the same website, the club goes on to confirm its opposition to
xenophobia and homophobia, as well as stating that "football is, today,
central to many people's ideas of community—and encouraging a sense
of belonging is crucial if minorities are to feel included." Clearly, the club
wishes to actively involve itself in struggles that affect working class
people, and the fact that a number of the club's supporters are featured on
the fascist Redwatch website is a testament to their efforts!

For football fans who despair at the influence of money on the game,
the progress that fan-controlled clubs have made proves that the process

of direct democracy and not-for-profit football is successful. The day has yet to come when a fan-controlled club reaches the Premier League, but perhaps Big Football and the money behind it will prove too strong for clubs such as Exeter City and Notts County who would not be able to compete financially for world-class players. Instead, the ambition for clubs such as AFC Liverpool, FC United and AFC Wimbledon is undoubtedly to reach at least the Football League, and many fans of the breakaway clubs would love to be drawn against the club that they broke away from in an FA Cup tie. The latter of these goals is merely the luck of the draw, but the former appears to be a not-too-distant prospect for AFC Wimbledon, who could be playing League football as early as 2011. For anarchists and fans alike, these clubs represent an aspect of everyday life that has been wrestled from capitalist hands and returned to the people, truly an example of creating a new 'society' inside the shell of the old. Apart from the largest Premier League clubs, the formation of a supporters' trust that can gain control of a majority of club shares and turns the club into a not-for-profit organisation is not an unrealistic prospect; this has occurred at Cambridge City, Exeter City, Stockport County, Raith Rovers (albeit with the help of Gordon Brown!) and Notts County, and is perhaps a less extreme version of a traditional factory occupation! Making the connections between fan-control and anarchism and stressing the damage being done to football by capitalism to fans could result in an increase of anti-capitalist sentiment amongst working-class football fans. Football and other sports are a part of the community, and as a part of the community, anti-sport anarchists need to be engaging with fans, not looking down on them and trying to force them to "better" themselves by rejecting sport. These alternative clubs are often defined by their solidarity with each other and their resistance to capitalism, something that anarchists should be congratulating and encouraging.

Some writers have sketched a concrete vision of football in a socialist society. John Reid wrote in *Reclaim the Game*:

> A Socialist society would guarantee and protect the existence of all clubs, League and non-League. Football clubs are an integral part of working class communities. Clubs would be community run and non-profit making. [. . .] Supporters would not just be involved in turning up to watch. There would be a proper club structure where people would enroll to the club of their choice for a nominal fee. [. . .] Under Socialism players would receive wages tied to the average wage of a skilled worker.[97]

Alternative Football Culture

Grassroots and Underground Football Culture

Not least due to the critique of the commercialization of football, people around the world have, for at least fifteen years, worked on forming an underground soccer culture, complete with its own clubs, networks, and tournaments.

Among the longest-running and best-known of the football lovers who have taken the step from criticizing the official game to founding their own radical/left-wing/socialist soccer club are the Bristol Easton Cowboys/Cowgirls.

▌ The Easton Cowboys and Girls Sports Club

Roger Wilson

A timeline
Easton, Bristol, England: July 1992, twenty punks, anarchists, hippies, asylum seekers and local kids set up a soccer team and enter a local League. They call themselves the Easton Cowboys.

Stuttgart, Germany: May 1993, the Cowboys attend their first football festival, forge themselves as a team and are inspired by the collective ideas of the German squatters and punks that host the event.

Bristol, England: August 1994, the Cowboys hold their first of many international football festivals, leading to the creation of a European network of teams.

Dorset, England: August 1998, over 1,000 people gather at an Alternative World Cup festival of football featuring a strange collection of teams from Germany, Belgium, France, Poland, Norway and the eventual winners a group of school kid soccer stars from Diepkloof, SOWETO, South Africa.

Chiapas, Mexico: May 1999, a group of Cowboys play tournaments in Zapatista rebel held territory. This leads to the formation of the solidarity group KIPTIK, which provides materials and volunteers for water and health projects.

Compton, South Central Los Angeles, USA: September 2000, a bunch of cricketers from England play the ex-gang members cricket team the Homies and the Popz. The Homies tour England the year after with a memorable stay in Bristol.

Hamburg, Germany: May 2002, inspired by our connections with the Bundesliga club FC St. Pauli and its women's football team, our own women's team, The Cowgirls, is formed.

Rif Mountains, Morocco: August 2003, through connections with the local Moroccan community, the Cowboys venture into Africa, grinding out some creditable results in the heat and dust.

Chiapas, Mexico: May 2006, we continue the close ties with the Zapatistas by bringing our new men and women's basketball teams to play in the rebel zones.

West Bank, Palestine: May 2007, the Cowboys tour Hebron, Bethlehem and Ramallah, with a memorable final match in the shadow of the Israeli apartheid "wall."

Devon, England: August 2007, on the 15th anniversary of the Club's formation we hold our largest international tournament yet featuring four different sports and amongst many others, our new anti-fascist friends FC Vova from Lithuania.

Sao Paolo, Brazil: May 2009, a mixed group of Cowboys and girls travel to Brazil to play Autônomos FC, an anarchist football team.

Bristol, England: February 2010, five hundred people attend a party which raises enough money in one night to help get the Autônomos FC from São Paolo to Europe for the summer tournaments.

Bristol, England: May 2010, the Zapatista solidarity group KIPTIK celebrates its 10th anniversary.

Football, Community, and Politics

In this essay, I am going to analyse how radical ideas such as autonomy, democracy, free social spaces and internationalism can be practically developed outside of the constraints of formal and explicit political activity. In this case, the means for testing and propagating these ideas was football and the organisational form employed was the "sports club."

My case study is the social and sporting community known as the Easton Cowboys and Cowgirls based in Bristol, England and "officially" founded in 1992. [A] This sports club currently has twelve league teams playing football, cricket, netball and basketball with several hundred players, supporters and friends. The club is closely linked with many local organisations in Bristol including campaigns to protect playing fields and open spaces, self-organised sports leagues and international solidarity groups. It also has connections with other networks of football teams and organisations in four continents of the world.

Some Terms and Explanations

To begin, it will be useful to explain some terms that are used in this essay relating to "community" and the "political."

Community (with a big 'C') is defined here in an objective sense as fixed geographical spaces where people live, work and socialise (neighbourhoods, barrios, projects, estates, streets etc.). In a more subjective sense, **community** (with a small 'c') refers to actual relationships between people. For example, these include sub-cultures (punks, skateboarders, football hooligans, ravers, etc.), informal networks based on similarity of social need (parents with young children, literacy and language groups etc.) or collectives bound to hobbies or interests (such as sports clubs, local history groups, reading circles etc.). It is important to understand how these two ideas of community are similar, how they differ and when they coincide in practice.

These definitions of community are drawn in order to allow analysis rather than to act as fixed points of reference. The idea of "community" is problematic in that it does not necessarily infer stasis, shared identity, cohesive action or even unity. Neither does it deny the possibility for these states or forms of activity to exist for moments or over longer periods of time. The real difference is that Community roots people spatially (whilst accepting that the physical boundaries are often difficult to locate), whereas community represents a non-spatial relationship between people.

In addition, two definitions of the word "political" are offered.

Consider **Politics** (with a big 'P'), this is also understood in an objective sense, a set of reified ideas, ideology or theory describing a worldview, ways of changing things or ways of living (for example Anarchism, Environmentalism, Socialism, Religious fundamentalism, Neo-liberalism etc.). In contrast the term **politics** (with a small 'p') has a more subjective sense, where the real nature of our lives conflicts or meets with our needs and desires as individuals or collectives of human beings; for example, our relationship to work, the State, the Community (or community) and our families, lovers and friends. To demonstrate the difference between these two, consider the example of absenteeism from work. This may exist on a day to day political level in our society as the individual or collective refusal of exploitation and alienation, but it only becomes Political when it is embodied in an ideology (or theory) which is then explained back to people (i.e. as, say, part of the concept of "class struggle" against capital-ism). The definitions are important because they are a crude attempt to explain the difference between reified ideas imposed from the "outside" (a big 'P') and those developed, in general, from our own experiences and from the "inside" (a small 'p'). These two ideas of the "political" can meet in important instants in our lives and have met many times in particular historical moments.

Table 1 below is an attempt to synthesize these four definitions of community and politics into a matrix in order to provide further examples of their intersections both practically and historically. The arrows illustrate the relationships I have discussed. The attempted path of some Political communities of the left are shown by the grey arrows, notably entry into the political Community with an ideology that supposedly will transform these bodies into Political Communities operating in a dual power scenario with the state. The sports club however offers a potential social space where a feedback relationship with both the political Community and the Political communities can operate in practice (shown by black arrows).

	Political	**political**
Community	Soviets, workers councils, anti-poll tax groups, Zapatista municipalities	Neighbourhoods, barrios, projects, favelas, estates
community	Anarchist, Socialist and Communist organisations	Sports organisations, social clubs, self-help groups

Table 1: Examples of the intersections between the definitions of community and politics

Some History

Some of us who founded our sports and social club originally came from an anarchist Political scene (a community). We had been politicised through a variety of means in the 1980s, initially through being involved in the punk community and its connections to the peace movement, animal rights, feminism and other "single" issues. Through this involvement and the important political events of the 1980s (the Miners' and Printers' strikes, inner city riots, civil disobedience against nuclear weapons, the repression of cultural activity such as "social centres," "raves" or "festivals" etc.) we developed a more coherent overall critique of the existing order, specifically capitalism, class divisions and the state.

Throughout this whole period we existed in a Political community defined by such ideological terms as Anarchism, Anarcho-syndicalism or Left Communism. Interestingly this particular Political community spent much of its time trying to make connections with its opposite. We actually wanted to be part of an authentic political Community that is involved in local autonomous neighbourhoods, organising against the state and capitalism without mediation by Political organisations, or in contrast ghottoised into sub cultural communities (like punk-rock or squatters'). Awareness of these contradictions led us to critique rival organisations, which we regarded as being far from "revolutionary."

So-called "revolutionary" organisations, typically Political parties of the left appeared only to want to recruit members and instil in them their crystallised ideology as the party line. We considered them to be inflexible, manipulative and uncritical. The leadership of these undemocratic organisations often treated the rank and file as merely foot-soldiers and strikers to be wheeled out to demonstrate or sell newspapers. In contrast, the sub-cultural communities from which many of us had come, appeared to spend most of their time wanting to appear different to the populace, usually by fashion, music and behaviour. [B] They encouraged exclusion, didn't want to communicate with the Communities they lived in, and even if they professed to be Political, joining was difficult as it involved subscribing to a fairly tight set of unwritten cultural rules. Despite having attempted to escape these two unsatisfactory poles in the mid-80s, we existed uneasily between them recognising that either of these critiques could still be applied to our own political groupings.

Burnout
In the early 90s a historical moment occurred where Political communities (such as Class War Federation and other class struggle orientated Anarchist and Ultra-left groups etc.) were actually confronted by the political Community. This was during the Poll Tax revolt with its popular semi-spontaneous campaign of civil disobedience; refusing to pay the tax, mass opposition to bailiffs, through to assaults on local council meetings in the provinces and a huge "riot" in central London. After the "victory" of this struggle, a partial reform and more importantly the removal of Margaret Thatcher and the right wing of the governing Tory party, the self-

organisation of the local Poll Tax groups began to collapse. Our generation of activists had been involved in activism for around ten years in various political struggles and many of us were pretty "burned out." Some of us were "tired," some were in prison, others were fighting long court cases and many of us had committed the ultimate activist crime of having long term relationships and even (gasp!) children.

We had tried to avoid becoming "24-hour activists" through the '80s, mostly without success, and now we wanted a bit of a "life." One of the few non-Political activities some of us took part in was playing kick-about soccer in Easton, the local Community that some of us lived in. This had been going on for several years and had united some punks, squatters, hippies, local youth and asylum seekers. In 1992 we helped form a football team and entered a local league. Without realising it, we set off a train of events that was to end in the strangest places.

Anatomy of the Easton Cowboys

I would like to isolate four ideas that had a direct link to the Political communities of the 1980s and characterised the development of what became the "Easton Cowboys" sporting organisation. These ideas were never explicit in the "Easton Cowboys" in the way they would have been in a Political organisation, but nevertheless played an important role in our new political community.

Autonomy

The idea of independent autonomous organisation, with no mediation by external bodies (either financially or politically) comes straight from the punk rock culture. The "get off your arse, learn three chords and start a band of the '70s" had exploded into a whole range of cultural and political organisations of the '80s (squatted buildings, social centres, gig halls, free festivals, travellers etc.). Through post-punk bands such as Crass and inspiration from the European squatting movements (Berlin, Amsterdam, Zurich) a whole generation of activists had been injected with a "go it alone" attitude that meant not waiting for permission or cash before acting to find social spaces. Despite being burned pretty badly in the 80s by police repression and problems with hard drugs, this culture stayed with the activists into the 90s and was melded first with the acid house and the "free party" scenes, and eventually "Reclaim the Streets" and the emerging anti-globalisation movement.

For us it took a different turn, becoming part of the culture of our small but growing social and sporting organisation. We were fiercely independent, raising our own money through whatever scams, gigs or parties we could come up with, refusing grants or sponsorship from businesses or municipal bodies and avoiding any kind of charity or "kind benefactors."

On a political level our "do it yourself" stance meant not being tied to any Political grouping (unlike some other lefty teams), being wary of being recuperated by local government or so called Community organisations and trying to control our relationship with the main-stream media as we became a "tasty" story for local and national TV, radio and the press.

Democracy and Organisation

Our experience of the hierarchical cliques and mafia type hierarchies of other football clubs we had played for or against cemented certain ideas we already had about democracy from our Political experience. From our very beginnings as a team we exercised player power, with open meetings electing the coach and other positions of responsibility within the club. This developed into mass assemblies of the whole club, recognition that we were a social and sporting organisation so that anybody could vote and attend these meetings even if they weren't a player and, until this very day, no formal membership. Along the way we picked up various skills as a group including the ability to chair meetings, a structure that allowed everyone to speak if they wanted and the ideas of delegation, rotation and responsibility. In addition, we created a flexible organisation that was able to throw up smaller groups to carry out specific tasks or organise events, which then dissolved afterwards, so preventing the crystallisation of leadership or too much bureaucracy. Our mottos were *"if we say we are going to do it, we do it"* and *"as much organisation as we need and no more."*

Our success with this democratic model (despite the hegemony of the neo-liberal ideas [C]) and the expansion of the club led to a large organi- sation that in turn generated various subsidiary special interest groups. These included Cowboys who were involved in local campaigns (such as battles over the development of playing fields, protecting asylum seekers, anti-fascist activities), social activities (Can-can dancers, art projects, his- tory groups) and international solidarity groups (Chiapas, Palestine, Brazil etc.). Unlike many formal Political organisations, the "Easton Cowboys" did not seek to absorb these groups into its structure or control them, but rather to create an environment where these activities were both advertised and open to involvement of the players and supporters. These self-organised sub-groups were autonomous but closely connected to the sports club as well as having wider links outside. This created a network of non-sporting activities that surrounded the Club, brought new players in from different social directions and offered lots of opportunities for involvement in more formalised political activity than just playing sport. These organisational relationships are modelled in Figure 1.

It is important to note that because the activity of a sports club is not inherently related to any particular sub-culture or political ideology it offers a space for people to meet from often quite unrelated backgrounds.

This social space and the unforced connections with the surrounding political sub-groups offered a bridge for players and supporters to enter into political activity when they chose, and usually as a result of discussion with other Cowboys in the less intimidating atmosphere of the Club (rather than a political meeting or public event). This linkage overcame many of the problems encountered by Political communities who found that their mere approach scared off or alienated many people.

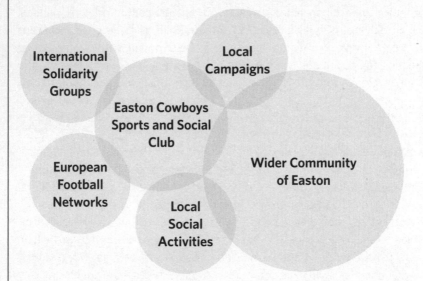

Figure 1: Schematic model of relationship between Easton Cowboys Sports Club and associated groups

Inclusivity

Class, race, gender, and sexuality issues abounded in the "radical" movements of the 1980s. The period was full of "anti" positions (anti-racism, anti-sexism etc.) predicated on the idea of the "personal is political" principally developed in the feminist movements of the 1970s. The Easton Cowboys culture was different in a subtle but important way. We aimed to try to create an atmosphere in the club that did not exclude people. This was quite different to the accusational attitudes of "political correctness" that some of us had faced from our previous Political lives. We did not get hooked up on words, instead we dealt with issues of sexism and racism within the club on a personal basis and only at the last resort took them to a formal meeting. [D] The key thing was not to try to suppress jokes or banter, but to create a more sensitive atmosphere. For example, making a joke about a "prostitute" meant recognising that the person sitting next to you was dating a prostitute. Saying something derogatory about lesbians was attacking your own fans or some of the women's football team. This is not always an easy process. The key to this approach was the understanding that behaviour and language does not always define belief and that personal change is born by experience and recognition of relationships, rather than by moral reproach or formal punishment. All of us developed and changed as a result.

The question of "inclusivity" is of direct relevance to the informal and formal exclusionary practices of sub-cultures and Political communities. The "Cowboys" were not conceived as an "anarchist" football team, instead we sought to interact with the Community we lived in as well as the sub-cultural groups and local Political communities. In our travels we have come across several "anarchist" football teams and have noted how their search for autonomy has actually been consciously or unconsciously exclusionary in that they immediately placed their sporting activities into a sub-cultural or Political milieu. [E] A related question concerns where a sports club socialises, the obvious option for "anarchists" is to situate this activity in the sub-cultural confines of a "social centre." In contrast, the "Cowboys" operated out of an ethnically mixed Jamaican run pub with a long history of involvement in the Community of Easton. [F] This social space offered a neutral meeting ground for lovers of football, political activists and the wider Community.

The "Easton Cowboys" sports club has always had a relatively healthy ethnic mix which was a result of our location in a mixed Community, the openness of the organisation and the nature of the "beautiful game." Soccer has an impressive capability to cross cultural and ethnic barriers, because it is simple, needs very little equipment and is ultimately a "dramatic" collective experience. Anybody can play it, anywhere in the world. It does not provide a solution to the problem of discrimination but it does offer "spaces" where prejudices can be understood and new relationships formed, sometimes merely because we play and party "together."

Before we joined the local football league we were well aware of the potential problems we might face as a bunch of punks and "long hairs" in a team with local Afro-Caribbean, Sikh kids and Iraqi refugees. For a start, we were in the middle of the "fall-out" from the first Gulf War and we also had the expectation of having to deal with racist elements in some opposing teams. However, we were politely surprised, most of the teams we played were fine and the incidents we had imagined were few and far between. When we did face racism or homophobia we were by degree violent or funny on the field of play. Opposing knucklehead twats never quite knew if they were going to get a head butt or their butt touched when they played the Cowboys! We refused the role of moral preachers; instead we talked to other teams with our banter and our boots.

Inevitably, a contradiction arose from our inclusivity. As more players arrived to sample the fun and the drama of Sunday football we were faced with the issue of having to exclude those who weren't "good enough" to get into our only league team. This was a critical moment and the dilemma was simple. Were we going to stick to our "anarchist" principles and let everyone play regardless of their ability or exclude some and effectively turn them away from the Club? The solution to this issue of balancing the need to win matches and progress in the league with the need to "include" came organically. When the number of players who weren't getting a regular game (and were openly complaining about it) grew to a critical mass, we started a second team. This solution was great as it created more "spaces" to play, strengthened the Club and, crucially, provided a place to blood new and young players. This process has continued apace over the years and the Club now has twelve male and female teams playing four different sports—Football, Cricket, Netball and Basketball—making it one of the biggest amateur sports organisations in the city.

Internationalism

Lastly, I want to talk about internationalism. I purposely write this with a small 'i,' because this aspect of the Cowboys was again never contrived, forced or Political.

Traditional municipal exchanges often involving the twinning of towns and cities rarely involve direct relationships between people. As with international connections through Trade Unions, Political parties or organisations, they are usually mediated in some way, either by formal bodies

or by the Politics involved. In contrast, our trips were direct interventions in both communities and Communities. I mean this in the sense that we visited and got to know teams like ourselves (squatters, punks, anti-fascists) as well as visiting teams that represented towns (Bad Muskau in East Germany, Lecknica in Poland etc.). There was never any mediating group or organisation lying between us and whom we were partying with. What drove us was the wonder of going to strange places to play football, a dream we believe to be in the minds of all those who kick a ball around. This "wonder" would lead us from Chiapas to Palestine, and to setting up international tournaments (developed from the German model) which would bring youths from SOWETO onto the same pitch as ravers from Leeds, squatters from Germany and old geezers from Poland.

The key conduit for all this was the sport. In Europe it was the reason to meet new (and now old) friends from many countries every year and party. With the indigenous Zapatistas in Mexico, soccer provided a way of "breaking the ice" that so many other goggling international delegations had failed to do. In Compton L.A., cricket provided the link between us and a community so divided from White America that no one quite believed that we went there. Ironically the only reason we knew about Compton before our visit was because the violence has been so commercialised by capital, through "Gangsta Rap," that you can buy the packaged product anywhere in the world. This was especially clear to the teenage Cowboys and girls who came with us to this mythological anti-Disneyland and were pleasantly surprised by the warmth and friendship offered. Wonder fused with football, cricket and basketball eventually led us to making contacts with communities in four continents.

Certainly the lesson from all this was that making international links is not difficult especially when you have football, cricket, dancing and partying involved. [G] Of most interest is whether it was possible to pass through to the next stage, where some permanence in concrete links, friendships and relationships is to be had. From this comes the beginning of global networks that may be able to transcend the nation-state and racial and cultural divisions. We feel as a club that we have taken a few small steps along the long road to the dream of a world human community.

What Does All This Mean?
My key point is here that some fundamental ideas that make up the basis of anarchist theory (autonomy, democracy, inclusivity and international-ism) were tested out in a new arena, the sports club, which had been pretty much ignored by the "revolutionary" movement. So whilst Political communities struggled with trying to get people to implement these ideas in their opposite, the political Community (mostly without much suc-cess), i.e. informal projects such as the Easton Cowboys Sports and Social

Club, were able to actually test these things in practice in a much more pragmatic sense. After all, arming any community with actual experience of these four ideas is always useful even if it is not overtly Political. In fact I would argue that it is precisely because it wasn't seen as being Political that these ideas were able to flourish and be tested in the "real world."

Football allowed the crossing of certain barriers (class, race and nation) because of its apparent neutrality and popularity. The oppositional political and cultural ideas of the 1980s were translated into a new social form in the 1990s allowing them to expand beyond the limitations of the "anarchist ghetto" of formal Political organisations or exclusionary sub-culture. This symbiotic relationship is the key to understanding the success of the "expanded sports club"; soccer the lubricant, progressive ideas the engine. [**H**]

"They've Given Up Serious Politics"

Several critiques were levelled at the The Easton Cowboys and Girls Sports Club by the Political community we emerged from and I would like to analyse them now.

Initially, the general response to our activities in the local Community from the anarchists was: they've given up serious politics to play football. To a certain extent this was true. We had in a sense given up the Political community we came from, but instead found, perhaps without at first realising it, an exciting and interesting project to replace it. Instead of the feeling that we were outsiders in our local Community, we began to feel much more included. Our contacts with people who lived locally were far less forced and we certainly appeared a lot less threatening to them. It is true that we weren't pushing our ideas up front in the normal Political manner and neither were we hiding them in the style of the Trotskyite Left. Instead we were just putting them into practice with a group of people who did not necessarily share a unified Political idea but understood the positive and exciting aspects of the ideas themselves. It is certainly true that the image and "otherness" of Political sub-cultures is a major barrier to the transmission of ideas, something we did not have to worry about as a sports and social club.

Ironically, some years after leaving the Political community, we had to rebuild contacts with this scene again to allow us to travel to Mexico and visit the Zapatista communities. In the process of meeting activists from this milieu, we noticed that they were clearly worried about us as a group. They had stereotypical ideas about what a sports club was about, imagining heavy drinking, sexist and racist men who would be "culturally unaware." We were even patronisingly told we would have to undergo affinity group training, as we would clearly be unable to organise ourselves to "tie our own shoe laces" let alone deal with the rigors of travelling through Chiapas. This was a very strange experience. Meeting the Political community from the other direction, we could clearly see the perception of many "ordinary" people who feel patronised and at the same time notice the fears in the Political community they are confronted with. What an odd situation, a group of activists who want change the world through popular revolution but are afraid of the very people who are (according to the theory) going to do it "by any means necessary." This was very revealing to us.

Keep It Local!

A second critique that came from more class-conscious anarchists and activists was related to our internationalism, particularly our visits to Chiapas and consequent solidarity work with the Zapatista communities. In the 80s a political view had arisen that not only had the middle classes come to dominate politics in general but also specifically "revolutionary" politics and part of that domination was their obsession with "glamorous" armed struggle in far off places. Particularly criticised in the 1980s were the solidarity groups that supported the Sandinistas, as well as the Salvadoran and Guatemalan guerrilla insurgencies. The general argument went that the further away and unconnected with your home nation a national liberation struggle was, the easier it was to get involved with it politically. The most unfashionable national liberation struggles were close to home and/or involved your own nation, such as the Republican struggle in Northern Ireland. In addition it was perceived that middle class people could easily get involved with this "serious" Politics because they were too scared to deal with working class people who lived just down the street. Consequently the more hardcore class-conscious anarchists orientated themselves to activity in their local working class communities and stayed well away from any "international solidarity" organisations. International activity of this sort was left to the "middle-class" left and the fluffier "ghettoised" anarchist scene.

When the Easton Cowboys along with other like-minded clubs from England, Germany and Belgium built up a network of like-minded (anti-racist/anti-fascist) European soccer teams in the mid-90s it passed under the radar of the Political scene. It was the intervention of the club in the Zapatista political struggle that caused the sparks to fly. We were accused of forsaking local Political activities to engage ourselves in "far off" glamorous struggles with no connection to our neighbourhood. On the face of it, this was true and certainly some of us who knew this critique very well had already turned the ideas around in our heads many times. Of course, the irony of the whole situation was that at first we had been accused of "giving up politics to play football" and now the Sports and Social club was being criticised like a regular Political organisation!

The clearest and most constructive criticism came from some older activists who pointed out that if we were going to get involved with the Zapatistas then we should at a minimum try to get "proper" people over to Chiapas. What they meant by this was, if the middle class dominated the international solidarity movements, then we should encourage people who would never normally get involved in "glamorous struggles" such as the Zapatistas to go over to Chiapas and participate. This is what we tried to do. After all we thought why shouldn't we get involved in international solidarity. Why should it be left to the middle classes? There has been a long history of international working class solidarity worldwide and we didn't understand why we, as a sports club, couldn't be part of that history. The club thus acted as a conduit for participation in international solidarity unfettered by rigid ideological constraints or the exclusionary practices of Political communities. The Cowboys who ventured abroad were both educated and moved by our contacts with the rebel campesinos of Chiapas, the ex-gang members of Compton and the football clubs of Palestine. That contact and solidarity work continues to this day, and will continue into the future.

Class Composition

I touched on this issue earlier but would now like to consider it from the perspective of some of the criticisms that have been levelled at us both internally and externally. Often, the more "inclusive" you make an organisation the more the above questions come to the fore. We have been accused at different times of being "all middle class," "run by a gang of 11" and "a liberal clique." Most of these criticisms again are ironic, as the Club was never set up to be an exclusively "working class" Political organisation. When the Club started the only motto we had which was exclusionary and actually a bit of a joke was *No Coppers, No Christians.*" [1] Other than that, we would take anybody! So the Club has always been pretty cross-class in its make up. It never pretended to be anything else. Consequently, we have sometimes run up against the problems of articulate, confident middle class people tending to take on positions involved in the running of the Club. The main difference between a formal Political organisation and us in dealing with this particular problem is the nature of amateur sport. Freezing February mornings trying to win a game of soccer with a hangover has never really attracted political careerists! This lack of day-to-day Political glamour plus a structure that has implemented rotational democracy has instead opened up opportunities for people to develop and learn about organisation and self-management and thereby gain personal confidence beyond that of most Political communities. Sport can be a great leveller. You don't need a University degree to coach or run a soccer team. You gain respect from the players and supporters around you for many positive things, understanding people, being able to organise events, making us all feel better when times are grim and winning matches. In fact, all the things that make up a community.

Limitations and Problems

Having been a conscious cheerleader for the Easton Cowboys organisation so far in this essay it is time to turn a critical eye towards the club and its activities. One fear that was expressed by some of the founders as the club grew related to losing our culture, politics and identity. Some argued that we should not expand, or at least not too fast, as the end result would be a club full of people who had no idea about its origins and ideas. This issue also related to the question of attracting "good" players who did not share our "principles." The counter argument suggested that the dynamic of change was good itself and that if our culture and ideas were strong enough then they would not be diluted by more people becoming involved, instead it was hoped that they would be developed. After all it was argued, people were joining because it was an exciting club to be involved in and because of its values, such as inclusivity. It is hard to make a judgement about this, even in hindsight, except to say that most of the political activities of the sub-groups have continued to this day and there has not been a major reaction against this from the expanded "membership" of the Cowboys. The majority of the critics who have been surprised at the lack of overt Political activity have usually come directly from a Political community expecting a football club full of *anarchists* rather than one that is putting some of these ideas into *practice*.

A more significant problem has been when the club has had to deal with anti-social behaviour, particularly homophobic or sexist language. A recent end of season awards party was marred by (drunken) scuffles after some younger male members of the club made offensive remarks to some of the women footballers. The immediate reaction was a huge debate on our website chat room, some of which degenerated into verbal abuse. This was followed by personal contacts between the involved parties and an Emergency General Meeting to discuss the issues. Some of the more Political elements regarded the incident as a justification of their criticisms that the Club was too inclusive and consequently it needed to "vet" new members as well as create a more rigid constitutional framework. Others reasoned that we should expect conflict from time to time because if there was none, then that would be a sign we were *not inclusive*. They also argued that formalising the process of resolving disputes such as these would hamper informal resolutions and frighten off some new Cowboys before they had a chance to change their behaviour. The tension between formal and informal interventions to deal with such incidents has been a constant and uncomfortable feature of our history and is interestingly a direct reflection of debates going on in wider society. [J]

It is important to state again that the Cowboys was never conceived of as a Political organisation though it may act as a conduit to and from such organisations. It is thus difficult to criticise it on the basis that its Politics have become diluted or that it has failed in its Political objectives. The real question is if the club is not Political then what is it? And the answer cannot be just "a sports club." The question is probably best dealt with by looking at what it has done that is of interest Politically and judging whether that continues or fades. The longevity of the Club's core values of autonomy, democracy, inclusivity and internationalism will be a marker of its success rather than a sign of the failure to achieve something more Political.

Onward to Victory . . .

To summarize, I would like to isolate the following points:

Football (and other sports) can go some way to breaking divisions of nation, race and culture whereas overtly Political interventions often fail.

Ideas such as autonomy, popular democracy, inclusivity, and internationalism can be practically explored outside of the confines of Political organisations.

It can be easier to test ideas like these when there is no overt Political approach. The ideas themselves are more important than political stances or labels.

It is useful to break out of your Political community and enter the political Community, and "expanded" sports clubs can be a short-cut to doing this.

Organisations such as sports clubs can provide social spaces for people to meet, which can overcome some facets of sub-cultural, race, class and gender divisions.

Clubs such as the Cowboys should not be judged on their ability to achieve Political objectives but in their capability to put radical ideas into practice and act as conduits for their spread both locally and globally.

Finally, there has never been a grand master plan with the Cowboys. Our adventures and political activity have evolved and developed in an unselfconscious way over time. There's a sense in which the club is one ever-unfolding social experiment. Most sports clubs or social organisations have a limited lifespan and often rise and fall pretty quickly, but nearly twenty years into the Cowboys I have no idea what or where it might lead to next or what the shape of the club might be in five years' time. Which, after all, mirrors the excitement of playing the "beautiful game." You never quite know what might happen next . . .

A For simplicity (and space), from here on in the "Easton Cowboys" or "Cowboys" refers to "The Easton Cowboys and Girls Sports Club" and thus to both male and female members of this organisation. It should be noted that the opinions expressed in this essay are those of the author only and do not represent the views of the Easton Cowboys sports club.

B Many activists rejected these exclusionary and "ghettoised" cultures, which they had joined as teenagers. The question arose, if we wanted to get involved in "real struggles," why did we want to make ourselves different to those with whom we wanted to engage? As a result, many Punks cut off their Mohicans or dreads, accepted more mainstream cultures and started to dress like the friends from their Communities. Having Politics, it was argued, was not a question of fashion.

C One of the most disturbing aspects of the 1990s was how successful the dominant ideology of the period had been in rubbishing and suppressing ideas about grass-roots democracy. Not only were many new Cowboys unused to concepts of popular democracy, despite the long tradition of such organisational forms in UK working class Political and social movements, but they often initially carried a general disdain for them.

D "Cunt" for example became a term of endearment rather than a basis for exclusion.

E For example, in Oakland, California I played football with the local "anarchist" team who did not want to join a local league because it was "too competitive" and was disinterested in playing against or even communicating with the African and Latino football teams on the adjacent pitches. This was an anathema to my "Cowboy" football sense.

F The public house "The Plough" in Easton has become a symbol of both inter-ethnic and international linkages and this culture has continued for more than twenty years.

G It should be noted that meteoric rise of the World Wide Web and the availability of E-mail during the formative years of the Cowboys had a major impact on our ability to create links with sports clubs and communities throughout the world.

H 2010 marked the 10th anniversary of KIPTIK, a solidarity group set up by players and supporters from the The Easton Cowboys and Girls Sports Club to help provide materials and technical support for water and health projects in Zapatista communities in SE Mexico. Recent links with communities in Palestine, Lithuania, and Brazil have also spawned both political and social activities.

I We have had to turn one prospective policeman away on the basis it was "best for him and us." As far as I am aware, we have not had any problems with Christians (so far)! The motto was then expanded by some of the punk elements to *"No Jugglers, No Drummers"* in response to the perceived "hippy like" activities associated with the rave scene. This rule has (unfortunately, in the author's opinion) not been enforced.

J For example, many argue that problems of racism and racial prejudice cannot be effectively addressed by litigation and municipal government policy; they are problems that have to be resolved within communities, between people.

Roger Wilson was one of the founding members of the The Easton Cowboys and Girls Sports Club. Thanks to this happy meeting of minds, he has spent more than twenty years playing football, basketball, and cricket in England and around the world. He currently lives a double life in Bristol as an engineer and historian.

Other alternative clubs in Europe include the Lunatics FC of Antwerp, Belgium, and the FC Vova of Vilnius, Lithuania. Copenhagen's Christiania has is own team, the Christiania Sports Club. Denmark is also home to the FK Utopia. In Stockholm, a team called Socialistiska patientkollek-

tivet, named after the radical German Socialist Patients' Collective of the 1970s, played in the Sunday Leagues for several years. A classic among anarchist teams is Switzerland's FC Bakunin, which was a mainstay of the "Alternative League Zurich," founded in the 1970s. There are also teams like Germany's Rijkaard Jugend [Rijkaard Youth], named after Frank Rijkaard, who famously spat at Rudi Völler during the 1990 Men's World Cup encounter between the Netherlands and Germany, and Standard Alu, a Sunday League team from Hamburg that values hitting the cross bar over scoring (*alu* is short for *aluminium*). Another interesting German club is Roter Stern Leipzig [Red Star Leipzig], founded in 1999 by autonomous activists and today well-established as a left-wing sports club. Its success triggered a number of Roter Stern teams across Germany, which also organize an annual tournament, co-sponsored by the left-wing journal *Jungle World*—some of the more recent Red Star clubs have little to do with radical politics, however, pursuing a rather liberal course.

▌ The FC Vova: An Antifascist Football Club in Lithuania

Interview with Paulius Grigaitis

What can you tell us about the history of the FC Vova?
It all started in 2004. A few punks posted a message on the Lithuanian punk-hardcore site *hardcore.lt*, trying to organize a Sunday football match in Vilnius. When a crowd illegally gathered on the small pitch of a Christian school, the team was born.

We kept on playing and lots of different people showed up: boys, girls, Lithuanians, Russians, Poles. Climbing over the fence every time and playing the best game in the world united us. We started to play more regularly, and eventually we had our first match against a team from out of town: a punk rock squad from Kaunas. We won 7-0! (We later lost 1 8 in Kaunas, but no one remembers . . .).

Then we went to Tabuns, an open-air DIY festival in Latvia. We needed a name and after some discussion we decided to follow in the footsteps of bands that chose beautiful girls names, like Shora, Nora, and Bora. We ended up calling ourselves FC Vova after our goalkeeper at the time (who let in way too many balls but was very nice and entertaining). Under that name we made it to the quarterfinals at the Tabuns Festival, and we have used it since.

Later that year, we also played at the Zabadaks Festival in Latvia. After the games had been moved from Saturday to Sunday due to torrential rain, we won the tournament—thanks to a minor straight edge influence within the team, we were the only ones to show up in the morning!

Since the tournaments in Latvia had been fun, we organized our own tournament at Lithuania's Darom Festival in 2005 and 2006. The first year, we lost the final to our main rivals from Kaunus. The second year, the final was never played because the festival was shut down after problems with the local mafia, so we all had to go fight the fuckers.

When a Sunday Football League started in Vilnius in 2005, we decided to join after some consideration. We were able to raise the registration fee through a benefit show—with many bands that include FC Vova members: Va Taip Vat, Pendelis, Toro Bravo, Frekenbok, Dr. Green, Sloppy Livin'—and sponsorship from my sister Eglė. As with every decent sponsor, we carried her name on our shirts—we made really nice stencils.

Joining the league was the right decision. We made more friends and even our fans started to organize! Today, we have different fan clubs like Kosmos, BB United, and Voverės, an all-female group challenging the male dominance. We can have up to two hundred supporters at games and our fans are among the liveliest in Lithuania, and this includes professional teams!

The big problems with the Sunday League today are that it has vastly expanded, that the rules have been tightened, and that it has gotten much more competitive. As a consequence, it sometimes sucks to play, and we are wondering whether we should start a 100 percent DIY league, like some friends in Minsk did, the capital of Belarus. But for now we are still in the Vilnius Sunday League and we are trying to make the best of it.

We also continue to play tournaments, and thanks to many international contacts we have made, we have traveled quite far. We have joined big events like the Mondiali Antirazzisti in Italy, and we have traveled to Belarus, Sweden, Germany, Belgium, Holland, England, Spain, and even Brazil.

It is important to note that we are not just a sports group; the social aspect is very important! We've had players from various countries and with various backgrounds, and the team is always changing, which helps us all to become more open-minded. Awareness about racism and all forms of discrimination is very important—in football as much as in everyday life. Our slogan is: *Love Football—Hate Fascism!*

Can you tell us more about the DIY league in Minsk?
It started a few years ago and is called the "Belarus Antifa Football League." It contains eight 5-a-side clubs and there are games every weekend.

Are there other teams in Eastern Europe like FC Vova?
There are other teams that have players with punk and Antifa backgrounds. But they are all longtime football supporters. With the FC Vova, it is different, because we have our own supporters. In other words, we have been able to attract punks and activists who had never been interested in football before. And we—players and supporters—are really many. So I like to think that the FC Vova is a bit special . . .

Speaking of football supporters: are there many active left-wing football fans in Eastern Europe?
In post-Soviet countries the majority of football supporters—hooligans or Ultras—are right-wing. All supporters hate communism, mostly because of the history.

Also in Lithuania, most fan groups are right-wing or at least patriotic. But these days many want to leave politics behind and just want to focus on supporting their team.

In Belarus, the supporters of the biggest club, Dinamo Minsk, are almost all right-wing racists, while the supporters of the biggest rival, FC Partizan Minsk, either have a hardcore and Antifa background or are antiracist hooligans—they are doing good work.

It is similar in Ukraine, where Dynamo Kiev has a lot of right-wing support, while their rivals Arsenal have a stronger Antifa base.

I should also add that hardly any antifascist, antiracist, and anarchist supporter in Eastern Europe would use the term "left-wing." It usually refers to remnants of the state socialist regimes, and most activists want to clearly distance themselves from that. You can also see this in the symbols that are being used—no one here would run around in a Che Guevara shirt ...

Do you think that football can support radical politics?
Yes. I think that football is a big part of many people's lives, so it is a great political vehicle in many ways. It can also help you to meet like-minded people—and the more we come together, the stronger we will be.

Paulius Grigaitis is a founding member of the FC Vova. You can find him in the streets of Vilnius, in London squats, or in São Paulo favelas.

Many underground and grassroots football clubs meet every year at the Alternative World Cup. In 2010, it was organized by the Republica Internationale FC of Leeds.

The Alternative Football World Cup, Republica Internationale FC, and Socialist Football

Interview with Rob Cook and Mick Totten

What is the Alternative Football World Cup?
Rob: The Alternative World Cup is a tournament for members of a loose network of teams from across Europe, including Germany, Belgium, Poland, Lithuania, and UK—but this time may well include a team from Brazil, and one from the U.S. The teams are considered "like-minded" in general politics and values, but not all have an overtly political basis to them. There have been annual summer tournaments between many of these teams since at least 1998. The idea is to share our values whilst we play football together, drink together, and organise various entertainment, all in a space where people can meet up, and be as they want to be. I would characterise the mood and spirit far more as "anarchist" than "socialist" or other labels.

What motivated you to host it in 2010?
Rob: I think the single most motivating reason to host the tournament is a feeling that it's "our turn." Over the years the teams have supported each other morally and sometimes financially, so sharing the load is important. Lots of people from our club have enjoyed the benefits of the hard work put in by others in places such as Hamburg and Antwerp, and feel it's time that we did the same. Some have developed a strong vision of how our tournament would look and feel.

Can you tell us more about Republica Internationale?
Rob: Republica Internationale FC was formed in 1983. But initially it was called, I believe, Woodhouse Wanderers, then the Rising Sun, then

Moscow Central, then Republica Highland. We finally became Republica Internationale in about 2001, mostly so that we would have a name we were happy with and that we wouldn't have to change every time we moved to a new pub!

From the start it was an avowedly "socialist football club" which didn't want to take part in established clubs which they perceived as frequently racist and sexist. My understanding is that the club was formed by a group of men who wanted to play football, but football was initially casual, but fairly quickly the club formed a team in the Leeds Sunday League.

Mick: I agree that the club was very much politically oriented in the beginning. After a few years, when some older original players left and new people had to be recruited, the political commitments were harder to guarantee and among some were not as strong as before. This caused some misunderstandings, and we decided to draft a socialist "constitution," which, since then, all of our players have to sign up and abide to.

So since then, all members have been committed activists?
Mick: Not necessarily. Our club is a "broad church" with lots of different views. Sharing our views and co-education is important. For those with stronger formed politics it is important to consider what motivated us and where we got our views from. Remembering this allows the club to create opportunities for newer, less political members to be exposed to alternative ideas which can change their lives. The question of how much political commitment was expected from the members has been an issue since then as well, and we had people leave the club because of that.

Rob: I would see this as an on-going division within the club—it's always there, but only occasionally becomes a problem for people. I think

this is one of the perhaps inevitable problems of seeking to combine politics with a competitive, macho, tradition-based sport.

Does the majority of members fall into any particular political group or are they affiliated with any particular organisation? "Socialism" is a broad term ...
Rob: Indeed, there's a range of opinions about what this means and sometimes there is discussion around that. There are many members now, especially younger ones, for whom the actual word "socialist" means nothing, even if they share broadly similar "left wing" values. Is it important to retain the word, and try to explain it, or to use appropriate words "left wing," "internationalist" etc. that may attract more people? This is an on-going debate.

Has the wide range of opinions ever created any particular problems?
Mick: Not often. It's all part of a healthy democratic debate really. Except for the time the anarchist members refused to recruit players from the Socialist Workers Party ... as they perceived them as fascist-left.

How about the class background of your members?
Mick: It's very mixed. We have members who went to private schools and fancy universities, and members who have a very strong working-class background.

This has never created problems either?
Mick: Again, not really. I think it has actually helped people to overcome class differences by learning from each other and helping out one another in different ways.

   Rob: I feel it sometimes overlaps with discussions about the level of aggression in the men's game.

What were some of the milestones in the history of the club?
Mick: Things really changed in the late '90s, when we discovered that there were similar football clubs out there—for a long time we didn't know! So that's when we started to network more and travel for different tournaments.

   Rob: In 1998 we participated in the first Alternative World Cup, organised by the Easton Cowboys of Bristol. In 2001, we took part for the first time in Mondiali Antirazzisti in Italy. Soon after we built very strong links with Sankt Pauli in Hamburg. Club members have also been on tours in Chiapas (Mexico), playing football with Zapatista rebels, and taken part in football tours of Palestine. In 2001, there was also an influx of women, which had a big impact on the club. Women quickly got involved in all areas, and elected positions, and Republica rapidly became a genuinely mixed club.

Mick: Women quickly became even in numbers with men. And now are probably more dominant in key organising positions, especially amongst younger members.

Rob: In 2006 we won the Coppa Mondiali Antirazzisti, for our "anti-racist work throughout the year." This was a highly motivating experience for many of us involved, and led to new or strengthened relationships with other clubs and tournaments.

Can you tell us a little more about the political work you do as a club?
Rob: First of all, I'd like to mention the democratic structure. We elect a coordinating committee, currently of ten people, and football captains, vice-captains and secretaries, none of whom are committee members. We have full club meetings about three times a year, and a number of social events. We also have an "ethical fund"—a pool of money in a specific account which supports political and educational development, which can be used as a shared resource across the network, and which members can apply to (in order to go on a tour if they can't afford to, or to organise an event, for example), which furthers our values.

Over the years, we have regularly organised a May Day tournament, historically mostly for "like-minded" teams, but perhaps more recently with an attempt to make it more community-orientated we have also organised specific community tournaments at Hyde Park Unity Day and in connection with Leeds Together 4 Peace.

We have a history of supporting campaigns. For example, some of us did some work in the club about fair trade and other consumer issues. In about 2005 one of the results was to agree that the club will buy fair trade goods, including footballs, whenever possible, and will never buy from Nestlé, McDonald's, Nike or Coca-Cola. This was a good way of educating members about various global issues, and another way of bring- ing politics into the club.

We have played in the pink of the Justin Campaign, to combat homophobia in sport, and in Palestine football shirts in support of the people of Gaza. This season, our men's team wears a shirt with the logo and slogan of the White Ribbon Campaign, which aims at men working to end men's violence against women. We intend to do something similar, perhaps for a variety of campaigns, each time we need a new kit.

Some club members have also regularly taken part in anti-fascist leafleting around Leeds, especially in the run-up to elections.

In 2009, we started running a monthly meeting called "The Left Wing," in which someone presents a specific issue in order to share information and educate others, and discuss individual and club political values and positions.

Apart from the "football vs. politics" debate you mentioned, what are other problems you've encountered?
Rob: There is from time to time a split, and can be heated discussion, about the extent to which it's OK, or even important, to be macho and aggressive on the pitch in the men's game, despite our values and constitution.

What do you mean by being "macho and aggressive" on the pitch?
Mick: Sunday League football in England can get pretty rough, especially men's, where aggression and violence are quite normal. So one question is: how do you respond to aggressiveness from the opposite team? Are you gonna let them get away with it, or do you respond in kind? Another question is when it comes within our own team? There have been different approaches and opinions within the club. Maybe that's also one of the issues where class does play a role. Our working-class players seem often more used to rough encounters in life and on the pitch and their reactions can differ from those with other values or those who have a more middle-class background. This can cause conflict.

How can football help us in pursuing principles of justice and equality?
Rob: The most obvious way that football can do this is that it brings people together by being "the universal game" (even if that is not entirely accurate). There's a fair chance that, as long as you're not too shy, you can join in a casual game of football anywhere in the world. This can bring down barriers. Also locally: in a tournament we organised in October 2009, a team of white "settled" children from a community in South Leeds played against a team of Gypsy and Traveller children. They were from a similar area of Leeds, but they'd never played each other before, and almost certainly held various prejudices about each other. They said afterwards that they may play each other again.

For me, football is a tool for pursuing social justice and equality. There are many such tools. Football happens to be an important one because it is so universal and popular. It can be used as "a way in" to so many different issues. I have seen it be empowering for numerous women in the club, many of whom have never played football before. It has brought many club members into contact with issues and people they have never come across before.

To me, it's important to acknowledge that while football can be used extremely positively for social change, this is by no means inevitable.

For example, I am frustrated by the macho and aggressive attitudes that persist in male football, even within our club, and the anger that is often created in connection to football. So at my worse times I feel that trying to work within football for social change is delusional, and it can feel like colluding with male violence and aggression, rather than challenging it.

Football also divides people. As such, it can also be a tool for people who seek to create division. For example, over the last year a far-right organisation called the English Defence League has deliberately timed demonstrations to be in cities when particular football matches are happening, as they recognise that they can rely on their supporters, and potential supporters, to be in that city that day. This is also strongly linked to the use of football to foment nationalism. For me, and many other people, this can make us very reluctant and passive supporters of the England football team.

Is this true for all of your members?
Mick: No, there is variety. In general, the more politically involved you are, the more critical you are of the nationalism involved in support-ing the English team. But "nationalism" in itself is a contested political issue, so there's a variety of takes. And some believe "Englishness" can be reclaimed from the far-right. Besides, we have a number of Irish and Scottish members (as well as other nationalities), and their perspectives are different too; because of historical oppression by the English and the sense of resistance through celebrating indigenous Celtic culture.

What is your perception of the professional game? Do you follow it at all?
Rob: I personally watch a certain amount of professional football on TV, but I no longer go to matches. I enjoy good football, but feel very uncom-fortable with the hatred and tribalism that is so often expressed by fans at matches. There is far less racism than there used to be when I was watching football in the 70s, but there is still a great deal of hostility. It is also incredibly expensive now to go to matches. I have very little interest in the media circus that follows every utterance of footballers and managers. For me, this has nothing to do with football, but only with the obsession with "celebrity."

My overall perception is that modern professionals are mostly extremely out of touch with the communities that idolise them and that they nominally represent. One day, if the trend continues, I believe this link will be broken, and there will be a real crisis for football. Vast money comes from television, and television needs people at the grounds, or the atmosphere of the matches is poor, and the whole experience of watching on TV would be radically worsened, so less people would watch, and the TV money would dry up. In many ways I would love that to happen!

As a club we have become less interested—we used, for example, to organise an annual event to coincide with watching the FA Cup final on TV. This has gone. When we come back to the pub from training, or a game, there is often a live match on TV, but many members pay little or no attention to it. I think there is also a gender divide on this issue. I know that several of the women players, even those who are very good players, have no interest at all in watching professional football.

Mick: Many members support Sankt Pauli and are regular visitors there because it's so uniquely anti-capitalist and some reject mainstream British support altogether in favour of Sankt Pauli.

What is your vision for football in a socialist society?

Rob: Now that's a big question! I have to say first that I don't foresee a socialist society coming around any time soon, so it's pretty academic.

I think the best way for me to see it is to focus on the good things of football. It's physical exercise, cheap and easy to play, pretty well anyone can do it, you can develop creativity and team spirit, and it can bring people together across huge barriers. That's all about the importance of "grassroots" football, and casual "parks" football. I would love to see that continually encouraged and developed. This could be through schools, and through increased access to resources (such as goalposts). But similarly to how I feel that football is just one tool, it is also not necessarily the best or only sporting activity that should be promoted in a socialist society. It is simply the most prominent one now.

I definitely do not think that it's a positive thing for a state—whether "socialist" or otherwise—to co-opt football. This is always very tempting for states to do, and may produce champions, but probably always mitigates against the sort of positive grassroots and casual play that I've mentioned.

Mick: For me, football will always be corrupted in capitalist society. But it's different elsewhere, like sport in general in Cuba. So football in its essence is mostly about community organisation and collective values, which can act as resistance under capitalism but as a foundation of civil society as part of Socialism. For me, playing the game is socialism. It's about the collective organisation and will of the majority triumphing over the contribution of any individual. It's a great metaphor for socialism.

Rob Cook and Mick Totten have been longtime members of Republica Internationale FC. Rob has worked in various roles promoting social justice in the voluntary sector in Leeds over the last twenty-five years, including in community development, fair trade, development education, and mental health. Mick has worked in community sport, community art, and education promoting the politicization and use of recreation for community development.

Constitution of the Republica Internationale FC

This Club recognises and supports the values of Socialism. Its members are committed to the promotion of Socialist ideas and actions. The following principles govern the Club's journey. There are about 100 teams that play in the Leeds Sunday Leagues. As far as we are aware ours is the only team playing under such a Constitution. Our uniqueness is precious and will be defended fiercely!

The club will not tolerate racist, homophobic, sexist, prejudicial, or abusive behaviour by any of its members.

The game should be played in good sporting spirit.

Whilst committed to the rigour of hard physical, competitive sport, players will not behave in an unacceptably aggressive or violent way.

Players should play in a camaraderie spirit of a team, co-operatively advise each other in a positive manner and never offer purely negative criticism.

Players should recognise that the game is played, first and foremost, for fun!

In Brazil, it is the Autônomos FC of São Paulo that has become the flagship of a radical football counterculture.

VAMÔ, VAMÔ... VAMÔ, VAMÔ...
VAMÔ, VAMÔ... TORCIDA AUTÔNOMA!

Football in Latin America and the Autônomos FC

Interview with Danilo Cajazeira

How important is football for everyday life in Latin America?
In almost all of Latin America—with the exception of countries where it isn't the most popular sport, like Venezuela or Cuba—we can say that football is perhaps the only thing that still belongs, at least in some way, to the people. It defines the only public field where all can have a say and an opinion that is no less important than that of the "specialists." Football has political importance for people's life. Organized supporters' groups can often put stronger pressure on the government than political interest groups. They also have a lot of experience in fighting the police . . .

Football is everywhere on the continent: from the poorest to the richest neighborhoods. But, as with everything in capitalism, football is more and more turned into exclusive entertainment for the elite. Everything is done to keep the poor from the stadiums. In countries with a long tradition of people fighting for their rights, this process meets many obstacles because supporters resist; but in other countries—like in Brazil, where people believe media claims that commercialization will make us a part of the First World—people behave in the way that good consumers are supposed to. As a consequence, football is increasingly disappearing from everyday life and turning into a televised spectacle. The participation of the people becomes reduced to discussing games the morning after.

How did the game develop historically? In Europe, football is often seen as a traditional working-class sport but this has changed through commercialization. How does this compare to Latin America?
The game was brought to Latin America by immigrants and by Latin American students who had spent some time in Europe. It first arrived in Argentina und Uruguay, where its development resembled that of Europe. It went from an elitist game played at private schools with a center on individual performance to being a collectively oriented people's game with a focus on passing and controlling the ball. In Brazil, football arrived later, and it was picked up by people in a different way: it was played on the streets and on the fields and dribbling was key. That's why you have two different schools of football in Latin America: the "passing game" vs. the "dribbling game."

To a large degree, football has always been a DIY affair in Latin America. Not because there was any such notion, but because people had to do everything themselves for football to exist: find a place to play, create teams, organize tournaments, and so on. For amateur teams, this is still the case. Poverty means finding ways to get by and it teaches people the values of solidarity. Historically, all over Latin America football clubs were the first public institutions that people actively got to participate in.

The development of professionalism has an ironic touch: it was the successful poor clubs that profited the most and drove the rich clubs out of business. The poor clubs became strong because they had many more players to pick from than the clubs who only chose players from affluent communities; besides, most poor clubs allowed black players at a time when this was a taboo for the rich. Professional football also seemed a promising way out of poverty, so there was a stronger economic incentive among the poor. The clubs of the poor also attracted larger crowds. In the end, we can say that it was poverty that made them succeed in professional football and that caused the rich clubs to disappear. However, it lies in the nature of competitive sports that only a few clubs can become truly successful, so many of the poorer clubs suffered under professionalism as well. Some had to fold completely as more and more football grounds gave way to factories during Brazil's industrialization.

How has football been used by the political powers on the continent?
Every dictatorship in Latin America has used the game for its interests. In Brazil, the victory at the 1970 World Cup was a big propaganda coup

for the military regime. It was even worse when the Argentineans won the 1978 World Cup. The victories had its contradictions, though: both times, the managers who had prepared the teams came from the left! João Saldanha, the Brazilian manager in 1970, was fired just before the World Cup started; César Luis Menotti, the Argentinean manager in 1978, was allowed to stay. Reportedly, he told his players before the final: "We aren't playing for the military generals in the stadium. We are playing for every worker of this country, for every missing person, and for every mother who has lost her child!"

Latin American governments tried to control all aspects of football early on. In Brazil, laws were created that made self-organization difficult. For example, players were forced to sign their names onto score sheets. But a huge part of the population was illiterate! The fact that such laws led to late-night literacy campaigns in improvised schools set up by football clubs is a striking example for the DIY character of the sport and the solidarity it created.

The rich always tried to manipulate the sport as well. When their teams were less and less successful, they started their own leagues—never with any success. They also joined forces to found the São Paulo FC, a club closely tied to powerful politicians and responsible for some of the most bizarre episodes in Brazilian football: once, the Governor of São Paulo state, who also happened to be the president of the São Paulo FC, arrived in a helicopter in the middle of a game to talk to the referee!

Nowadays, political control, economic exploitation, and consumerism strongly overlap. The media has turned the lives of professional players, referees, managers, and presidents into soap operas, endlessly reporting about their personal affairs. It's all about inventing drama to make money. Of course football is still exploited politically in very direct ways as well: politicians support certain teams to boost their campaigns, they promise sponsorship and new pitches for amateur teams, etc.

Has football also been a medium for dissidents and revolutionaries?
In many ways. In the beginning, communists and anarchists were against the game, saying that it divided the working class by pitting workers against workers. But with the game growing so rapidly, they noticed that it had the potential to unite people. Communist and anarchist teams were created. Some of the professional clubs that exist in Argentina, Brazil, and Uruguay today were originally founded by communists and anarchists. Many amateur teams have the same history. For example, there are several teams in São Paulo with the name May 1. In Uruguay, there was even an anarchist league in the 1920s called Federación Roja del Deporte [Red Sports Federation]; it included teams like La Comuna, Soviet, Libertad, Leningrado, Guardia Roja, etc.

Today, the Zapatistas use football as a tool of resistance and political propaganda. They frequently approach professional clubs with requests to play against them, putting the clubs' slogans of "solidarity" and "anti-racism"—often little more than cheap campaigns—to the test.

What do you think of professional managers and players who profess to left-wing ideas, like César Luis Menotti or Diego Maradona?
It's a complex issue. But I'd much rather have them than the jerks running FIFA or the Latin American football associations! Maradona has really become an icon for left-wing football fans, even in Brazil—Pelé, for example, never did any good for the people outside of the pitch. It helps when folks like Menotti and Maradona speak out about left-wing issues, even if it's all a bit contradictory.

In the 1980s in Brazil, we saw the perhaps biggest left-wing experiment ever in professional football. We were still living under the military dictatorship when some players of Corinthians, the most popular club in São Paulo, initiated the so-called "Corinthians Democracy." The initiative was also supported by their coach and the club's management. All decisions concerning the team—from the players to be signed to the salaries being paid—were made democratically. The club also participated in demonstrations against the dictatorship and promoted democracy in its journal and even on its jerseys. Mandatory pre-game hotel accommodation was abolished, returning autonomy and responsibility to players who were often treated like children.

The Corinthians won the São Paulo State Championships twice in a row and got international recognition. Meanwhile, they were frantically attacked by the Brazilian media, and even by some other players. The movement ended when two of the most influential figures left in 1984: Sócrates, who had announced that he would leave Brazil if democracy was not reestablished, went to Italy, and Casagrande went to play for São Paulo FC.

During the few years of Corinthians Democracy, the club not only gained moral prestige, it was also able to sort out its financial problems. To this day, no similar experiment has been conducted—at least not on this scale.

Almost all of the team's players are still politically active—unfortunately, some have become professional politicians ...

How about radicals who write about football, like Osvaldo Bayer and Eduardo Galeano?
Galeano is awesome! I always say that Galeano's books should be compulsory reading for kids in football schools! Bayer is great too. Both manage to attract a radical as well as a mainstream audience.

I think that intellectuals in general have much to contribute to sports, since sports can be a revolutionary way of changing society. Of course Galeano and Bayer have no influence on the actual management of football clubs, but they inspire people to resist the tendencies that turn football from a game into a business. We don't want to consume football, we want football to be ours! It was ours before capitalism took it away.

Tell us about Autônomos FC. When was the club founded? What are its ambitions?

Autônomos FC was founded in May 2006 by a bunch of punks who were tired of other punks questioning their passion for football and of football fans questioning their passion for punk. We thought it'd be easiest to simply blend both; we figured that the passion for DIY punk mixed with the passion for football could only make us stronger. We had experience from playing 5-a-side DIY tournaments. When Autônomos was officially founded, we first played against 7-a-side teams in the city of São Paulo. Over time, more and more people joined because of our open structure and our communal decision-making processes, and we changed to an 11-a-side team, playing the "real game."

We were never an exclusively "anarchist" team, but always a "self-managed" one. There was never a need to put our principles into writing because we were always assured of them: anti-racism, anti-homophobia, anti-merchandise, solidarity, self-management. Active participation in the affairs of the club is as important as football skills. Self-management is not always easy. It demands everyone's dedication and responsibility.

The club's ambition was to play football and to spread the message that if everyone can play football, everyone can participate in the development of society. Now that we have grown, we think about bigger things, like having our own pitch and maybe writing a journal. Today, we have two 11-a-side men's teams and one 5-a-side women's team, and at every game more people show up.

After an anarchist news agency from São Paulo State had come to interview us, we were able to get in touch with more left-wing people who see revolutionary potential in the sport. I hope that Autônomos can one day contribute to changing both football and society—at least in São Paulo. How? Don't ask! We have no program. We find our way day by day ...

Are there similar clubs in Latin America?

I don't know of any other club in Latin America that works in the same way. Some political groups have football teams. In São Paulo, for example, the communist students had a team called Máquina Vermelha, which means "Red Machine." We have played against them, it was fun.

I am always looking for other Latin America clubs like ours, because I would love to organize an Alternative World Cup, like the one that's organized every year in Europe. Maybe we can call that the big ambition of Autônomos FC. In fact, I recently found out about the Club Social, Atletico y Deportivo Ernesto "Che" Guevara in Argentina! We have already discussed to arrange a meeting, to exchange experiences, and to organize an Alternative South America Cup!

You mentioned the political power of football supporters' groups in Latin America. Are some of them decidedly left-wing? Is there an equivalent to the European Ultra movement?
There is one faction among Corinthians supporters, the Movimento Rua São Jorge, which is left-wing and critical of modern football. They try to organize an association for different supporters' groups to defend their interests and they have strong links with Via Campesina and the MST, Brazil's Landless Workers' Movement, which is probably the major social movement in the country. Corinthians' major supporters' group was founded by left-wing university students in the 1960s, but it would be a stretch to call it left-wing today.

As far as Ultras go, there is at least one group, the Ultras Resistência Coral; they support Ferroviário AC, a Brazilian team from Ceará State. But there isn't any Ultra movement as such, there are rather groups that know about Ultras and admire them—often, however, mainly the violence.

How do you think that football can contribute to a better world?
Football, as I see it, reflects life. You find—at least metaphorically—all aspects of life in the game. It's the modern version of Ancient Greek theatre: it involves drama, individual contribution, collective contribution, and people rising from the bottom of society, overcoming all obstacles. Football teaches us many important things about life, even in its competitive aspect: the winner never crushes the loser for good. Football, like life, is cyclical: today's defeat becomes tomorrow's victory. We are never done!

Furthermore, at a time when everything has become ephemeral, football retains its geographical and historical power: it ties identities to places, and it teaches us that history is made by everybody, everyday. Football builds on this history, an *oral* history. I learned about the past of my team from older people, and I feel that this past is also mine.

If you add up all these aspects, it is easy to see how football can be revolutionary. Instead of dividing people, it brings them together. Of course we can't ignore the fights and the deaths caused by football supporters around the world. But this is a result of capitalism; it is an expression of capitalist competition. In a world where every place is your place, where you don't have to fear losing it to another person, the kind of hatred leading to such incidents is impossible. The problem is much bigger than football. In fact, football can open up ways to a different world: it has a few very simple and easily understood rules, it can be played everywhere and requires very little material, and it is open to everyone. It is the only sport in the world where a much worse team can beat a supposedly undefeatable team—and in the next game, everything changes again. As I said, football is like life: what happened can't be changed and becomes history, but from history we can learn and we can proceed to new things. And we can do this *together* with our rivals on the football field: we can grow with them instead of fighting them. This might sound romantic, but I refuse to live without romance.

Danilo Cajazeira is a geographer, teacher, anarchist, Corinthians supporter, and founding member of Autônomos FC. He lives in São Paulo.

In North America, there have been a few Anarchist Soccer Leagues and the Anarchist Football Association in the Midwest of the United States. Among radical soccer clubs are Chicago's Black and Red Football, the San Francisco Bay Area's Kronstadt FC, and Austin's Texas Anti-Border(s) Patrol. Soccer competitions have also included teams like the Riot Soccer Club, Maknovist City, Emma Goldman Anarchist Feminist Club, and Dynamo Kropotkin. In many cities across the United States and Canada, anarchists get together for games of soccer regularly.

■ Soccer Teams Go on a Revolutionary Kick: Communists Play Anarchists in Berkeley

SF Gate, September 15, 2003
Tanya Schevitz

In some ways, the soccer game played in North Berkeley Sunday afternoon was a typical matchup with cheerleaders, hearty competition, a rousing band and proud parents on the sidelines.

But the anarchists vs. the communists soccer match veered off pretty quickly from there.

The Brass Liberation Orchestra, a patchwork band of musicians, played everything from saxophones to drums and a tuba, getting the crowd going with a lively rendition of "Internationale," an anthem of communists and socialists, while players jumped up and down and raised their fists in the air.

The cheerleaders chanting "Give me an A, A, A for Anarchy," wore black motorcycle boots and fashioned their pom-poms from strips of a black garbage bag. One shimmied into a makeshift black skirt—and because of the cold, donned a friend's black pullover, which she said reeked of the puke-like smell of aged spilled beer.

Instead of advertising, the sign on the sidelines of Gabe's East field was painted half black for the anarchists and half red for the communists, reading "For a World Without Borders. For a World Without Bombs."

And there was gloating at the game—over the collapse of the World Trade Organization talks.

But the idea behind the game was a noble one, players said: to bring people together from across the political spectrum to build a community around the values they share—and to have fun, of course.

The two teams were born from the protests against the war in Iraq earlier this year. Many of the soccer players had protested in the streets together during the days before and after the start of the war and they wanted to make sure they stayed together.

"There is a history of political tension between the anarchists and the communists, but we are united on our opposition to U.S. wars abroad and at home on poor people, working people, people of color," said Chris Crass, 29, of San Francisco, a member of the anarchist team and an organizer of anti-racist and political workshops.

And so, the activists—men, women and even a six-year-old boy—settled on the creation of two teams.

The anarchist team, Kronstadt FC, was named for the 1921 revolt of workers of the Kronstadt army base against the Communist government in Russia. The players wore black T-shirts with the insignia of an A with a circle around it, a black star and a soccer ball.

The communist team, Left Wing, sported shiny jerseys in Communist red, of course, with a fist holding a flag with a red star.

There were players from various organizations across the Bay Area, from the San Francisco Women Against Rape to SOUL, a youth organizing group, and the Campaign for Renters Rights.

Sunday's game was actually the second match.

The first game, held Aug. 17 in Piedmont, tied 2-2 after it was shut down by local officials because the teams were playing on the field without permission.

Anarchist Soccer Rules

The Austin Chronicle, June 9, 2006
Diana Welch

Let's get one thing straight about anarchism: Though there is little doubt that those who call themselves anarchists want to drastically change the way the world is run, they're not a bunch of black-clad nihilists plotting their way toward chaos. At the most basic, anarchism (derived from the Greek "without ruler") is the belief that an anti-authoritarian society based on mutual aid and self-governance is not only preferable to what we've got now to what we've got now, but also a viable alternative. Not surprisingly, the folks in charge of "what we've got now" don't exactly cotton to that idea, and anarchism has long been given a bad rap. Recently, local groups associated with anarchism got a scare when it was revealed to a UT law class that Food Not Bombs and Austin Indymedia—two examples of everyday folks creating parallel structures outside of state-sponsored society—were considered worthy of inclusion [on] the FBI's Central Texas "Terrorist Watch List." (Immediately following the incident, spokespeople for the FBI, both local and national, claimed they weren't aware of any such list, though UT student Elizabeth Waggoner wrote a detailed recounting of Special Agent Charles Rasner's presentation to her class on ... Austin Indymedia!)

With that sort of heat, one wouldn't necessarily expect local anarchists to gather in public parks thrice weekly for a friendly game of soccer. But, in an attempt to bridge the gap between alternative and mainstream social groups, gather they do. According to a 33-year-old anarcho-athlete named Simon, the Sunday games at the Rosewood Recreation Center are best for newcomers to attend, regularly attracting anywhere from 45 to 70 folks of varying ages, genders, ethnicities, and skill levels. "Everyone compliments everyone else, even if it's someone on the opposing team who has made a great play," Simon says of the anarchist model of competitive sportsmanship. "And, it's not like people are running around with the ball in their hands. On the field, there are rules. Just no rulers."

It is from this weekly phenomenon of people playing friendlylike that Austin's anarchist soccer team, the Texas Anti-Border(s) Patrol, formed. This July, the TABP will head to the 10th annual Mondiali Antirazzisti (Anti-Racist World Cup) in Montecchio, Italy, the first team from the Americas to do so.

"A central part of the Anti-Racist World Cup is to share information on local struggles," says Cale Layton, an organizer of the upcoming Anarchist Soccer Movie Screening and Fundraiser at MonkeyWrench Books. "We're planning on bringing a multimedia presentation on the Minutemen and the increasing xenophobia in the U.S., and we're asking people in Austin to [come] share their ideas on what we should present about these issues." Though the players will be paying their own way to and from the Mondiali, this outdoor screening of the documentary Football and Fascism (with beer!) hopes to raise money for the team's print materials, which will be shared with 192 teams from all over the world, including Albania, Germany, Burkina Faso, Cameroon, Czech Republic, Ukraine, Israel, Switzerland, and the United Kingdom.

Giving Hegemony a Red Card: Anarchist Soccer Club Takes Sports Beyond Winning and Losing

The McGill Daily, September 14, 2009
Anna Leocha

Wednesday nights in the northeast corner of Parc Notre Dame de Grace, wedged between Cote St. Antoine and Girouard just north of the dog run, Alex Megelas waits patiently on a tuft of grass for followers (read: enthusiasts) of what he has termed his Anarchist Soccer Club. Through a particularly non-hierarchical version of soccer, the club aims to combat "the discriminatory practices that are often part of organized sports...such as sexism, homophobia, and machismo."

Essentially, the Anarchist Soccer Club eradicates the hierarchy that normally exists in organized sports by stripping the game of its traditional rules. This means no score keeping, no boundaries, no team captains, and no hands (Psych! Handballs are totally allowed!). Anything and everything is allowed, except for aggressive behaviour and bad-attitudes—which Megelas explains you are able to "call people out on." Teams are picked using a number system (1, 2, 1, 2) and tend to be very flexible. Players sub in for people who aren't on their "team," and because rest/socializing/Gatorade breaks are frequent, teams tend to morph and be modified as the night goes on.

Though it may seem all fun-and-games, the Anarchist Soccer Club is righteously attributed to a specific set of values. By utilizing the highly connotative term "anarchist," the club has politicized the sport of soccer, in reaction to the discrimination they see in sports, and the divisive sentiments that organized sports can foster (i.e. "I love this team because it is mine; I hate this team because it is not mine"). With this in mind, people join the club because it is a space where they know they will feel safe and understood. Most importantly, it is a space where they can truly enjoy themselves and the game of soccer without having to worry about inequity.

"I come because it's fun and the people are friendly," says Ovidiu, a seventeen-year-old from NDG who has been playing with the club for only two weeks. "It's more fun than playing with people who are serious, and it's better than having to pay money for a team."

Ovidiu's group included two other local teenage boys and an eight-year-old, the younger brother of one of Ovidiu's friends. Part of the openness of the program includes accepting all age groups. On Wednesday nights, it's perfectly normal to see a fifteen-year-old playing with—never against—a fifty-year-old.

Some participants don't even like soccer. According to Layla AbdelRahim, a self-proclaimed anarchist, organized sports are restrictive and thus violent, limiting the body's potential to enjoy other sorts of pleasure. AbdelRahim appreciates the Anarchist Soccer Club's relaxed, congenial ethos, while whole-heartedly embracing the program's implicit disorder. She goes to let her young daughter run around and to build relationships with people she describes as "exploding with good energy and chaos ."

The question is: Do sports have the unbounded potential to bring disparate groups together in harmony? Megelas and his crew think not. The World Cup is a spectacle; the Olympics are a capitalist commodity. International sporting events aren't capable of bridging significant gaps. But within the local community, the Anarchist Soccer Club is proof that peace, love, and understanding can be as integral to the game of soccer as that little black-and-white orb. You've heard it before, people: "It's not about winning or losing—it's about having fun."

Numerous grassroots football tournaments of interest for radicals have been organized, some of them as annual events, some for a number of years, some as one-timers. A fairly random international selection includes the Antifascist Football Tournament in Toruń, Poland, the Antifa Soccer Cup in Lünen, Germany, the *Dai un calcio al razzismo* [Kick Racism] festival in Udine, Italy, Matches and Mayhem in Chicago, the Uprising tournament in New York City, the Anti-Racism World Cup in Belfast, Northern Ireland, the Poor People's World Cup in Cape Town, South Africa, and the *Frihetliga Fotbollscupen* [Libertarian Football Cup] in Stockholm, Sweden.

Stockholm's "Libertarian Football Cup"

Interview with Jan-Åke Eriksson

What is Stockholm's "Libertarian Football Cup"?
The Libertarian Football Cup is an enormously unorganized affair, in which the winner wins the dubious privilege of organizing next year's event. This means that some years are great, and others—well, not that great. But I guess that's part of the charm.

Do you know much about the history of the event? Where does the idea come from?
Not really sure. The first cup was organized in 1989 by the people who edited the anarchist journal *Brand*. Why they wanted to do it, I have no clue.

I first participated in 1994. At the time, it was all very much about beer and punk. Many people played in Doc Marten's boots. About seven or eight years ago, the tournament became more serious, Sunday League teams showed up, and the games became rather competitive—which took away from the festival atmosphere and the joy a bit.

You've been involved in organizing the event in recent years. Is there anything that's of particular importance to you?
I've been part of the organizing group for two years now, and I have tried to get some of the original spirit back. Sunday League teams are no longer allowed, the players must be in some way connected to the extra-parliamentary left, and there have to be both men and women on each team.

Why do people from the extra-parliamentary left meet for a soccer tournament?
I believe—or hope!—that we all share certain basic values. Political work, demonstrations, protests, boycotts, and fights with the police, neo-Nazis, sexists, and other scum can be very demanding. That's why I think that meeting for non-political activities is important.

Can football help the left in general?
Certainly. To have fun, to dance, to fool around, and to play football strengthens community. And that, in turn, helps left-wing politics.

Jan-Åke Eriksson lives in a collective house in Stockholm and works as a photographer for the syndicalist weekly *Arbetaren* [The Worker]. He is also a wicked goalkeeper.

Radical soccer tournaments have also taken place at political protests. In Japan, the Rage Football Collective (RFC) arranged the Anti-G8 Football Cup during the resistance against the G8-meeting in Hokkaidō in 2008.

▋ Interview with Tokyo's Rage Football Collective (RFC)

What is the Rage Football Collective?

The Rage Football Collective was established in 2008 while we were busy preparing protests against the G8 summit held that year in Toyako, Hokkaido, in the northern part of Japan. Some football fans who had met at political rallies and demonstrations launched a mailing list to discuss what we could do against the summit, and the list grew to about eighty people. The idea was to use football to communicate with the protesters who would gather at the G8 and to protest the globalization of capitalism.

So you organized games during the G8?

We had one international football session at Toyama Park in Tokyo, and another one at the anti-G8 Tobetsu camp in Toyako. In Tokyo, about forty people showed up, half of them activists from overseas: there were players from Korea, Malaysia, Australia, the Basque Country, France, Germany, the U.S., the UK, etc. At both events, Japanese and non-Japanese activists, regardless of their football skills, had a great time. We organized the games according to less competitive, "anarchist" ideas, like mixing sides etc.

The G8 summit was two years ago, the RFC still exists—what have you been doing since?

Although the anti-G8 movement gave us the opportunity to create the RFC, our goal was not limited to the event. Our vision was to work daily for the creation of alternative spaces for sports in Japan, especially football. Politically and ideologically, sports in Japan, including football, have been dominated by nationalist and capitalist interests. We wanted to create spaces for people who oppose the status-quo.

Although the age of the people on our mailing list ranges from twenty to about forty-five, the core group falls into the so-called "lost generation" of Japan: people in their late twenties and early thirties who have been facing a difficult work situation in a stagnant economy. So, apart from playing football, we have been active in various fields: organizing unions for precarious workers; anti-war and anti-military activism; anti-nuclear movements, anti-globalization; support for homeless people, immigrants, and indigenous people; anti-poverty activities; anti-death penalty; gender/alternative family movements; alternative economies; community spaces, etc. The list is long.

As of May 2010, we're especially involved in the protest against the "Nikezation" of Myashita Park, a small but culturally famous park in Tokyo's Shibuya district. Nike and the Shibuya municipal government decided—without any public consent—to turn this public park into a *Nike Park*, charging a high entrance fee. Football lovers, skateboarders, street musicians, wannabe actors, students, homeless people, and mothers with prams will all be kicked out. We have staged mini-football matches several times in protest.

We've also been playing matches with a Japanese homeless football team, "Nobushi [Stray Samurai] Japan," which joined the Homeless World Cup for the first time in 2009. The Nobushi team is organized by homeless people and a supporters' group related to the *Big Issue* magazine.

We also did a workshop at the Cultural Typhoon Festival in 2009, discussing the potentials of football as a form of resistance. We ended up playing "anarchist" games, open to anyone who was there: street vendors, people who walked their dogs, kids from the neighborhood—we played for more than three hours, and we will be back at the Cultural Typhoon Festival in 2010!

In general, we use our mailing list both to coordinate football games and to exchange political ideas. Our games are never restricted to people on the list. We often play with immigrant kids, and passers-by are always welcome!

The biggest and best-known of the annual get-togethers of progressive and radical football fans and players is the *Mondiali Antirazzisti* (Antiracist World Cup), an event that has been held every year in Reggio Emilia, Italy, since 1997. Today, it has reached legendary status among left-wing football supporters.

Mondiali Antirazzisti—the "Antiracist World Cup"

Interview with Carlo Balestri

Can you tell us about the history of the Mondiali Antirazzisti? What were the intentions behind the event?

The idea was born in 1997. We were mainly looking for an innovative way to counter the racism that was prevalent all over Europe at the time. We wanted to contribute to an antiracist presence in football stadiums, but we also wanted to work directly with migrants, getting a sense for the daily

problems they were facing. We wanted to dismantle stereotypes about Ultras, who were all seen as racists, *and* about migrants, who were all seen as illegals with criminal intentions. The Mondiali was the idea we came up with—it seemed like a natural way to combine the two.

Judging from the event's success, the idea we had wasn't so bad. Part of the success also came from the informal channels of communication that spread the word. This has brought new people to the Mondiali and has extended its target audience, while the original idea always remained the same.

Speaking of the Mondiali's success: what are its most important aspects?
As far as making the Mondiali a laboratory for the fight against racism is concerned—and this is not reduced to the actual tournament but extends to projects that are conceived there—I think that it went beyond anything that we could have ever imagined. Today, the Mondiali has become a central event for antiracist activism in Europe.

Needless to say, our ultimate goal is to see an Antiracist World Cup become unnecessary because there is no more racism. However, it will still take some time to get there . . .

Can you give us a short impression of teams that play at the Mondiali?
This is no easy task. We have always aimed at a diversity of people and this is reflected in the teams. However, we have seen some trends over the years. For example, the age of the participants has decreased and youth culture has become an obvious feature—although we still have players in their sixties! During the last few years, the participation of Ultra groups has also gone down a bit, while there are more teams coming from anti-racist organizations. The numbers of players from migrant communities are also increasing. We try to adjust the tourna-ment's structure every year to the participants. This year we had 204 teams . . .

Despite the diversity, I suppose it's the fight against racism that all share as a vision . . .
Yes. And the fight against discrimination in general. Of course some participants are much more active than others. There are some teams that mainly focus on the fun aspect of the Mondiali. But we try to get everyone involved in the values

of the event as deeply as possible.

What is the role that football can play in our communities from a progressive perspective?
Football is a universal language. It is a way of communicating that knows no language bar-

rier and that transgresses many physical barriers as well. At the Mondiali, the priority is not competition, but building relationships. The football that is played is a football of flexibility, meaning that no one will be excluded from the game, no matter the skill level.

Do you think that there is a strong divide between the professional, commercialized game and what we might call a "grassroots football movement?"
I think there is a big divide, even if amateur football often tries to emulate the professional game. At the Mondiali, we try to counter this tendency. We want to strengthen football as a model of integration and communication. In fact, a fair number of teams who have come to play have changed their attitude as a result of our efforts.

What is your future vision for the Mondiali Antirazzisti—and for football in general?
The hope for the Mondiali is to create a sort of "Social Forum for Sports": a place where ideas of social change can be developed through participating in various types of sports as well as in cultural events and workshops. All of this has to be organized on a grassroots level and without hierarchies. People have to find common ways and they have to exchange experiences.

As far as football in general goes, the current system creates a strict division between a few big clubs that become globally televised phenomena and the rest. The latter will only have one chance to survive: they must reconnect with their fans by allowing them to participate in the management. To me, this is the only possible future for football. The current system will not last.

Carlo Balestri is a co-founder and organizer of the Mondiali Antirazzisti and active in the fan initiative Progetto Ultrà.

On a final note, the Swiss activists of "Brot & Aktion" [Bread and Action] proved particularly innovative on the occasion of the 2008 Men's European Championship: from July 4 to 6, 2008, they occupied Zurich's Hardturm Stadium to celebrate "Brotaektschen," a three-day people's sports festival "without sponsoring and security forces."[98]

Football for Radicals

Competitiveness and How to Play the Game

One of the most critiqued aspects of soccer from a left-wing perspective is its competitiveness. No matter the level, the values, or the political consciousness involved, there are winners and losers in football. How do radicals deal with is? There are a few possible answers . . .

1. One can enjoy soccer without playing games. This can mean simple kickabouts in the park or fancy juggling, today often referred to as "freestyle." Variations include Kung-Fu Football (which Shaolin monks use to woo tourists) and Capoeira Football (which has already been exploited by a Nike ad).

2. One can turn the competitive aspect of the game into a positive contribution to social life. This relies on the cathartic function of competitive sports: they allow venting aggression, easing tension, and resolving conflict in a socially acceptable manner. No society will ever be free of these phenomena, and it is much healthier to deal with them in a regulated form than to ignore them. Hence, as long as people respect the basics of sportsmanship and the game's outcome, the competitive aspect of soccer can be beneficial for a balanced community life.

3. One can diminish the social implications of winning and losing. There are no particular rewards or reprimands. Winning and losing are just part of a game that is more enjoyable to play if there is something at stake—and nothing more.

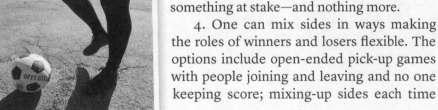

4. One can mix sides in ways making the roles of winners and losers flexible. The options include open-ended pick-up games with people joining and leaving and no one keeping score; mixing-up sides each time

someone scores; and having teams rotate: a team that concedes a goal makes space for another team, etc.

There is also the concept of three-sided soccer, allegedly developed by the Danish Situationist Asger Jorn.

An Introduction to Three-Sided Football

Leaflet by the Association of Autonomous Astronauts (East London Branch)

It appears that the first person to come up with the idea of 3-sided football was Asger Jorn, who saw it as a means of conveying his notion of trialectics—a trinitarian supercession of the binary structure of dialectics. We are still trying to discover if there were any actual games organised by him. Before the

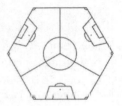

London Psychogeographic Association organised its first game at the Glasgow Anarchist Summer School in 1993, there is little evidence of any games being played.

There is, of course, the rumour that Luther Blissett organised an informal league of youth clubs that played 3-sided football during his stint at Watford in the early Eighties. Unfortunately, our research has found no evidence to support this. Nevertheless, Blissett's name will probably remain firmly linked to the 3-sided version of the game, even if in an apocryphal fashion.

The key to the game is that it does not foster aggression or competitiveness. Unlike two-sided football, no team keeps a record of the number of goals they score. However they do keep a tally of the goals they

WHILE PLAYING THREE SIDED FOOTBALL WE LOST THE BALL

Paul P.

concede, and the winner is determined as the team which concedes least goals. The game deconstructs the mythic bi-polar structure of conventional football, where an us-and-them struggle mediated by the referee mimics the way the media and the state pose themselves as "neutral" elements in the class struggle. Likewise, it is no psycho-sexual drama of the fuckers and fucked—the possibilities are greatly expanded!

The pitch is hexagonal; each team being assigned two opposite sides for bureaucratic purposes should the ball be kicked out of the play. The blank side is called the frontside. The side containing the orifice is called the backside, and the orifice is called a goal. Should the ball be thrust through a team's orifice, the team is deemed to have conceded a goal—so in an emblematic fashion this perpetuates the anal-retentive homophobic techniques of conventional football whereby homo-erotic tension is built up, only to be sublimated and repressed.

However the trialectic appropriation of this technique dissolves the homo-erotic/homo-phobic bipolarity as a successful attack will generally imply co-operation with the third team. This should overcome the prominent resistance to women taking their full part in football.

Meanwhile the penetration of the defence by two opposing teams imposes upon the defense the task of counterbalancing their disadvantage through sowing the seeds of discord in an alliance, which can only be temporary. This will be achieved through exhortation, body language, and an ability to manoeuvre the ball and players into such a position that one opposing team will realize that its interests are better served by breaking off the attack and allying themselves with the defending team.

Bearing in mind that such a decision will not necessarily be immediate, a team may well find itself split between two alliances. Such a situation opens them up to the possibility of their enemies uniting, making maximum use of this confusion. 3-sided football is a game of skill, persuasion and psychogeography. The semicircle around the goal functions as a penalty area and it may be necessary to use it for some sort of offside rule which has yet to be developed.

Publication year unknown, presumably mid-1990s

The Social Values of Football: A Theoretical Approach

"Football, as the embodiment of a need to communicate and to share, is one of the greatest concepts of humanity." This bold statement glared from a radical website dedicated to the game a few years ago.[99] Equally daring is Carlos Fernández's suggestion that "bringing football and anarchism together is a natural, symbiotic thing," formulated in his quintessential anarchist elegy to football, "Pitched Battles: Football and Anarchy."

Pitched Battles: Football and Anarchy

Carlos Fernández

In the Aguascalientes IV of Zapatista territory, we played football between two long, wood-plank dormitories, aiming for netless goals with sagging crossbars. The ball would often fly onto the buildings' roofs. This would not take it out of play, but instead lead to a brief struggle underneath the eaves to capture the ball as it rolled down. Those were crazy moments, charged with unreality because we played all out in the middle of a poverty alien to visitors like me, and even as military planes made their regular flyovers. On that field of strangeness in Mexico, some of us, visitors and hosts, came to know each other—if only slightly, at least sincerely. Football, played to fit the circumstances, opened connections between us, across barriers of languages, values, and even fitness. I was having a hard time with the altitude.

There are certain powerful ways in which the football field, or pitch, duplicates the social field. First, as history; it is a location of social activity. Nationalities, classes, and smaller social identities act out passionately on and around the pitch. Next, as collective formation; groups assemble into myriad shapes on and off the pitch, as elsewhere in societies. Football can touch off the powerful emotions that drive affiliations like teams, fan clubs, hooligan gangs, and beyond. Third, as style, the ways individuals and their communities or societies state their uniqueness; in football, this occurs mostly in the styles of play. Maybe most famously, Brazil produced a fluid kind of game obviously developed from capoeria, the Afro-Brazilian martial art. Fourth and most importantly, the football field reproduces the interdependence that characterizes the social; when people enthusiastically participate in the sport, they redefine it and themselves.

I do not seek to romanticize or intellectualize play here. I hope to inspire a way of looking at football (or any game) as a very real elaboration of people's philosophies, politics, and hopes. This makes it an important site of production of power relations. On the pitch, power is named, shared, contested, and felt. Its distribution never settles until the whistle blows. We need an anarchist attack on the sport's wider fields of form and organization. Kicking a ball around can be made as anarchist as barricading a street or forming a co-op.

How Can Football be Anarchist?

To begin, we can be sure that anarchists have played football as long as either has been around. The relationship is often explicit, as in the early 20th century, when the club now known as Argentinos Juniors was called the Chicago Martyrs and another club was begun in a Buenos Aires anarchist library. We can also condfidently guess that some of the Barcelona team that toured North America in 1937, raising money for the Republic, would identify themselves with their city's anarchists. And, one should question, were the striking professional players in Paris of May 1968 very different from the students or workers when they demanded their own part of freedom? Could the anti-authoritarian fans of St. Pauli leave their politics at the stadium gates or forget football before a meeting or protest? If many spaces and actions are often anarchist primarily by association, then football has an old anarchist face.

Also, people's love for the game has translated into their love for freedom and justice, as in the case of the '42 Dynamo Kiev team, the Algerians who quit French teams as their country fought for independence, or non-white European professionals like Ruud Gullit, who've taken stands against racism, greed, and fascism. As people have reproduced their values, identities, and desires within the game, they've stretched football into something more. Telling from their website *www.chumba. com/_footie.html*, Chumbawamba sponsors the Wetherby Athletic, a youth team, out of their passion for the game. Yet, their politics come out right on the kids' jerseys, emblazoned with the word "anarchy."

Politics do not appear as aberrations or accidents in football. They are part of people's interaction with the game. The sport retains its shape as a game from the heights of a World Cup final to games played on uneven fields in rebel Mexico. Its players, basic rules, and objectives remain the same. The sport changes in how people come together around its fundamental elements. The Barras Bravas of South America; the hooligans, ultras, and carnival fans of Europe—these provocative fringes of fandom suggest that new, energetic cultural forms can emerge from the football field. Although we won't fill stadiums very soon, the same is happening today among anarchists. Anarchist football appeared in the last few years with, unsurprisingly, no single name, style, or organization. In the US mid-Atlantic region, people play as the Anarchist Soccer League. On the west coast, anarchists and others play without names.

In the Midwest, the Arsenal, Riot, and Swarm play as the Anarchist Football Association. The last is an association or federation or network only by the minimum definitions of the terms. Some meet weekly, some yearly. The games last one or two hours. What happens before, during, or after follows no set outline. In a peculiar anarchist way, this new face of football repeats the history of the sport, the way collective politics and passion fuse on the pitch.

The Anarchist Football Association, as an example, can be considered a hypothetical, proposed, or working form for anarchist community. It might be nothing more than an anagram on patches worn by a bunch of people or it might be a real, large, but latent anarchist constituency. Its Chicago affiliate, ostensibly the most organized one (with a phone list, uniforms, schedule, etc.), includes individuals whose frequency of play, degrees of friendship, and political beliefs all vary widely. Outside the Association, an assortment of very non-regulation games are played in cities such as Portland, Berkeley, and San Francisco. This range of inci- dence points to a mutual redefinition of anarchism and football. Each one is transformed by joining the other. Anarchist games cleave football away from the commodification pushed by Nike, Major League Soccer, and [the] Federation of International Football Associations. And they give anarchism another rejuvenated cultural formation, a new shape for its expression.

What is a cultural formation? Fantasy might be an unavoidable term for what I'm trying to describe. And it's not one that I would immediately throw out. When I discovered Profane Existence in high school and saw the photos of huge European black blocs, I imagined that it would feel incredible to participate in such a collective action. A couple of years later, I unexpectedly joined the black bloc in a march against the Gulf War. I was hooked. Ever since, my ties to and identification with anarchists have wavered, but every upswing has hinged on such ambiguous images and fleeting moments of community. All the exchange, cooperation, and affinity that occur on the football field can serve the same functions of identification and loyalty.

Anarchist football can express collective identities through teams, specifically in how they practice anarchist ideals and build collective skills. Deciding on positions and strategies without a coach, training without pressure, using players of all skill-levels; who could accomplish these beside anarchists? And couldn't we use the communication skills and other cooperative skills in football in our direct actions? One skill that experienced football players often know is support. On the field, a player supports others by putting herself where her teammates can pass to her in order to keep the ball away from defenders or to advance it up the field. This technique involves awareness of where your comrades are and what they might do. During extra-legal work, such skills make actions faster, tighter and safer. Many other parts of playing football can feed into our tactics, and the reverse can also be true. A teammate of mine alludes to this mutual relationship in her declaration, "We kick. We run. We kick ass. We run away."

Non-technical aspects of football can also reinforce our collective political efforts, especially on a long term basis. For example, the idea of affinity as a strategic organizing principle—people taking political action in small groups based on mutual trust—is an anarchist innovation, but one which can be hard to realize. Playing football together regularly can provide a concrete sense of affinity. All the communication and coopera- tion that make up the game congeal into a feeling of mutual trust and understanding, a feeling that, once known, can be more easily achieved in other contexts. It's a beautiful thing when a few people together make an impact greater than the sum of their parts. If we don't see it enough in politics, we can at least find it in the best examples of football.

In one moment during Cameroon's near-victory over England in a 1990 World Cup quarterfinal, affinity took on a real, visible shape. The attack that put Cameroon one goal ahead was thrilling not only because it shamed one of the best teams, but also because it was executed so brilliantly. That Cameroon's play was both a thing of plain beauty and an underdog's success suggests how a moment of affinity can be poetic and concrete. In a recent Chicago Arsenal game, a teammate's simple pass surprised the other team and suddenly put our team into a fast break. After a couple more passes, we scored, as stunned as our opponents. Aren't such lucky chains of events the way we often imagine resistance, if not revolution, might happen? The magic of play touches the revolutionary imagination like poetry or art: It can spark a vision and feeling of things changing.

Of course, football doesn't appeal to everyone. But neither does any art or other cultural expression. What good does it do for revolution if its appeal isn't universal? The question is not a zero-sum situation, where we should either use the sport or discard it. The game can be changed. We can build team cohesion and skills with more in mind than just winning games. We can make it fun for more people, even for those who don't play. The potential of football as a part of political struggles requires that the sport be opened up again.

Skilling, sharing, and affinity must be made inclusive. On the football field, anarchist teams should adjust the pace and mood to keep new players involved. The game allows this by its fluid nature: offense can involve more passing than sprinting and defense can concentrate on containing its opponents. This general advice needs to be made more specific with regards to gender. Women should be a part of every team and all macho behavior should be kept off the field. It would be a great day when sexist put-down used against players, a common aspect of professional play, would be replaced with banter like, "Don't be such a male chauvinist! Pass the ball!" (I'm sure it would be catchier, though.)

Toward a Conclusion
It seems to be about simplicity: Football, at its heart, is a simple game, and anarchism, from the heart, is a simple wish. The sport's fundamental ease has taken it around the world and dragged us with it. It's one of the most wonderful things when we meet someone new at a game, or our bonds strengthen at dinner or a bar after we play. If the football field is essentially a meeting place for play, it must then extend to wherever people enjoy being with each other. That's where anarchy might start, or at least where

it can blossom. When the idea of self-organization can be made obvious by how a goal is scored or how a team trains, anarchism seems like no great feat. Bringing football and anarchism together is a natural, symbiotic thing. The pitch, what Gramsci called a "great open-air kingdom of human loyalty," needs to be made ours.

Carlos Fernandez is a Chicago-based activist. This article was first published in *Arsenal: A Magazine of Anarchist Strategy and Culture*, no. 1 (Spring 2000.)

Soccer is a complex game and there are probably as many problematic implications as there are liberating ones—however, the latter exist, and it is important for radical fans to tease them out. While football might not be revolutionary per se, it *can be* part of the revolution—reducing football to an opiate of the masses, to a capitalist Shangri-La, and to a reactionary breeding ground of nationalism and sectarianism is short sighted. There are values inherent in football that can help us form and establish communities based on direct democracy, solidarity, and, let us not forget, fun.

Football is a quintessential team sport. There are team events in track and field, skiing or archery, but most of them are summaries of individual performances. In football—like in other quintessential team sports: basketball, volleyball, hockey, etc.—there is no individual performance independent from the team. Even the success of long individual dribbles usually depends on teammates leading defenders astray, opening up space, etc. Likewise, free kick specialists could not score if teammates had not been fouled within reasonable distance to the goal. It is not surprising that the performances of individual players often vary significantly with different teams: some excel in their clubs but disappoint in their national sides, some improve greatly when they change their team, etc. At the same time, there is not only space for individual skill and creativity, but the success of the team is dependent on these qualities.

The Pass and Albert Camus

Wally Rosell

The ball has no attribute of power. The passer does not *own* the ball; he *possesses* the ball in the sense of Proudhon.

The passer remains the master of the act. As in libertarian society, he is free to do what he wants. However, he cannot exist alone, he cannot progress alone, and he cannot survive alone. Here is where the principle of mutual aid comes into play, as explained by Peter Kropotkin.

The pass is an altruistic act, in which the freedom of the passer ("I give the ball to those I want to give it to, at a time of my choosing") is entirely dependent on the existence of his teammates.

The individual act of passing receives its only meaning from the purpose it serves for the group. To pass ("to give") means to affirm the trust in one's teammates; it expresses the confidence that they will use the gift of the pass for the benefit of the collective. This is the essence of political activism. To pass the ball is essentially the same as to distribute a pamphlet or to put up a poster: the activist trusts that those who read it will turn it into something useful.

The act of passing is the antipode of a nihilist or a Stakhanovist act; it is a creative act. Technical skills are indispensable, as in all arts, but without creativity there can be no pass: the conditions are never exactly the same—each pass is unique.

Contrary to popular belief, the higher the level of the game and the stronger the opposition, the more individual creativity is needed for a team to succeed. It is the unexpected, the improbable, the *impossible* pass that liberates one's teammates and that advances the team. It is the ability of the passer to understand the context of a specific situation that turns him into an anarcho-Camusian individual instead of a robot. In the words of Camus, he becomes an "altruistic individualist."

If a libertarian poster is a poster that makes you think with your eyes, a libertarian sport is a sport that makes you think with your body. Intelligence in movement was always of utter importance to Albert Camus.

Wally Rosell has contributed numerous articles about the meaning of sports as a learning tool for libertarian praxis in *Le Monde libertaire*, the journal of the French *Fédération anarchiste*. This text is an excerpt of the talk "Albert Camus, les anarchistes et le football" [Albert Camus, the Anarchists, and Football], presented at the Rencontres Méditerranéennes Albert Camus in Lourmarin, France, 2008. Translated by Gabriel Kuhn.

In order to be great players, footballers have to show individual responsibility and discipline. For the collective to work, they need to fulfill the role that they are given. They can change it—say, a defender starts to play more offensively if the team is looking for an equalizer late in the game—but this has to happen in accordance with the team: everyone needs to know, and approve, of the tactical changes not to make the changes hazardous.

Unfortunately, even these most essential of footballing values, taught by managers for decades, are under threat in today's professional game. Most players are so concerned with their individual careers that they mean much more to them than their team's achievements. There is often little loyalty to the team. In this context, let us revisit the much-discussed Hope Solo incident at the 2007 Women's World Cup. Solo, a goalkeeper for the U.S. team, was surprisingly benched by manager Greg Ryan before the semifinal against Brazil, although she had been a solid keeper up to that point. Veteran Briana Scurry replaced her, had a bad day, the U.S. lost 0-4, and Solo declared afterwards that it was "obvious" that the coach had made the wrong decision and that "there is no doubt in my mind that I would have made those saves." As a consequence, she was not allowed to sit on the bench during the bronze medal game, was banned from the bronze medal ceremony, and had to return to the U.S. on a separate plane. Although substituting Solo was a ridiculous coaching decision and the retributions perhaps overly harsh, there is no denying that her statements breached an unwritten soccer code: no matter your individual disappointment and frustration, you do not publicly lash out at a teammate. In the end, such behavior can only come from valuing one's own interests over that of the collective.

The lack of fair play might be one of the biggest threats to the credibility of professional soccer overall. The degree to which cheating has become accepted is ridiculous. Getting away with fooling the referee or committing a "tactical" foul is seen as an accomplishment rather than as an embarrassment. At the 2010 Men's World Cup, it was disheartening to watch Uruguay striker Luis Suárez celebrate Ghana's missed penalty after he had prevented a last-minute Ghana goal with an intentional hand ball. To raise your arms in the heat of the moment is one thing—to then celebrate the act ecstatically is something different. It is as appalling as the theatrical agony after allegedly being hit by an opponent.

A related problem is a lack of compassion. German goalkeeper Toni Schumacher's nonchalant reaction to knocking Patrick Batiston unconscious during the 1982 Men's World Cup semifinal between Germany and France stands as a reminder for what football must not be. When Jens Lehmann writes in his 2010 autobiography *Der Wahnsinn liegt auf dem Platz* [Madness Lies on the Pitch] that this was an inspirational moment for his career because of Schumacher's "fearlessness," it explains a lot about what's wrong with footballers like Lehmann.

In fact, compassion must be extended to referees as well. While some of them can be unappealing authoritarians, many are in it for the love of the game, just like players, managers, and spectators. To demand of them to never ever make a mistake is ridiculous. The game has become incredibly fast and intricate, and it is impossible to see everything. Unless there will be major changes in the refereeing of football matches, mistakes will be made. No single linesman will ever be able to call all offside decisions correctly—not ever. Players make mistakes all the time too. The problem is that referees' mistakes often decide games.

Apart from a reform in the refereeing system—additional referees and video monitoring are the most obvious options—some rule changes should be considered as well: NBA-style goaltending could be introduced, penalty kicks could be moved to the 18-yard line, temporary suspensions of players could substitute red cards, etc. It is true that part of soccer's popularity derives from the fact that the game's rules have essentially been the same for more than a century, yet there have been many, often significant, rule changes that have not hurt the sport: in the last twenty-five years alone, new regulations have made it harder for goalkeepers to delay the game, most importantly the banning of the return pass; the number of substitutes has been changed; criteria for red cards have been tightened; it is no longer off-side to be level with the last defender, etc. In short, a number of things can be done to make the game more exciting, more credible, and more just.

Under ideal circumstances, football is a perfect environment in which to experience—and to experiment with—the combination of individual freedom and social responsibility. Furthermore, just like in society, people with many different skills have to work together to make a team successful. Ten Maradonas would not make a World Cup winning side. For a Maradona to shine, others have to do plenty of work that he is not able to do: form a solid defense line, run down loose balls, tackle opponents, win headers (without using the "Hand of God"), and so forth. There are many examples in football history of a team of "no names" beating a star-studded side simply because the players made the most of their abilities as a team. Football teaches people to combine their individual talents in the way most beneficial to the social good.

On this basis, writers have often stressed the positive role that football can play for socialist politics. Before the opening match of the 2010 Men's World Cup in South Africa, Castro Ngobese, spokesperson for South Africa's National Union of Metalworkers declared: "The opening match should serve as defiance to the barbaric, immoral and exploitive Capitalist system, for football by its nature promotes communalism and sharing—key elements of Socialism."[100]

Ideally, the sense of collectivity earned from playing football extends beyond one's team. First of all, it ought to encompass opposing players. The notion of "sportsmanship" may have overtones of gallantry and patriarchy, but the implied values of mutual respect, consideration for others, and modesty are important values for any radical endeavor. "Opponents" in football should be seen as "comrades"; much can be gained from this, not least an understanding for the priority of common values over temporary opposition. If the same principle was embraced in radical debate, our movements would know less division and, consequently, be stronger.

The sense of collectivity in football ought to encompass a team's supporters as well. Originally, football clubs were very much integrated into their socio-geographic surroundings, and the term "supporters" could be taken literally: they would show up at practice, talk to the players, boost their morale, cheer for them, accompany them on away games, etc. Football culture was indeed participatory and not reduced to the eleven players on the field. The common German description of the supporters as the "twelfth player" is very telling. Unfortunately, much of this has changed for the worse in the consumer-oriented fan culture of today. Concrete relationships between players and fans are basically a thing of the past. It has rightfully been said that many of today's football fans identify with a team the same way they identify with their Nike sneakers—and they "support" the club in the same way too, namely by buying stuff, in this case overpriced tickets, merchandise, and pay-TV packages.

Where football still brings people together in a very tangible way is at big international tournaments. While the media mostly focuses on tiny minorities of violence-prone fans and occasional skirmishes, the vast majority of soccer fans attend such tournaments in a spirit of joy, openness, and camaraderie. At all the big soccer events, you see fans from different countries socialize, spend time together, exchange addresses, and become friends. Otherwise, their paths might have never crossed.

Soccer fans have done much more to open borders, to create international alliances, and to overcome prejudice and bigotry than what both the tabloids and the cranky leftist soccer critics want to make us believe. Community is still created on the terraces as well, especially where left-wing fan initiatives are active, and in grassroots and underground soccer clubs.

Furthermore, like laughter and music, soccer, as the world's most popular sport, is a global language. All traveling soccer players have innumerable stories to tell about pick-up games with people whom they had never met before, who spoke languages they did not understand, and whose social and cultural backgrounds were different to theirs—nonetheless, they were able to share instant moments of joy and kinship. Besides, soccer's popularity makes it a worldwide reference point. It allows you to strike up conversations across all national, ethnic, cultural, and economic boundaries. You can discuss England's goalkeeping problems no matter whether you are in Kuala Lumpur, Cape Town, or Santiago de Chile—and all on equal footing! Soccer is indeed a universally applicable ice-breaker.

Apart from collective learning experiences and community-building, having fun is perhaps a trivial, yet also a crucial part of the soccer experience, both as a player and as a spectator. And it must not be belittled as "non-political" either—if Emma Goldman wants to dance in her revolution, others should have the right to kick a ball around.

Finally, there is health. Unless it is played in an overly competitive spirit, which puts unnecessary stress on one's body and endangers others, football, like any sport, contributes to individual and collective well-being.

Conclusion

"I enjoy making revolution! I enjoy going to football!"
—*Antonio Negri*[101]

Extra Time: Appendix to the Second Edition

Ultras in Middle East Uprisings: 2011-2013

Right about the time the first edition of *Soccer vs. the State* was released in 2011, football supporters made headlines around the world. During the occupation of Cairo's Tahrir Square, which eventually led to the resignation of Egypt's president Hosni Mubarak, Ultras of Cairo's two biggest clubs, Al Ahly and Zamalek, were at the forefront of street battles with security forces and Mubarak's supporters. They were widely hailed as one of the most important forces in the overthrow of the regime. When, on February 1, 2012, over 70 Al Ahly supporters were trapped and killed at Port Said Stadium after being attacked by opposing fans, security forces were suspected of tolerating, or even orchestrating, the massacre.

Football supporters were back in the news as a politically significant force in 2013, when supporters of Istanbul's three biggest clubs—Fenerbahçe, Galatasaray, and Beşiktaş—were centrally involved in the Gezi Park occupation, a milestone in the formation of Turkey's contemporary protest movement.

Neither of these examples makes football supporters a progressive force in general. The supporters involved in the protests in Egypt and Turkey were not necessarily representative of all of the countries' supporters, and even within their own ranks political views and affiliations varied. Football-supporters-turned-political-actors have also stood and fought alongside reactionary forces, for example during the 2013–2014 conflict in Ukraine. What has been proven, however, is the potential that lies in alliances of football fans and political activists.

▊ Ultras Bolster Protesters in Battles on Cairo's Tahrir Square

James Dorsey

Militant soccer fans bolstered this weekend the ranks of demonstrators in Cairo's Tahrir Square demanding an end to military rule in a re-enactment of the protests that ousted President Hosni Mubarak in February.

Like early this year, the ultras—militant, highly politicised, violence-prone fan groups modelled on similar organizations in Serbia and Italy—took the lead in confronting military police seeking to clear Tahrir Square. Within an hour of their arrival on late Saturday afternoon, police retreated from the square as battles continued for several hours on the side streets.

"The Ultras are here. I know that because they're the only ones facing the CSF [Egypt's paramilitary Central Security Force] with force while singing their [anti-security police] hymns," tweeted a protester from Tahrir. "The ultras are kicking the police's ass," tweeted another protester.

The ultra's sayaadin or hunters similar to the battles in February on Sunday hurled tear gas canisters fired by the police back into the ranks of the law enforcers. The tactic that worked against Mr. Mubarak's police and security forces early this year failed however to stop the military police from forcing demonstrators out of the square in a mass stampede.

Nonetheless, once they had regrouped, the ultras led thousands of protesters back into Tahrir. The ultras quickly erected barricades in preparation of expected further clashes that this weekend caused at least one death and the injuring of hundreds of others.

Protesters had called for the street battle-hardened ultras to join them as the battle for Tahrir raged through the afternoon on Saturday, with skirmishes spreading through Cairo's warren of tight streets and smaller squares.

The ultras—supporters of arch rival, crowned Cairo clubs Al Ahly SC and Al Zamalek SC—played a key role in the protests that toppled Mr. Mubarak. They have since been vocal in their demand that the military which succeeded the ousted president stick to its pledge to lead Egypt to elections within six months. That timetable has already slipped with the first stage of elections scheduled for November 28, nine months after the downfall of Mr. Mubarak.

Ultras have clashed repeatedly with security forces in recent months and in September led protesters in an attack on the Israeli embassy in Cairo that forced Israel to evacuate its diplomatic personnel. Israel's ambassador returned to the Egyptian capital this weekend.

Fuelled by a belief that they own the stadium as the only uncondi-tional supporters of their team, the ultras garnered their street fighting experi-ence in years of weekly battles with the police and rival fans. Much like hooligans in Britain whose attitudes were shaped by the decaying condition of stadiums, Egyptian ultras were driven by the Mubarak regime's attempt to control their space by turning it into a virtual fortress ringed by black steel.

The struggle for control produced a complete breakdown, social decay in a microcosm. If the space was expendable, so was life. As a result, militant fans would confront the police each weekend with total aban-donment. It was that abandonment that won them the respect of many Egyptians and that they brought early this year and again on Sunday to Tahrir Square. It was also coupled with their street battle experience what enabled them to help protesters early this year break down barriers of fear that had kept them from confronting the regime in the past and cemented resolve this weekend on Tahrir Square.

The joining of forces of arch rival ultras from Ahly and Zamalek, who for much of the past decade fought one another viciously early this year in the struggle to topple Mr. Mubarak and again this weekend serves as an indication of how deep-seated the demand is for the military to relinquish control.

James M. Dorsey is a senior fellow at the S. Rajaratnam School of International Studies at Nanyang Technological University in Singapore. His award-winning blog *The Turbulent World of Middle East Soccer* has been up since 2011. His book of the same title was published in 2016. This article appeared on the blog on November 21, 2011.

■ When Ultras Shook the Turkish Government

Ekim Çağlar

May 2013: Hooliganism is a hotly debated issue among politicians and pundits in Turkey. Many demand urgent measures against violence among soccer fans. On May 12, twenty-year-old Fenerbahçe supporter Burak Yıldırım was stabbed and killed by a group of Galatasaray fans.

Only a few weeks later, the situation is very different. A people's uprising has made it clear that supporters of different teams aren't out to kill each other. The uprising began with the occupation of Gezi Park near Taksim Square in central Istanbul. It brought together a wide variety of groups and proved that football supporters were as capable in mobilizing people as political organizations—or more so.

Differences between the terraces and the streets disappeared. During the uprising, we didn't know whether we were first and foremost football supporters or protesters. We learned to, literally, tie together the scarves of different clubs and join ranks in protesting the government. Soon, the name "Istanbul United" was on everybody's lips, with the supporters of Istanbul's three biggest football clubs coming together as one. There will, no doubt, never be a club called Istanbul United, but the scarves and shirts that combined the three clubs' colors and emblems sold very well, together with the gas masks and spray paint peddled by innovative street vendors around Taksim.

Frustration

I was among those who guarded Gezi Park around the clock already a week before the occupation turned into a mass protest. Even we were surprised when it happened. Religious and ideological divisions were suddenly put aside. Various ethnic and religious communities gathered together with nationalists, communists, LGBT people, and football supporters. It was the first time that a coalition of this kind drove political questions in Turkey together.

The uprising has sometimes been referred to as a revolt of middle-class youth. This simplifies things. The traditional workers' organizations were as much present as the homeless and glue-sniffing kids who have always made Gezi Park their home after sunset. Even if it rarely translated into concrete demands, all protesters shared the feeling that they were being suffocated by the ruling Justice and Development Party, AKP. The AKP was taking away people's freedom, their space to develop and to grow as the people they were.

Many of the football supporters involved might not have cared all that much about a small grassy area in the middle of Istanbul. But they were frustrated over new restrictions on the consumption of alcohol, rising ticket prices, and the banning of away supporters. The uprising allowed them to channel their frustration into political protest. Whatever reason the different participants had to get involved, the result was an inclusive movement everyone could identify with.

"Spray Your Tear Gas!"

The first wave of police repression only intensified the ties between the different groups protesting. Overcoming fear is a bonding experience. An old football chant turned into Turkey's new, unofficial anthem:

Sık bakalım, sık bakalım—Spray, spray
Biber gazı sık bakalım—Spray your tear gas
Kaskını çıkar—Take off your helmet
Copunu bırak—Drop your baton
Delikanlı kim bakalım—Then we see who has heart and courage

From the terraces to the streets: the chant made us hoarse but was kept alive by everybody else. It was a wake-up call for the political organizations of old that had increasing difficulties to reach the people. Football supporters were no longer seen as fanatical hooligans but as an important faction of a popular mass protest. Several factors had made this possible.

Creativity and Self-Confidence

The rhetoric of the terraces is less predictable than that of the traditional left. Humor and satire are key elements. The chants and slogans used by football supporters are creative and make people laugh, which, in turn, boosts their energy in confronting the police.

Football supporters also exude self-confidence. For many of them, political protests might have been new, but they adapted quickly while building barricades and singing songs of courage. They brought with them the optimism that is a part of the football experience, expressed in phrases such as "Each game starts at 0–0," and "The ball is round." Whenever I expected a long night out on the streets, I wore my match scarf. It's my lucky charm (even if I also wore it when I was teargassed and shot in the back with rubber bullets during the clearing of Gezi Park on June 15). The protesters believed in victory largely due to the optimism spread by football supporters. People came prepared as if it was a match day.

Courage and Experience

Mobilization among football supporters and political activists shares many features. To gather one's troops for home games every other week, to arrange meetings, and to prepare choreographies is very similar to getting ready for a political rally. Chants on the terraces aim to bring strength to your team and to demoralize the opponent. The feeling that what you do makes a difference is as essential for the football supporter as it is for the political protester. These shared experiences made communication between different groups in Gezi Park surprisingly easy.

Finally, football supporters know the police and its apparatus of repression. Among the political activists in Gezi Park only those who had been around for a long time had firsthand experience with state violence. Many of the younger activists felt relief when football supporters were close by. Similar dynamics could be observed during the 2011 uprising in Egypt against president Hosni Mubarak. Ultras from Al Ahly (Ultras Ahlawy) and Zamalek (Ultras White Knights) were up front during clashes with the police and Mubarak supporters due to their longstanding experience with police violence.

Politics Come into Play

When the uprising in Turkey became more and more politically charged, the Ultras reacted differently. Members of Galatasaray's UltrAslan and of Fenerbahçe's Genç Fenerbahçeliler were present in Gezi Park, but officially the groups distanced themselves from the protests after a few days. Beşiktaş supporters did not. This was not surprising, considering that Çarşı, founded in 1982, has long been Turkey's most political and influential Ultra group.

Çarşı had gathered public attention with spectacular actions before, for example when they prepared a choreography against the construction of nuclear power plants in 2007 together with Greenpeace. Çarşı was a major reason why the terraces of Turkish football stadiums were increasingly recognized as arenas for social movements. Academics and intellectuals began to show interest in the phenomenon as well. Sociologist Sema Tuğçe Dikici's 2013 book on Çarşı (*Çarşı: Bir Başka Taraftarlık*) is one of the most interesting results.

Masters of the Uprising

Çarşı has long been known to take a stand against racism, fascism, homophobia, and gentrification.

Çarşı supporters have also been recognized for impressive showings at May Day parades. When, during the Gezi Park uprising, one of them climbed an excavator, yelled chants through its loudspeaker system, and started chasing the water cannons truck of the police, legendary status was guaranteed. Whenever the police attacked, people were looking for black-and-white scarves to be sure that the first line of defense would not break. Arguing shopkeepers could threaten one another with lines such as: "Cool it, or I will call Çarşı!"

Çarşı is the closest you get to a social movement in Turkey's football stadiums. The vast majority of Çarşı members are left-leaning; most of them are communists and anarchists. Çarşı's popularity makes it a prototype for an inclusive and socially conscious Ultra group.

It is characteristic that Güneş, commonly known as *abla*, big sister, runs one of the Çarşı shops in the densely populated Beşiktaş neighborhood. Güneş is a little older than most of us. She always invites us in for tea when she sees us and never ceases to talk about "our wonderful boys who stand up to the police." She is an important part of Çarşı, a group that doesn't have regulations or membership cards, and is open to anyone.

Stubbornness and Hope

Ultras can be a part of social change. Çarşı are the flag-bearers of political Ultra groups in Turkey. The marches they organized during the uprising from the Beşiktaş neighborhood to Gezi Park gathered hundreds of thousands of supporters from different teams as well as ordinary citizens who had come to appreciate the wittiness of Çarşı slogans as well as the Bengal flares. My cousin, who has no interest in football and roots for Fenerbahçe if she has to, did not miss a single one of the marches. Many others joined to express their disapproval of the government or to simply drink beer and have a good time.

During the Gezi Park protests, Çarşı stood for joy, hope, and resilience. Whenever we left the house with our black-and-white scarves, we were cheered by our neighbors, the older ladies looking out their windows. It was ironic that Beşiktaş' black-and-white added so much color to the uprising. It goes to show what creativity can do.

Repression and Progress

A few weeks into the uprising, twenty Çarşı members were arrested. It was unsettling, but it confirmed how influential the group had become. The same was true when deputy prime minister Bülent Arınç falsely claimed that Çarşı had abandoned the protests after ten days. Later, he denied the comment, but the government aimed to break the protesters' morale by spreading unfounded rumors about one of the protest's biggest sources of inspiration.

One year after the uprising, Çarşı was under much pressure. Thirty-five members had been charged with treason. Social movements and the country's progressive cultural establishment rallied behind them. The defendants' first court appearance was on December 16, 2014. During the proceedings, protesting Beşiktaş supporters were joined not only by political dissidents, but also by Ultras from other clubs. In stadiums across Europe, banners expressed solidarity with the accused. The trial was widely considered a show of force by the government; Human Rights Watch described it as a judicial farce.

On December 16, it was decided to postpone further proceedings to April 2015, and the accused's travel bans were lifted. Eventually they were freed from all charges.

No Opiate of the People

Today, football jerseys and scarves are as common a sight at political rallies in Turkey as party emblems and Che Guevara shirts. Football terraces have become a  platform for radical democratic grassroots organizing. There are several—more or less explicitly—progressive supporter groups: Şimşekler (Adana Demirspor), FenerbahCHE and Sol Açık (both Fenerbahçe), Halkın Takımı (Beşiktaş), Tekyumruk (Galatasaray), YaBasta (Göztepe), KemenCHE (Trabzonspor), and Karakızıl (Gençlerbirliği). Some of them are very influential, others are small, but they all prove that supporters are becoming increasingly political. The groups appear at May Day rallies and have supported Halil İbrahim Dinçdağ, an openly gay referee who has been banned from officiating matches by the Turkish Football Association. Football, once referred to by intellectuals as "an opiate as effective as religion," has become a political factor in Turkey. Supporters' calls for social change can be neither denied nor ignored.

What to Expect

Political supporter groups started to appear on the terraces of Turkish stadiums in the early 2000s. Their impact peaked during the 2013 uprising. Even government-friendly Ultras, concentrated in the Kasımpaşa neighborhood, the childhood home of Prime Minister Recep Tayyip Erdoğan, have been influenced by this. With the help of the police, they have chased protesters with bats and hatches, wearing their club's blue-and-white jerseys. On International Women's Day, Bursaspor supporters attacked a rally, injuring ten women. The politicization of the terraces is as much a fact as the political division among them. Rivalry is not a thing of the past. Conflict has to be expected, in particular, when progressive groups become more visible among government-friendly crowds. There are other factors to be considered as well: the introduction of a highly unpopular electronic ticketing system in 2014 has driven many supporters from the stadiums, but it has also given Ultras a new cause to unite around.

We can only speculate about what will happen in the long run. What we do know is that Ultras have become a political force to be reckoned with. And the government is aware of it

Ekim Çağlar is a Swedish-Turkish journalist and author of the book *Propagandafotboll* (2016). This article appeared as "När ultras skakade den turkiska regeringen" on *anarkism.nu* in the spring of 2015. Earlier versions were published in the Norwegian soccer magazine *Josimar* and the Swedish quarterly *Brand*. Translated by Gabriel Kuhn.

■

Protest, Intervention, Change: Activism in Soccer

In the preface to this edition, we have listed some of the most prominent examples of activism in soccer of recent years. Here we want to look at three of them more closely: the popular protests in Brazil ahead of the Men's World Cup in 2014; the story of Deniz Naki, a footballer who has become a new icon among radical football supporters; and the case of Malmö FF supporter and antifascist Showan Shattak, who has become a symbol for politically conscious fans when he was almost killed during a confrontation with neo-Nazis on International Women's Day in 2014.

▐ Neither a Raving Festival nor a Stormy Protest: After the World Cup, Social Movements in Brazil Draw Mixed Conclusions

Gesa Köbberling

President Dilma Rousseff had promised the *copa das copas*, the best World Cup ever. In the eyes of most Brazilians, it wasn't. The crisis and organizational chaos that Rousseff's opponents from the right had announced, did not occur. But the "country of football" wasn't engulfed by soccer fever either. No matter how much the media tried to hype the event, the population remained aloof, even distant.

There were no mass protests disrupting the tournament. Protests that did occur were largely ignored by the media. What had happened to the movement that only a year earlier, in June 2013, had demanded hospitals and schools instead of stadiums living up to "FIFA standards"? The movement that denounced forced evictions and police violence? The movement that had been able to prevent the raise of public transport fees?

Social Inequality

In June 2013, when the FIFA Confederations Cup was held in Brazil as a
test case for this year's World Cup, millions of people protested across the
country. The protests originated in March, after the city of Porto Alegre
had raised public transport fees. In April, due to massive resistance, the
decision was revoked. This success instigated a popular movement that
targeted a variety of social ills. Brazilian activists give a variety of reasons
why it was not rekindled during the World Cup.

First, mass demonstrations have not been a feature of everyday life
in Brazil since the days of the military regime and the democracy movement of 1983–1984. The expectation that the momentum of the June 2013
protests could be maintained until the summer of 2014 was unrealistic.

Second, the political profile of the 2013 protests became blurry. By
June, when the number of participants peaked, the progressive demands
for better public transport, education, health services, and the "right to the
city" had been replaced by a general frustration with the status quo, the
alleged incompetence of the government, and widespread corruption. It
was "good form" to partake in the protests. Meanwhile, the political right,
eager to oust the Workers' Party from government, was trying to co-opt
them.

When participation in the protests subsided, the protests regained
their leftist profile. The social movements that had emerged in Brazil
during the early 2000s and local groups kept them alive with the help
of loosely connected grassroots committees. The different issues that
people focused on coalesced in a critique of the development plans for
the 2014 FIFA World Cup and the 2016 Olympic Games. It was commonly
understood that Brazil's marginalized communities would pay the price.
The sports events became symbols for the ongoing social inequality in
the country and for prioritizing the interests of transnational corporations.
People were engaged in different struggles: *favela* residents fought for
better living conditions and an end to endemic violence as well as forced
evictions, while nationwide movements demanded reforms of the education system. One reason for the protest movement not having been able to
mobilize large crowds in 2014 might have been its clear left-wing profile.

Controversies within the Movement

Another reason for the relatively low number of protests was repression.
All protests that did occur were met by police in riot gear. In 2013, the
repression galvanized the movement; it provoked people who made police
violence one of the main issues they rallied against. But when a journalist
was killed by a flare thrown by a protester, there was widespread concern
for a spiral of violence and the movement became divided. The media
exploited the image of the "menacing black bloc." Militant forms of protest

had little support within the movement, and the fear for violent confrontation was a strong demobilizing factor.

The diversity of the movement might have also turned from strength to weakness. Brazilian activists seem undecided on this. There was substantial disagreement over whether to embrace the slogan "There Won't Be a World Cup"; many activists thought that football should be used as a positive reference point instead. There was also disagreement with regard to the Workers' Party. Some protesters did not want to weaken the party ahead of the general elections in October, while others rejected all party politics.

Finally, one must not underestimate the Brazilian people's emotional attachment to football and the World Cup. While a small faction of the left hoped for an early exit of the *Seleção*—a novelty in Brazil—the majority of activists were not interested in boycotting the tournament. Rather then joining a protest, they wanted to see a game with their friends.

The protests that did occur were diverse. In Rio, a march to the Maracanã Stadium was held under the motto "There Won't Be a World Cup." It was stopped by police using tear gas, pepper spray, and rubber bullets. Protesters smashed windows and threw rocks and Molotov cocktails. Four rallies were organized under the motto "Our World Cup Happens in the Streets." The aim was not to prevent or disrupt the World Cup, but to use the event to spotlight social woes (not least for international football fans) with the help of artistic interventions and street football tournaments. There was also a march under the slogan "The Festival in the Stadiums Is Not Worth the Tears in the Favelas." It was organized by favela residents who wanted to bring the protests against the militarization of their neighborhoods from the city's periphery to the rich parts of town where the tourists gathered. The march went from the Copacabana to the favela of Pavão-Pavãozinho. Participants carried coffins and crosses made out of cardboard and displayed images of police violence and of people murdered in the favelas, almost all of them young Black males. The police met the protests with little concern for the law. Alleged ringleaders were preemptively arrested and accused of forming "terrorist" organizations. Security forces responded with particular violence to all protests in the vicinity of the Maracanã Stadium.

Even if the numbers of people participating in the 2014 protests were lower than expected, the 2013 protests did have an impact on the public reception of the World Cup. No matter how much the media tried to stir up a World Cup frenzy, it was never felt on the streets. Protest slogans such as "This Is Not Our World Cup" clearly resonated with many Brazilians. It was hard to have a conversation about the World Cup without someone pointing out that it was only the white upper class who could afford to attend games in the stadiums. Despite their great love for football, Brazilians agreed that the money that had been spent on the tournament should have rather been invested in health services and education. FIFA's disregard for human rights was seen as a disgrace.

Football no longer functioned as a national umbrella that made class differences in Brazil disappear. This unifying function had been undermined for years, with ticket prices constantly rising and supporter groups being harassed by the police. The expenses for the World Cup and the submission to FIFA's demands were seen as a logical consequence of this development. Instead of football concealing social contradictions, it was now highlighting them. The people's reception of the World Cup made it clear that these contradictions were no longer accepted.

Networks of Social Movements

With the 2016 Olympic Games approaching, Rio awaits yet another major sports event. More stadiums are being built, and there will be more forced evictions and relocations. At least, the protest movement has forced the local government to enter negotiations with residents, also about compensation packages.

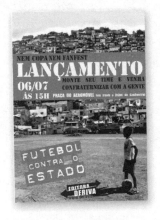

In the past fifteen years, many social movements emerged in Brazil independently from the organizations of the traditional left. These movements have developed their own forms of political practice as well as strong networks. Grassroots organizations in the favelas, NGOs, and progressive scholars unite to make left-wing criticism of the neoliberal agenda a part of everyday political debate, not without success. A movement that had, at times, lost direction and was threatened by right-wing co-optation has proven resilient and regained its left-wing roots. Activists in Rio de Janeiro are certain about one thing: even after the World Cup, the protests will continue.

Gesa Köbberling is a psychologist based in Freiburg, Germany. During the 2014 Men's World Cup, she attended a conference on football and social movements in Porto Alegre and rekindled old friendships as well as her love for community organizing in Rio de Janeiro. This article appeared as "Weder rauschendes Fest noch Protesturm" in *analyse & kritik*, no. 596, August 19, 2014. Translated by Gabriel Kuhn.

■ A Prisoner of Football: An Interview with Deniz Naki

Moritz Ablinger and Jakob Rosenberg

"I don't want to go to prison because of a tattoo." Deniz Naki has to be careful with how he expresses himself—even on his body. On his lower left arm it says *azadi*, freedom; the hand below is adorned by an image of Ernesto "Che" Guevara. Naki calls Che "an international freedom fighter." The Amed SK striker himself is under surveillance by the Turkish state. In April 2017, he received a suspended prison sentence of eighteen months because of "terrorist propaganda." Naki had dedicated the victory in a 2015 cup match to the victims of the Turkish-Kurdish conflict. In 2014, when the Islamic State attacked the town of Kobane in Syrian Kurdistan, Naki expressed his support for the Kurdish forces in an online post.

In July 2017, Naki visits Vienna. He is the celebrity guest at a festival arranged by FEYKOM, an umbrella organization for Kurds in Austria. While the former St. Pauli player signs autographs and poses for selfies, a stall nearby sells the Amed shirt bearing his name. Our interview is interrupted several times, as people come to shake his hand. When we ask for the reason of his popularity in the Kurdish diaspora, the answer does not come from Naki but his sidekick Murat: "Everybody knows him. He is a role model. He doesn't mince his words and says what people think."

In 2013, you left Germany's second league to play in Turkey. Was it hard to adjust?
I had political problems in Turkey right from the start. I have been there for four years. For one and a half years I played for Gençlerbirliği in Ankara. When the attack on Kobane happened, I posted something online and was attacked by three men on the street. I returned to Germany and did not play football for about eight months. I had no intentions of returning to Turkey, but with Amed it was different. Amed is a Kurdish club. The president, the management, and 85 percent of the players are Kurds. When they got in touch, it was an easy decision to join them. I arrived in a war zone. Things are calmer at the moment, but you never know when and where the next bomb is going to explode. In the spring of 2016, I was suspended from the league for twelve weeks and got involved in everyday life in Diyarbakır, as Amed is called in Turkish. I saw people dying. What do you do? You have to speak out.

In April, you were sentenced to prison, but it seems you still want to return. Why?
I am bound to return to Amed. At the first trial, I was freed from all charges. At the second trial, both the judge and the prosecutor were the same, but I received a suspended prison sentence of eighteen months

and twenty-two days, with a probation period of five years. You don't have to do anything in Turkey to go to prison. But, honestly, I would rather be in prison than on probation for five years. They wanted to make an example of me. They want me to be quiet. But I won't be quiet for five years.

Don't you feel restricted at all because of the sentence?
No. It doesn't matter whether I get five or ten years on probation. I have done nothing wrong. We as a people want peace. If that is a crime, I am ready to commit it. When someone says, "We want peace, not war," and then you call him a terrorist, I am happy to be a terrorist.

Your lawyer considered an appeal. What is the current status?
Who would I appeal to? The judge? The state? The judge had already freed me from all charges. Then he felt the heat from above.

Have you become politically more conscious in Turkey?
I wouldn't say that I have become more conscious. I followed the developments in Turkey when I was living in Europe, too. But it's a big difference when you're on the ground. I have seen bombs being dropped and people die. I have carried dead bodies. It affects you deeply. If you see it on television, yes, it also affects you, but there is always something you can do for distraction. When you're in the middle of it, you don't have that option.

Is it your calling to create more awareness of the Turkish-Kurdish conflict?
If I can be a voice for my people, I am happy to be that voice. I am well known. It is an advantage that I have played in the Bundesliga, of course. If I have a problem, people support me. I still get support from St. Pauli, which I much appreciate.

Isn't it also a disadvantage that you are well known, since it means you have many eyes on you?
Of course. It means that the people in Turkey who don't like me are aware of what I'm doing. I am loved by the people in the east of the country, but not in the west. I have to be careful when I move there, especially now. The Kurdish people are proud of me, which means that those who oppose me are waiting for any mistake I might make.

Are you worried for your safety?
I only leave Diyarbakır for away games. Then, I must be prepared for anything. It could be prison or worse. But I have decided to follow this path, and I didn't make that decision just a year or two ago. I come from

a political family and I was raised with politics. My father is a political refugee, he hasn't been able to visit Turkey for forty years.

Are your parents proud of you? Are they worried?
I am not doing anything wrong. Of course, my mother worries. When things are really bad, she calls me every night, asking me how I am and telling me to be careful. My father's motto is: "When you decide to do something, you have to stand for it." I have chosen the same path he chose.

You mean you returned to Turkey to continue his struggle?
That's right. Imagine my father saying: "Stop and focus on football!" My response would be: "You were tortured, you were imprisoned, and you were forced to flee to Germany." What would he say then?

At away games, you and your teammates are called terrorists and PKK supporters. How different is your life from that of an ordinary football player?
We are abused and ridiculed. People throw things at us, and I am always the center of attention. In the beginning, it bothered me, but then I developed a different attitude: the more I am attacked, the more motivated I become. I have to give my answer on the pitch. In Bursa, I was cursed by twenty thousand supporters—after I had scored my second goal, everyone was quiet. That is the best response. But it is difficult, it's not like it was with St. Pauli. When we played with St. Pauli against Hansa Rostock, fierce rivals, I planted a St. Pauli flag on the pitch. But security is high in German stadiums, I didn't have to worry about anyone storming onto the pitch to go after me. If I planted a Kurdish flag on the pitch in Bursa or Erzurum, people would come down from the stands, burn the flag, and, most probably, kill me. When we played in Erzurum, there were thirty thousand people in the stadium, but only about a thousand policemen.

Do you feel protected by the police?
Truly, the police unsettles me. At away games, they can even attack us. You always have to ask yourself: Who is your friend? Who really helps you? In the end, we can only trust ourselves. It's twenty-five men against everybody else. Should a supporter attack me, I wouldn't hide behind a policeman and say: "Protect me!" I know that he'd want to go after me as well.

Do you get support from other fans? Beşiktaş, for example, has a left-wing supporter group with Çarşı.
Yes, there are some left-wing fans, but when it comes to Amed, we have no friends. Our friends are other clubs in the east, but they play in lower leagues. Otherwise, there are just individual fans who stand behind us.

How about the Gezi Park movement?

The Gezi Park movement? What shall I say about that? They gathered in front of a tree and said: "You are not supposed to cut down that tree." I respect that, it was a protest movement, and it was attacked by the state. That's all fine, but, at the same time, people died in Diyarbakır, in Sur, in Cizre, in Nusaybin. Why did no one protect them? Why did no one mobilize one hundred thousand people and build a barricade? When you can organize an uprising because of a tree but decide to remain silent when people are killed, I am not interested in your movement.

In February 2016, you were suspended for twelve games, and your club was fined 150,000 euros. Does the Turkish Football Federation want to prevent Amed from being promoted to the second league?

Of course. Amed has got more attention in two years than other clubs in their entire existence. The Turkish Football Association and the politicians do everything they can to prevent us from being promoted. They think: "If the club already causes problems in the third league, what would happen if they advanced all the way to the first?" Our games would be shown on television, also in Europe. People would see how we are treated. Many still don't know. That's why our fans record matches on their mobile phones. When Diyarbakir was a war zone, we could at least bring some joy into people's lives.

Don't you ever think: "I shouldn't be playing football right now, there are more important things to do"?

After everything I experienced, I no longer had any desire to play football. I wanted to go in a completely different direction—something I cannot talk about now. If we do another interview in ten years, and I am no longer in Turkey, I will tell you what I would have liked to do. But I think I can make our people happy with football. I have to keep on playing, even if I don't want to.

Are you a prisoner of football?

Exactly. There aren't many who would put up with this. It is no fun to be abused by a crowd of thirty thousand people. They abuse my mother, my siblings, my entire family. They abuse my culture and my religion. But if I stopped, I would feel like I surrendered. I would be telling people: "Okay, I am afraid. I will stop. You will get rid of me, and I will get rid of you." Instead, I will stay and say: "You are wrong. Me, I have done nothing wrong. That's why I'm here. You can scream and shout as much as you want."

As Amedspor racked up the wins in the Turkish Cup in early 2016, the historic city center of Diyarbakır, Sur was under a ruthless curfew and siege.

Hundreds were killed, mostly civilians

and much of the neighborhood was flattened.

Since the ceasefire had fully broken down, far-right politicians began to stoke the simmering racist flames

and to nationalists, Amedspor became the enemy.

an illegal team with a fan base of terrorists.

Amedspor Director of Football, Servet Evrol described games as "war missions."

Away games greeted the team with seas of Turkish flags, nationalist banners and their fans with torrents of racist abuse and violence.

How long do you intend to stay?

I will stay until the people say: "It's enough; you can go now." Neither the club's president nor the management can send me away, only the people. If the people say, "We have had enough of you and want you to leave," then I will leave. But I hope this won't happen.

Do you expect further problems with the Turkish Football Association?

If they start suspending me for any nonsense, it will only hurt the club. If that happens, I will stop with football completely. In Turkey, I would never get another offer, even though I am good enough to play in the first league. I have talked to clubs from the first league whose managers wanted me to come, but they can't risk this because of the fans.

Why aren't there more other outspoken players?

There are many Kurdish players in Turkey's first league. But what they care about are their careers and their salaries. I don't want to name names, but this includes players who play for the Turkish national team and are admired by the fans. Of course, the fans only admire them because they keep their mouths shut. They would no longer be admired if they spoke out against the government and its actions. I know this, because I have experienced it. When women and girls were sold on the markets in Kobane, when children were raped and men beheaded, I said: "Wait a minute, what is happening here?" That was all I did.

What would happen to the players you mentioned if they spoke out?

Their days in the first league would be over. I could have also kept quiet and prioritized my career and my salary. But then I could no longer look at myself in the mirror. I might not earn as much as other players, and I might not have the same career. But when we face the Kurdish people, I am the one they will embrace. This love you cannot buy with money, not even if you are multibillionaire.

Update March 2018: During a visit to Germany in January 2018, Deniz Naki escaped an assassination attempt when a car he was traveling in was shot at several times. He moved to a safe house and decided not to return to Turkey. Shortly thereafter, the Turkish Football Association banned him for life from playing football in the country due to "ideological propaganda."

This interview originally appeared under the title "Gefangener des Fußballs" in *Ballesterer*, no. 124, September 2017. Translated by Gabriel Kuhn.

▍Kämpa Showan!

PM Press blog, December 12, 2016
Gabriel Kuhn

While returning home from celebrating International Women's Day on March 8, 2014, a group of left-wing activists in Malmö, Sweden, was confronted by neo-Nazis. Among the activists was Showan Shattak, a well-known antifascist organizer and supporter of Malmö FF, the town's main football club and one of Sweden's most successful. Showan was stabbed and brutally beaten. A severe head injury threatened his life, and he was in an induced coma for a week. After seven operations and months of rehabilitation, he still suffers from exhaustion, lack of concentration, and attention deficits to this day.

Although three more activists were stabbed, with another receiving life-threatening injuries, Showan became the attack's public face. The slogan Kämpa Showan! (Fight Showan!) spread quickly on social media, banners in support of the attacked appeared in football stadiums across northern Europe, and antifascist rallies were organized in numerous Swedish towns. A friend of Showan summarized the phenomenon thus:

> Suddenly, a snowball started rolling and, next you thing you knew, it had turned into an avalanche. There was no strategic plan. I think it was a combination of him being a very open, social, and well-connected person and the broad resistance against fascism that exists. No one knew if Showan had wanted any of that, but now it was too late. It could no longer be stopped.

The quote is from a newly released book documenting a history that has brought left-wing politics and football supporters' culture together in the public eye like few others. Lavishly illustrated and beautifully designed, *Ingen jävla hjälte* (No Fucking Hero) was written by the journalist Andreas Rasmussen, a friend of Showan's from neighboring Copenhagen. He states in his introduction:

> Neither Showan nor I like it when struggles or movements are represented by individuals. Still, it felt right to write this book. Showan has become a symbol for struggles and movements. Large parts of society associate him with the struggle against homophobia and racism, with the city of Malmö, and with the football club Malmö FF. This is why it feels appropriate that he gets to tell his story and who he is, what he has experienced and how he looks at life and the world.

Rasmussen weaves together Showan's family history (his parents fled Iran in the 1980s), the relationship to his former girlfriend Charlotte (also stabbed during the 2014 attack), his politicization and embrace of Malmö

FF, and the events of March 8, 2014, as well as their aftermath in a patchwork-like book divided into several short chapters. Nothing is explored in depth, but the result is a very readable, telling, and often touching insight into Swedish society and politics, the extra-parliamentary left, and (albeit to a lesser degree) football culture.

The book ends with the trial against two of the neo-Nazis responsible for injuring Showan and his friends. The main defendant had hidden for two years in Ukraine, presumably with the help of fascist companions. Eventually, he was arrested and extradited to Sweden. He was sentenced to three years in prison for assault, but was not convicted for attempted murder. His co-defendant was freed from all charges. The decisions raised many eyebrows in Sweden, especially considering the more severe sentences handed out to militant antifascists in recent years.

Even if you don't read Swedish, flip through *Ingen jävla hjälte* if you ever get the chance. The photographs and the artwork alone are worth it. Kämpa Showan! Kämpa Malmö!

Trial update: After the book had gone to print, a Swedish court of appeals reversed the original sentences: the defendant arrested in Ukraine was now freed from all charges, while his co-defendant was sentenced for assault, receiving a three-year prison term.

■

The FIFA Scandal of 2015

On May 27, 2015, the day before FIFA's 65th congress, Swiss police entered a luxury hotel in Zurich and arrested seven FIFA officials accused of fraud. This triggered a tale that has all the ingredients of a compelling true-life crime story: with several law enforcement agencies across the world involved, the FBI and Interpol included, bribes and corruption were disclosed as common features of FIFA operations, affecting all major tournaments. Billions of dollars were distributed among a feudal elite of soccer bureaucrats. The tale entails FIFA-officials-turned-informants (most notably, the influential U.S. soccer administrator Chuck Blazer), high-profile trials, witness intimidation, the mysterious death of a defendant, undisclosed internal investigations, and heads rolling at FIFA headquarters (albeit without much impact on the organization's structure). In the first edition of this book, I described FIFA as "an extremely powerful and rich organization, rife with corruption and oligarchic structures and tied into many political and economic interests." If any proof for this assessment was needed, it was provided by the events of 2015 and their consequences.

What essentially triggered the investigations leading to the legal crackdown on FIFA was the bizarre awarding of the 2022 Men's World Cup to Qatar. The U.S., also a bidder, felt snubbed and the FBI got involved. Since the World Cup was awarded to Qatar in 2010, the country has been criticized for the atrocious conditions under which migrant workers are building stadiums and infrastructure. Despite occasional concessions by the Qatar government—including a reform of the infamous *kafala* system, which essentially leaves migrant workers without rights and under full control of their employers—the lives of migrant workers in Qatar are still defined by cramped housing, low wages, poor safety standards, lack of union representation, and legal discrimination. In its "State of the World's Human Rights" report of 2017–2018, Amnesty International offered a sobering conclusion: "Third-party auditors highlighted some progress on projects for the football World Cup in 2022, but identified abuses of migrant workers at all 10 of the contractors they investigated."

▋ FIFA's Corruption Scandal–Let's Take Back the Game

Ryan Reilly

On May 27, the world of international soccer was rocked by yet another corruption scandal. Fourteen top ranking officials of FIFA, soccer's world governing body, were indicted by the United State Department of Justice on a variety of charges including racketeering, money laundering, and wire fraud. The charges stem from bribes and kickbacks paid out for media deals and vote buying associated with major world tournaments, including the World Cup. Recently appointed U.S. Attorney General Loretta Lynch charged, "These individuals and organizations engaged in bribery to decide who would televise games, where the games would be held, and who would run the organization overseeing organized soccer worldwide." Swiss authorities are also investigating FIFA officials with their investigation centered on corruption relating to the awarding of the 2018 and 2022 World Cup tournaments to Russia and Qatar respectively.

FIFA was founded in 1904 to help further the spread of what would become the world's most popular game by codifying the rules. Today, FIFA has become an undemocratic cesspool of corruption and sexism controlling the game of soccer. Where once it helped standardize the rules of a game that swept the international working class, it now acts as a brutal tool of capitalism, sweeping aside communities and the game's traditions in the name of profits for the world's largest corporations.

As if to thumb its nose toward human rights, FIFA awarded 2018 and 2022 World Cups to Russia and Qatar. Despite launching a "Say No to

Racism" campaign, FIFA awarded the 2018 World Cup to Russia despite that country's dismal record on LGBTQ rights. Perhaps even more scandalously, the 2022 World Cup was awarded to Qatar though that country had no infrastructure to host such a huge event. To rectify that Qatar has imported hundreds of thousands of migrant workers, many from Nepal. To FIFA's and Qatar's eternal shame thousands of workers have already lost their lives building stadiums, roads and other related projects. Already, *The Nation* reports that up to 1,200 migrant workers have died.

New Beginning?

Fans across the world are looking to the corruption probes to finally clean up the corruption within FIFA. Corruption scandals have become almost commonplace for FIFA, though this time seemed different for two reasons: The number of indictments handed down is unprecedented; and the arrests came a mere two days before the vote to reelect the 17-year incumbent Sepp Blatter as President of FIFA. Blatter's presidency has been riddled with scandal, yet he won this year's vote despite the storm raging around him. Then, in another shock to the soccer world, Blatter announced that he would be resigning his presidency just four days after the vote.

This announcement has encouraged soccer fans around the globe that perhaps a new beginning was possible for FIFA. Blatter presided over decades of corruption. The general outlines were apparent to all, but the sordid details are only now seeing the light of day. Blatter, despite overseeing anti-racist campaigns, has maintained sexist attitudes in regards to the women's game. When asked how the women's game could be made more popular, he infamously stated, "They could, for example, have tighter shorts." In a cruel ironic twist of fate the Women's World Cup was slated to start a few days after the indictments, whose drama could well overshadow some of the world's best athletes and soccer players on the biggest stage of their careers. In many ways it truly encapsulates how FIFA officials have treated women soccer players as second class citizens.

The twin investigations by U.S. and Swiss authorities and Sepp Blatter's subsequent resignation will see a superficial new beginning for FIFA. How far the investigation and the effort to root out corruption remains to be seen; certainly the first charge of the next president will be to end some of the most corrupt and obvious payoffs and kickbacks. Will the next FIFA regime signal a new day for women's soccer? With a closed, undemocratic system—even the presidents of each national soccer organization, like US Soccer, are not elected—it remains to be seen how much public pressure can force reforms to the global game.

The problems of FIFA run much deeper than a few bad apple officials and a misogynistic president. Sepp Blatter's predecessor, João Havelange summed it up pretty well when he said, "I came here to sell a product

called football, and my intention is for this
product to reach as many consumers as it can,
and for its price to constantly grow." Under
Havelange and Blatter soccer fans became
"consumers," while the organization aimed to
squeeze as much money from them as possible, for the highest possible profit. Millions of
people around the world watch and play soccer.
By monopolizing control over soccer FIFA has
amassed massive amounts of revenue. According to Forbes.com, total
revenue for the 2014 was a whopping $2 billion!

Under capitalism the games we love are monetized and used to
generate massive amounts of profit. Soccer is no different. FIFA is not in
business "For The Game. For The World," as their slogan reads. While
most FIFA officials probably did not join in order to reap the rewards of a
corrupt organization the logic of running FIFA as a business in a capitalist
world dictates that profit and money come before love for the game itself.

It is estimated that nearly a billion people watched the final game of
the 2014 World Cup between Germany and Argentina. That represents
a massive captive audience for the sponsors of the World Cup such as
Coca-Cola, Adidas, Visa, Hyundai, and Budweiser, and the rest of the
who's who of corporate sponsors. These corporations are more than
willing to pay FIFA handsomely for the exclusive rights to advertise in the
stadiums, on television and radio broadcasts, and to put FIFA's logo on
their products. Of course they do not pay because they love soccer. They
pay because a billion people will view the corporations' advertising while
watching the game they love.

FIFA Needs You, You Don't Need FIFA
Host countries of the World Cup and other tournaments are expected
to provide what are called "FIFA quality stadiums." The expectations are
that not only should the stadiums be world class but also the surrounding
infrastructure needs to be state of the art and the local areas need to be
made safe for visiting dignitaries and travelling fans. Often these demands
lead to abuses. The deaths of migrant workers in Qatar illustrate that
perfectly. In preparing for the 2014 World Cup, Brazilian officials displaced
hundreds of thousands of residents of the historic favela neighborhoods. It
cost Brazil $15 billion total to host the tournament with most of that being
taxpayer funded. Jules Boykoff, a former professional soccer player and
current political science professor at Pacific University, calls this "celebration capitalism," where public-private partnerships are created in a mood
of excitement for the games so that "the public pays and the private
profits."

In the lead up to the 2014 World Cup in Brazil, for which Brazil spent $11 billion on public works projects alone, the people of Brazil took exception to how this "celebration capitalism" took advantage of their love for the game of soccer. Protestors demanded "FIFA quality schools," "FIFA quality hospitals," and "FIFA quality homes," etc. The money spent on stadiums, some of which were practically abandoned after the World Cup, could have been spent on improving the infrastructure and social programs for millions of Brazilians. Even members of the Brazilian national team voiced their support for the protests. Neymar wrote on his Facebook page, "I always had faith that we wouldn't need to get to the point of 'going to the street' to demand better transport, health services, education and security. I also want a fairer, safer, healthier and more honest Brazil." The late Uruguayan journalist and author Eduardo Galeano summed it up perfectly:

> Brazilians, who are the most soccer-mad of all, have decided not allow their sport to be used anymore as an excuse for humiliating the many and enriching the few. The fiesta of soccer, a feast for the legs that play and the eyes that watch, is much more than a big business run by overlords from Switzerland. The most popular sport in the world wants to serve the people who embrace it.

Millions of working class people the world over embrace soccer as a refuge from the hardships of everyday life. Those who seek to use their love of the game to reap massive amounts of profit threaten to ruin the game. Fans should demand not only an end to FIFA corruption and abuses in places like Brazil and Qatar but control of the game itself. The money generated by soccer could be used for socially beneficial programs including building soccer facilities for everyone to use and enjoy regardless of ability to pay. The Brazilian protestors were correct in calling for FIFA quality hospitals/schools/homes. The money is there but under capitalism that money goes to a very few select individuals within FIFA and their corporate sponsors.

There is little point to having faith in FIFA reforming itself.

Fans could create democratic structures that could organize leagues and tournaments locally, nationally and globally. Fan organizations could ultimately demand the municipalisation of club teams so that they are run for the benefit of the areas in which they are located. For example, Barcelona Football Club has an ownership structure that consists of fans purchasing a membership in the club and electing an assembly of delegates to run the club. The Green Bay Packers do not have a single ownership but are likewise owned by the people who love the team. That is the only reason the Packers have been able to stay and thrive in North America's smallest major league sports market.

While the indictments by the U.S. Justice Department are a good start in exposing and cleaning up the corruption inherent in FIFA, it should be noted that this is the same Justice Department that refuses to expose and clean up the corruption inherent on Wall Street. Loretta Lynch can order the arrests of soccer officials and sports marketing directors but cannot order FIFA to be more democratic. Only by joining together in mass movements to demand a full investigation of FIFA corruption and the replacement of big business ownership with community control can working class soccer fans begin to truly democratize the game they love.

Ryan Reilly writes on sports and politics and tweets at @Ryan_Reilly78. This article was originally published by *Socialist Alternative*, June 30, 2015.

Why Is the 2022 World Cup Being Held in a Country That Practices Modern-Day Slavery?

Michelle Chen

This summer, the populist fervor of Brazil's World Cup sparked riotous street protests against the country's economic hierarchy. But the 2022 World Cup in Qatar is being built in an even more unequal country, and there will likely be little public unrest, just vast expanses of deserts and skyscrapers, where the country's poorest workers are forced to toil in silent captivity.

In this miniature oil empire, a tiny elite lords over an impoverished majority of imported workers. Now that thousands of those migrants are constructing the state-of-the-art arenas and gleaming modern transit hubs of world football, rights advocates are pushing for an abolition of Qatar's medieval labor regime.

Human rights activists estimate the true costs of the World Cup in terms of the rising migrant death toll, estimated at about 1,200 nationwide since the World Cup was awarded, projected to reach 4,000 by the time the games begin. According to advocates, the harsh labor conditions at the game sites and surrounding infrastructure have led to a massive fatality rate; causes range from construction-related injuries to cardiac arrest to suicide.

In recent weeks, the Qatari government has presented reform plans such as strengthening employment contract law, improving housing standards and better regulating wage payments. Though it has shown more openness to labor reform than other Persian Gulf states, the government disappointed advocacy groups by stopping short of endorsing a minimum wage or unionization rights, and providing no set timetable for policy changes. Recently, the Qatar Foundation, a quasi-governmental think tank, issued one of the most extensive analyses yet of migrant labor issues, with similar reform recommendations, but still did not endorse the radical changes that rights groups have demanded.

Though the reform proposals encourage greater transparency and oversight of employers, along with international collaboration with migrant's home countries, they basically leave intact (aside from a name change) the traditional structure of labor sponsorship, known as the kafala system, which activists say is at the root of the mistreatment and exploitation of migrants.

Investigations by media and advocacy groups like the International Trade Union Confederation (ITUC) and Human Rights Watch have revealed that workers bound by kafala, mostly from South Asia, often live in squalid encampments, labor all day in hazard-prone, sweltering building sites and often suffer fraud and wage theft. But the social and political isolation cuts the deepest. Workers are legally captives of their employers, blocking them from changing jobs or leaving the country.

The Qatar Foundation's report, authored by the migration studies scholar Ray Jureidini, recommends developing "standardized ethical recruitment practices in the labor sending countries" and cutting down on excessive recruitment fees that put migrants in heavy debt. The report also recommends standardization and transparency in contracting. Nonetheless, it does not address workers' needs for freedom of movement and the autonomy to break from an employer or leave the country. It also dismisses the idea of an equal pay law, arguing that "Qatari citizens have the highest GDP in the world," so comparable wages for poor foreigners would be unfeasible.

Activists warn that whatever the law states, migrants in the kafala system typically have almost no legal recourse against abusive employers or protection from retaliation for challenging authority. The ITUC's report on Qatar labor quotes a driver from the Philippines: "We are afraid to complain to the authorities. We see that workers who do complain are either blacklisted, deported or threatened. Our managers told us that workers who go on strike get deported within 12 hours."

Even when migrant contract workers lose their jobs, they may end up stranded indefinitely if their employer does not give permission for them to return home. Workers who run away or are "abandoned" by their bosses might wind up homeless, unemployable and trapped on foreign soil.

Besides the World Cup labor camps, female household workers are even more vulnerable to abuse, as well as sexual violence. Thousands of domestic workers reportedly flee their bosses each year. A domestic worker, who ran away from a boss who had raped her, told the ITUC: "When I see a Qatari man, I am always afraid because I am thinking they will catch me and put me in jail, and send me to the Philippines. Running away from your sponsor is very difficult because I don't have any legal papers, and then I cannot get a good job."

Rights groups say the problem of migrant labor in Qatar is not simply that laws are not followed or enforced but that contracts are often used to control workers rather than to establish a mutual partnership, and thus lock them into an extremely oppressive system.

Union activists have called for a full abolition of the kafala system and guarantees of a minimum wage, freedom of assembly and collective bargaining, in accordance with international labor standards. The ITUC has even pushed for a rerun of the Qatar vote to stop the games altogether.

ITUC General Secretary Sharran Burrow tells *The Nation* via e-mail that the Qatar Foundation's latest recommendations will be toothless unless migrants are guaranteed equal treatment and access to justice:

> None of the reforms proposed in the Qatar Foundation report are going to work without rule of law, including a competent and fully staffed labour inspectorate and a functional judiciary. If you look at the thousands of workers trapped in deportation centres, or with unsolved complaints, this is nowhere in evidence in Qatar. Once again, Qatar has shown a blind spot on the fundamental right of freedom of association. Not a word is mentioned in the Qatar Foundation report about Qatar meeting its international obligations.

But another challenge to reform is Qatar's social and cultural anxiety about the country's huge demographic imbalances. Qatar has one of the highest ratios of migrants to citizens, with foreign workers making up some 85 percent of the population.

James Dorsey, longtime observer of Mideast soccer politics and senior fellow at Nanyang Technological University in Singapore, says that while the "enlightened autocracy" that rules Qatari society might be open to basic improvements in working conditions, the fundamental shift needs to begin on a cultural level. If Qatari officialdom ultimately decides to broach political issues like union rights and freedom of association, he says, it would follow "as a consequence of" other social and political restructuring as the country faces the fallout of minority rule.

At the same time, change is being accelerated by public pressure, as Qatar faces greater worldwide scrutiny in its bid to gain "soft power" through cultural and commercial investments.

"What the Qataris are realizing is that their winning of the right to host the World Cup not only gave them leverage, but gave others leverage," Dorsey tells *The Nation*. "So suddenly . . . groups like Amnesty and Human Rights Watch, they have moral authority," amid the public outcry over worker deaths. "The ITUC," he adds, "potentially has 175 million members in 153 countries, presumably a majority of those members are football fans, so it can actually move bodies."

The upshot of World Cup 2022 is that in the glaring spotlight of football's globalized populism, Qatar is finally being held to account for labor abuses that would otherwise be dismissed as just the cost of doing business. And fans around the world will now see that their fellow workers have paid the ultimate price for a few days of sporting spectacle.

Michelle Chen writes for *The Nation*, *Dissent*, and *In These Times*. She tweets at @meeshellchen. This article was originally published by *The Nation*, July 23, 2014.

The People's Football Congress

Call-out, June 2015
David Goldblatt

The King is heading for exile, many of his courtiers are in the tower or on the run, but the ancien régime remains intact. The world's national football associations, many of whose senior executives are enmeshed in the ever widening web of corruption and bribery, and few of which are accountable to anyone or anything, remain the kingmakers.

However, neither they nor FIFA own football. They hold it in trust for the rest of the world. The meanings and values that coalesce around the game are not produced by them, by football associations nor even by the great clubs and their super stars.

Football matters because people have chosen to invest it with meaning by playing, organising and following it. The crowds that populate the stadium of this planet are not mere consumers but chorus, commentator and an essential component of the spectacle and ritual that makes it the global game.

But we—the global communities of grassroots players, fans, amateur officials and coaches—are not consulted or represented by our football associations anywhere in the world. Nor have we any reason to think that they are capable of making enlightened decisions that favour the common good over private, and venal interests.

If we want this to change we have to let them know, in person.

We propose that alongside the extraordinary FIFA congress that will elect the next president, to hold the People's Football Congress. (People FC for short?)

In common with, and inspired by the World Social Forum, the congress will create a space in which the global civil society of players and fans, individuals and NGOs, social and political football activists, from every continent, can gather, communicate, play football, protest and have an inordinate amount of fun.

People FC will meet on the day before FIFA congress and offer, in many different ways, an alternative vision of the governance of world football. On the day of the FIFA congress, the People FC will help organise a day of protest, pranks, and alternative commentary on the events in the Palace.

Various factors prevented the People's Football Congress from taking place in 2015. But the vision expressed in this call to action is as relevant as it was then. David Goldblatt is the author of *The Ball Is Round* and is currently hosting the Al-Jazeera football podcast *The Game of Our Lives*.

Keeping It Real: Alternative Football Cont.

Many people are working on alternatives to the FIFA-controlled game of soccer in the form of community clubs and grassroots leagues—a potential basis for a People's Football Congress should the idea ever bear fruition. On the following pages, we will look at four examples in more detail: the ongoing efforts of the Easton Cowboys and Cowgirls in Bristol, England; 17 SK, a community sports club in Stockholm, Sweden; Futbolistas L.A. and the Left Wing Fútbol Collectives network in the U.S.; and the "Wild League" in Vienna, Austria.

■ Review of *Freedom Through Football: The Story of the Easton Cowboys and Cowgirls*

Alpine Anarchist Productions, December 2012
Gabriel Kuhn

Within alternative sports circles, the Easton Cowboys and Cowgirls of Bristol have reached quasi-legendary status. Among the various sports clubs prioritizing community building, solidarity, and fun over competition and profit, the Easton Cowboys and Cowgirls stand out as one of the longest running, biggest, and most influential. Now, on the twentieth anniversary of their foundation, we are presented with a history of the club in book form. Will Simpson and Malcolm McMahon have risen to the task, providing us with all the crucial facts, reports of the club's major activities, analyses of its inner workings, entertaining anecdotes, and numerous pictures and illustrations, including state-of-the-art DIY flyers from the earliest days. Since the original Cowboys were a football team and since footballers remain the strongest contingent within the club (with no less than seven active teams), the focus on soccer is not surprising; however, we also learn about Cowboys and Cowgirls playing cricket, netball, basketball, and even, during a short-lived attempt in the 1990s, rugby. In telling the club's story, the authors do not gloss over the problems that all social projects of this kind inevitably encounter—here, they include death, substance addiction, and internal conflict. Simpson and McMahon handle these difficult issues with remarkable care and dignity.

The idea of sports clubs focusing on community rather than competition is not new. In fact, it is at the heart of the original amateur ideal. The problem with traditional amateurism, however, is twofold: 1. It often had a class bias, where the ideal was primarily sustained by those who could afford it, that is, by people who had no need to earn money from playing sports. 2. It was apolitical, pretending that sports can be played in an environment supposedly unaffected by society's power structures. What distinguishes conscious clubs like the Easton Cowboys and Cowgirls from this tradition is that they fall into neither trap: the non-profit approach to sports is not based on class privilege but on a general discomfort with commercialization and careerism, and—while moral policing is shunned— there is a strong awareness of sports' ability to uphold, *but also to undermine*, dominant power structures. It is here where these clubs become legitimate descendants of the early twentieth-century workers' sports clubs that were crucial for working-class culture before nationalism, war, and consumer society set an end to one of the most genuine popular attempts at social change.

Even if unintended, this legacy is also expressed in the Easton Cowboys and Cowgirls calling themselves a "Sports and Social Club," which evokes the memory of the many Spanish and Latin American Clubes Sociales y Deportivos. While some of the latter were committed to sobriety, however, the "all-pervading love of beer" and of other stimulants features strongly in *Freedom Through Football*. There are some bright spots for straight edge readers, though: not only did the Cowboys get inspired to form a futsal team after playing at a straight edge punk festival in Brazil, but their first trip through alcohol-free EZLN territory in Mexico also brought surprising realizations: "Incredibly, despite all our fears and worries about the army, the checkpoints, guns, heat and insects, we had achieved everything we set out to do. We had even proved that we can function for a week without alcohol. In fact, we all realised that [there] was no possible way we could have coped with the march of death, the

21 games of football and the physical exertions that were required of us *with* alcohol. That and a week's worth of clean mountain air in our lungs meant that we all returned to San Cristóbal feeling on top of the world." Who would have thought?

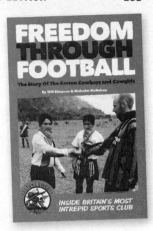

Since *Freedom Through Football* is an inside history, it is inevitable that some parts will mainly appeal to readers familiar with Bristol and its surroundings, with the neighborhood of Easton, with the delightful characters that have written Cowboys and Cowgirls' history, and with The Plough, the pub that has always served as the club's headquarters (its former landlord, Cliff Bailey, even provides a preface). This familiarity is far from a requirement for enjoying the book, however. There are plenty of tales highly relevant for both the sports fan and the grassroots organizer. This involves the Cowboys and Cowgirls' tours of Chiapas (the second one involving a figure modestly introduced as "a young Bristol street artist called Banksy"), Palestine, Brazil, and other regions as much as local campaigns in support of so-called illegal immigrants or in opposition to the all-out assault on the commons.

It also involves reflections on how a sports club—or any social project, for that matter—can live up both to certain ethical standards and to the virtue of inclusivity. This is never an easy thing to do, since the interpretation of ethical standards will always differ when people from a wide variety of backgrounds unite. Furthermore, as the authors note, "there has never been a Cowboys manifesto that you have to sign up before joining," despite a commitment to certain principles ("opposition to racism, sexism and homophobia being a very significant one"). Since it is not surprising that these matters have caused tensions among Cowboys and Cowgirls, it is particularly encouraging that they have not led to serious rupture, but, in the authors' opinion, to the club becoming "stronger." The reason was a willingness to dialogue and to actually put inclusivity into practice. Far too often, inclusivity is proclaimed as an ideal, while it is at the very same time undercut by excluding practices. In this light, the Easton Cowboys and Cowgirls have set a remarkable example for any kind of social organizing, one that many activists can, and must, learn from.

The Easton Cowboys and Cowgirls have already left a strong legacy. In 1993, they organized the first Alternative Football World Cup, an event that exists to this day and a crucial factor in the emergence of a worldwide alternative football network reaching from São Paulo, Brazil, to Vilnius, Lithuania. They also kickstarted international solidarity projects like Kiptik (Tzeltal for "inner strength") whose self-proclaimed aim is "to support the Zapatista struggle directly through the construction of drinking water systems, ecological stoves, health and mural projects." Not least, they have had a long-lasting impact on the community of Easton. Best of all, there is no sign of stopping!

Everyone is encouraged to join Easton Cowboys and Cowgirls' history by attending their games and tournaments, by supporting their campaigns, or simply by visiting The Plough. Everyone is also encouraged to read *Freedom Through Football*, which should not be missing on the bookshelf of anyone interested in sports, social justice, and having a good time—it's rare to find a more fitting package.

A second edition of *Freedom Through Football: The Story of the Easton Cowboys and Cowgirls* was released in 2017. An additional chapter chronicles the club's exploits since the original release, which have included the prevention of club members being deported, fundraising efforts to support a netball player whose daughter was diagnosed with cancer, and a Cowgirls soccer team touring the West Bank in 2014. In the words of the authors: "To be continued . . ."

Community Football: 17 SK

Gabriel Kuhn

On the basis of the social values entailed in grassroots football, people around the world have established more sophisticated versions of the pick-up game variety, mainly in founding projects providing a more organized framework, with reserved playing fields, regular hours, and individuals taking on responsibility for basic equipment (balls, goals, jerseys). The casual character of the game does not change, however: scores are not necessarily kept, sides are switched around, rules are flexible and decided upon democratically, and referees are replaced by self-responsibility. Often, the motivation is to make use of football's social values in the context of local community organizing and social work. One recent example is 17 SK, a community sports club founded in Stockholm in early 2011.

17 SK emerged from Nätverket Linje 17, a network of community projects along the southern end of Stockholm's subway line 17. Nätverket Linje 17 describes itself as "an umbrella for different initiatives and activities of local groups focusing on a variety of issues, from organizing talks to involvement in local schools and collective gardening."

In this context, the idea behind 17 SK was, in the words of the initiators, to "create an environment in which people can play sports with a sense of community and without competitive pressure. We also want to use sports' potential to bring people together, to get to know one another, and to share joy, laughter, and exercise." Flyers including this credo, and an enchanting artwork by Fiona Moyler, borrowed from an article about "Revolutionary Football" in the Irish *RAG: Anarcha-Feminist Magazine*, were distributed in the neighbourhood to launch the project.

The results have exceeded all expectations. 17 SK started with one mixed game a week. Soon, a women's game and training session, open to transgender people, was organized on another evening, then a second mixed game on the weekend, and finally a football school for children, including kids at the tender age of two. All this happened within a few months, when a total of about one hundred people, ranging in age from twelve to sixty-five, had attended the games, the majority not tied to activist circles and hailing from a variety of countries rarely seen represented together at local political meetings: apart from Sweden, there were players from Argentina, Austria, England, Gambia, Greece, Iceland, Ireland, Italy, Russia, Somalia, the U.S., and other countries I now forget.

The level of competitiveness is kept at bay by the project's guiding principles. Switching sides has proven to be a very easy manner of avoiding the winner-loser pattern. Rules are kept to a minimum, and the standard points of contention (throw-ins, corner kicks, role of goalkeepers, etc.) are decided collectively on the spot depending on the number of players, the size of the field, and other factors. Most games have been played on a patch of grass next to the fields of the local football club where portable goals and water are available, allowing the players to make use of often undervalued public resources, which fits in nicely with the anti-privatization sentiments of the Linje 17 network.

The biggest challenge for the mixed games was avoiding the neighbourhood's "football lads" from taking over the event. Even in Sweden, where women's soccer enjoys a comparatively high status among the population, a strong gender imbalance is deeply embedded in the game and football tends to be an area in which masculine hierarchies are established and defended. Despite pledges of "inclusiveness" and "non-competitiveness," this can also spill into projects like 17 SK. However, very gentle countermeasures proved to make a big difference. After a couple of weeks, four "guidelines" were established that prevented some of the most problematic behaviour from recurring and thereby making the games much more welcoming for people with less football experience, which was one of the main goals of 17 SK from the very beginning. These guidelines, repeated at the beginning of every game, were:

1. No hard physical play: no tackles, no high kicks, etc.
2. No hard shots with the potential of injuring people
3. Encouragement between players rather than critique
4. Responsibility to include everyone in the game

Especially number four turned out to be of great importance. Even with the best intentions, it is easy to pass the ball to friends or players you consider most likely to score rather than to newcomers or less experienced players. However, the insistence on the guidelines together with a raised level of awareness proved effective in the long run, and while it would be foolish to claim that all problems were overcome at the end of the 2011 outdoor season, the 17 SK games had turned much more inclusive and enjoyable for everyone—at times, women outnumbered men even in the mixed games.

Establishing a women's group, "17 Sisters," was another means to counter the gender imbalance inherent in football and to provide more space for women to play. There is an overlap between the mixed games and the women's group, with some women participating in both. Others prefer to play only in the women's games. Among other things, 17 Sisters has contributed to thirty-year-olds playing football for the first time in an environment they actually enjoy. The success has been huge. Now, there is a 17 Sisters Facebook group with close to fifty members, and indoor facilities have been organized to continue weekly games during the winter. This is a pioneering effort within 17 SK, which will hopefully inspire more indoor activities next winter—significant in a country like Sweden.

Meanwhile, "17 Kids," the children's football school, has been enjoyed both by the children and their parents who self-manage the school. Not only can children at the youngest age participate, there is also a conscious effort not to let gender determine early divisions (personally, I consider five-year old boys naming Sweden's Lisa Dahlqvist as their favourite player a huge step forward), and not to exclude anyone for "lack of talent" or "lack of ambition," making the common joy in playing the most important aspect instead.

With the first outdoor season finished, there are, of course, plenty of discussions about how to proceed with 17 SK. So far, no 17 SK team has been formed to play in competitions. Shall one, in the future, participate in *Korpen*, a Swedish variety of Sunday Leagues, or at least in amateur tournaments around town? Or would this violate the non-competitive credo? Can the "community project" continue, while a Sunday League team might emerge from it? If so, can both projects carry the same name?

For 17 SK, these questions will be answered in the future. Other grassroots football projects already field teams in Sunday Leagues and amateur tournaments. Many of them prove that this does not necessarily mean to betray football's social values—in fact, it can be a vehicle to promote them.

This summary of 17 SK's first season was part of a longer article titled "Grassroots Football: Values, Examples, Potentials," published by *STIR Magazine*, November 30, 2011. In the spring of 2018, 17 SK still exists. Some groups have folded, others have been added. The soccer groups still form the core, playing year-round. 17 Sisters partook in a tournament in 2013, but apart from that the club's activities have remained non-competitive. I was on the coordinating committee until 2015. A longer evaluation of the club, written by another coordinator, Klara Dolk, and myself has appeared under the title "Stockholm's 17 SK: a case study in community football" in *Sport in Society* 18, no. 4, May 2015.

About Left Wing Fútbol: How We Play

futbolistasla.org, March 2018

The Left Wing style of fútbol is different from what you will find in most pick-up games or organized soccer leagues. Here we are intentional about playing fútbol in the way we envision the world—cooperative, compassionate, just, fair, and equal—and we strive to reflect these values on the field. Our style of play is best exemplified by the score of every game, 2–2. We care about and prioritize play that is about the process, which means passing and sharing the ball, working together, building our skills, building camaraderie, and having fun.

The Left Wing space is inclusive and welcoming of all of those who want to play. Those of all skill levels, identities, orientations, cultures, races, genders, ages, and abilities are invited to play with us.

To maintain the Left Wing style of fútbol, we have agreements that generations of Left Wing Futbolistas have endorsed:

No slide tackling. We don't want anyone to get hurt.

Take a step back on 50/50 balls. If two players are converging on a ball and both have an equal chance of winning it, someone needs to step back and yield to the other.

Play to each other's skill level. If you are more advanced than your opponent, give them the opportunity to handle the ball without charging at them to take the ball from them. Likewise, give players who may not be as advanced as you a chance to develop by challenging them appropriate to their skill level (i.e., don't patronize them).

No trash talk. Unless it's funny or you know the person. In other words, nothing is so important that we need to communicate with each other in anger or spite.

Anyone can stop play if we aren't living up to our agreements. If egos arise or if any of our agreements or values are breeched, individuals in the collective are encouraged to stop the game, talk, and recalibrate so that everyone feels comfortable and supported on the field.

Manifesto of the Wilde Liga Wien

wildeligawien.wordpress.com, February 2018

The Wilde Liga Vienna Collective formed in February 2017, inspired by the "colorful" and "wild" leagues of Germany (*Bunte und Wilde Ligen*), the tradition of "popular football" in Italy (*calcio popolare*), and non-competitive soccer tournaments held in a spirit of solidarity such as Vienna's Ute Bock Cup, the Mondiali Antirazzisti in the region of Emilia, Italy, and the No Racism Cup in Lecce, Italy.

Based on our understanding of football, we want to give people the opportunity to play the sport outside of club structures and rules imposed by the Austrian Football Association. This means friendly games *without performance angst* and *without referees.* It implies that the teams and players themselves are responsible for what is happening on the pitch. This is only possible if arguments, fouls, and interferences from onlookers are kept at bay, and if we meet one another with respect and a willingness to compromise. Overly ambitious and self-righteous forms of behavior are obstacles to this. Fairness and consideration for everyone's physical well-being are key principles for enjoying football in a carefree and pleasurable environment.

Problems with opposing teams shall be resolved in peaceful ways when they occur. This can be a challenge for some: we expect all participants to see the players on the other side of the pitch not as adversaries, or even enemies, to be beaten by all means necessary (permitted or not), but rather as peers, fellow spirits, and sometimes friends, with whom we want to share fun and dignity in a fair and friendly game of football. At the end of an encounter, everyone should be looking forward to another game in a year's time, or during tournaments at an earlier stage. If you should run into a fellow league player in the village of Vienna, in a bar or strolling along the Danube River, it should be a meeting with someone you know and respect based on a common footballing experience.

The football we play shall be characterized by equal rights, diversity, and mutual respect, no matter one's gender, sexual orientation, religion, or place of origin! With our project, we want to contribute to breaking down the dominance of cis-men in football. Our goal is soccer beyond gender bar-

riers! We can only make this happen collectively. *All genders welcome!* is a guideline we are strongly committed to.

Reclaim public space! is another guideline. We consciously want to play games in public space. Commercial interests shall be pushed to the sidelines.

The Wilde Liga Wien is self-organized and based on principles of direct democracy. All decisions are made collectively. When, where, and how we play is decided by the teams together. All teams, initiatives, organizations, networks, and individuals that commit to the wild league's colorful spirit are invited to participate. Those who do not (yet) have a team are also welcome. *Amateurs of all districts, unite!*

How do we play?

The rules of the Wilde Liga Wien are established by all teams together. However, they only serve as suggestions and can be adjusted for each match by the teams playing one another. Our credo is: *Permitted is what gives you pleasure and doesn't hurt others.* Team uniforms, for example, *can* be used but are not required. Soccer cleats are not allowed. We prefer to see shoes designed for artificial grass, indoor soccer, or running. Needless to say, you can also play in your bare feet. An important factor in deciding on your footwear is the opinion of the groundskeeper. *Our principles of fair play must be extended to groundskeepers!*

We suggest a playing time of 40 minutes (2 × 20) and teams of five outfield players and a goalkeeper. Players can be substituted at any time and as often as desired.

Players are not bound to particular teams. We embrace the *polyplayer!* Teams can also loan players from other teams, but you should not bring in club players just to raise your team's performance.

We suggest ignoring the offside rule and the back-pass rule. Goalkeepers should be free to handle the ball within their zone as they please. Unintentional hand balls should not lead to free kicks and penalties.

These suggestions apply as long as the teams playing each other have not made other agreements. In the case of technical flaws (a perennial favorite: the incorrect throw-in), we should all be generous as long as no one draws an unfair advantage. After all, we also want people to participate who still need to fine-tune their motor skills.

Matches shall be played in a way that makes officials unnecessary. In the spirit of our league, no team will accept an unjust advantage; instead, they will admit to rule violations even if not called on them. In the case of a disagreement, the teams are expected to come to a conclusion in a reasonable manner. Ideally, things are settled right there and then by the players immediately involved. If they prove incapable of doing so, it is a good idea to simply pass the ball to the opposing team and get on with things.

All problems that occur on the field must be solved by the teams involved. If that is not possible, the problems can be discussed at a Wilde Liga meeting. As a basic rule: it is the *responsibility of each team* to avoid this. If games have to be abandoned, neither team will be awarded points.

Teams are expected to respect the spirit of the Wilde Liga. If their opponents feel that this has not been the case, the issue will be discussed at the next Wilde Liga meeting. Teams can also challenge points that have been awarded to opponents who have acted inappropriately. In extreme cases, teams can be expelled from the league. Any such decision can only be made at a Wilde Liga meeting.

Yellow and red cards do not exist. If players act out, their own team will have to ensure that they leave the pitch. Tactical fouls—and intentional fouls in general—are harmful; so are provocations and insults. Players misbehaving in the heat of the moment are expected to apologize and to promise to improve their conduct. Otherwise, they ought to be replaced by another player and feel ashamed.

How is the Wilde Liga organized?

There will be Wilde Liga tables that can be read in various ways. They not only list results but also provide information on *fair play*. At the end of the season, teams leading the fair play table will be awarded, while no one will be awarded for the highest number of victories. Instead, we will celebrate *each other* at an after-party that we will organize collectively.

Since there is no binding schedule, teams have to agree on when to play each other. Once such an agreement has been made, the teams will do everything (really everything!) for the game to take place. The decision to cancel games must not be taken lightly. Also, all teams should be willing to meet the teams that want to play them. If two or three of your best players cannot make it, this is no reason to cancel a game. Only personally delivered cancellations are acceptable. (Telephone, yes; email or voicemail, no.) If teams are indeed forced to cancel a game, they must do so in time to give their opponent the opportunity to meet a different opponent. It is no fun for people to reserve a day for a game of soccer and then have no one to play with. If a team misses a game because its members slept in or if they forget to cancel a game at least 48 hours before kickoff, the opponent will be awarded a 5-0 victory, unless it agrees to reschedule the game.

There will be a Wilde Liga calendar for each season. Ideally, all teams will have played all other teams by the end of it. On match days, both (!) teams shall send the results to the Wilde Liga's email account.

For the first three weekends of the season, we can offer pitches. For subsequent weekends, we have to find pitches together. That is why it is so important that *all teams are active participants in the league*! If you have any suggestions for pitches, please email us. We are looking for natural and artificial grass to celebrate (six-a-side) soccer without being forced to empty our bank accounts.

Wilde Liga meetings

Each team should help shape the Wilde Liga. Our rules will be constantly readjusted. In order to coordinate the league, team representatives will come together in regular meetings.

The Wilde Liga meetings are the league's central decision-making body. It is here that the league's ambition and structure will be defined and redefined. The meetings are based on solidarity and mediation, and we aim to make decisions by consensus.

At the meetings, we will exchange experiences, draw schedules, and deal with organizational questions. If serious problems occur, meeting participants will try to find a solution. That's why it is important that *each team sends at least one representative* to each meeting.

The social significance of the meetings must not be underestimated either. People who regularly share a beverage get to know each other and become good companions on the pitch.

Forward! And don't forget: *The dignity of the ball is inviolable!*

Translated by Gabriel Kuhn.

Challenging Male Dominance One Strike at a Time: The Women's Soccer Rebellion

Public recognition of women's soccer has been slowly but steadily increasing for many years. Hundreds of women professionals can today make a living from playing the sport, and international tournaments fill stadiums

and receive broad media attention.
Women soccer fans have also received
more recognition, not least through
the website *This Fan Girl* and the exhibition *Fan.tastic Females: Football Her.
Story*. However, the gaps between the
men's and the women's game remain

enormous. For example, the money invested by UEFA in the Women's
Champions League is less than 1 percent of what it invests in the men's
tournament.

In recent years, women players have taken it into their own hands to
bring about change. In 2015, a U.S. tour by the Australian team got canceled when players went on strike demanding better pay and facilities. In
2016, the Nigerian team held out in a hotel in Abuja for several days until
the national football association paid them outstanding wages. In 2017, a
longstanding dispute over the financial compensation of players on the U.S.
women's team, which included five top players filing a complaint with the
U.S. Equal Employment Opportunity Commission, was settled. That same
year, Scottish players maintained a media blackout ahead of the European
Championship in order to protest the way they were treated by the Scottish
Football Association. In Brazil, three players resigned from the team when
their complaints about discrimination against women players were ignored.

Right around the same time, things came to a head in Europe, when
the runner-up of the 2017 European Championship, the team of Denmark,
went on strike, missing two scheduled matches, one of them an important qualifier for the 2019 World Cup. The demands of the Danish players were the usual: better pay, better facilities, better travel arrangements,
equal treatment to the men's team. The strike was a huge issue in Denmark.
The Danish Language Council declared *kvin-
delandsholdet*, the "women's national team,"
the Word of the Year. Eventually, the dispute
was settled, not least because the Danish
men's team had sided with the women players, offering to rechannel funds allocated
to them. In December 2017, the respective
captains of the Norwegian men's and wom-
en's teams signed an agreement with the
Norwegian FA that guarantees equal pay for
all Norwegian internationals. In club football, a similar example has been set by the
English lower-league side Lewes FC, which
has decided to share its budget equally
between the men's and the women's teams.

The professionalization of the women's game entails many positive aspects, including better conditions to train and perform as well as the possibility to make a living from playing the sport you love. Yet it is a double-edged sword, not least for people looking for alternatives to the commercialized men's game. For many fans of women's soccer, professionalization threatens aspects that appeal to them: pleasing grounds rather than multi-purpose arenas; a festive rather than testosterone-driven atmosphere; fair play instead of diving, faking injury, and committing tactical fouls. But women's football must not become a projection surface for dreamy fans frustrated with the developments of the men's game. Women playing football must have the same professional opportunities as men. The trend of the world's leading football clubs investing more money into their women's sides contributes to this. In Europe, until the early 2000s, the leading women's teams all belonged to clubs that focused predominantly, or even exclusively, on their women's teams. Sweden's Umeå IK and Germany's Turbine Potsdam are two outstanding examples. The clubs that meet in the 2018 Women's Champions League semifinal are Manchester City, Chelsea, VfL Wolfsburg, and Olympique Lyon—in other words, clubs whose men's sides have long been powerhouses in European football. Even if big clubs only allocate a fraction of their budget to women's teams, they are usually able to provide better facilities and salaries than women-only clubs. It is telling that the attempt to launch an independent women's top club in Sweden, Tyresö FF, ended in a fiasco: a few days after the team played in the final of the 2014 European Women's Champions League, it went bankrupt. Yet the big clubs taking charge of women's football further undermines the appeal of independent women's football and cements the gap between the men's and the women's game.

It is difficult not to be impressed by clubs such as Sheffield's AFC Unity, which not only take pride in their independence but also in being based on progressive values and their involvement in community projects. AFC Unity runs programs such as Solidarity Soccer, which helps "emphasise that football can be a force for good, increasing confidence in life and interpersonal skills and body image," and Football for Food, which gathers donations for food banks and raises awareness about food poverty.

With the media tapping into nationalism, the biggest tournaments of women's soccer, the World Cup, the European Championship, and the Olympics receive broad public attention today. However, this is not yet reflected at the club level. Everyday passion for football remains largely reserved for men's teams and leagues. Here, deeply patriarchal football culture still rules supreme. It will be hard to change this, unless there is broad social change undermining the values of patriarchy itself, including hierarchy, competition, and aggressiveness. Luckily, grassroots football culture at its best does exactly that. A true football revolution can only be a women's revolution.

■ The Danish Women's National Team Strike of 2017

Interview with Tine Hundahl, March 2018

How much attention did the strike receive in Denmark, and how did the media and the public react?
The conflict started shortly after the team won the silver medal at the European Championship. The tournament was its big public breakthrough, and the players were the entire country's darlings. There were countless receptions upon their return. So it was big news when the conflict with the Danish Football Association erupted. Danish media covered it very closely. The conflict between the men's U21 and the FA, which played out at the same time, was almost ignored. All focus was on the women.

There was very little sympathy for the FA. How could they deny improvements to the women's team after such a big success? The public stood firmly behind the players. During the Euro, the media had told many stories about the players performing on such a high level despite keeping jobs or being full-time students. When the men's team negotiated their payments with the FA in 2015, they had little support; they were regarded as overpaid professionals who should consider it an honor to play for their country. The few times similar sentiments were expressed with regard to the women's team, they were shut down quickly. The women players had already sacrificed a lot to be available for the team.

No one understood how the FA could cancel the World Cup qualifier against Sweden. It was a bad move that seemed to confirm that it was not interested in a constructive solution and was even willing to jeopardize the women's success. It was a big relief when FA officials finally returned to the negotiation table.

Apparently, even LO, the Danish Trade Union Federation, got involved. Can you tell us more about the union support the players received?
Trade unions are still strong in Denmark. It is an important aspect of the "Danish Model" that trade unions and employers reach agreements without involving legislators. The football players' union SPF was an actor in the conflict from the beginning. Not only did it seek better conditions for the women's team, but it was also very concerned about the FA's attempt to undermine its right to collective bargaining. This would have had serious consequences not only for all national football teams but for competitive sports in Denmark in general. Unsurprisingly, the women players got support from prominent athletes, not least the men's football team. High-profile politicians also took their side. Even FIFpro, the world players' union, urged the Danish FA to return to the negotiation table after the game against Sweden had been canceled. The relationship between the players' union and the FA has been strained for a long time, which

probably contributed to the conflict escalating. In the end, LO as well as Denmark's Sports Confederation got involved to help sort things out.

What were the consequences? How much has this changed football in Denmark, both for women and men?
It's too early to say. For the men, not much has changed. Among women players, it has left the feeling that not even a silver medal at the Euro guarantees them the recognition and respect they deserve; the flowery speeches and the free champagne they were treated to no longer shine so brightly. What the Danish Football Association and the clubs around the country must do now is to revive the positive attention that women's football received after the Euro. A real effort must be made to develop women's football, also at the club level. This requires both attracting bigger sponsors and improving the conditions that women footballers train and play under.

Tine Hundahl is active in the Danish Football Supporter Association and the UEFA Women in Football Leadership Programme.

Introducing AFC Unity, the Left-Wing Feminist Football Club

Will Magee

The reality for many women's football clubs in England is that they are treated as subordinate to their male counterparts. While the women's game has more exposure than ever—owing to the success of the England national team—and public interest seems to be at an all-time high, the landscape for women's club football in England is still intermittently bleak.

Mere days before the beginning of the last Women's Super League season, Notts County Ladies were folded because, in the words of Notts County chairman Alan Hardy, it would have been "financial suicide" to keep the team going. Just imagine the furor and the subsequent fundraising effort had the same been said of the men's operation. A couple of months ago, Sunderland Ladies were booted off their Academy of Light training pitches in favor of the men's development sides. While some clubs—notably Manchester City—have invested heavily in their women's set-up, the majority of women's sides are left in little doubt that they are considered less important than their affiliated men's teams.

While many would point to the disparity in profits between the men and women's game as the reason for this—reductive as that comparison might be—the fact is that women have been marginalized historically in English football. If the women's game is behind the men's in terms of profile and revenue, it may have something to do with the fact that it was actively suppressed for almost 50 years. In 1921, supposedly jealous of the high crowds in attendance at women's matches and anxious they would become a vehicle for women's suffrage, the FA banned women's teams from playing at its member stadiums. This ban was not lifted until the late-1960s, while underinvestment, exclusion and hostility towards women's football have continued into the modern day.

Certainly, when it comes to exclusion and hostility, the women involved with indie team AFC Unity have taken matters into their own hands. Founded in 2014, based in Sheffield and run as a not-for-profit organisation, the club has an ethos which enshrines all that is best about the grassroots tradition of women's football. They stress inclusion and equality as core values, they eschew the dog-eat-dog attitude that characterises so many other clubs, and they put themselves at the heart of the local community. What's more, the club is first and foremost about female empowerment; in part a reaction to all the years the women's game has been put second to the men's.

Unlike most other women's football clubs, AFC Unity is a standalone enterprise and not affiliated to a men's outfit. This is a point which its co-founders, Jay Baker and Jane Watkinson, are keen to stress. Jay is the manager of the club and was, until 2015, the only man on the Board of Directors (his resignation to focus on his managerial duties means the club now has an all-female board), while Jane is involved in the day-to-day running of the club and also plays for the first team. According to Jane, the idea of a women's team going it alone is hard for some people to get their heads around. "The FA still describe us as AFC Unity Women's, and it's like: 'You don't need to put *Women's*.' We're an independent women's football club—nobody says 'Arsenal Men's.'"

For Jane, that independence is part of what makes the club a feminist endeavor. "With the club, giving women power is at the center of it," Jane says. "Even with the coaching, the running of the club and so on, the big thing is to create an environment where women take on key roles, feel comfortable having a voice and having a say in how the club is run, and what we are going to do campaign-wise."

As one part of its community work the club has collected supplies and raised awareness for local food banks in a "Football For Food" campaign, with players encouraged to get involved with and help organize the volunteering effort. AFC Unity also pride themselves on their social conscience, which is reflected as much by what they do off the pitch as what they do on it.

Take a look at the club's badge and it's not difficult to infer which way the club leans politically. Sporting a red star adorned with the word "Integrity," the club wears its left-wing values (almost literally) on its sleeve. Jay explains that it felt important to make the club a socialist as well as feminist undertaking, just another way in which the "Red Stars" are a reaction against the status quo of English football.

"I'm a Doncaster Rovers fan, I was involved with the Supporters' Trust there, and the more I found out about football at a higher level, the more I became disenchanted with it," Jay says. "That led me to really want to do something at a grassroots level, and get football back to what it was supposed to be originally: the love of the game, a connection to the local community and that community reflected in the collectivism of a football team."

"The team is predominantly left-leaning to center-left, with a few Corbynistas in the side and certainly lots of Labour voters," Jay laughs. "A lot of the players work in social care, as doctors and nurses and so on, so I think we tend to attract a certain type, but we're not dogmatic . . . We've said, 'Let's look at the football first, see how that connects to the community, and then talk about what we care about,' instead of setting some sort of political criteria."

Nonetheless, the club is unashamed in promoting its collective ideals through football. Outside of the first team, AFC Unity run reserve training sessions for women of all abilities through a programme called "Solidarity Soccer." They have played friendlies against like-minded groups, like Clapton Ultras and Republica Internationale, and even give discounts to trade union members as their own symbolic contribution to the labour movement.

For many of the players who make up their 25-woman first team squad, this is what sets AFC Unity apart from other women's teams and gives the club its unique appeal. Sarah Choonara, a member of the first team who's been involved with its trade union initiative, talks passionately about the attraction of the club's social and political side.

"It's one of the things that makes you feel very committed to the club, in that they're very visible in supporting things like LGBT rights, workers' rights and the 'Football for Food' campaign, while they're also very aware of the politics behind these issues," Sarah says. "Stuff like the discount for union members . . . It's fantastic to play for a club which holds that stuff in high regard.

That said, the club is serious about its commitment to inclusion, with Jane and Jay both emphasising that there's no political benchmark for participation. This is certainly the impression given by Sophie Mills, another AFC Unity first teamer who has been with the club almost since its inception. "What set AFC Unity apart was just how friendly and supportive they were when I joined . . . They don't tolerate people being rude to each other and creating a negative atmosphere," Sophie says. "As well as that, you're the main focus, where I think in a lot of places the women's team is almost an afterthought . . . There is a political element to the club, but we don't stand around in training talking politics or anything like that."

The focus on mutual respect, fairness and good sportsmanship come up time and time again in conversation with members of the club. Jane, for instance, quit football in her teens despite playing at a high level, put off by the disciplinarian attitude of her coaches and a prevalent survival-of-the-fittest worldview. AFC Unity is intended to be the opposite of that, an antidote to the bullying culture that so often thrives in competitive sport. In keeping with its socialist roots, the team is all about collective responsibility, as opposed to singling players out for criticism and abuse.

Though it is an indie club with only a few seasons under its belt, the staff and players at AFC Unity are showing that women's football can be done differently. Not only are they providing an alternative to people put off by the prevailing norms of the game, they are doing so in a manner which puts the women who play for them first. Add to that their political awareness and undercurrent of fierce idealism, and it's clear that their corner of Sheffield is graced with a pretty special football team. There's a long way to go in the fight against the marginalization of women in football, but it's through grassroots efforts like this that real change will be made.

Will Magee is a journalist specialising in sport and politics, with bylines in *VICE*, the *Independent*, the *Mirror*, the *i Paper*, and various other outlets. This article was originally published by *VICE UK*, January 9, 2018.

Reflections and Outlook: Three Interviews

After the release of *Soccer vs. the State* in 2011, I was given the opportunity to speak my mind on the game in various forums. People asked very interesting and challenging questions that have helped me sharpen my views and articulate them more clearly. I want to conclude this edition with three of the interviews I was able to do. While some repetition is inevitable, I have selected conversations that focus on certain aspects of the game in more detail. They also provide insight into my personal footballing experience, my understanding of the sport, and my expectations for its future.

▌Discussing *Soccer vs. the State* in Ireland

Workers Solidarity Movement website, May 8, 2011
Interview by Ciaran M.

> **"The revolution will inevitably awaken in the British working class the deepest passions which have been diverted along artificial channels with the aid of football."**–Leon Trotsky.

Football comes in for much negative criticism from the left, mainly criticisms similar to Trotsky's above, deriding it as cathartic and a distraction. Yet in recent years, we've seen iconic events like the "Football Revolution" in Iran, the Greek riots following the death of Alexandros Grigoropoulos, where Panathinaikos fans fought against the police side by side with anarchists and the Al-Ahly Ultras in Egypt and their apparent hand in revolution there. How influential has football been in Rebellions and amongst the rebellious throughout history?
Football has been attracting the masses around the world for over a century. Where masses gather, the powerful lose control—unless we're talking about orchestrated mass gatherings, which are characteristic of fascist and authoritarian regimes. But this doesn't really work with football, since it is hard to orchestrate a football game. Football is too unpredictable.

Authoritarian regimes have always used the prestige that derives from football victories for political purposes, but they have had a hard time to use football as a general propaganda tool. The Nazis abandoned national encounters altogether after an embarrassing loss to Sweden in Berlin in 1942.

And it is not only the game that is unpredictable. So are football crowds. You never know which direction their desires might take. There is always a potential for rebellion—unfortunately, there is also always a potential for reactionary celebrations of the status quo. Neither football nor football fans are rebellious per se. We have radical supporters, we have fascist supporters; we have football teams that spur nationalism, we have football teams that spur international solidarity. At the right moments, the rebellious side comes through, as in the examples you mentioned and in many others: long before the current uprising in Libya, the terraces of Libyan football stadiums turned into spaces of dissent whenever Gadaffi-favoured teams were playing; in the 1980s, Polish workers made regular use of football stadiums to express support for the then illegal trade union Solidarność; in fact, the very first steps to regulate the game of football in the early 19th century was caused by regular anti-authoritarian riots in connection with the inter-village football games at the time.

Football does have the cathartic and distracting dimensions that many leftists deride, no doubt. But it also has a subversive dimension. The challenge for radical football-loving activists is to fuel the latter.

I've read about football's spread from England across continental Europe through the export of labour in the late 19th and early 20th century and how football shirts of teams on the continent can often be traced back to workers from English towns and their teams. Did you come across much of this, or across any teams founded by unions/socialists or anarchist workers?
The fact that many teams on the European continent were founded by Englishmen is not only reflected in the club's colours, but also in their names: AC Milan, Athletic Bilbao, and the First Vienna FC are only some examples. The pattern even extends beyond Europe to clubs such as Argentina's Newell's Old Boys or Uruguay's Montevideo Wanderers.

Although many of the English-named clubs were founded by English businessmen, the international spread of football was very much connected to migrant workers. Where the British established themselves as the main colonial power—in North America, Oceania, and South Asia—they also managed to establish the sports preferred by the establishment, namely rugby and cricket (which, in North America, turned into baseball and American football). Where British migration was mainly labour-related, football was the clear number one.

The question of whether football was originally a working-class sport is a tricky one to answer, as capitalist interests have always been involved. But it has certainly been the working-class that has carried the game, being responsible for its worldwide popularity.

The question about clubs founded by socialists allows for an interesting observation regarding the left's historical relationship with football. This relationship has always been ambivalent. While there was strong objection to football by those who mainly saw it as an opiate of the masses, there were also socialists who early on saw football's potential for working-class organizing. Football clubs provided the possibility for workers to gather outside the workplace, to self-organize, and to gain self-esteem—all necessary components for working-class resistance.

This tendency was probably strongest in Argentina where the early 20th century saw the foundation of clubs like Mártires de Chicago (1904; later Argentinos Juniors, Diego Maradona's first professional team), Chacarita Juniors (1906), and El Porvenir (1915). Also in this case, the club's colours sometimes recall the origins. The Chacarita Juniors, founded on May 1 in an anarchist library, are still playing in red-and-black!

In general, though, the colours of today's football clubs are only vague indicators for their political past. The heritage is probably most pronounced in Britain, where red continues to indicate working-class roots, and green Catholic/Irish heritage.

Bill Shankly once said: "The socialism I believe in is everybody working for the same goal and everybody having a share in the rewards. That's how I see football, that's how I see life." Are their many characters like Shankly or professed socialists like Brian Clough left in the game or has capitalism succeeded in nullifying the growth of characters like them?

PM PRESS

JUST BOOKS COLLECTIVE

Soccer vs. The State

Radical politics and football

PM author Gabriel Kuhn finishes his tour of Ireland with the launch of his new book 'Soccer Vs The State: Tackling Football and Radical Politics' - a look at how football has maintained it's image as the game of the working class, despite turning into a multi-million pound industry rampant with corruption, shady deals and commercialisation.

FRONT PAGE BAR (upstairs)

8PM SUNDAY 15th MAY

Free entry

Folks like Shankly and Clough have always been in the minority. There have been few outspoken socialist managers in the history of professional football. And even their legacy is often tainted. Clough, for example, was a blatant racist and homophobe. It is true, though, that it seems even less likely today to find managers of this sort who profess to socialist politics—although folks like Alex Ferguson do, for whatever it's worth.

One obvious problem is that the world of professional football is so saturated with money and the notion of success that it is simply difficult to remain credible as a socialist. Ferguson is a case in point, I believe. Even if you hold on to your ideals, you certainly have to make a lot of compromises—which will eventually compromise your ideals too.

Of course most of those who have strong ideals will never reach the position of an Alex Ferguson to begin with. Not necessarily because of a lack of knowledge or skill, but because the world of professional football is too rough, too competitive, and too greedy for most politically aware folks. Even if they love football and pursue a professional career, they are more likely to be cut or to give up themselves than players who see no problem in having corporate logos splashed across their chests, in earning more money in a year than entire working-class families in a lifetime, and in being expected to "fight" in order to "beat" their opponents. That's why you find many socialists drawn to today's DIY football underground that is documented in one of the main chapters of *Soccer vs. the State*.

Politically, there has been an interesting dichotomy between the rising influence of capitalism in football and the strike back against it. The "Spirit of Shankly" group fought against the ownership of Liverpool by Tom Hicks and George Gillett and Wimbledon fans fought (and won) the rights to ownership of their teams name after the teams owners sought

to relocate their team 90 KM away from its home. These are just two examples of the fight against the capitalist destruction of the ideals of the sport. Is this something that is happening worldwide?

Absolutely, you have these tendencies everywhere. One of the interesting aspects of football is the fact that, historically, clubs weren't corporations but community organizations. There was often a strong personal link between players and supporters, even on the highest level. This was still apparent in the 1970s. Malmö FF played in the 1979 European Cup Final with ten players born in the town itself—a town of 300,000 people. This is unthinkable today. It also leaves many supporters who try to regain a sense of community frustrated. You don't have to be left-wing to feel that way.

I should add, though, that these sentiments are not without their problems, as any glorification of the past has its conservative implications, but football supporters' anti-corporate stances should be inspiring for any left-wing activist.

The global spread of Sky Sports has certainly contributed to this: that many teams have become brands rather than what they used to be— local teams supported mainly by local fans. Their has been a backlash against this with many teams having armies of "armchair" fans, disen- chanting many "local" football supporters and leaving space for teams like FC United of Manchester. Is this something we can expect to see more in football?

I believe so. Again, the community aspect of football has been one of the backbones of its popularity, and there remain many supporters who embrace it. At the same time, we can't ignore the fact that many people buy into brands—literally. "Modern football" sells. On a global scale, the popularity of the game has further increased over the last twenty years, not least due to cable TV, celebrity culture, and brand identity. People are trained to be consumers, whether that relates to Nike sneakers or Manchester United jerseys.

We must not forget, however, that we can't condemn all the con- sequences of modern football. Romanticizing the "pure" working-class past of football is not only false because such purity never existed, it also means romanticizing a time when terraces were almost exclusively male and white. Today, football audiences have become more diverse. Traditionalism, no matter the context, is hardly a left-wing value. Change and development belong to progressive politics, and there is no problem with things changing and developing. The question is how things change and develop. And this is where modern football has a lot to answer for, as it has created not only an unsavoury commercial spectacle but also new forms of exclusion, mainly along economic lines.

It has also created a difficult situation for the thousands of professional footballers who are not part of the limelight: the vast majority of today's professionals do not earn millions of euros a year; they rather live precarious lives with a complete lack of economic. This is particularly pronounced in the case of football migrants from Africa whose European residency permits are often handled by their clubs. Effectively, this makes them modern-day bondsmen. In other words, the workers' side of the coin—meaning unionization and so on—has not kept up with the professional formation of the game. Modern football exemplifies all that neoliberalism stands for. And it's not a pretty sight!

Understandably, realities like these drive politically aware fans away from the game. My prediction for the future is that we will see the deepening of an already apparent rift between the professional, commercialized game and the abovementioned DIY football underground.

While the interest of this interview is obviously going to lean towards the left-wing elements of football, there is an obvious right-wing element, not least with Berlusconi's ownership of Milan. Would you say his interest is merely profit driven or does he play on the team in the same way he harnessed the idealism and imagery of "Forza Italia?" How right-wing are the structures that govern the sport?
I think we are dealing with two phenomena when we speak of the right-wing dimensions of football. One is the capitalist structure itself. As I tried to point out, modern football is part of the neoliberal enterprise and the right-wing agenda of individualism, competition, free market economy, etc. The other phenomenon is the direct involvement of right-wing politicians and organizations in football.

As stated above, football is powerful because it attracts the masses. Hence, it is attractive for politicians who try to benefit from football's popularity and who exploit the game for their own interests. Sometimes this works, sometimes it doesn't. For Berlusconi, it works because Milan is successful. If this wasn't the case, the outcome might be very different.

The motivations for the involvement of right-wing politicians in football are complex. Some might do it for political purposes. Some might be interested in financial profits. And some might simply like football—unfortunately, the game attracts all sorts of people.

While the structures that govern the sport may be right-wing, would you agree with the idea that stadiums themselves are social spaces where anti-establishment politics thrive?
Absolutely. Football terraces are among the public spaces that are the hardest to control for authoritarian regimes. Individuals become relatively

anonymous, there is a certain sense of chaos, and the dynamics of passionate crowds are always threatening. History provides many examples for protest in football stadiums that would have been impossible otherwise. Catalan and Basque stadiums during the Franco regime are probably the best examples; others include Austrian football grounds during the annexation by Nazi Germany and Ukrainian stadiums at the times of the Soviet Union.

Would you say football has been a good way of building international solidarity? I know offhand about the "Alerta" network of Celtic/St. Pauli/ Livorno/Athletic Bilbao/Hapoel Ultras (amongst others) and their stand against fascism and racism.

I think that this is one of the most intriguing aspects of football and one of the most underrated by left-wing critics. In left-wing circles, there is often a strong focus on the nationalism that football generates. Of course this is a problem. Yet even at the most contested international tournaments, like the World Cup or the European Championships, the number of fans who socialize and make friends with fans from other countries far outweighs the number of those who seek trouble. Football is indeed an "international language" and one of the most effective—and healthy!—social icebreakers. No matter where in the world you are, if you join a pick-up game, or even just discuss football, the result might easily be long-lasting relationships—and, in any case, you will leave with the experience of having connected with strangers.

Networks like Alerta are just the most obvious and organized expressions of this. They also fit the worldwide connections of grassroots football teams, which allow the Easton Cowboys and Cowgirls from Bristol to tour Palestine and Chiapas, and the Autônomos FC from São Paulo to develop a tight bond with the FC Vova from Vilnius. Needless to say, such connections open up many possibilities for effective international activism.

Ultra and casual cultures are much derided in the mindset of many. And yet Ultra culture goes hand in hand with antifascism in many countries. How much of this did you come across in writing the book?

The politics of football supporters are of course a crucial part of the book. I'd distinguish between Ultras and casuals, though. The latter are more of a subculture that developed around football with members who often have little to say about the game itself. With Ultra groups it's different. Football really is the heart of most Ultras' lives, they are passionate about the sport, they want to be recognized as an active part of it, and they try to influence its course. Ultra culture has also become a global phenomenon, while the casuals have largely been confined to Britain.

Ironically, most Ultra groups are decidedly "apolitical," which basically means they don't want to subscribe to a particular ideology or to be affiliated with any party or other political interest group. This has good and bad consequences. The good ones are that it's hard for right-wing extremists to infiltrate them. The bad ones are that Ultras do not take explicitly left-wing stances—except for the few that are decidedly antifascist, but those are a minority. Fortunately enough, the decidedly right-wing Ultra groups are a minority too.

Most Ultra groups carry elements that veer both to the left and to the right of the political spectrum. On the left, we have a deep mistrust of police and institutional authority, a critique of corporate capitalism, an emphasis on creative expression, and a sense of self-organization and self-determination; on the right, we have traditionalism, territorialism, a rigid notion of loyalty, and internal hierarchies. For activists, this ambiguity is a challenge. It is wrong to claim Ultra culture as radical—however, there is radical potential. In order to strengthen it, we need to build solid connections. As Gerd Dembowski, spokesperson for BAFF, the German "Alliance of Active Football Fans," says in his interview in *Soccer vs. the State* [see p. 149], it has become mandatory for activists to establish close ties with Ultra groups if they want to maintain an influence on football supporter culture in general.

Fascist dominated Ultras groups often support a different team from the same city. Is the divide easy to distinguish in many places?
Usually, it is. I mean, the symbols and slogans are pretty clear. It is notable, though, that political alliances can shift. In some cities, of course, the boundaries are rather clearly drawn. In Hamburg, for example, it is near impossible for right-wingers to organize around the FC St. Pauli, and so the Hamburger SV becomes their natural outlet. However, there is left-wing organizing at the Hamburger SV, too. In Munich, 1860 has been the traditional darling of the left with its working-class roots and close ties to St. Pauli. Yet, in recent years one of the most progressive Ultra groups in the Bundesliga, the Schickeria, has formed among Bayern Munich supporters. In England, the Chelsea fan base has significantly shifted from the strong right-wing currents of the 1980s. In Milan, left-wing support has in a sense always gone back and forth between Inter and AC—the latter still having some explicitly left-wing supporters despite the Berlusconi presidency. In Madrid, Real counts as Franco's former darling, yet, today, Atlético has the more explicit neofascist supporters. So while there are certain historical trajectories, there is always politically contested space. This also means that there is always a chance for radical fans to make a difference!

Last year, the English FA tried to get ten volunteers for and advertisement campaign against homophobia in Football. Not one volunteer came

forward. **This year, there was the much publicized sacking of two sports commentators over their comments about a lineswoman. Are Sexism and Racism rife in football? Have you come across many teams such as St. Pauli (whose Ultras have their own women's section) to boot "isms" out of the game?**

Racism, sexism, and homophobia have been intrinsic parts of football culture for a good century. A lot has changed in the last twenty years, partly because of grassroots initiatives within the football world and partly because of general social developments. Also football associations have jumped on the bandwagon with various, at least nominal, campaigns against racism and sexism—homophobia still seems to be the most difficult issue to tackle. In any case, it takes time to overcome deeply rooted prejudice. There is still a lot of bias in the football world towards men who don't fit the prevalent norms of masculinity. Racism rears its ugly head time and time again, and anti-Semitism is rampant whenever teams with Jewish roots, like Ajax Amsterdam or MTK Budapest, take the field. A lot remains to be done to really make a fundamental change.

Homophobic prejudices are perhaps most pronounced. It is extremely difficult to be openly gay in the world of football, at least for male players—female players are often assumed to be lesbian anyway, so it is perhaps easier to accept when they actually are. Overall, the fight against homophobia has been very painful. The story of Justin Fashanu, the first professional player to come out in 1990, is very tragic. As we know, it ended with Fashanu's suicide in the US in 1998. Soccer vs. the State includes a moving piece about the gay Dutch referee John Blankenstein, who dedicated a lot of his time and energy to fighting homophobia, which included fighting personal abuse and discrimination.

There have been interesting developments recently in Sweden, where I live. The cover story of the February 2011 issue of *Offside*, an outstanding Swedish football magazine, was dedicated to Anton Hysén, Sweden's first gay player to come out. Anton is the son of Glenn Hysén, who was one of Sweden's most prominent players of the 1980s, which adds another interesting layer to the story. The immediate response to the interview has been very positive, and we can only hope that it helps change attitudes towards gay footballers in Sweden and beyond!

You had a brief flirtation with a semi-professional career and yet turned your back on playing the game for a life in academics and politics. Did you come across racism and homophobia in the game? Did anything spur you to make that choice to quit?

Homophobia defined the football culture I grew up in. It was much more than something "you'd come across." I don't think I went through a single training session without someone being called a "faggot" for a missed tackle or a botched pass. Being a faggot was basically the antithesis of being a footballer. To be a gay footballer was hence by definition impossible. Unfortunately, this is an attitude that many famous managers and players have held throughout their careers.

Sexist and racist comments, mainly in the form of "jokes," were also an everyday part of my experience. However, this only played a small role in my decision to quit. I found there were ways to challenge these patterns, to throw others off by questioning the "fun" they engaged in, and to make a difference, even if tiny. What bothered me more were the authoritarian structures of the clubs, the intrigues and power games, the lack of personal support for players and their treatment as mere assets, the haggling over salaries and transfer sums, and the influence of owners and sponsors on a game they knew nothing about. In short, it just became an unpleasant environment to be in on a daily basis. And there were personal reasons, too. I simply wanted to have more time for studying, activism, and travelling. The only thing that might have kept me going at the age of nineteen would have been a first league contract. But I wasn't offered one, and since then I've been playing football for nothing but the fun.

One of my favourite quotations on the game comes from Albert Camus: "All that I know most surely about morality and obligations, I owe to football." As a last question, I'll ask you your favourite!
I think I'd have to go with the German comedian Klaus Hansen, who said: "Football is like democracy: twenty-two people play and millions watch." It might sound like a condemnation of the game. But I see it as a call to action!

Militancy and the Beautiful Game

Recomposition, March 3, 2016
Interview by Scott Nicholas Nappalos

You played soccer competitively at one point in your life. How did being in the world of sports as a profession impact your relationship and view of the game?
It had a strong impact on me. I was very disappointed with the social dynamics of it. There was a lot of dishonesty and deceit. I don't want to paint too negative a picture, but professional sports is full of people with their own interests—club owners, sponsors, managers—who care very little about the athletes themselves. This is particularly problematic in relation to young athletes who are unexperienced, naive, and easily exploitable, but it can also concern older players who, after years of dedication, are nonchalantly dropped if they no longer yield the results

required. It is certainly a world where performance weighs much more than friendship or mutual respect. "Camaraderie" is upheld as a value, but it is often reduced to a mere public relations ploy or even a means to force players into submission. There is also competition among athletes, of course, but I felt this was offset by a sense of solidarity that also exists, at least among some.

Again, I don't want too paint too negative a picture, and there were many moments when I really enjoyed playing and spending time with my teammates, but the overall structure was disheartening; and I would not say this if my experiences hadn't been confirmed by many other athletes I've talked to over the past 25 years. Needless to say, differences between countries and individual sports exist, and if you're fortunate enough to get to work with people treating you decently your experiences will be different; not all owners and managers are bad. But there exists a pattern. Basically, we are dealing with a microcosm of capitalism at its worst: at the end of the day, competition rules, and success is all that matters. To survive in an environment like this, certain qualities are needed: strong egos, self-confidence, high competitiveness, and a personality able to handle critique and even abuse. Professional athletes might range from devout Christians to hard-partying "bad boys," but they all share certain characteristics; and if you don't share these characteristics, you will have a hard time finding a place in their world. None of this, of course, says anything about the games they are playing. The games are great. They just need to be liberated from an unhealthy environment.

What made you start thinking about sports as a topic for political study?
To be honest, it's mainly the attempt to combine two passions, in that case publishing and sports. I love putting books together, everything from conceptualizing them to working with the texts to being involved in the layout. I did plenty of zines over the years, and, in a way, the books are just an extension. When you work with established publishers you have access to more resources. For example, doing a book with over a hundred full-color illustrations, such as *Playing as If the World Mattered*, would have been impossible to do on my own. So that's one part. The other part is sports, which I like to play, watch, and discuss. In that sense, it was a natural combination.

But there's more to it. I also think sport is an underrated subject within the radical left. Think about all the books that we have not only on political organizing and economic theory but also on music, visual arts, or even food. Where are the books on sport? And sport is a subject that millions of people, not least working-class people, are very excited about. Dave Zirin has almost a monopoly on radical sports writing, and he does an excellent job, but his work focuses mainly on the US and the big professional leagues. There is still a lack of coverage when it comes to international angles and grass-roots initiatives. In other words, I felt that they were voids to be filled. Judging from the mostly positive feedback I've received, others felt the same. And there is an increasing number of radical authors coming out with writings on sports. Matt Hern did a book for AK Press, *One Game at a Time*, and *Freedom Through Football* is a great history about the Easton Cowboys and Cowgirls of Bristol, a pioneering community sports club with a radical edge. It's all very promising.

The IWW had some intersections with sports through members who were professional athletes, for instance Nicolaas Steelink, who you write about in *Soccer vs. the State*, but I've also read that the union participated in soccer leagues with socialists and communists in the 30s. Do you know anything more about the history and context of these radical sports leagues in the US?

Workers' sport wasn't as big in the US as in Europe, where the headquarters of both the international socialist and communist sports organizations were based, namely the Socialist Workers' Sport International and the Red Sport International. Nonetheless, there was a workers' sport movement in the US, too, and wobblies were involved in it, for example in the foundation of the Labor Sports Union of America in 1927, where they worked alongside socialists of other stripes. However, the Labor Sports Union of America was soon in control of communist agitators and became the US chapter of the Red Sport International. As such, it was behind the probably best-known workers' sport event organized in the US, the so-called Chicago Counter-Olympics of 1932, an alternative to the "bourgeois" Olympics held in Los Angeles that same year.

Unfortunately, the history of socialist sports in the US hasn't been studied much and plenty remains to be uncovered. In radical circles, we probably wouldn't know about Nicolaas Steelink today if Dutch journalists hadn't traced his journey from football pitches in Holland to soap boxes in California. I'm sure many other inspiring stories remain to be told; let's hope we'll get to hear them soon.

In your books and interviews you've referenced briefly debates among anarchists that happened in places like Germany and Argentina in the early days of soccer. What were the positions amongst anarchists towards the game at that time? Clearly the situation has been radically

transformed with the consolidation of professional sports as multibillion-dollar industry, but are the corollaries of the same debates today?

I think that the critique of sport's commercialization is particularly pronounced today, since its wheels have been turning frantically over the past thirty years. It was already an issue in the early twentieth century, however, especially with regard to the first corporate sponsorship deals and the betting industry. Yet, the bigger issue for left-wing critics was sport's alleged role in distracting the masses from political organizing. The Romans would have called it "bread and circuses," and the Marxists called it "the opium of the people." Many anarchists shared those sentiments, and even those who didn't often ignored sports as a supposedly apolitical and unimportant means of leisure. One of the most revealing aspects of the relationship between anarchism and sport is the latter's almost complete absence from anarchist publications. But there have always been anarchists who criticized the rejection of sports as elitist and who stressed sport's political potential in terms of uniting people, strengthening communal values, challenging class structures, and so on. Essentially, both leftist anti-sport and pro-sport arguments have remained the same during the past hundred years.

Each era seems to have its political challenges that emerge within the world of athletics that reflects the broader social conflicts of its day: perhaps it was collectivity and the anarchist clubs in South America at the turn of the century, black liberation and anti-colonial struggles in athletes in the 1960s. Where should we be situating things events today like the FIFA corruption scandals, Brazil and South Africa's anti–World Cup protests, and the Missouri college football anti-racism strike (to give a few non exhaustive samples)?

I think what we see today expresses both a growing mistrust of authority and a stronger sense of entitlement among the masses. People are fed up with corrupt and unaccountable rulers and they are not afraid to show it. Unfortunately, this doesn't automatically translate into sweeping political change, as we are facing very complex power structures, but we live in times of strong social movements and protests, which implies widespread grassroots organizing. Even if common visions and strategies have yet to be developed to be effective on a broad scale, these are very encouraging signs. Luckily, challenging the forms in which sports are administered and played is a part of this process.

Are there any more texts on sports you're working on now? Things in the sports world we should be paying attention to?

I have completed a small book about how, in the early twentieth century, the workers' sport movement was tied into the European working class movement's overall ideas of social transformation. The book focuses on the writings of Julius Deutsch, who was the president of the Socialist Workers' Sport International. It will be out with PM Press this year under the title *Antifascism, Sports, Sobriety: Forging a Militant Working-Class Culture*. I have also outlined a book about Europe's grassroots soccer culture, but realizing it would require a lot of traveling, which, in turn, needs both time and money, so I'm not sure when that will happen.

In terms of what we should pay attention to, it certainly entails the abovementioned protest movements in sports, but also the increasing awareness among athletes regarding the corruption and misconduct of sports authorities. Sport's international governing bodies are under increasing pressure, whether it's FIFA, the IOC, or the International Association of Athletics Federations (IAAF). This opens up exciting prospects. Imagine high-profile athletes coming out in support of Soccer World Cup or Olympic Games boycotts. It would raise sports protests to a whole new level with far-reaching consequences for society as a whole. Let's hope we'll get there soon.

On Modern Football and How an "Implosion" Is the Only Way the Sport Can Save Itself

Doing the Rondo, October 20, 2017
Interview by Shirsho Dasgupta

Soccer, both in England and in the United States, began in the schools and universities of the affluent. How then did it emerge as a sport that we generally identify with the working classes?
Football started out at schools and universities, but factory owners soon realized its potential in pacifying the work-force: the game channeled workers' energies into sports rather than protest, it empowered them, and factory teams led to a stronger identification with their employers. All of this applied to players and spectators alike. Besides, football is very easy to play: the rules are simple and you need neither expensive equipment nor special grounds. A game of football can be improvised pretty much anywhere. This is one of the main reasons why it became the world's most popular sport.

Finally, once it was professionalized, it provided one of the few viable career options for working-class folks outside of the factory. Therefore, football did indeed become a working-class sport in the early twentieth century, although it was always controlled by the upper classes

You write in *Soccer vs. the State* that in South America football is generally considered to be "play" while in Europe it is "work." What would you

say is the reason behind this distinction? Is it because in South America the whole idea of "work" itself perhaps has overtones of colonialism, exploitation or oppression?

I think I referred to common perceptions regarding the differences between European and South American football. I myself would not draw such lines, as they are clearly simplistic. But perhaps these perceptions do include an anti-colonial element: colonizers, and European nations in general, are associated with rigid regimes of work, which many see reflected in their approach to football. German teams, for example, have long been very successful, but their success has often been attributed to "discipline," "organization," and a "fighting spirit" rather than technical skills and creativity. In this context, playfulness appears rebellious, something that has long been associated with South American teams, particularly the Brazilian one, which indeed played more attractive football than most European teams in the post-World-War-II era. Today, these differences are largely gone, but the common perceptions persist. When Dunga became Brazil's manager in 2006, his focus on defense and efficiency was considered a betrayal of the Brazilian game, not least in Brazil itself.

Would you agree that perhaps this conceptualization is strange given the fact that South American fans care more about winning than perhaps Europeans in general? After all, South American fans have a reputation of booing or hissing at their own teams when they do not play well—in a sense they are perhaps, more unforgiving than fans of Europe.

Some people would say that this is simply a result of South Americans being more passionate about football than Europeans. Needless to say, we have to be very careful with such assumptions, as they reek of racial stereotypes: the "emotional" South American vs. the "rational" European. Sports commentators still use such clichés routinely: they criticize non-European players—especially African ones—for their apparent lack of discipline and tactical understanding, or dirty play, and for losing their temper.

In general, I don't think there is that much of a difference in how supporters relate to the game globally. There are differences from country to country depending on numerous factors, and it's hard to make out any patterns. In Europe, for example, you find some of the worst fan violence in Sweden, a country usually known for its level-headed and reserved population. It's all rather complicated.

In Soccer vs. the State, you mention that the sport played an important role in the decolonization of Africa, especially in Ghana and Guinea. But how exactly did football help? Is it not, at the end of the day, a "European" sport? Why did the leaders of the anti-colonial movement not seek to use any other game, perhaps even a sport which is native to Africa?

Perhaps ironically, football helped for the very reason that it wasn't an African sport but a global one. Africans being able to compete with nations from all continents, including colonizing nations, meant a lot for national self-esteem. Even decades after independence, the symbolic value of this remained strong. Senegal's victory over France at the 2002 World Cup, for example, has played a significant role for modern Senegalese identity, although the country had become independent from France 42 years earlier. Cameroon player Roger Milla summed up the overall sentiment well when he commented on Cameroon's successful run at the 1998 World Cup: "An African head of state who leaves as the victor, and who greets with a smile the defeated heads of state! . . . It's thanks to football that a small country could become great."

Young Africans, some even children, are lured and often brought to Europe with deceitful promises. They leave everything behind, often pay huge sums of money despite their poverty and then in Europe, they find that they do not have a future in football (which may be for a variety of reasons). Many call it a "slave trade," yet Daniel Künzler, whom you interviewed yourself, refuses to call it so. Do you agree? Or do you think while the situation might not be exactly the same, it certainly is analogous?
I concur with Künzler when he finds the term "slave trade" inappropriate to describe the transfer of African football hopefuls to Europe. It trivializes the horrors of the slave trade. Young African footballers are not forced at gunpoint to leave their countries, they aren't put in chains and crammed onto boats for journeys many of them won't survive, their legal status is not simply that of property, etc. So, there are significant differences.

However, there are enormous problems involved in the global trade of African footballing talent, and they are tied to colonial history. Young African players leave their families and chase their dreams because they have few other options to improve their lot. Very often this happens under dubious circumstances. Many young African players arrive abroad in a very vulnerable position, and the many unscrupulous people involved in the football industry take advantage of that. Many a gifted African player ends up on the streets of Europe without money or documents; others are entirely dependent on the whims of erratic club owners. None of

these dynamics will change before the global political and economic order changes. However, things can be done to mitigate the consequences. Organizations such as Foot Solidaire have done great work.

On that note, today's footballing academies take in a lot of youngsters, yet of course, only a few are signed by clubs, especially the bigger ones. Why is it so? Has our new obsession with data and football analytics something to do with this trend?

Data and analytics might provide a new framework for selecting some players and weeding out others, but the fact that many talented young-sters never earn a professional contract simply has to do with high compe-tition. The money generated by football has multiplied during the past 25 years, which also means that more money is invested in youth football and academies. Today, you have thousands of incredibly well schooled players at the age of 17 or 18, but there are only so many open spots on the rosters of professional teams. Many players simply don't make the cut. And among those who do, many are out of a contract again within a few years when new and better players have come up through the ranks.

In the 1970s, if you made it to the roster of a professional team, you could count on a professional career of 10 to 15 years as long as you avoided serious injury. Today, the average career span is three to four years; there is an enormous turnover. Only the players at the absolute top can build successful careers into their 30s.

What about the grassroots development programmes? While it is true that they have perhaps "discovered" a lot of talented footballers from remote villages, many of these programmes are funded and run by corporate entities. In India for example, big mining companies encroach upon tribal lands and evict them from their homes and then set up foot-ball programmes under a mandate of "Corporate Social Responsibility." Jacinta Kerketta in a poem highlighted how these programmes are used to lure tribal children away from education because the companies know that an educated child might protest against them.

It is an excellent poem. I find football to be a wonderful game with lots of liberating potential, but we have to be realistic: football also serves, and always has, as an opiate for the masses. There is no doubt about that.

Programs that supposedly help the poor, while in fact only creating new forms of dependence and exploitation, are pervasive, also in football. I am sure that there are people involved in these programs whose heart is in the right place, and some of the programs might indeed do some good, for example if they encourage young girls to play football. But we have to scrutinize them very carefully—and we should be suspicious every time a program is sponsored by FIFA or any of its subsidiaries.

With the increase in televised games, more and more people throughout the world are actively watching the game. Yet while a number of developing countries had always followed the sport, fan support seems to be changing. For example, in India while the older generations generally supported Brazil or Argentina during the World Cup, for a majority of today's youth (who are growing up watching the European leagues) it is more natural to support Germany or England or Spain. Can this be interpreted as the beginnings of a radical universalism—the previously colonized has "forgiven" white Europe and is willing to stand beside it as comrades? Or is it another symptom of a Eurocentric global order?

I think mainly the latter, perhaps with a tint of the former.

In general, I believe it is a result of the stronger marketing power of European nations. Asia is the market that rich European clubs woo for the most right now. Summer tours of the continent have become a main feature of the clubs' pre-season routine, although they take an enormous toll on the players who are already facing an ever more expanding schedule during regular season. At the same time, European clubs sign Asian players to secure television time in the players' home countries. In the near future, we will see more and more Chinese players in Europe, for example. The modern football industry follows the laws of the market.

But, yes, it might also be the case that "post-colonial" identities are taking shape in formerly colonized countries, especially among the middle classes. Shedding anti-colonial sentiments might be a way of saying that you've become equal and that there is no reason to harbor resentment; it is self-affirming rather than self-deprecating. Perhaps this is a form of "radical universalism," although I would leave it to others to make that argument.

Stadiums previously used to serve as meeting places for the working class. However, today as the prices of tickets continue to rise, football-watching is increasingly becoming an activity for the affluent. As a cheaper substitute, during international tournaments, FIFA generally prepares for a "fan zone," which is basically a viewing area with a big screen. However, entry to these zones, which are always in public spaces, is restricted—making these spaces private. So faced with these twin obstacles, will the working class nature of the game soon be destroyed?

I would argue that at the level you're describing (big international tournaments and the big national leagues) the working-class character of the game has already been destroyed. In England, most working-class fans can no longer afford tickets; they gather in the pub to watch games instead. Football has become popular enough to attract masses of middle- and upper-class people as customers, and since they have more money to spend, they receive priority over working-class supporters (who, of course, are still expected to buy expensive pay-TV packages and jerseys with sponsors' logos splashed across the chest). Ironically, the "working-class charm" of football remains a selling point for the middle- and upper-class customers. Maybe we can call this "classploitation." The good news is that the working-class character of the game will always survive at the grass-roots level: in the alleys, backyards, and meadows of the planet.

So now that the majority of soccer fans increasingly depend on televisions or the radio, can we foresee a situation like the one described by Borges in his short story "Esse Est Percipi"?

I guess we're entering the philosophical realm, as in: how is the media affecting our perception of the world? Professional sports is a theater, no doubt, and there is plenty of deception, from doping to match fixing to an ever growing disparity in resources and assets. One reason why people love theater is that deception can make life more bearable. In situationist terms, modern football is a near-perfect spectacle. Borges raises the specter in his story.

As a sort of resistance to the "new football economy," a lot of "alternate" or "fan-owned" clubs have sprung up throughout the world. But should the football fan be content with these alternate spaces? Is it not a tacit acceptance that the mainstream footballing world cannot be recovered from corporate/right-wing interests? Would you say that while alternate clubs are fine, the real fight lies in reclaiming all of football from aforementioned interests?

Of course, and I think most of the people involved in alternative football clubs would agree with that. Ideally, clubs run by supporters, embracing values of solidarity, and not buying into the consumerist doctrine would form the nucleus of an entirely new sports world. Needless to say, it is hard to create such a world unless there is fundamental political, economic, and cultural change, but these clubs make their contribution in the field of sports—which is a field as contested and politically relevant as any other, if not particularly so due to the attention it receives and the passions it arouses.

On the topic of corporate ownership, what do you think will be the impact of the success of RB Leipzig in Germany? Germans after all take a lot of pride in their 51–49 ownership rule. Do you think the Bundesliga will slowly adopt the Premier League model wholesale?

I don't think the Bundesliga will go the way of the Premier League, because I believe the so-called 50+1 ownership rule—meaning that a club's members will always have just over 50% of decision-making powers—won't fall. Germans are too aware of it being an important piece of the puzzle that makes the Bundesliga the most popular league in the world measured by attendance. However, the rule is increasingly undermined in order to do away with the average member's influence. RB Leipzig is a prime example. Membership criteria and fees are so prohibitive that the club has less than twenty members with voting rights, all of them close associates of Red Bull tycoon Dietrich Mateschitz.

In other clubs, we face the typical problems of electoral politics: members may be able to cast votes when administrative positions are up for grabs (often with only one serious contender), but they have no influence over the club's everyday affairs. Furthermore, big sponsors often enough threaten to withdraw their support if their expectations aren't met. In other words, the 50+1 rule is far from ideal, but it at least keeps the possibility of a more democratic and participatory football culture alive, even on the professional level, something exemplified by FC St. Pauli more than by any other club.

On that note, what are your opinions on the Bosman Ruling?
When Belgian professional Jean-Marc Bosman went to the European Court of Justice in the early 1990s because a transfer fee demanded by his club RFC Liège stopped him from continuing his career in France even though his contract with RFC Liège had expired, he caused a complete overhaul of the football transfer system. Not only are players now free agents at the end of their contracts, but restrictions on signing players from foreign countries were also scrapped. The Bosman Ruling strengthened the position of professional footballers vis-à-vis their employers. That's positive. At the same time, the ruling had some problematic consequences. In football, too, the rich benefit more from "free trade" than the poor. Nowadays, it is possible for the big leagues to secure all of the world's most promising football talent at a very young age, while the foundation of top-quality football in other countries is eroded. The same is true on a domestic level: small clubs lose their best players to the big clubs very early on. As a result, the gap between the strong and the weak in football grows by the year, economic injustice increases further, and competition becomes more boring. None of this is the fault of the Bosman Ruling per se, which was correct, but it also fit the neoliberal agenda perfectly.

Since today's footballing calendar is fixed according to television schedules, sometimes a team might end up playing 3–4 matches in a space of 8–10 days. What do you think is the toll that it takes on the players themselves?
No one would deny that the toll is enormous. Germany went with a B-team to this year's Confederation Cup in Russia, because the team

manager Joachim Löw considered the big stars overplayed (the fact that Germany won the tournament might confirm that the stars on the other teams were overplayed, too). All of the big club teams that play in three competitions each year (the national league, the national cup, and the continental cup) have large rosters that allow for rotation among the starting eleven. It's the only way to keep up with the schedule. Needless to say, you need to have plenty of money to afford a star-studded roster of 20+ players. It's yet another factor that contributes to the increasing gap between the top and the bottom tiers of modern football. But each game means a lot of money for the rich, which is most important. Look at the ridiculous decision to extend the World Cup to 48 participating nations. The only good thing is that the football industry is headed for an overkill: eventually, even the most loyal of fans will become victims of over-saturation. The biggest hope for modern football to end is an implosion.

Perhaps the greatest resistance against corporate football has been offered by ultras groups especially in Europe and Latin America. What are the differences and parallels between the ultras in the two continents?
Very hard for me to say since I have not been able to keep up with the development of Ultra groups in Latin America. My sense is that Ultra culture remains centered in Europe—Latin America has its own supporter cultures. But, obviously, the Ultras' dedication and ability to turn even the most boring of games into an event due to their choreographs, banners, and chants, have attracted football supporters in Latin America as well. As always, the media likes to focus on the violence displayed by some Ultras, but the overall culture is very positive. Many Ultra groups are also clearly anti-racist and anti-fascist, even if their hierarchical organization, territorial claims, and macho tendencies clash with leftist ideals.

In terms of Ultra culture extending beyond Europe's borders, it might be most interesting to look to East Asia and North Africa, where the influence seems strongest, albeit in different ways. In East Asia, it is mainly the aesthetics that are introduced to the big leagues, while in North Africa it is the politics—mainly the Ultras' resistance to surveillance, police violence, and the political exploitation of the game—that define much of the supporter culture in the region. The role that the Egyptian Ultras played in the uprisings of 2011 are only the most famous example.

Can football, often called an "opiate of the masses" ever serve as an agent of the left? Can it possibly build solidarity given that its essence is competition—something that is often referred to as protracted war?
I don't think the competition is the problem. The war metaphors are silly and overused. Most games we play have a competitive element. It is what

makes them fun. We are competitive beings in the sense that we define what we are capable of in comparison to what others are capable of. We would never know if we were fast runners if we didn't compare our running speed to that of others, something that children do in a playful manner. The problem is when competition loses its playfulness and becomes the engine of all activity. It is not surprising that football has gone that way since pretty much anything does in a capitalist society. In a socialist society, the competitive element would be kept at bay. In fact, football contains many aspects that contradict it: collaboration, respect, fair play. It also serves as a universal language, akin to music or dance. If these aspects are at the center of the football experience, it can without doubt contribute to progressive social developments. The alternative football clubs are a case in point.

Finally, what is the future of the game?

As I said, football will always survive at the grassroots level, as a natural way for people to get together, exercise, develop social skills, have fun, and so on. Many things remain to be done to make this experience all-inclusive, especially with respect to the gender imbalance that still haunts the sport, but I think there's been improvement in the last decades and I hope we'll continue on this path. Things are more difficult at the professional level. There, prospects are dire. The modern football industry is still exploring and conquering new markets, it is ruled by a quasi-feudal organization run by crooks, FIFA, and it will remain exploited both by ruthless corporations and politicians. However, as I have also hinted at above, I think that modern football culture is nearing a tipping point; it is growing too big for its own good. Eventually, the circus will have replaced the game entirely and the bubble will burst. This, without doubt, will be a reason to celebrate.

Resources

Reading Material

Some of the books listed here have alternate titles due to the differing usage of "football" and "soccer" across the English-speaking world. The differences are usually minimal.

There is a legion of publications about soccer. It is utterly impossible to provide an exhaustive overview, so I will limit myself to books and periodicals that may be most relevant to the readers of this book.

For a general history of the game, David Goldblatt's *The Ball Is Round: A Global History of Football* (first published in 2006, several editions since) is a great choice. Imposing in its scope, well structured, and very readable, it serves as a major reference guide to anyone interested not only in soccer, but also in the game's intricate relationship with society and politics. If you cannot make it through a thousand pages, then James Walvin's *The People's Game: History of Football Revisited* (first published in 1994, second and revised edition in 2000), Bill Murray's *The World's Game: A History of Soccer* (1998), and Eric Midwinter's *Parish to Planet: How Football Came to Rule the World* (2007) all provide shorter overviews. For more specific chapters of soccer history, Chris Taylor's *The Beautiful Game: Journey through Latin American Football* (1998), Andrei Markovits and Steven Hellerman's *Offside: Soccer and American Exceptionalism* (2001), Alex Bellos's *Futebol: The Brazilian Way of Life* (2002), Paul Darby's *Africa, Football, and FIFA: Politics, Colonialism, and Resistance* (2002), Peter Alegi's *African Soccerscapes: How a Continent Changed the World's Game* (2010), Steve Bloomfield's *Africa United: How Football Explains Africa* (2011), and David Goldblatt's *Futebol Nation: A Footballing History of Brazil* (2014) are all recommended. The intriguing story of the Robben Island prison's soccer leagues has been documented in Chuck Korr and Marvin Close's *More Than Just a Game: Soccer vs. Apartheid* (2010). Among the innumerable books on individual soccer clubs, Barry Flynn's *Political Football: The Life and Death of Belfast Celtic* (2009) is one that stands out for the politically inclined reader.

Simon Kuper's *Football Against the Enemy* (1994) and Franklin Foer's *How Soccer Explains the World* (2004) both contain well-written stories about the intersections of soccer and social life by two traveling journalists. *Soccernomics* (2009), written by Kuper and Stefan Szymanski, contains many interesting facts, though your head might start spinning if you're not all that used to numbers and statistics. *The Global Game: Writers on Soccer* (2008), edited by John Turnbull, Thom Satterlee, and Alon Raab, contains a wide variety of texts on soccer—everyone will find something to their liking. The stand-out work for soccer from a left-wing perspective is Eduardo Galeano's *El fútbol a sol y sombre* (1995), published in English as *Soccer in Sun and Shadow* (1998). It is a wonderful book, full of enticing tales about football, particularly in Latin America.

Among the progressively oriented football books in English, most focus on the commercialization of the game. Particularly notable are John Reid's *Reclaim the Game* (first published in 1992, new edition in 2005), *A Game of Two Halves? The Business of Football* (1999), edited by Sean Hamil, Jonathan Michie, and Christine Oughton, David Conn's *The Beautiful Game? Searching for the Soul of Football* (2005), and Matthew Bazell's *Theatre of Silence: The Lost Soul of Football* (2008). The commercialization of contemporary football, particularly in England, is also the theme of recent books by David Goldblatt, *The Game of Our Lives: The Meaning and Making of English Football* (2014), and by James Montague, *The Billionaires Club: The Unstoppable Rise of Football's Super-Rich Owners* (2017). Decan Hill has made a name for himself with investigations into the highly complex world of match-fixing. His acclaimed 2010 release *The Fix: Soccer and Organized Crime* was followed up in 2013 by *The Insider's Guide to Match-Fixing in Football*. An insight into the uncanny world of financial transactions in the soccer industry is provided by the online platform *Football Leaks: Football and TPO Whistleblowing*.

Andrew Jennings has been providing insights into the mysterious workings of FIFA for a long time. His book *Foul! The Secret World of FIFA: Bribes, Vote Rigging and Ticket Scandals* was published in 2006, and since the FIFA scandal of 2015 broke, he has presented us with *The Dirty Game: Uncovering the Scandal at FIFA* (2015) and, together with Bonita Mersiades, *Whatever It Takes: The Inside Story of the FIFA Way* (2018). Additional books covering the FIFA scandal include Heidi Blake and Jonathan Calvert's *The Ugly Game: The Qatari Plot to Buy the World Cup* (2015) and David Conn's *The Fall of the House of FIFA: The Multimillion-Dollar Corruption at the Heart of Global Soccer* (2017).

Since 2011, there has been a remarkable rise in the publication of politically oriented soccer books. Events in the Middle East have been covered by James Montague in *When Friday Comes: Football, War and Revolution in the Middle East* (2013), and by James Dorsey in *The Turbulent World of Middle East Soccer* (2016). Dave Zirin has looked at developments in Brazil in *Brazil's Dance with the Devil: The World Cup, the Olympics, and the Fight for Democracy* (2014). Andrew Downie has dedicated a book to one of the most prominent left-wing footballers of all time with *Doctor Socrates: Footballer, Philosopher, Legend* (2017). Nick Davidson has written the first full-length book in English about the FC

St. Pauli with *Pirates, Punks, and Politics—FC St. Pauli: Falling in Love with a Radical Football Club* (2014). Cofounder John-Paul O'Neill has told the somewhat turbulent story of the FC United of Manchester in *Red Rebels: The Glazers and the FC Revolution* (2017). Will Simpson and Malcolm McMahon's account of the Easton Cowboys and Cowgirls, *Freedom Through Football: The Story of the Easton Cowboys and Cowgirls* (2012; second edition 2017) is featured in this book. Phil Scraton's *Hillsborough: The Truth* (2016), Mike Nicholson's *The Hillsborough Disaster: In Their Own Words* (2016), and the book *Hillsborough Voices: The Real Story Told by the People Themselves* (2017), edited by Kevin Sampson with the Hillsborough Justice Campaign, document the resilience of football supporters and the people of Liverpool in the face of media smears and a police cover-up.

Additional soccer books released in English in recent years that may be of interest to readers of this book include Emy Onuoura's *Pitch Black: The Story of Black British Footballers* (2015) and Oliver Kay's *Forever Young: The Story of Adrian Doherty, Football's Lost Genius* (2016), addressing the strain that competitive football puts on many young players. People fascinated with the often sensationalized aspect of fan violence may want to look at James Bannon's *Running with the Firm: My Double Life as an Undercover Hooligan* (2014). Of renewed interest considering the many soccer-related migrant and refugee initiatives of recent years is also Warren St. John's popular *Outcasts United: An American Town, a Refugee Team, and One Woman's Quest to Make a Difference* (2009).

In 2010, Ted Richards has compiled a football book in the never-ending series of "Philosophy-and-xy" publications; for those interested, *Soccer and Philosophy: Thoughts on the Beautiful Game* (2010) might be worth a look. In 2017, prominent philosopher Simon Critchley presented his own take on the matter in *What We Think about When We Think about Soccer* (2017). Academically inclined readers can indulge in the *Soccer and Society* journal, which has been published since the year 2000. In 2015, the journal *Sport in Society* released an issue titled "DIY Football: The Cultural Politics of Community," which covers various community clubs featured in this book.

There is a vast array of great non-English soccer literature. In German, excellent football books from a left-wing perspective are produced by Die Werkstatt and various radical publishers. Among the uncountable publications on the FC St. Pauli, a recent standout is Fabian Fritz and Gregor Backes's *FC Sankt Pauli: Fußballfibel* (2017). In Swedish, Erik Niva's articles—collected in various anthologies—are outstanding. In Spanish, there is Osvaldo Bayer's *Fútbol argentino* (1990). In French, there is *Le Temps du "Miroir": Une autre idée du football et du jour-nalisme* (1982) by François Thébaud, longtime editor of the left-leaning magazine *Miroir du football*; *Les enragés du football: L'autre Mai 1968* (2008) by François-René Simon, Alain Leiblang, and Faouzi Mahjoub, about the turbulent events of 1968; and the graphic novel *Un maillot pour l'Algerie* (2016), which tells the story of the FLN team during the independence struggle. In Italian, there are great books about fan culture like Nanni Balestrini's *I furiosi* (1994), Valerio Marchi's *Ultrà. Le sot-toculture giovanili negli stadi d'Europa* (1994), and Giovanni Francesio's *Tifare contro. Una storia degli ultras italiani* (2008).

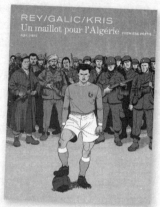

Among literary approaches, Nick Hornby's *Fever Pitch* (1992), the account of an incurable Arsenal fan, might be the most widely read soccer book of all, but if you insist on reading Hornby, I'd recommend *High Fidelity* instead. Cristiano Cavina is an Italian writer who captures the beauty of amateur football. One of his books, *Un'ultima stagione da esordienti* (2006), tells the story of the AC Casola, a side competing within a regional league in the fading days of leftist resistance in the 1980s. Existentialists might enjoy Peter Handke's *Die Angst des Tormanns beim Elfmeter*

(1970), published in English as *The Goalie's Anxiety at the Penalty Kick* (1972). Thomas Hoeffgen's *African Arenas* (2010) is a wonderful picture book about football pitches in Africa.

Football magazines abound. Interesting articles in English can be found in various local zines, the well-established *When Saturday Comes*, and the quarterly *The Blizzard*, founded in 2011.

Films

All titles given for foreign-language films are the ones used for international distribution. If films have not been distributed internationally, their original foreign-language titles are listed.

A fair number of soccer-themed films are available, but you have to do a lot of digging before you find anything satisfactory. *Goal!* (2005/2007/2009), the rags-to-riches story of Los Angeles youngster Santiago Muñez, is probably the most successful, and there are three parts—you need a lot of dedication. *The Golden Ball* (1994), based on the life of Guinean star player Salif Keïta, follows a similar theme and is a much better choice.

For intellectual viewers, there is Wim Wenders's *The Goalkeeper's Fear of the Penalty* (1972, also known as *The Goalie's Anxiety at the Penalty Kick*), based on the Peter Handke novel. *Victory* (1981, also known as *Escape to Victory*) stars Sylvester Stallone as a very disoriented goalkeeper in a World War II POWs' game against a Nazi squad; it is worth a few laughs if you like that kind of stuff. Of much higher quality is *Gregory's Girl* (1981), an endearing coming-of-age film set around a Scottish youth football team.

Those Glory Glory Days (1983) captures the obsession of writer Julie Welch and her friends with Tottenham Hotspur in the early 1960s. *When Saturday Comes* (1996) is a British version of rags-to-riches: less glamorous, less cheesy, but still not too exciting. *Fever Pitch* (1997) is based on the Nick Hornby novel.

The Cup (1999) is a charming film featuring young Tibetan students from a monastery in the Himalayas who are determined to watch the 1998 Men's World Cup Final. In *The Great Match* (2006), "tribal peoples" try to watch the 2002 Men's World Cup Final between Brazil and Germany, but unfortunately the film is laden with clichés. *A Shot at Glory* (2000) is an underdog story about a small Scottish club making a run for the Scottish Cup title. Purely for aesthetic reasons, *Mean Machine* (2001), a prison soccer drama, and *Shaolin Soccer* (2001)—the title says it all—might please a few viewers.

Bend It Like Beckham (2002) certainly has cheesy elements, but it was an important contribution to addressing both sexism and racism in football. The German film *Guys and Balls* (2004) and the Icelandic flick *Eleven Men Out* (2005) tackle homophobia in football, both from a humorous angle. More somber is the documentary *Forbidden Games: The Justin Fashanu Story* (2017). It focuses on the relationship between Justin, the first professional footballer to come out as gay, and his estranged brother John, also a former professional footballer.

Merry Christmas (2005) tells about the Christmas Truce on the Western Front in 1914, including a football match between British and German troops. *Miracle Match* (2005, also known as *Game of Their Lives*) proves that any U.S. victory can be turned into patriotic mush, even in soccer; the movie is about the team that "miraculously" beat England at the 1950 Men's World Cup. The Germans have similar schmaltz with *The Miracle of Bern* (2003), a reference to their unexpected 3–2 win over Hungary at the 1954 Men's World Cup final.

Buenos Aires, 1977 (2006, also known as *Chronicles of an Escape*) is based on a script by former semi-professional goalkeeper Claudio Tamburrini, who was held captive by the Argentinean military regime in 1977. *Offside* (2006) portrays Iranian women trying to sneak into a World Cup qualifier in Tehran; the film was prohibited in Iran.

The Damned United (2009) tells the story of Brian Clough's short spell as manager at Leeds United; it has been widely criticized for confusing fact with fiction. Ken Loach's *Looking for Eric* (2009) is a brilliant effort, with Eric Cantona playing himself as a muse for the depressed postal worker Eric Bishop.

There are a number of hooligan movies to choose from, which focus on tough guys beating up people and on tough guys talking about beating up people. There are *The Football Factory* (2004), *Green Street Hooligans* (2005, also known as *Green Street* or simply *Hooligans*), *The Rise of the Footsoldier* (2007), *Cass* (2008), *Awaydays* (2009), *Green Street (Hooligans) 2* (2009), and *The Firm* (2009). A hooligan-themed movie that puts the focus on masculinity rather than on the exploitation of violence is *Hata Göteborg* (2007), a DIY project by a group of twenty-somethings from the Swedish town of Helsingborg—highly recommended!

There are numerous interesting documentaries about football:

Football as Never Before (1971) is an experimental project following George Best in real time during a game between his Manchester United and Coventry City. *Zidane: A 21st Century Portrait* (2006) follows the same pattern, capturing Zinedine Zidane with seventeen cameras during a single match in April 2005. A conventional documentary about George Best, titled *George Best: All by Himself*, was released in 2016. *Maradona by Kusturica* (2008) is a portrayal of Diego Maradona by acclaimed Serbian filmmaker Emir Kusturica that includes plenty of material about Maradona's political ideas and activism. *Football Rebels* (2012), presented by Eric Cantona, portrays five professionals, Sócrates among them, who have spoken out on social and political issues. *Tom Meets Zizou* (2011) tells the story of how Thomas Broich, once hailed as the future of German football but growing increasingly weary of Bundesliga demands, finds a less demanding footballing environment in Australia.

Kill the Referee (2009, also known as Referees at Work) is a fascinating, close-up study of match officials during the 2008 Men's European Championship. The Referee (2010) follows the preparations of Swedish referee Martin Hansson for the 2010 Men's World Cup, which took a dramatic turn after he missed Thierry Henry's handball during France's decisive qualifier against Ireland.

Football's Fight Club (2002), The Real Football Factories (2006), and The Real Football Factories International (2007) are TV programs on hooliganism.

The Game of Their Lives (2002) traces the history of the sensational 1966 World Cup team of North Korea. Munidal '78, la historia paralela (2003) looks at the 1978 Men's World Cup in Argentina in its sociopolitical context. Communism and Football (2006) looks at the impact of politics on football in the former state socialist countries of Eastern Europe. Futebol de Causas (2009) chronicles the political significance of the Portuguese club Académica de Coimbra in the late 1960s and early 1970s. The role of the Ultras in the Turkish Gezi Park protests of 2013 has been documented in Istanbul United (2014).

The Other Final (2003) is a pleasant film about the two lowest-ranked FIFA teams, Bhutan and Montserrat, meeting on the morning of the 2002 Men's World Cup Final. Goal Dreams (2006) documents the run for the 2006 Men's World Cup of the Palestinian football team. Next Goal Wins (2014) accompanies the team of American Samoa trying to recover from a 0–31 loss against Australia in a 2011 World Cup qualifier. Desert Fire and the World Cup Rebels (2016) focuses on the impossibility of the Kurdish national team to qualify for the World Cup, as it is not recognized by FIFA.

Dare to Dream: The Story of the U.S. Women's Soccer Team (2005) is an interesting HBO documentary, although the U.S. hype becomes at times unbearable. Once in a Lifetime: The Extraordinary Story of the New York Cosmos (2006) gives us the tale of the legendary New York City soccer club. Assyriska: A National Team Without a Nation (2006) is an account of the Assyrian football club from Södertälje, Sweden. After the Cup: Sons of Sakhnin United (2010) investigates the outfall of the sensational 2004 Israeli Cup win of the predominantly Arab side of Bnei Sakhnin. The Return to Homs (2013) features the controversial Syrian goalkeeper-turned-rebel-commander Abdul Baset al-Sarout.

Kicking It (2008) is a great film about the history of the Homeless World Cup. *Gringos at the Gate* (2010) documents the soccer rivalry along the U.S.-Mexican border. *Pelada* (2010) is an intriguing film that follows U.S. soccer enthusiasts playing pick-up games in twenty-five countries.

The Railroad All-Stars (2006) depicts a soccer team founded by sex workers in Guatemala City in 2004. *Football Under Cover* (2008) accompanies the Berlin-Kreuzberg women's team of BSV Al-Dersimspor in its games against Iran's women's national side. *Pizza Bethlehem* (2010) depicts an all-female soccer team in the multicultural Bethlehem neighborhood of the Swiss capital Bern. *Refugee 11* (2017) follows the exploits of a refugee football team with members from fifteen countries in a small German town.

Fahrenheit 2010 (2009) takes a critical look at the 2010 Men's World Cup in South Africa (South African TV stations refused to air the film). *Soka Afrika* (2011) investigates the often-harsh conditions under which African footballers are traded and forced to play on other continents. *Dirty Games* (2016) takes a broad look at corruption and exploitation in sports. *The Workers Cup* (2017) reports from Qatar, portraying the migrant workers who build stadiums and infrastructure for the 2022 Men's World Cup.

John Cleese's *The Art of Football from A to Z* (2006) is expectedly humorous and will appeal to Monty Python fans. Readers are also encouraged to find the Monty Python clip "Philosophers' World Cup."

Music

Musicians have always been close to football. Elton John has been serving Watford in different roles since the 1970s. Richie Blackmore, Robert Plant, and Rod Stewart are all big football fans—the latter even pursued a professional career once upon a time. Iron Maiden regularly fielded a team during concert tours. Chumbawamba sponsored the Wetherby Athletic Under-14 side. Weezer dedicated the song "Represent" to the U.S. men's soccer team. The Old Firm Casuals, fronted by Rancid guitarist and vocalist Lars Frederiksen, recorded an anthem for the San Jose Earthquakes titled "Never Say Die," and Rancid drummer Branden Steineckert wrote the tune "Believe" for his hometown team Real Salt Lake. The numerous artists who have worn St. Pauli shirts or accessories on stage include the Asian Dub Foundation, Sascha Konietzko of KMFDM, Andrew Eldritch of Sisters of Mercy, Georg Hólm of Sigur Rós, and Alex Rosamilia of the Gaslight Anthem.

The possibly biggest musical icon for football fans is Bob Marley. The slogans "Football Is Music"and "Football Is Freedom" are ascribed to him. Tragically, a toe injury from a football game was directly linked to the illness that would eventually cost him his life. A soccer ball was among the items he was buried with. The connections between soccer and reggae remain: Ezra Hendrickson, a native of St. Vincent and the Grenadines and longtime MLS player, regularly wore a Bob Marley shirt underneath his jersey. In the Caribbean, soccer games are often combined with reggae and dancehall festivals. In New Caledonia, reggae and football are the cornerstones of Kanak youth culture.

There are hundreds of songs about football—the worst being those performed by national teams before big tournaments. Underneath a lot of forgettable tunes, some gems can be found. In the early 1970s, Gilberto Gil wrote "Meio de Campo," a beautiful song dedicated to the "rebel footballer" Afonsinho. Charly García wrote a "Maradona Blues" after Maradona's expulsion from the World Cup in the U.S. Another highly recommended South American football tune is Jorge Ben's "Ponta de Lança Africano (Umbabarauma)." Some artists have dedicated whole albums to football. Outstanding are *Scientist Wins the World Cup* (1982) by dub legend Scientist, and the Wedding Present's *George Best* (1987), the band's best-selling record to date. London-based reggae producer Adrian Sherwood was behind the The Barmy Army album *The English Disease* (1989), which incorporated a football crowd chant into every song.

In the 1990s, many punk and indie bands wrote football songs. "Hier kommt Alex" by the Fortuna Düsseldorf fans Tote Hosen was originally a tribute to the *Clockwork Orange* character but soon became an anthem for longtime Fortuna manager Alexander Ristić. The Spanish Oi! band Ska-P released a song to honor their club Rayo Vallecano, "Como un rayo." With the help of the comedians David Baddiel and Frank Skinner, the Lightning Seeds produced "Three Lions," one of the few decent English football songs with mainstream success. Ash put a photo of Eric Cantona kicking the Crystal Palace supporter Matthew Simmons on the cover of their single "Kung Fu."

In 1996, a classic among antifascist hooligan albums was released by the Oppressed, namely *Music for Hooligans*. "Strachan," dedicated to the Scottish midfielder Gordon Strachan, was a popular song for the Hitchers. In Argentina, ska punk band Las Manos de Fillippi wrote a song about the 1978 World Cup, "La selección nacional." Turbonegro recorded a special German version of "I Got Erection" for the FC St. Pauli. Chumbawamba's "Tubthumping" became an unofficial anthem for the 1998 Men's World Cup in France, and the group rejected a lucrative advertisement deal with Nike. "Holigan" was a catchy fan anthem released by the Turkish ska punk band Athena, which went on to represent Turkey at the 2004 Eurovision Song Contest; they also released an album celebrating the one-hundredth anniversary of Fenerbahçe Istanbul.

In the year 2000, the Dutch outfit Discipline released the *Hooligan's Heaven* EP; the title song became a crowd favorite. Discipline also wrote songs like "Everywhere We Go" and "Red and White Army," which used to be played at the home games of PSV Eindhoven. In 2003, another classical hooligan album was released by The Business, *Hardcore Hooligan*, including songs like "Hand Ball" (a reference to Diego Maradona's goal against England in 1986), "Southgate (Euro 96)," "England 5—Germany 1," and "Terrace Lost Its Soul." Meanwhile, Oi! band Guardia Negra dedicated a song to the Argentinean club Atlanta, entitled "Bohemios" after the club's nickname, on their album ¡Adrenalina!.

In 2004 the Italian punk rock band Los Fastidios released the ultimate antifascist football supporter anthem (save pacifists): "Antifa Hooligans." The band, die-hard fans of the local amateur club Virtus Verona, released another football-dedicated record in 2007, *Un calcio ad un pallone*; it includes a dedication to Cristiano Lucarelli and a cover of the Liverpool

fans' legendary "You'll Never Walk Alone."
In 2005, Swedish punk band Millencolin
released "My Name is Golden," a song
dedicated to Zlatan Ibrahimović, who
shares Millencolin singer Nikola Šarčević's
Yugoslav background.

In 2006, punk rock veterans Sham
69 and the Special Assembly challenged
the official English World Cup song
with "Hurry Up England—The People's
Anthem." Manu Chao, an ardent football fan, released the popular "La Vida
Tómbola," dedicated to Diego Maradona
and featured in Emir Kusturica's film about Maradona; Manu Chao had
already released a Maradona-dedicated track with his band Manu Negra,
"Santa Maradona."

In 2008, the British DJ Richy Pitch, who had been living in Ghana for a
couple of years, gave us "Football Jama," inspired by African football supporters. In 2009, Mexican rock band Maldita Vecindad released a passionate manifesto for people's football with "Fut Callejero (Pura Diversion)."

Interesting records came out in connection with the 2010 Men's World
Cup in South Africa. In England, indie legend Mark E. Smith recorded
"England's Heartbeat" with Shuttleworth. Ghana's Wanlov the Kubolor
released *Yellow Card: Stomach Direction*, and a number of tunes were produced that criticized the corporate interests involved in the World Cup and
the modern game in general: Nomadic Wax, DJ Magee, and DJ Nio joined
up for the *World Cup* EP, the Chomsky Allstars released "The Beautiful
Gain," and hip hop outfit EWOK recorded the track "Shame on the Game."

Among the many football song sampler, the ones recommended for
radical fans are BAFF's *Music for the Terraces* (2003), and two St.-Pauli-
dedicated releases: *Der FC St. Pauli ist schuld, . . . dass ich so bin* (1998), *We
Love St. Pauli* (2007), and *St. Pauli Einhundert* (2010), a monumental 5-CD
box set celebrating the club's one-hundredth anniversary with one hundred
songs by one hundred bands and a one-hundred-page booklet.

A standout among football-related songs of recent years is Matt Fishel's
"Football Song," released in 2010 and featured on Fishel's first album *Not
Thinking Straight* (2013). It tells about a gay student's perception of his
school's football team and his crush on the team's captain. The video features players from Stonewall FC, Britain's highest-ranked gay football club.
Entertaining are the homages to Zinedine Zidane by Vaudeville Smash
(feat. Les Murray) and to Zlatan Ibrahimović by Sanjin & Youthman.

With *45football.com*, there is now also a blog dedicated to football-
related records.

Online

Football Associations

Fédération Internationale de Football Association (FIFA): **www.fifa.com**
Asian Football Confederation (AFC): **www.the-afc.com**
Confédération Africaine de Football (CAF): **www.cafonline.com**
Confederation of North, Central American and Caribbean Association
Football (CONCACAF): **www.concacaf.com**
Confederación Sudamericana de Fútbol (CONMEBOL): **www.conmebol.com**
Oceania Football Confederation (OFC): **www.oceaniafootball.com**
Union of European Football Associations (UEFA): **www.uefa.com**
Confederation of Independent Football Associations (ConIFA):
www.conifa.org

Football Clubs

AC Omonia Nicosia: **www.acomonia.com**
Altona 93: **www.altona93.de**
Argentinos Juniors: **www.argentinosjuniors.com.ar**
AS Livorno: **www.livornocalcio.it**
Athletic Bilbao: **www.athletic-club.net**
Ajax Amsterdam: **www.ajax.nl**
Bnei Sakhnin: **www.sakhnini.net**
Celtic Glasgow: **www.celticfc.net**
Chacarita Juniors: **chacaritajuniors.org.ar**
Corinthians: **www.corinthians.com.br**
Dalkurd FF: **www.dalkurd.se**
El Porvenir: **www.clubelporvenir.com.ar**
FC Barcelona: **www.fcbarcelona.com**
FC St. Pauli: **www.fcstpauli.com**
FC United of Manchester: **www.fc-utd.co.uk**
Forest Green Rovers FC: **www.forestgreenroversfc.com**
Hapoel Tel Aviv: **www.hapoelta-fc.co.il**
Pumas: **www.pumas.mx/**
Racing Club: **www.racingclub.com.ar**
Rayo Vallecano: **www.rayovallecano.es**
SD Eibar: **www.sdeibar.com**
SV Babelsberg 03: **www.babelsberg03.de**
Tennis Borussia Berlin: **www.tebe.de**
Türkiyemspor Berlin: **www.tuerkiyemspor.info**
Vasco da Gama: **www.crvascodagama.com**
Virtus Verona: **www.usvirtusbv.it**

Fan-Owned and Community Clubs

AFC Liverpool: **www.afcliverpool.tv**
AFC Wimbledon: **www.afcwimbledon.co.uk**
AKS Zły: **www.aks-zly.pl**
Austria Salzburg: **www.austria-salzburg.at**
Autônomos FC: **www.facebook.com/Autônomos-FC**
Bristol Easton Cowboys/Cowgirls: **eastoncowboys.org.uk**
BSV Al-Dersimspor: **www.bsv-aldersim.eu**
Christiania Sports Club: **www.csc1982.dk**
FC United of Manchester: **www.fc-utd.co.uk**
FC Vova: **www.facebook.com/FCVOVA**
FK Utopia: **www.fkutopia.dk**
Flying Bats Women's Football Club: **www.theflyingbats.com**
Futbolistas L.A.: **www.futbolistasla.org**
Hapoel Katamon Jerusalem: **www.katamon.co.il**
HFC Falke: **www.hfc-falke.de**
Lewes FC: **www.lewesfc.com**
Republica Internationale FC: **www.republica-i.co.uk**
Roter Stern Leipzig: **www.roter-stern-leipzig.de**
Seitenwechsel: **www.seitenwechsel-berlin.de**
Wrexham AFC: **www.wrexhamafc.co.uk**

Organizations and Projects

Common Goal: **www.common-goal.org**
European Gay and Lesbian Sport Federation: **www.eglsf.info**
Fan.tastic Females: Football Her.Story: **www.fan-tastic-females.org**
Football Against Racism in Europe: **www.farenet.org**
Football Unites, Racism Divides: **www.furd.org**
Gol de Letra: **www.goldeletra.org.br**
International Gay and Lesbian Football Association: **www.iglfa.org**
Kick It Out: **www.kickitout.org**
Moving the Goalposts: **www.mtgk.org**
Neven Subotić Foundation: **www.nevensuboticstiftung.de**
Show Racism the Red Card: **www.srtrc.org**
Soccer in the Streets: **www.soccerstreets.org**
Soccer without Borders: **www.soccerwithoutborders.org**
Streetfootball World: **www.streetfootballworld.org**
This Fan Girl: **www.thisfangirl.com**

Supporters' Groups & Networks

Alerta: **nomattimen.wordpress.com/alerta-network**
Bündnis aktiver Fußballfans (BAFF): **www.aktive-fans.de**

Çarşı: **www.forzabesiktas.com**
Clapton Ultras: **www.claptonultras.org**
Commando Ultra 84: **www.commandoultra84.com**
Coordination Nationale des Ultras: **cnu07.free.fr**
F_in—Frauen im Fußball: **www.f-in.org**
Football Supporters' Federation: **www.fsf.org.uk**
Gay Football Supporters Network: **www.gfsn.org.uk**
Green Brigade: **greenbrigade.proboards.com**
Gruppo di Strade: **peristeristreetgroup.blogspot.com**
Hillsborough Justice Campaign: **www.facebook.com/HJCOfficial**
Queer Football Fanclubs: **www.queerfootballfanclubs.eu**
Radical Fans United: **rfu.blogspot.com**
Spirit of Shankly: **www.spiritofshankly.com**
St. Pauli Fanladen: **www.stpauli-fanladen.de**
Ultrà Sankt Pauli: **usp.stpaulifans.de**
Ultras Hapoel: **www.ultrashapoel.com**

Grassroots Leagues and Tournaments

Alternative Liga Zürich: **www.fsfv.ch**
Amputee Football World Cup: **www.worldamputeefootball.com**
Anti-Racism World Cup, Belfast, Northern Ireland:
www.facebook.com/arwcbelfast
Come Together Cup: **www.come-together-cup.de**
Homeless World Cup: **www.homelessworldcup.org**
Mondiali Antirazzisti: **www.facebook.com/mondialiantirazzisti**
Ute Bock: **www.utebockcup.at**
Wilde Liga Wien: **www.wildeligawien.wordpress.com**

Publications

11Freunde: **www.11freunde.de**
Ballesterer: **ballesterer.at**
Die Werkstatt: **www.werkstatt-verlag.de**
Le Miroir du football: **www.miroirdufootball.com**
TÁL: **www.talfanzine.com** (retired)
When Saturday Comes: **www.wsc.co.uk**

Blogs

45football: **www.45football.com**
Doing the Rondo: **www.doingtherondo.com**
Football Derbies: **www.footballderbies.com**
Football Is Radical: **www.footballisradical.com** (on hiatus)
Football Leaks: **www.footballleaks2015.wordpress.com**

From a Left Wing—The Cultural Politics of Soccer:
fromaleftwing.blogspot.com (retired)
In Bed with Maradona: **www.inbedwithmaradona.com**
In Sun and Shadow: **www.insunandshadow.com**
Obscure Music and Football: **obscuremusicandfootball.wordpress.com**
(retired)
Philosophy Football—Sporting Outfitters of Intellectual Distinction:
www.philosophyfootball.com
The Turbulent World of Middle East Soccer:
www.mideastsoccer.blogspot.com

Bands

Los Fastidios: **www.losfastidios.com**
Ska-P: **ska-p.com**

Notes

1   Tom Clark, "Camus, Zidane and Absurdity of Football," *Tom Clark: Beyond the Pale*, http://tomclarkblog.blogspot.com/2010/06/camus-zidane-and-absurdity-of-football.html.

2   "Football and Class Struggle: Interview with Toni Negri," by Renaud Dély and Rico Rizzitelli for *Libération*, https://libcom.org/library/negri-football-class-struggle.

3   John Turnbull, "A Soccer Player's Escape From Argentina . . . Into Philosophy," *The Global Game*, http://www.theglobalgame.com/blog/2008/08/a-soccer-players-escape-from-argentina%C2%A0-into-philosophy [2019: no longer active].

4   Claudio Tamburrini, "The Right to Celebrate," *Idrottsforum*, http://www.idrottsforum.org/features/tamburrini/tamcla_argentina.html.

5   For an overview see the chapter "Chasing Shadows: The Prehistory of Football," in David Goldblatt, *The Ball Is Round: A Global History of Football* (London: Viking, 2006), 3–18.

6   Peter Marsh et al., *Football Violence and Hooliganism in Europe*, Word doc, available at *Redwhite*, www.redwhite.ru/fans/books/hools/fv2.doc.

7   "History of Football Violence," *The Football Network*, http://footballnetwork.org/violence/history-of-violence/.

8   "History of Football," *Icons: A Portrait of England*, http://www.icons.org.uk/theicons/collection/fa-cup/biography/history-of-football [2019: no longer active].

9   "Football Violence in History," *Social Issues Resource Centre*, http://www.sirc.org/publik/fvhist.html.

10   "Cambridge Rules," *Spartacus Educational: Encyclopedia of British Football*, https://spartacus-educational.com/Fcambridge.htm.

11   Marsh et al., *Football Violence and Hooliganism in Europe*.

12   Chris Bambery, "Marxism and Sport," *International Socialism* 73 (1995), http://www.pubs.socialistreviewindex.org.uk/isj73/bambery.htm.

13   Ibid.

14   "The History of Women's Football," *The Football Association*, http://www.thefa.com/womens-girls-football/history.

15   Tamir Bar-On, "The Ambiguities of Football, Politics, Culture and Social Transformation in Latin America," *Sociological Research Online* 2, no. 4, http://www.socresonline.org.uk/2/4/2.html.

16   Ian Syson, "How Soccer Explains the World: A Review," *The Age (Australia)*, http://www.theage.com.au/articles/2004/09/15/1095221654997.html?from=moreStories.

17   "He's in the Pink: Interview with Simon Kuper," by John Turnbull for *The Global Game*, http://www.theglobalgame.com/blog/2005/08/hes-in-the-pink-interview-with-simon-kuper [2019: no longer active].

18   Franklin Foer, *How Soccer Explains the World: An Unlikely Theory of Globalization* (New York: Harper Collins, 2004), 241.

19   Dorian de Wind, "Conservative Rage at Soccer and World Cup Is Nothing New," *Huffington Post*, June 28, 2014, https://www.huffingtonpost.com/dorian-de-wind/conservative-rage-at-socc_b_5540546.html.

20   Steven Wells, "The Truth the Soccerphobes Refuse to Face," *Guardian,* January 17, 2008, http://www.guardian.co.uk/sport/blog/2008/jan/17/thetruththesoccerphobesref.

21   Bar-On, "The Ambiguities of Football, Politics, Culture and Social Transformation in Latin America."

22   Jan Dunkhorst, "Linker Fußball? Rechter Fußball? César Luis Menotti als Utopist des Wahren, Guten und Schönen im Fußballsport" [Left-wing Football? Right-wing Football? César Luis Menotti as the Utopian of the True, Good, and Beautiful in the Game of Football], *Lateinamerika Nachrichten,* https://lateinamerika-nachrichten.de/artikel/linker-fussball-rechter-fussball/.

23   Simon Kuper and Stefan Szymanski, *Soccernomics* (New York: Nation Books, 2009), 272.

24   Bambery, "Marxism and Sport."

25   "Quotations about Soccer," *The Quote Garden,* http://www.quotegarden.com/soccer.html.

26   John Williams, "Football, Politics and War," *Leicester Mercury Columns,* April 4, 2003.

27   Bambery, "Marxism and Sport."

28   Eric Hobsbawm, *Nations and Nationalism Since 1780: Programme, Myth, Reality* (Cambridge: Cambridge University Press, 1990).

29   Simon Kuper, "It's Here—The One Show That Unites the Globe," *The Age (Australia),* May 31, 2002, http://www.theage.com.au/articles/2002/05/31/1022569835379.html.

30   Bar-On, "The Ambiguities of Football, Politics, Culture and Social Transformation in Latin America."

31   "Germany vs. Sweden," *The Unofficial Football World Championships,* http://www.ufwc.co.uk/2010/07/germany-vs-sweden-1942.

32   John C. Turnbull, Alon Raab, and Thom Satterlee, eds., *The Global Game: Writers on Soccer* (Lincoln: University of Nebraska Press, 2008), 189–94.

33   Kuper and Szymanski, *Soccernomics,* 135.

34   Ibid., 134–35.

35   Goldblatt, *The Ball Is Round,* 322.

36   John Turnbull, "A Soccer Player's Escape from Argentina . . . Into Philosophy."

37   Andrew Feinstein, "The Rise of the Tenderpreneurs, the Fall of South Africa," *New Statesman,* June 7, 2006, http://www.newstatesman.com/africa/2010/06/south-world-anc-party-zuma.

38   Dale T. McKinley, "South Africa: The Myths and Realities of the FIFA Soccer World Cup," *Africafiles,* http://www.africafiles.org/article.asp?ID=23856.

39   Erik Niva, *Den nya världsfotbollen* [The New World Football] (Stockholm: Modernista, 2008), 249.

40   Terry Eagleton, "Football: A Dear Friend to Capitalism," *Guardian,* June 15, 2010, http://www.guardian.co.uk/commentisfree/2010/jun/15/football-socialism-crack-cocaine-people.

41   Eric Wegner, "Gedanken zur Fußball-WM 1998. Fußballsport zwischen Massenkultur, kommerzieller Kickerei und nationalistischer Instrumentalisierung" [Thoughts on the 1998 Soccer World Cup: Football between Mass Culture, Commercial Kickabouts, and Nationalist Instrumentalization], *Revolutionär Sozialistische Organisation,* http://www.sozialismus.net/agm/home/flugschriften/f6_fussball.htm.

42   "Workers of the World United: Football and Socialism," *Socialist Party: Portsmouth Branch,* http://socialistpartyp.wordpress.com/2010/07/07/workers-of-the-world-united-football-and-socialism.

43   "'Fußball ist eine Art von Krieg. Jeder muss kämpfen, um zu gewinnen.' (Johann Cruyff)," ['Football is a kind of war. Everyone has to fight to win.' (J.C.)], *Forum Radikaldemokratische Politik,* http://www.radikaldemokraten.de/archiv/materialien/flugblaetter/fussball-ist-eine-art-von-krieg-jeder-muss-kaempfen-um-zu-gewinnen.

44   Marsh et al., *Football Violence and Hooliganism in Europe.*

45   See, for example, Simon Kuper, "Celtic and Rangers, or Rangers and Celtic," in *Football Against the Enemy* (London: Orion, 1994), 205–19.

46   Kuper, *Football Against the Enemy,* 113.

47 John Turnbull, "Pride of Lions: Iraqi Asian Cup Victory Reminds a Civilization What Normal Feels Like," *The Global Game*, August 9, 2007, http://www.theglobalgame.com/blog/2007/08/pride-of-lions-iraqi-asian-cup-victory-reminds-a-civilization-what-normal-feels-like [2019: no longer active].

48 Pascal Boniface and Lilian Thuram, "Pour la Coupe du monde de football de 2018 en Israël et Palestine!" *Institut de Relations Internationales et Strategiques*, December 12, 2007, currently available at http://www.palestine-solidarite.org/analyses.Pascal_Boniface.121207.htm.

49 "The Team," *Search for Common Ground*, http://www.sfcg.org/programmes/cgp/the-team.html.

50 www.streetfootballworld.org.

51 "Football Violence in History."

52 "Media Coverage of Football Hooliganism," *Social Issues Resource Centre*, http://www.sirc.org/publik/fvmedia.html.

53 Marsh et al., *Football Violence and Hooliganism in Europe*.

54 "Fig Fact-Sheet Four: Hooliganism," *Live inSoccer*, http://liveinsoccer.blogspot.com/2008/01/fig-fact-sheet-four-hooliganism-what-is.html.

55 "History of Soccer," *Oakville Men's Soccer Club*, http://www.soccerweb.ca/HistoryofSoccer.html.

56 "Fact Sheet 10: The 'New' Football Economics," *Department of Sociology: Sports Resources, University of Leicester*, archived at https://web.archive.org/web/20110305215453/www.le.ac.uk/snccfr/resources/factsheets/fs10.html.

57 Eduardo Galeano, *Soccer in Sun and Shadow* (London/New York: Verso, 2003, revised edition, translated by Mark Fried), 95.

58 John Reid, *Reclaim the Game: The Death of the People's Game*, www.socialistparty.org.uk/ReclaimTheGame/reclaimthegame1.htm.

59 Ibid.

60 Ibid.

61 Ibid.

62 Ibid.

63 Ibid.

64 Bambery, "Marxism and Sport."

65 Ibid.

66 Feinstein, "Rise of the Tenderpreneurs, the Fall of South Africa."

67 Patrick Bond, "Red Cards for Fifa, Coke and South African Elites," *Counterpunch*, https://www.counterpunch.org/2010/06/14/red-cards-for-fifa-coke-and-south-african-elites/.

68 Ashwin Desai and Patrick Bond, "South Africa's own goal," *Red Pepper*, http://www.redpepper.org.uk/South-Africa-s-own-goal.

69 Susan Galleymore, "World Cup Soccer 2010: Shame on the Beautiful Game," *OpEdNews*, http://www.opednews.com/articles/World-Cup-Soccer-2010-Sha-by-Susan-Galleymore-100608-993.html.

70 Feinstein, "Rise of the Tenderpreneurs, the Fall of South Africa."

71 "Fact Sheet 4: Black Footballers in Britain," *Department of Sociology: Sports Resources, University of Leicester*, archived at https://web.archive.org/web/20110309045510/http://www.le.ac.uk/snccfr/resources/factsheets/fs4.html.

72 Martin Jacques, "Football and Race: The Shame in Spain," *Guardian*, May 8, 2005, http://www.guardian.co.uk/sport/2005/may/08/europeanfootball.football.

73 Reid, *Reclaim the Game*.

74 Andrew Gumbel, "Gadaffi's Soccer Foes Pay Deadly Penalty," *The Independent*, http://www.independent.co.uk/news/gadaffis-soccer-foes-pay-deadly-penalty-1328829.html.

75 "Missed the Goal for Workers: the Reality of Soccer Ball Stitchers in Pakistan, India, China and Thailand," *Clean Clothes Campaign*, https://cleanclothes.org/resources/recommended-reading/ilrf-soccerball-report.pdf/view.

76 Barney Ronay, "Anyone Want to Play on the Left?," *Guardian*, April 25, 2007, http://www.guardian.co.uk/football/2007/apr/25/sport.comment1.

77   "Berti Is Back," August 10, 2006, *11Freunde*, https://www.11freunde.de/artikel/fussball-3088.

78   "Juan Verón," *Tripod*, http://2sexyfootballers.tripod.com/veron.html.

79   "The Day Magic Wowed Wembley," *FIFA*, https://www.fifa.com/news/y=2013/m=11/news=the-day-magic-wowed-wembley-2227730.html.

80   "The Brains behind the Magical Magyars," *FIFA*, https://www.fifa.com/news/y=2007/m=4/news=the-brains-behind-the-magical-magyars-510979.html.

81   Reid, *Reclaim the Game*.

82   Ronay, "Anyone Want to Play on the Left?"

83   David Künstner, "El Flaco—ein Mann der Linken. Cesar Luis Menotti, argentinischer WM-Coach 1978," [El Flaco, A Man of the Left: César Luis Menotti, Argentina's World Cup Coach 1978] *Secarts*, https://www.secarts.org/?id=173&lang=de.

84   Bar-On, "The Ambiguities of Football, Politics, Culture and Social Transformation in Latin America."

85   Sophie Ari and Jo Tuckman, *Guardian*, October 18, 2004, "Soccer Stars Support Guerrillas," http://www.guardian.co.uk/world/2004/oct/19/mexico.

86   Kuper, *Football Against the Enemy*, 108.

87   Renato Ramos, "Interview with Agência de Notícias Anarquistas," *Midia Libertaria*, http://www.midialibertaria.jex.com.br/anarquia/futebol+sempre+foi+opio+e+paixao.

88   "Football is Faster than Words: Interview with Orhan Pamuk," by Christoph Biermann and Lothar Gorris for *Spiegel Online*, June 4, 2008, http://www.spiegel.de/international/europe/spiegel-interview-with-orhan-pamuk-football-is-faster-than-words-a-557614.html.

89   "A Brief History," *The Celtic Football Club*, http://www.celticfc.net/pages/history.

90   "Fact Sheet 6: Racism and Football", *Department of Sociology: Sports Resources, University of Leicester*, archived at https://web.archive.org/web/20090630162409/http://www.le.ac.uk/sociology/css/resources/factsheets/fs6.html.

91   Reid, *Reclaim the Game*.

92   Bar-On, "The Ambiguities of Football, Politics, Culture and Social Transformation in Latin America."

93   A special thank you to Jonas Gabler, who has shared many insightful comments on the Ultra phenomenon. Jonas is the author of *Ultrakulturen und Rechtsextremismus. Fußballfans in Italien und Deutschland* [Ultra Cultures and the Extreme Right. Soccer Fans in Italy and Germany (2009) and *Die Ultras: Fußballfans und Fußballkulturen in Deutschland* [The Ultras: Soccer Fans and Soccer Cultures in Germany] (2010), both published with Cologne's PapyRossa Verlag.

94   "Die Fans wollen mitreden" [The Fans Want to Have a Say], *Frankfurter Rundschau*, http://www.fr.de/politik/spezials/doku---debatte/fussball-die-fans-wollen-mitreden-a-1181094

95   Christian Gottschalk, "Vorwort" [Preface], *Viervierzwei*, http://www.viervierzwei.de/index2.php?mode=viewcat&cat_id=3 [2019: no longer active].

96   "Fact Sheet 7: Fan 'Power' and Democracy in Football," *Department of Sociology: Sports Resources, University of Leicester*, archived at https://web.archive.org/web/20100821184842/http://www.le.ac.uk/so/css/resources/factsheets/fs7.html.

97   Reid, *Reclaim the Game*.

98   The entire communiqué in German can be found here: http://www.raumpflege.org/index.php?pressecommunique_brotaektschen [2019: no longer active].

99   From www.soccernova.com, which has since gone offline.

100   Patrick Bond, "Six Red Cards for FIFA," June 12, 2010, *ZSpace*, https://zcomm.org/zcommentary/six-red-cards-for-fifa-by-patrick-bond/.

101   "Football and Class Struggle: Interview with Toni Negri," by Renaud Dély and Rico Rizzitelli for *Libération*, https://libcom.org/library/negri-football-class-struggle.

Images

84 *Les enragés du football: L'autre mai 68* was published in 2008, recalling the
footballers' occupation of the French Football Association headquarters on May
22, 1968, and reflecting on its consequences. Two of the authors, Alain Leiblang
and Faouzi Mahjoub, took part in the occupation. *Editions Calmann-Lévy*

86 Panel discussion organized by War on Want: Fighting Global Poverty, London
Gareth Kingdon/War on Want

92 *Personal Archive*

94 Club Atlético Atlanta, the "Jews" of Argentina's football league. Villa Crespo is the
historically Jewish neighborhood of Buenos Aires. *www.caatlanta.com.ar*

95 *F_in—Frauen im Fußball*

98 *F_in—Frauen im Fußball*

99 (left) "Choreography" of Antidiskriminierungs-AG, SV Werder Bremen
Antidiskriminierungs-AG, SV Werder Bremen; (right) "Choreography" of Infamous
Youth, SV Werder Bremen *Infamous Youth, SV Werder Bremen*

102 *Queer Football Fanclubs*

103 *Queer Football Fanclubs*

104 Team Seitenwechsel. Tanja Walther-Ahrens third from right *Courtesy of Tanja
Walther-Ahrens*

105 (top) "Berlin has a ball/bullet for everyone." Radicals welcome the 1974 Men's
World Cup in Germany. *HKS 13/http://plakat.nadir.org*; (bottom) Ullevi Stadium
Gothenburg, 2009 *B.J.L.*

106 *Jafar Panahi Productions, Filmcoopi Zurich*

108 FoulBall Campaign *BBA and International Labor Rights Forum*

112 (top) *Muzy Corp*; (bottom) Volker Ippig *FC St. Pauli*

116 (top) A.S. Livorno supporters *UltrasTifosi/ultras-tifo.tk*; (below) *Personal Archive*

117 "Lucarelli, I love you" *loungerie/flickr*

119 *blogdellospor.blogspot.com*

122 *R.S. Grove*

124 *R.S. Grove*

126 "Oleguer—We Are on Your Side" *joacuso.blogspot.com*

133 (top) "Beyond Logic, Beyond Reason, I Give You My Life and My Heart"—
Supporters of Racing Club, Buenos Aires *fedematos/Foro Racing*; (bottom) "Rayo
Vallecano: Pride of the Working Class" *Personal Archive*

134 Poster announcing a football match between English trade unionists and
Catalonia's "Youth Front" during the Spanish Revolution. According to
Wally Rosell, such matches were organized regularly and were often rather
competitive—especially when communists met anarchists. *Courtesy of Wally Rosell*

137 St. Pauli, Millerntor Stadium *Selim Sudheimer*

138 St. Pauli, Millerntor Stadium *Selim Sudheimer*

139 St. Pauli, Millerntor Stadium *Selim Sudheimer*

145 *Personal Archive*

147 BAFF Congress 1994 *BAFF Archive*

148 Gerd Dembowski with his "Scheiss-WM 2006" [Fucking 2006 World Cup]
shirt, which caused many unpleasant encounters in the streets of Berlin *Jana S.
Dembowski*

151 Call for a demonstration against the planned Germany vs. England encounter in
Berlin on April 20 (Adolf Hitler's birthday), 1994 *HKS 13/http://plakat.nadir.org*

152 "No to Racism and Sexism in the Stadium" *Personal Archive*

154 A kind of German soccer copwatch campaign: "Trust is good, control is better/
Football supporters observe the police/Enragés—a movement of the angry and
furious" *Personal Archive*

Inserts

About the author

Gabriel Kuhn is a former semi-professional soccer player who lives as an independent author and translator in Stockholm, Sweden. Among his publications with PM Press are *Sober Living for the Revolution: Hardcore Punk, Straight Edge, and Radical Politics* (2010); *Playing as if the World Mattered: An Illustrated History of Activism in Sports* (2015); and *Antifascism, Sports, Sobriety: Forging a Militant Working-Class Culture—Selected Writings by Julius Deutsch* (2017).

ABOUT PM PRESS

PM Press was founded at the end of 2007 by a small collection of folks with decades of publishing, media, and organizing experience. PM Press co-conspirators have published and distributed hundreds of books, pamphlets, CDs, and DVDs. Members of PM have founded enduring book fairs, spearheaded victorious tenant organizing campaigns, and worked closely with bookstores, academic conferences, and even rock bands to deliver political and challenging ideas to all walks of life. We're old enough to know what we're doing and young enough to know what's at stake.

We seek to create radical and stimulating fiction and nonfiction books, pamphlets, T-shirts, visual and audio materials to entertain, educate, and inspire you. We aim to distribute these through every available channel with every available technology— whether that means you are seeing anarchist classics at our bookfair stalls, reading our latest vegan cookbook at the café, downloading geeky fiction e-books, or digging new music and timely videos from our website.

PM Press is always on the lookout for talented and skilled volunteers, artists, activists, and writers to work with. If you have a great idea for a project or can contribute in some way, please get in touch.

PM Press
PO Box 23912
Oakland, CA 94623
www.pmpress.org

PM Press in Europe
europe@pmpress.org
www.pmpress.org.uk

FRIENDS OF PM PRESS

These are indisputably momentous times—the financial system is melting down globally and the Empire is stumbling. Now more than ever there is a vital need for radical ideas.

In the years since its founding—and on a mere shoestring— PM Press has risen to the formidable challenge of publishing and distributing knowledge and entertainment for the struggles ahead. With over 300 releases to date, we have published an impressive and stimulating array of literature, art, music, politics, and culture. Using every available medium, we've succeeded in connecting those hungry for ideas and information to those putting them into practice.

Friends of PM allows you to directly help impact, amplify, and revitalize the discourse and actions of radical writers, filmmakers, and artists. It provides us with a stable foundation from which we can build upon our early successes and provides a much-needed subsidy for the materials that can't necessarily pay their own way. You can help make that happen—and receive every new title automatically delivered to your door once a month—by joining as a Friend of PM Press. And, we'll throw in a free T-shirt when you sign up.

Here are your options:

- **$30 a month** Get all books and pamphlets plus 50% discount on all webstore purchases

- **$40 a month** Get all PM Press releases (including CDs and DVDs) plus 50% discount on all webstore purchases

- **$100 a month** Superstar—Everything plus PM merchandise, free downloads, and 50% discount on all webstore purchases

For those who can't afford $30 or more a month, we have **Sustainer Rates** at $15, $10 and $5. Sustainers get a free PM Press T-shirt and a 50% discount on all purchases from our website.

Your Visa or Mastercard will be billed once a month, until you tell us to stop. Or until our efforts succeed in bringing the revolution around. Or the financial meltdown of Capital makes plastic redundant. Whichever comes first.

Playing as if the World Mattered: An Illustrated History of Activism in Sports

Gabriel Kuhn

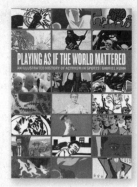

ISBN: 978-1-62963-097-7
$14.95   160 pages

The world of sports is often associated with commercialism, corruption, and reckless competition. Liberals have objected to sport being used for political propaganda, and leftists have decried its role in distracting the masses from the class struggle. Yet, since the beginning of organized sports, athletes, fans, and officials have tried to administer and play it in ways that strengthen, rather than hinder, progressive social change. From the workers' sports movement in the early twentieth century to the civil rights struggle transforming sports in the 1960s to the current global network of grassroots sports clubs, there has been a growing desire to include sports in the struggle for liberation and social justice. It is a struggle that has produced larger-than-life figures like Muhammad Ali and iconic images such as the Black Power salute by Tommie Smith and John Carlos at the 1968 Mexico Olympics. It is also a struggle that has seen sport fans in increasing number reclaiming the games they love from undemocratic associations, greedy owners, and corporate interests.

With the help of over a hundred full-color illustrations—from posters and leaflets to paintings and photographs—*Playing as if the World Mattered* makes this history tangible. Extensive lists of resources, including publications, films, and websites, will allow the reader to explore areas of interest further.

Being the first illustrated history of its kind, *Playing as if the World Mattered* introduces an understanding of sports beyond chauvinistic jingoism, corporate media chat rooms, and multi-billion-dollar business deals.

"Gabriel Kuhn dismantles the myth that sports and politics do not belong together."
—Mats Runvall, *Yelah*

"Creativity and solidarity are as indispensable in sport as they are in social struggle. If you have any doubt, read this book."
—Wally Rosell, editor of *Éloge de la passe: changer le sport pour changer le monde*

"Gabriel Kuhn is not concerned with moral reflections about how to approach sports and politics. Instead, he provides practical examples of how sport is already politicized and portrays supporters—and even athletes—as progressive social forces."
—Ekim Çağlar, *Flamman*

Antifascism, Sports, Sobriety: Forging a Militant Working-Class Culture

Julius Deutsch
Edited and translated by Gabriel Kuhn

ISBN: 978-1-62963-154-7
$14.95   128 pages

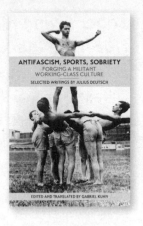

The Austromarxist era of the 1920s was a unique chapter in socialist history. Trying to carve out a road between reformism and Bolshevism, the Austromarxists embarked on an ambitious journey towards a socialist oasis in the midst of capitalism. Their showpiece, the legendary "Red Vienna," has worked as a model for socialist urban planning ever since.

At the heart of the Austromarxist experiment was the conviction that a socialist revolution had to entail a cultural one. Numerous workers' institutions and organizations were founded, from education centers to theaters to hiking associations. With the Fascist threat increasing, the physical aspects of the cultural revolution became ever more central as they were considered mandatory for effective defense. At no other time in socialist history did armed struggle, sports, and sobriety become as intertwined in a proletarian attempt to protect socialist achievements as they did in Austria in the early 1930s. Despite the final defeat of the workers' militias in the Austrian Civil War of 1934 and subsequent Fascist rule, the Austromarxist struggle holds important lessons for socialist theory and practice.

Antifascism, Sports, Sobriety contains an introductory essay by Gabriel Kuhn and selected writings by Julius Deutsch, leader of the workers' militias, president of the Socialist Workers' Sport International, and a prominent spokesperson for the Austrian workers' temperance movement. Deutsch represented the physical defense of the working class against its enemies like few others. His texts in this book are being made available in English for the first time.

"An almost completely forgotten episode in labor history."
—Murray Bookchin, author of *Anarchism, Marxism and the Future of the Left*

"A foretaste of the socialist utopia of the future in the present."
—Helmut Gruber, author of *Red Vienna: Experiment in Working-Class Culture, 1919-1934*

"The insurrection of February 1934 . . . left behind the glorious memory of resistance to fascism by arms and not merely by speeches."
—E.J. Hobsbawm, author of *The Age of Extremes: The Short Twentieth Century, 1914-1991*

Sober Living for the Revolution: Hardcore Punk, Straight Edge and Radical Politics

Edited by Gabriel Kuhn

ISBN: 978-1-60486-051-1
$22.95   304 pages

Straight edge has persisted as a drug-free, hardcore punk subculture for 25 years. Its political legacy, however, remains ambiguous—often associated with self-righteous macho posturing and conservative puritanism. While certain elements of straight edge culture feed into such perception, the movement's political history is far more complex. Since straight edge's origins in Washington, D.C. in the early 1980s, it has been linked to radical thought and action by countless individuals, bands, and entire scenes worldwide. *Sober Living for the Revolution* traces this history.

It includes contributions—in the form of in-depth interviews, essays, and manifestos—by numerous artists and activists connected to straight edge, from Ian MacKaye (Minor Threat/Fugazi) and Mark Andersen (*Dance of Days*/Positive Force DC) to Dennis Lyxzén (Refused/The (International) Noise Conspiracy) and Andy Hurley (Racetraitor/Fall Out Boy), from bands such as ManLiftingBanner and Point of No Return to feminist and queer initiatives, from radical collectives like CrimethInc. and Alpine Anarchist Productions to the Emancypunx project and many others dedicated as much to sober living as to the fight for a better world.

"Perhaps the greatest reason I am still committed to sXe is an unfailing belief that sXe is more than music, that it can be a force of change. I believe in the power of sXe as a bridge to social change, as an opportunity to create a more just and sustainable world."
—Ross Haenfler, Professor of Sociology at the University of Mississippi, author of *Straight Edge: Clean-Living Youth, Hardcore Punk, And Social Change*

"An 'ecstatic sobriety' which combats the dreariness of one and the bleariness of the other—false pleasure and false discretion alike—is analogous to the anarchism that confronts both the false freedom offered by capitalism and the false community offered by communism."
—CrimethInc. Ex-Workers' Collective

The Football Factory

John King

ISBN: 978-1-62963-116-5
$16.95   296 pages

The Football Factory is driven by its two main characters—
late-twenties warehouseman Tommy Johnson and retired
ex-soldier Bill Farrell. Tommy is angry at his situation in
life and those running the country. Outside of work, he
is a lively, outspoken character, living for his time with a
gang of football hooligans, the excitement of their fights
and the comradeship he finds with his friends. He is a
violent man, at the same time moral and intelligent.

Bill, meanwhile, is a former Second World War hero who helped liberate a
concentration camp and married a survivor. He is a strong, principled character
who sees the self-serving political and media classes for what they are. Tommy and
Bill have shared feelings, but express their views in different ways. Born at another
time, they could have been the other. As the book unfolds both come to their own
crossroads and have important decisions to make.

The Football Factory is a book about modern-day pariahs, people reduced to the
level of statistics by years of hypocritical, self-serving party politics. It is about the
insulted, marginalised, unseen. Graphic and disturbing, at times very funny, The
Football Factory is a rush of literary adrenalin.

"Only a phenomenally talented and empathetic writer working from within his own
culture can achieve the power and authenticity this book pulses with. Buy, steal or
borrow a copy now, because in a short time anyone who hasn't read it won't be worth
talking to."
—Irvine Welsh, author of Trainspotting

"King's novel is not only an outstanding read, but also an important social document. . .
. This book should be compulsory reading for all those who believe in the existence, or
even the attainability, of a classless society."
—Paul Howard, Sunday Tribune

"Bleak, thought-provoking and brutal, The Football Factory has all the hallmarks of a
cult novel."
—Dominic Bradbury, The Literary Review

"This is a chronicle of a lost tribe—the white, Anglo-Saxon heterosexual who is fed up
with being told he is crap. It is the story of a flight from fear by a group of Londoners who
have seen the present and know it does not work. . . . King writes powerfully with a raw
realism and clear grasp of a culture which has been denied but cannot be ignored."
—Hugh MacDonald, Glasgow Herald

Girl Gangs, Biker Boys, and Real Cool Cats: Pulp Fiction and Youth Culture, 1950 to 1980

Edited by Iain McIntyre and Andrew Nette with a Foreword by Peter Doyle

ISBN: 978-1-62963-438-8
$29.95   336 pages

Girl Gangs, Biker Boys, and Real Cool Cats is the first comprehensive account of how the rise of postwar youth culture was depicted in mass-market pulp fiction. As the young created new styles in music, fashion, and culture, pulp fiction shadowed their every move, hyping and exploiting their behaviour, dress, and language for mass consumption and cheap thrills. From the juvenile delinquent gangs of the early 1950s through the beats and hippies, on to bikers, skinheads, and punks, pulp fiction left no trend untouched. With their lurid covers and wild, action-packed plots, these books reveal as much about society's deepest desires and fears as they do about the subcultures themselves.

Girl Gangs features approximately 400 full-color covers, many of them never reprinted before. With 70 in-depth author interviews, illustrated biographies, and previously unpublished articles from more than 20 popular culture critics and scholars from the US, UK, and Australia, the book goes behind the scenes to look at the authors and publishers, how they worked, where they drew their inspiration and—often overlooked—the actual words they wrote. Books by well-known authors such as Harlan Ellison and Lawrence Block are discussed alongside neglected obscurities and former bestsellers ripe for rediscovery. It is a must read for anyone interested in pulp fiction, lost literary history, retro and subcultural style, and the history of postwar youth culture.

Contributors include Nicolas Tredell, Alwyn W. Turner, Mike Stax, Clinton Walker, Bill Osgerby, David Rife, J.F. Norris, Stewart Home, James Cockington, Joe Blevins, Brian Coffey, James Doig, David James Foster, Matthew Asprey Gear, Molly Grattan, Brian Greene, John Harrison, David Kiersh, Austin Matthews, and Robert Baker.

"Girl Gangs, Biker Boys, and Real Cool Cats *is populated by the bad boys and girls of mid-twentieth-century pulp fiction. Rumblers and rebels, beats and bikers, hepcats and hippies—pretty much everybody your mother used to warn you about. Nette and McIntyre have curated a riotous party that you won't want to leave, even though you might get your wallet stolen or your teeth kicked in at any given moment."*
—Duane Swierczynski, two-time Edgar nominee, author of *Canary* and *Revolver*

The Explosion of Deferred Dreams: Musical Renaissance and Social Revolution in San Francisco, 1965-1975

Mat Callahan

ISBN: 978-1-62963-231-5
$22.95   352 pages

As the fiftieth anniversary of the Summer of Love floods the media with debates and celebrations of music, political movements, "flower power," "acid rock," and "hippies", *The Explosion of Deferred Dreams* offers a critical re-examination of the interwoven political and musical happenings in San Francisco in the Sixties. Author, musician, and native San Franciscan Mat Callahan explores the dynamic links between the Black Panthers and Sly and the Family Stone, the United Farm Workers and Santana, the Indian Occupation of Alcatraz and the San Francisco Mime Troupe, and the New Left and the counterculture.

Callahan's meticulous, impassioned arguments both expose and reframe the political and social context for the San Francisco Sound and the vibrant subcultural uprisings with which it is associated. Using dozens of original interviews, primary sources, and personal experiences, the author shows how the intense interplay of artistic and political movements put San Francisco, briefly, in the forefront of a worldwide revolutionary upsurge.

A must-read for any musician, historian, or person who "was there" (or longed to have been), *The Explosion of Deferred Dreams* is substantive and provocative, inviting us to reinvigorate our historical sense-making of an era that assumes a mythic role in the contemporary American zeitgeist.

"Mat Callahan was a red diaper baby lucky to be attending a San Francisco high school during the 'Summer of Love.' He takes a studied approach, but with the eye of a revolutionary, describing the sociopolitical landscape that led to the explosion of popular music (rock, jazz, folk, R&B) coupled with the birth of several diverse radical movements during the golden 1965-1975 age of the Bay Area. Callahan comes at it from every angle imaginable (black power, anti-Vietnam War, the media, the New Left, feminism, sexual revolution—with the voice of authority backed up by interviews with those who lived it."
—Pat Thomas, author of *Listen, Whitey! The Sights and Sounds of Black Power 1965-1975*

"All too often, people talk about the '60s without mentioning our music and the fun we had trying to smash the state and create a culture based upon love. Mat Callahan's book is a necessary corrective."
—George Katsiaficas, author of *The Imagination of the New Left: A Global Analysis of 1968*

Wobblies and Zapatistas: Conversations on Anarchism, Marxism and Radical History

Staughton Lynd and Andrej Grubačić

ISBN: 978-1-60486-041-2
$20.00   300 pages

Wobblies and Zapatistas offers the reader an encounter between two generations and two traditions. Andrej Grubačić is an anarchist from the Balkans. Staughton Lynd is a lifelong pacifist, influenced by Marxism. They meet in dialogue in an effort to bring together the anarchist and Marxist traditions, to discuss the writing of history by those who make it, and to remind us of the idea that "my country is the world." Encompassing a Left libertarian perspective and an emphatically activist standpoint, these conversations are meant to be read in the clubs and affinity groups of the new Movement.

The authors accompany us on a journey through modern revolutions, direct actions, anti-globalist counter summits, Freedom Schools, Zapatista cooperatives, Haymarket and Petrograd, Hanoi and Belgrade, 'intentional' communities, wildcat strikes, early Protestant communities, Native American democratic practices, the Workers' Solidarity Club of Youngstown, occupied factories, self-organized councils and soviets, the lives of forgotten revolutionaries, Quaker meetings, antiwar movements, and prison rebellions. Neglected and forgotten moments of interracial self-activity are brought to light. The book invites the attention of readers who believe that a better world, on the other side of capitalism and state bureaucracy, may indeed be possible.

"There's no doubt that we've lost much of our history. It's also very clear that those in power in this country like it that way. Here's a book that shows us why. It demonstrates not only that another world is possible, but that it already exists, has existed, and shows an endless potential to burst through the artificial walls and divisions that currently imprison us. An exquisite contribution to the literature of human freedom, and coming not a moment too soon."
—David Graeber, author of *Fragments of an Anarchist Anthropology* and *Direct Action: An Ethnography*

"I have been in regular contact with Andrej Grubačić for many years, and have been most impressed by his searching intelligence, broad knowledge, lucid judgment, and penetrating commentary on contemporary affairs and their historical roots. He is an original thinker and dedicated activist, who brings deep understanding and outstanding personal qualities to everything he does."
—Noam Chomsky